T0073245

Advanced API Security

OAuth 2.0 and Beyond

Second Edition

Prabath Siriwardena

Apress®

Advanced API Security: OAuth 2.0 and Beyond

Prabath Siriwardena
San Jose, CA, USA

ISBN-13 (pbk): 978-1-4842-2049-8   ISBN-13 (electronic): 978-1-4842-2050-4
https://doi.org/10.1007/978-1-4842-2050-4

Managing Director, Apress Media LLC: Welmoed Spahr
Acquisitions Editor: Jonathan Gennick
Development Editor: Laura Berendson
Coordinating Editor: Jill Balzano

Cover image designed by Freepik (www.freepik.com)

Distributed to the book trade worldwide by Springer Science+Business Media New York, 233 Spring Street, 6th Floor, New York, NY 10013. Phone 1-800-SPRINGER, fax (201) 348-4505, e-mail orders-ny@springer-sbm.com, or visit www.springeronline.com. Apress Media, LLC is a California LLC and the sole member (owner) is Springer Science + Business Media Finance Inc (SSBM Finance Inc). SSBM Finance Inc is a **Delaware** corporation.

For information on translations, please e-mail rights@apress.com, or visit http://www.apress.com/rights-permissions.

Apress titles may be purchased in bulk for academic, corporate, or promotional use. eBook versions and licenses are also available for most titles. For more information, reference our Print and eBook Bulk Sales web page at http://www.apress.com/bulk-sales.

Any source code or other supplementary material referenced by the author in this book is available to readers on GitHub via the book's product page, located at www.apress.com/9781484220498. For more detailed information, please visit http://www.apress.com/source-code.

Printed on acid-free paper

This book is dedicated to my sister Deepani,
who backed me all the time!

Table of Contents

About the Author

 **Prabath Siriwardena** is an identity evangelist, author, blogger, and VP of Identity Management and Security at WSO2. He has more than 12 years of industry experience in designing and building critical identity and access management (IAM) infrastructure for global enterprises, including many Fortune 100/500 companies. As a technology evangelist, Prabath has published seven books. He blogs on various topics from blockchain, PSD2, GDPR, IAM to microservices security. He also runs a YouTube channel. Prabath has spoken at many conferences, including RSA Conference, KNOW Identity, Identiverse, European Identity Conference, Consumer Identity World USA, API World, API Strategy and Practice Conference, QCon, OSCON, and WSO2Con. He has traveled the world conducting workshops and meetups to evangelize IAM communities. He is the founder of the Silicon Valley IAM User Group, which is the largest IAM meetup in the San Francisco Bay Area.

Acknowledgments

I would first like to thank Jonathan Gennick, Assistant Editorial Director at Apress, for evaluating and accepting my proposal for this book. Then, I must thank Jill Balzano, Coordinating Editor at Apress, who was very patient and tolerant of me throughout the publishing process. Alp Tunc served as the technical reviewer—thanks, Alp, for your quality review comments, which were quite useful. Also I would like to thank all the external reviewers of the book, who helped to make the book better.

Dr. Sanjiva Weerawarana, the Founder and former CEO of WSO2, and Paul Fremantle, the CTO of WSO2, are two constant mentors for me. I am truly grateful to both Dr. Sanjiva and Paul for everything they have done for me.

My wife, Pavithra, and my little daughter, Dinadi, supported me throughout this process. Thank you very much, Pavithra and Dinadi.

My parents and my sister are with me all the time. I am grateful to them for everything they have done for me. Last but not least, my wife's parents—they were amazingly helpful.

Although writing a book may sound like a one-man effort, it's the entire team behind it who makes it a reality. Thank you to everyone who supported me in many different ways.

Introduction

Enterprise APIs have become the common way of exposing business functions to the outside world. Exposing functionality is convenient, but of course comes with a risk of exploitation. This book is about securing your most important business assets or APIs. As is the case with any software system design, people tend to ignore the security element during the API design phase. Only at the deployment or at the time of integration they start worrying about security. Security should never be an afterthought—it's an integral part of any software system design, and it should be well thought out from the design's inception. One objective of this book is to educate the reader about the need for security and the available options for securing APIs.

The book guides you through the process and shares best practices for designing APIs for better security. API security has evolved a lot in the last few years. The growth of standards for securing APIs has been exponential. OAuth 2.0 is the most widely adopted standard. It's more than just a standard—rather a framework that lets people build solutions on top of it. The book explains in depth how to secure APIs from traditional HTTP Basic authentication to OAuth 2.0 and the profiles built around OAuth, such as OpenID Connect, User-Managed Access (UMA), and many more.

JSON plays a major role in API communication. Most of the APIs developed today support only JSON, not XML. The book focuses on JSON security. JSON Web Encryption (JWE) and JSON Web Signature (JWS) are two increasingly popular standards for securing JSON messages. The latter part of the book covers JWE and JWS in detail.

Another major objective of the book is to not just present concepts and theories but also to explain concepts and theories with concrete examples. The book presents a comprehensive set of examples to illustrate how to apply theory in practice. You will learn about using OAuth 2.0 and related profiles to access APIs securely with web applications, single-page applications, native mobile applications and browser-less applications.

I hope this book effectively covers a much-needed subject matter for API developers, and I hope you enjoy reading it.

CHAPTER 1

APIs Rule!

Enterprise API adoption has exceeded expectations. We see the proliferation of APIs in almost all the industries. It is not an exaggeration to say a business without an API is like a computer with no Internet. APIs are also the foundation for building communication channels in the Internet of Things (IoT) domain. From motor vehicles to kitchen appliances, countless devices have started communicating with each other via APIs.

The world is more connected than ever. You share photos from Instagram in Facebook, share a location from Foursquare or Yelp in Twitter, publish tweets to the Facebook wall, connect to Google Maps via the Uber mobile app, and many more. The list of connections is limitless. All this is made possible only because of public APIs, which have proliferated in the last few years. Expedia, Salesforce, eBay, and many other companies generate a large percentage of their annual revenue via APIs. APIs have become the coolest way of exposing business functionalities to the outside world.

API Economy

According to an infographic[1] published by the ACI Information Group, at the current rate of growth, the global Internet economy is around 10 trillion US dollars. In 1984, at the time the Internet was debuted, it linked 1000 hosts at universities and corporates. In 1998, after almost 15 years, the number of Internet users, globally, reached 50 million. It took 11 years since then to reach the magic number 1 billion Internet users, in 2009. It took just three years since then to get doubled, and in 2012 it reached to 2.1 billion. In 2019, more than half of the world's population—about 4.3 billion people—use the Internet. This number could further increase as a result of the initiatives taken by the Internet giants like Facebook and Google. The Internet.org initiative by Facebook,

---

[1]The History of the Internet, http://aci.info/2014/07/12/the-data-explosion-in-2014-minute-by-minute-infographic/

© Prabath Siriwardena 2020
P. Siriwardena, *Advanced API Security*, https://doi.org/10.1007/978-1-4842-2050-4_1

1

launched in 2013, targets to bring together technology leaders, nonprofits, and local communities to connect with the rest of the world that does not have Internet access. Google Loon is a project initiated by Google to connect people in rural and remote areas. It is based on a network of balloons traveling on the edge of space and aims to improve the connectivity of 250 million people in Southeast Asia.[2]

Not just humans, according to a report[3] on the Internet of Things by Cisco, during 2008, the number of things connected to the Internet exceeded the number of people on earth. Over 12.5 billion devices were connected to the Internet in 2012 and 25 billion devices by the end of 2015. It is estimated that by the end of 2020, 50 billion devices will be connected. Connected devices are nothing new. They've been there since the introduction of the first computer networks and consumer electronics. However, if not for the explosion of the Internet adoption, the idea of a globally connected planet would never take off. In the early 1990s, computer scientists theorized how a marriage between humans and machines could give birth to a completely new form of communication and interaction via machines. That reality is now unfolding before our eyes.

There are two key enablers behind the success of the Internet of Things. One is the APIs and the other is Big Data. According to a report[4] by Wipro Council for Industry Research, a six-hour flight on a Boeing 737 from New York to Los Angeles generates 120 terabytes of data that is collected and stored on the plane. With the explosion of sensors and devices taking over the world, there needs to be a proper way of storing, managing, and analyzing data. By 2014, an estimated 4 zettabytes of information was held globally, and it's estimated, by 2020, that number will climb up to 35 zettabytes.[5] Most interestingly, 90% of the data we have in hand today is generated just during the last couple of years. The role of APIs under the context of the Internet of Things is equally important as Big Data. APIs are the glue which connect devices to other devices and to the cloud.

---

[2]Google Loon, http://fortune.com/2015/10/29/google-indonesia-internet-helium-balloons/

[3]The Internet of Things: How the Next Evolution of the Internet Is Changing Everything, www.iotsworldcongress.com/documents/4643185/3e968a44-2d12-4b73-9691-17ec508ff67b

[4]Big Data: Catalyzing Performance in Manufacturing, www.wipro.com/documents/Big%20Data.pdf

[5]Big data explosion: 90% of existing data globally created in the past two years alone, http://bit.ly/1WajrG2

The API economy talks about how an organization can become profitable or successful in their corresponding business domain with APIs. IBM estimated the API economy to become a $2.2 trillion market by 2018,[6] and the IBM Redbook, *The Power of the API Economy*,[7] defines API economy as *the commercial exchange of business functions, capabilities, or competencies as services using web APIs*. It further finds five main reasons why enterprises should embrace web APIs and become an active participant in the API economy:

- Grow your customer base by attracting customers to your products and services through API ecosystems.

- Drive innovation by capitalizing on the composition of different APIs, yours and third parties.

- Improve the time-to-value and time-to-market for new products.

- Improve integration with web APIs.

- Open up more possibilities for a new era of computing and prepare for a flexible future.

Amazon

Amazon, Salesforce, Facebook, and Twitter are few very good examples for early entrants into the API economy, by building platforms for their respective capabilities. Today, all of them hugely benefit from the widespread ecosystems built around these platforms. Amazon was one of the very first enterprises to adopt APIs to expose its business functionalities to the rest. In 2006 it started to offer IT infrastructure services to businesses in the form of web APIs or web services. Amazon Web Services (AWS), which initially included EC2 (Elastic Compute Cloud) and S3 (Simple Storage Service), was a result of the thought process initiated in 2002 to lead Amazon's internal infrastructure in a service-oriented manner.

---

[6]IBM announces new solutions for the API economy, http://betanews.com/2015/11/05/ibm-announces-new-solutions-for-the-api-economy/

[7]*The Power of the API Economy,* www.redbooks.ibm.com/redpapers/pdfs/redp5096.pdf

The former Amazon employee, Steve Yegge, shared accidentally an Amazon internal discussion via his Google+ post, which became popular later. According to Yegge's post,[8] it all began with a letter from Jeff Bezos to the Amazon engineering team, which highlighted five key points to transform Amazon into a highly effective service-oriented infrastructure.

- All teams will henceforth expose their data and functionality through service interfaces.

- Teams must communicate with each other through these interfaces.

- There will be no other form of interprocess communication allowed: no direct linking, no direct reads of another team's data store, no shared memory model, no backdoors whatsoever. The only communication allowed is via service interface calls over the network.

- It doesn't matter what technology is used. HTTP, Corba, Pubsub, custom protocols—doesn't matter.

- All service interfaces, without exception, must be designed from the ground up to be externalizable. That is to say, the team must plan and design to be able to expose the interface to developers in the outside world. No exceptions.

This service-based approach leads Amazon to easily expand its business model from being a bookseller to a global retailer in selling IT services or cloud services. Amazon started exposing both EC2 and S3 capabilities as APIs, both in SOAP and REST (JSON over HTTP).

---

[8]Steve Yegge on Amazon, `https://plus.google.com/+RipRowan/posts/eVeouesvaVX`

Salesforce

Salesforce, which was launched in February 1999, is a leader in the software-as-a-service space today. The web API built around Salesforce capabilities and exposing it to the rest was a key success factor which took the company to the state where it is today. Salesforce kept on using platforms and APIs to fuel the innovation and to build a larger ecosystem around it.

Uber

Google exposes most of its services via APIs. The Google Maps API, which was introduced in 2005 as a free service, lets many developers consume Google Maps to create much useful mashups by integrating with other data streams. Best example is the Uber. Uber is a transportation network company based out of San Francisco, USA, which also offers its services globally in many countries outside the United States. With the Uber mobile application on iOS or Android (see Figure 1-1), its customers, who set a pickup location and request a ride, can see on Google Maps where the corresponding taxi is. Also, from the Uber driver's application, the driver can exactly pinpoint where the customer is. This is a great selling point for Uber, and Uber as a business hugely benefits from the Google Maps public API. At the same time, Google gets track of all the Uber rides. They know exactly the places of interests and the routes Uber customers take, which can be pumped into Google's ad engine. Not just Uber, according to a report[9] by Google, by 2013 more than 1 million active sites and applications were using Google Maps API.

---

[9]A fresh new look for the Maps API, for all one million sites, `http://bit.ly/1NPH12z`

Figure 1-1. *Uber mobile app uses Google Maps*

Facebook

Facebook in 2007 launched the Facebook platform. The Facebook platform made most of the Facebook's core capabilities available publicly to the application developers. According to the builtwith.com,[10] the Facebook Graph API was used by 1 million web sites across the Internet, by October 2019. Figure 1-2 shows the Facebook Graph API usage over time. Most of the popular applications like Foursquare, Yelp, Instagram, and many more consume Facebook API to publish data to the user's Facebook wall. Both parties mutually benefit from this, by expanding the adaptation and building a strong ecosystem.

---

[10]Facebook Graph API Usage Statistics, `http://trends.builtwith.com/javascript/`
`Facebook-Graph-API`

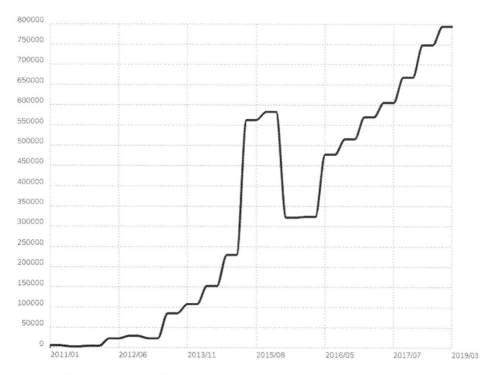

Figure 1-2. *Facebook Graph API usage statistics, the number of web sites over time*

Netflix

Netflix, a popular media streaming service in the United States with more than 150 million subscribers, announced its very first public API in 2008.[11] During the launch, Daniel Jacobson, the Vice President of Edge Engineering at Netflix, explained the role of this public API as a broker, which mediates data between internal services and public developers. Netflix has come a long way since its first public API launch, and today it has more than a thousand types of devices supporting its streaming API.[12] By mid-2014, there were 5 billion API requests generated internally (via devices used to stream the content) and 2 million public API requests daily.

---

[11]Netflix added record number of subscribers, `www.cnn.com/2019/04/16/media/netflix-earnings-2019-first-quarter/index.html`

[12]API Economy: From systems to business services, `http://bit.ly/1GxmZe6`

Walgreens

Walgreens, the largest drug retailing chain in the United States, opened up its photo printing and pharmacies to the public in 2012/2013, via an API.[13] They started with two APIs, a QuickPrints API and a Prescription API. This attracted many developers, and dozens of applications were developed to consume Walgreens' API. Printicular is one such application developed by MEA Labs, which can be used to print photos from Facebook, Twitter, Instagram, Google+, Picasa, and Flickr (see Figure 1-3). Once you pick your photos from any of these connected sites to be printed, you have the option to pick the printed photos from the closest Walgreens store or also can request to deliver. With the large number of applications built against its API, Walgreens was able to meet its expectations by enhancing customer engagements.

Figure 1-3. *Printicular application written against the Walgreens API*

---

[13]Walgreens API, https://developer.walgreens.com/apis

Governments

Not just the private enterprises but also governments started exposing its capabilities via APIs. On May 22, 2013, Data.gov (an initiative managed by the US General Services Administration, with the aim to improve public access to high-value, machine-readable datasets generated by the executive branch of the federal government) launched two initiatives to mark both the anniversary of the Digital Government Strategy and the fourth anniversary of Data.gov. First is a comprehensive listing of APIs that were released from across the federal government as part of the Digital Government Strategy. These APIs accelerated the development of new applications on everything from health, public safety, education, consumer protection, and many more topics of interest to Americans. This initiative also helped developers, where they can find all the government's APIs in one place (`http://api.data.gov`), with links to API documentation and other resources.

IBM Watson

APIs have become the key ingredients in building a successful enterprise. APIs open up the road to new business ecosystems. Opportunities that never existed before can be realized with a public API. In November 2013, for the first time, IBM Watson technology was made available as a development platform in the cloud, to enable a worldwide community of software developers to build a new generation of applications infused with Watson's cognitive computing intelligence.[14] With the API, IBM also expected to create multiple ecosystems that will open up new market places. It connected Elsevier (world-leading provider of scientific, technical, and medical information products and services) and its expansive archive of studies on oncology care to both the medical expertise of Sloan Kettering (a cancer treatment and research institution founded in 1884) and Watson's cognitive computing prowess. Through these links, IBM now provides physicians and nurse practitioners with information on symptoms, diagnosis, and treatment approaches.

---

[14]IBM Watson's Next Venture, `www-03.ibm.com/press/us/en/pressrelease/42451.wss`

Open Banking

API adaptation has gone viral across verticals: retail, healthcare, financial, government, education, and in many more verticals. In the financial sector, the Open Bank[15] project provides an open source API and app store for banks that empower financial institutions to securely and rapidly enhance their digital offerings using an ecosystem of third-party applications and services. As per Gartner,[16] by 2016, 75% of the top 50 global banks have launched an API platform, and 25% have launched a customer-facing app store. The aim of Open Bank project is to provide a uniform interface, abstracting out all the differences in each banking API. That will help application developers to build applications on top of the Open Bank API, but still would work against any of the banks that are part of the Open Bank initiative. At the moment, only four German banks are onboarded, and it is expected to grow in the future.[17] The business model behind the project is to charge an annual licensing fee from the banks which participate.

Healthcare

The healthcare industry is also benefiting from the APIs. By November 2015, there were more than 200 medical APIs registered in ProgrammableWeb.[18] One of the interesting projects among them, the Human API[19] project, provides a platform that allows users to securely share their health data with developers of health applications and systems. This data network includes activity data recorded by pedometers, blood pressure measurements captured by digital cuffs, medical records from hospitals, and more. According to a report[20] by GlobalData, the mobile health market was worth $1.2 billion in 2011, but expected to jump in value to reach $11.8 billion by 2018, climbing at an impressive compound annual growth rate (CAGR) of 39%. The research2guidance[21]

---

[15]Open Bank Project, `www.openbankproject.com/`

[16]Gartner: Hype Cycle for Open Banking, `www.gartner.com/doc/2556416/hype-cycle-open-banking`

[17]Open Bank Project connector status, `https://api.openbankproject.com/connectors-status/`

[18]Medical APIs, `www.programmableweb.com/category/medical/apis?&category=19994`

[19]Human API, `http://hub.humanapi.co/docs/overview`

[20]Healthcare Goes Mobile, `http://healthcare.globaldata.com/media-center/press-releases/medical-devices/mhealth-healthcare-goes-mobile`

[21]Research2guidance, `http://research2guidance.com/the-market-for-mobile-health-sensors-will-grow-to-5-6-billion-by-2017/`

estimated the market for mobile health sensors to grow to $5.6 billion by 2017. Aggregating all these estimated figures, it's more than obvious that the demand for medical APIs is only to grow in the near future.

Wearables

Wearable industry is another sector, which exists today due to the large proliferation of APIs. The ABI Research[22] estimates that the world will have 780 million wearables by 2019—everything from fitness trackers and smart watches to smart glasses and even heart monitors, in circulation. Most of the wearables come with low processing power and storages and talk to the APIs hosted in the cloud for processing and storage. For example, Microsoft Band, a wrist-worn wearable, which keeps track of your heart rate, steps taken, calories burned, and sleep quality, comes with the Microsoft Health mobile application. The wearable itself keeps tracks of the steps, distances, calories burned, and heart rate in its limited storage for a short period. Once it's connected to the mobile application, via Bluetooth, all the data are uploaded to the cloud through the application. The Microsoft Health Cloud API[23] allows you to enhance the experiences of your apps and services with real-time user data. These RESTful APIs provide comprehensive user fitness and health data in an easy-to-consume JSON format. This will enhance the ecosystem around Microsoft Band, as more and more developers can now develop useful applications around Microsoft Health API, hence will increase Microsoft Band adaptation. This will also let third-party application developers to develop a more useful application by mashing up their own data streams with the data that come from Microsoft Health API. RunKeeper, MyFitnessPal, MyRoundPro, and many more fitness applications have partnered with Microsoft Band in that effort, for mutual benefits.

---

[22]The Wearable Future Is Hackable, `https://blogs.mcafee.com/consumer/hacking-wearable-devices/`

[23]Microsoft Cloud Health API, `https://developer.microsoftband.com/cloudAPI`

Business Models

Having a proper business model is the key to the success in API economy. The IBM Redbook, *The Power of the API Economy*,[24] identifies four API business models, as explained here:

- *Free model*: This model focuses on the business adoption and the brand loyalty. Facebook, Twitter, and Google Maps APIs are few examples that fall under this model.

- *Developer pays model*: With this model, the API consumer or the developer has to pay for the usage. For example, PayPal charges a transaction fee, and Amazon lets developers pay only for what they use. This model is similar to the "Direct Revenue" model described by Wendy Bohner from Intel.[25]

- *Developer is paid directly*: This is sort of a revenue sharing model. The best example is the Google AdSense. It pays 20% to developers from revenue generated from the posted ads. Shopping.com is another example for revenue sharing business model. With Shopping. com API developers can integrate relevant product content with the deepest product catalogue available online and add millions of unique products and merchant offers to your site. It pays by the clicks.

- *Indirect*: With this model, enterprises build a larger ecosystem around it, like Salesforce, Twitter, Facebook, and many more. For example, Twitter lets developers build applications on top of its APIs. This benefits Twitter, by displaying sponsored tweets on end user's Twitter timeline, on those applications. The same applies to Salesforce. Salesforce encourages third-party developers to extend its platform by developing applications on top of its APIs.

---

[24]*The Power of the API Economy*, www.redbooks.ibm.com/redpapers/pdfs/redp5096.pdf
[25]Wendy Bohner's blog on API Economy: https://blogs.intel.com/api-management/2013/09/20/the-api-economy/

The API Evolution

The concept behind APIs has its roots from the beginning of computing. An API of a component defines how others would interact with it. API stands for application programming interface, and it's a technical specification for developers and architects. If you are familiar with the Unix or Linux operating system, the man command shouldn't be something new. It generates the technical specification for each command in the system, which defines how a user can interact with it. The output from the man command can be considered as the API definition of the corresponding command. It defines everything you need to know to execute it, including the synopsis, description with all the valid input parameters, examples, and many more. The following command on a Unix/Linux or even on a Mac OS X environment will generate the technical definition of the ls command.

```
$ man ls
NAME
     ls -- list directory contents
SYNOPSIS
     ls [-ABCFGHLOPRSTUW@abcdefghiklmnopqrstuwx1] [file ...]
```

Going little further from there, if you are a computer science graduate or have read about operating systems, you surely have heard of system calls. System calls provide an interface to the operating system's kernel, or a system call is how a program requests a service from the underlying operating system. Kernel is the core of the operating system, which wraps the hardware layer from the top-level applications (see Figure 1-4). If you want to print something from the browser, then the print command, which initiated from the browser, first has to pass through the kernel to reach the actual printer connected to the local machine itself, or remotely via the network. Where kernel executes its operations and provides services is known as the kernel space, while the top-level applications execute their operations and provide services in the user space. The kernel space is accessible for applications running in the user space only through system calls. In other words, system calls are the kernel API for the user space.

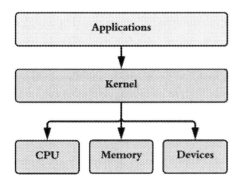

Figure 1-4. *Operating system's kernel*

The Linux kernel has two types of APIs: one for the applications running in the user space and the other one is for its internal use. The API between the kernel space and user space can also be called the public API of the kernel, while the other as its private API.

Even at the top-level application, if you've worked with Java, .NET, or any other programming language, you've probably written code against an API. Java provides Java Database Connectivity (JDBC) as an API to talk to different heterogeneous database management systems (DBMSs), as shown in Figure 1-5. The JDBC API encapsulates the logic for how your application connects to a database; thus, the application logic doesn't need to change whenever it connects to different databases. The database's connectivity logic is wrapped in a JDBC driver and exposed as an API. To change the database, you need to pick the right JDBC driver.

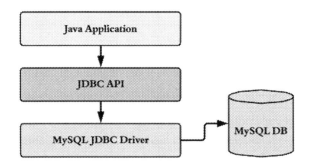

Figure 1-5. *JDBC API*

An API itself is an interface. It's the interface for clients that interact with the system or the particular component. Clients should only know about the interface and nothing about its implementation. A given interface can have more than one implementation, and a client written against the interface can switch between implementations seamlessly and painlessly. The client application and the API implementation can run in the same process or in different processes. If they're running in the same process, then the call between the client and the API is a local one—if not, it's a remote call. In the case of the JDBC API, it's a local call. The Java client application directly invokes the JDBC API, implemented by a JDBC driver running in the same process. The following Java code snippet shows the usage of the JDBC API. This code has no dependency to the underneath database—it only talks to the JDBC API. In an ideal scenario, the program reads the name of the Oracle driver and the connection to the Oracle database from a configuration file, making the code completely clean from any database implementations.

```java
import java.sql.Connection;
import java.sql.DriverManager;
import java.sql.PreparedStatement;
import java.sql.SQLException;

public class JDBCSample {

public void updataEmpoyee() throws ClassNotFoundException, SQLException {
 Connection con = null;
 PreparedStatement prSt = null;
    try {
     Class.forName("oracle.jdbc.driver.OracleDriver");
     con = DriverManager.getConnection("jdbc:oracle:thin:@<hostname>:<port
     num>:<DB name>", "user", "password");
     String query = "insert into emp(name,salary) values(?,?)";
     prSt = con.prepareStatement(query);
     prSt.setString(1, "John Doe");
     prSt.setInt(2, 1000);
     prSt.executeUpdate();
     } finally {
         try {
            if (prSt != null) prSt.close();
            if (con != null)  con.close();
          } catch (Exception ex) {
```

```
            // log
          }
        }
}
}
```

We can also access APIs remotely. To invoke an API remotely, you need to have a protocol defined for interprocess communication. Java RMI, CORBA, .NET Remoting, SOAP, and REST (over HTTP) are some protocols that facilitate interprocess communication. Java RMI provides the infrastructure-level support to invoke a Java API remotely from a nonlocal Java virtual machine (JVM, which runs in a different process than the one that runs the Java API). The RMI infrastructure at the client side serializes all the requests from the client into the wire (also known as *marshalling*) and deserializes into Java objects at the server side by its RMI infrastructure (also known as *unmarshalling*); see Figure 1-6. This marshalling/unmarshalling technique is specific to Java. It must be a Java client to invoke an API exposed over Java RMI—and it's language dependent.

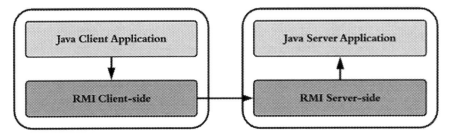

Figure 1-6. *Java RMI*

The following code snippet shows how a Java client talks to a remotely running Java service over RMI. The Hello stub in the following code represents the service. The rmic tool, which comes with Java SDK, generates the stub against the Java service interface. We write the RMI client against the API of the RMI service.

```
import java.rmi.registry.LocateRegistry;
import java.rmi.registry.Registry;

public class RMIClient {
```

```
public static void main(String[] args) {
    String host = (args.length < 1) ? null : args[0];
    try {
        Registry registry = LocateRegistry.getRegistry(host);
        Hello stub = (Hello) registry.lookup("Hello");
        String response = stub.sayHello();
        System.out.println("response: " + response);
    } catch (Exception e) {
        e.printStackTrace();
    }
}
}
```

SOAP-based web services provide a way to build and invoke a hosted API in a language- and platform-neutral manner. It passes a message from one end to the other as an XML payload. SOAP has a structure, and there are a large number of specifications to define its structure. The SOAP specification defines the request/response protocol between the client and the server. Web Services Description Language (WSDL) specification defines the way you describe a SOAP service. The WS-Security, WS-Trust, and WS-Federation specifications describe how to secure a SOAP-based service. WS-Policy provides a framework to build quality-of-service expressions around SOAP services. WS-SecurityPolicy defines the security requirements of a SOAP service in a standard way, built on top of the WS-Policy framework. The list goes on and on. SOAP-based services provide a highly decoupled, standardized architecture with policy-based governance. They do have all necessary ingredients to build a service-oriented architecture (SOA).

At least, that was the story a decade ago. The popularity of SOAP-based APIs has declined, mostly due to the inherent complexity of the WS-∗ standards. SOAP promised interoperability, but many ambiguities arose among different implementation stacks. To overcome this issue and promote interoperability between implementation stacks, the Web Services Interoperability (WS-I)[26] organization came up with the Basic Profile for web services. The Basic Profile helps in removing ambiguities in web service standards. An API design built on top of SOAP should follow the guidelines Basic Profile defines.

---

[26]The OASIS Web Services Interoperability Organization, www.ws-i.org/

Note   SOAP was initially an acronym that stood for Simple Object Access Protocol. From SOAP 1.2 onward, it is no longer an acronym.

In contrast to SOAP, REST is a design paradigm, rather than a rule set. Even though Roy Fielding, who first described REST in his PhD thesis,[27] did not couple REST to HTTP, 99% of RESTful services or APIs today are based on HTTP. For the same reason, we could easily argue, REST is based on the rule set defined in the HTTP specification.

The Web 2.0 trend emerged in 2006–2007 and set a course to a simpler, less complex architectural style for building APIs. Web 2.0 is a set of economic, social, and technology trends that collectively formed the basis for the next generation of Internet computing. It was built by tens of millions of participants. The platform built around Web 2.0 was based on the simple, lightweight, yet powerful AJAX-based programming languages and REST—and it started to move away from SOAP-based services.

Modern APIs have their roots in both SOAP and REST. Salesforce launched its public API in 2000, and it still has support for both SOAP and REST. Amazon launched its web services API in 2002 with support for both REST and SOAP, but the early adoption rate of SOAP was very low. By 2003, it was revealed that 85% of Amazon API usage was on REST.[28] ProgrammableWeb, a registry of web APIs, has tracked APIs since 2005. In 2005, ProgrammableWeb tracked 105 APIs, including Google, Salesforce, eBay, and Amazon. The number increased by 2008 to 1000 APIs, with growing interest from social and traditional media companies to expose data to external parties. There were 2500 APIs by the end of 2010. The online clothing and shoe shop Zappos published a REST API, and many government agencies and traditional brick-and-mortar retailers joined the party. The British multinational grocery and merchandise retailer Tesco allowed ordering via APIs. The photo-sharing application Instagram became the Twitter for pictures. The Face introduced facial recognition as a service. Twilio allowed anyone to create telephony applications in no time. The number of public APIs rose to 5000 by 2011; and in 2014 ProgrammableWeb listed out more than 14,000 APIs. In June 2019, ProgrammableWeb

---

[27]Architectural Styles and the Design of Network-based Software Architectures, `www.ics.uci.edu/~fielding/pubs/dissertation/top.htm`

[28]REST vs. SOAP In Amazon Web Services, `https://developers.slashdot.org/story/03/04/03/1942235/rest-vs-soap-in-amazon-web-services`

announced that the number of APIs it tracks eclipsed 22,000 (see Figure 1-7). At the same time, the trend toward SOAP has nearly died: 73% of the APIs on ProgrammableWeb by 2011 used REST, while SOAP was far behind with only 27%.[29]

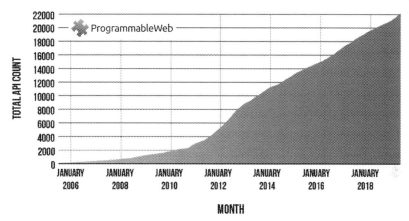

Figure 1-7. *The growth of APIs listed on ProgrammableWeb since 2005*

The term API has existed for decades, but only recently has it been caught up in the hype and become a popular buzzword. The modern definition of an API mostly focused on a hosted, web-centric (over HTTP), public-facing service to expose useful business functionalities to the rest of the world. According to the *Forbes* magazine, an API is the primary customer interface for technology-driven products and services and a key channel for driving revenue and brand engagements. Salesforce, Amazon, eBay, Dropbox, Facebook, Twitter, LinkedIn, Google, Flickr, Yahoo, and most of the key players doing business online have an API platform to expose business functionalities.

---

[29]SOAP is Not Dead, http://readwrite.com/2011/05/26/soap-is-not-dead---its-undead

API Management

Any HTTP endpoint, with a well-defined interface to accept requests and generate responses based on certain business logic, can be treated as a naked API. In other words, a naked API is an unmanaged API. An unmanaged API has its own deficiencies, as listed here:

- There is no way to track properly the business owner of the API or track how ownership evolves over time.

- API versions are not managed properly. Introduction of a new API could possibly break all the existing consumers of the old API.

- No restriction on the audience. Anyone can access the API anonymously.

- No restriction on the number of API calls by time. Anyone can invoke the API any number of times, which could possibly cause the server hosting the API to starve all its resources.

- No tracking information at all. Naked APIs won't be monitored and no stats will be gathered.

- Inability to scale properly. Since no stats are gathered based on the API usage, it would be hard to scale APIs based on the usage patterns.

- No discoverability. APIs are mostly consumed by applications. To build applications, application developers need to find APIs that suit their requirements.

- No proper documentation. Naked APIs will have a proper interface, but no proper documentation around that.

- No elegant business model. It's hard to build a comprehensive business model around naked APIs, due to all the eight reasons listed earlier.

A managed API must address all or most of the preceding concerns. Let's take an example, the Twitter API. It can be used to tweet, get timeline updates, list followers, update the profile, and do many other things. None of these operations can be performed anonymously—you need to authenticate first. Let's take a concrete example (you need to have cURL installed to try this, or you can use the Chrome Advanced REST client browser plug-in). The following API is supposed to list all the tweets published by the authenticated user and his followers. If you just invoke it, it returns an error code, specifying that the request isn't authenticated:

```
\> curl https://api.twitter.com/1.1/statuses/home_timeline.json
{"errors":[{"message":"Bad Authentication data","code":215}]}
```

All the Twitter APIs are secured for legitimate access with OAuth 1.0 (which we discuss in detail in Appendix B). Even with proper access credentials, you can't invoke the API as you wish. Twitter enforces a rate limit on each API call: within a given time window, you can only invoke the Twitter API a fixed number of times. This precaution is required for all public-facing APIs to minimize any possible denial of service (DoS) attacks. In addition to securing and rate limiting its APIs, Twitter also closely monitors them. Twitter API Health[30] shows the current status of each API. Twitter manages versions via the version number (e.g., 1.1) introduced into the URL itself. Any new version of the Twitter API will carry a new version number, hence won't break any of the existing API consumers. Security, rate limiting (throttling), versioning, and monitoring are key aspects of a managed business API. It also must have the ability to scale up and down for high availability based on the traffic.

Lifecycle management is another key differentiator between a naked API and a managed API. A managed API has a lifecycle from its creation to its retirement. A typical API lifecycle might flow through Created, Published, Deprecated, and Retired stages, as illustrated in Figure 1-8. To complete each lifecycle stage, there can be a checklist to be verified. For example, to promote an API from Created to Published, you need to make sure the API is secured properly, the documentation is ready, throttling rules are enforced, and so on. A naked business API, which only worries about business functionalities, can be turned into a managed API by building these quality-of-service aspects around it.

---

[30]Twitter Health, https://dev.twitter.com/status

Figure 1-8. *API lifecycle*

The API description and discoverability are two key aspects of a managed API. For an API, the description has to be extremely useful and meaningful. At the same time, APIs need to be published somewhere to be discovered. A comprehensive API management platform needs to have at least three main components: a publisher, a store, and a gateway (see Figure 1-9). The API store is also known as the developer portal.

The API publisher provides tooling support to create and publish APIs. When an API is created, it needs to be associated with API documentation and other related quality-of-service controls. Then it's published into the API store and deployed into the API gateway. Application developers can discover APIs from the store. ProgrammableWeb (`www.programmableweb.com`) is a popular API store that has more than 22,000 APIs at the time of this writing. You could also argue that ProgrammableWeb is simply a directory, rather than a store. A store goes beyond just listing APIs (which is what ProgrammableWeb does): it lets API consumers or application developers subscribe to APIs, and it manages API subscriptions. Further, an API store supports social features like tagging, commenting, and rating APIs. The API gateway is the one which takes all the traffic in runtime and acts as the policy enforcement point. The gateway checks all the requests that pass through it against authentication, authorization, and throttling policies. The statistics needed for monitoring is also gathered at the API gateway level. There are many open source and proprietary API management products out there that provide support for comprehensive API store, publisher, and gateway components.

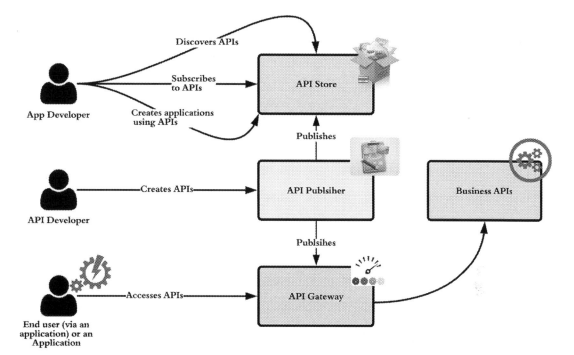

Figure 1-9. *API management platform*

In the SOAP world, there are two major standards for service discovery. Universal Description, Discovery, and Integration (UDDI) was popular, but it's extremely bulky and didn't perform to the level it was expected to. UDDI is almost dead today. The second standard is WS-Discovery, which provides a much more lightweight approach. Most modern APIs are REST-friendly. For RESTful services or APIs, there is no widely accepted standard means of discovery at the time of this writing. Most API stores make discovery via searching and tagging.

Describing a SOAP-based web service is standardized through the Web Service Definition Language (WSDL) specification. WSDL describes what operations are exposed through the web service and how to reach them. For RESTful services and APIs, there are two popular standards for description: Web Application Description Language (WADL) and Swagger. WADL is an XML-based standard to describe RESTful or HTTP-based services. Just as in WSDL, WADL describes the API and its expected request/response messages. Swagger is a specification and a complete framework implementation for describing, producing, consuming, and visualizing RESTful web services. With more than 350,000 downloads per month, of Swagger and Swagger-related tooling, the Swagger specification is promising to be the most widely used format for describing APIs.[31] Figure 1-10 shows the Swagger definition of the Swagger Petstore API.[32]

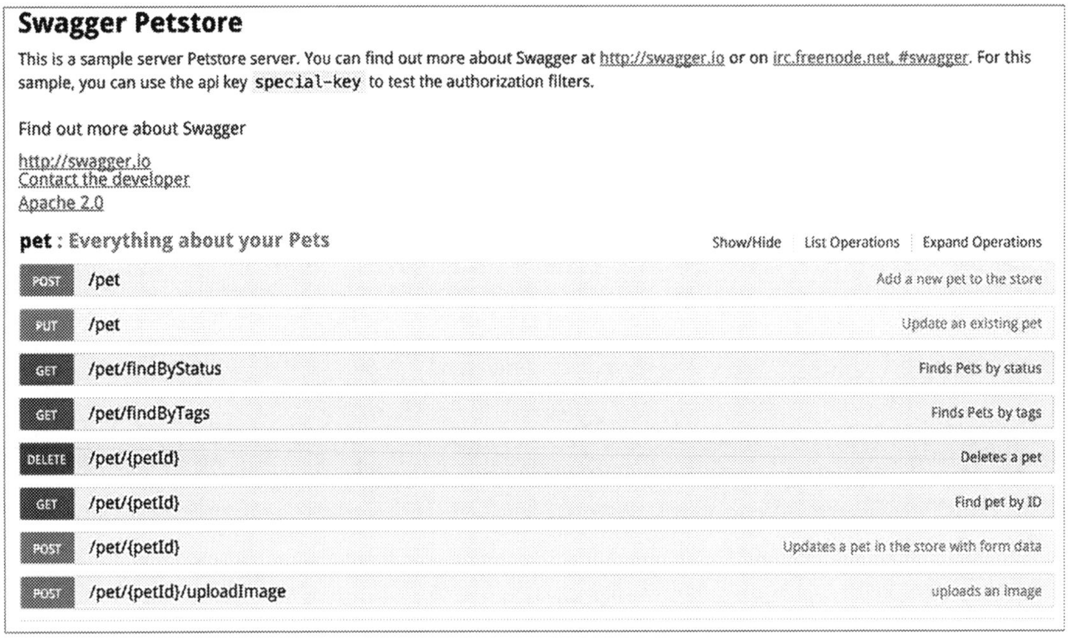

Figure 1-10. *Swagger definition of the Swagger Petstore API*

Based on the Swagger 2.0 specification, the OpenAPI Initiative (OAI) has developed an OAI specification involving API consumers, developers, providers, and vendors, to define a standard, a language-agnostic interface for REST APIs. Google, IBM, PayPal, Intuit, SmartBear, Capital One, Restlet, 3scale, and Apigee got involved in creating the OpenAPI Initiative under the Linux foundation.

---

[31]Open API Initiative Specification, `https://openapis.org/specification`

[32]Swagger Petstore API, `http://petstore.swagger.io/`

MANAGED APIS AT NETFLIX

Netflix started its journey as a DVD rental service and then evolved into a video streaming platform and published its first API in 2008. In January 2010, Netflix API recorded 600 million requests (per month), and in January 2011, the number rose up to 20.7 billion, then again after a year, in January 2012, Netflix API was hit with 41.7 billion requests.[33] Today, at the time of this writing, Netflix handles more than one third of the entire Internet traffic in North America. It's a widespread service globally over 190 countries in 5 continents, with more than 139 million members. Netflix API is accessed by thousands of supported devices, generating billions of API requests per day.

Even though Netflix API was initially developed as a way for external application developers to access Netflix's catalogue, it soon became a key part in exposing internal functionality to living room devices supported by Netflix. The former is the Netflix's public API, while the latter is its private API. The public API, when compared with the private API, only attracted a small number of traffic. At the time Netflix decided to shut down the public API in November 2011, it only attracted 0.3% of the total API traffic.[34]

Netflix uses its own API gateway, Zuul, to manage all its API traffic.[35] Zuul is the front door for all the requests from devices and web sites to the back end of the Netflix streaming application. As an edge service application, Zuul is built to enable dynamic routing, monitoring, resiliency, and security. It also has the ability to route requests to multiple Amazon Auto Scaling Groups as appropriate.[36]

The Role of APIs in Microservices

Going back to the good old days, there was an unambiguous definition for *API* vs. *service*. An API is the interface between two parties or two components. These two parties/components can communicate within a single process or between different processes. A service is a concrete implementation of an API using one of the technologies/standards available. The implementation of an

---

[33]Growth of Netflix API requests, https://gigaom.com/2012/05/15/netflix-42-billion-api-requests/

[34]Top 10 Lessons Learned from the Netflix API, www.slideshare.net/danieljacobson/top-10-lessons-learned-from-the-netflix-api-oscon-2014

[35]How we use Zuul at Netflix, https://github.com/Netflix/zuul/wiki/How-We-Use-Zuul-At-Netflix

[36]Zuul, https://github.com/Netflix/zuul/wiki

API that is exposed over SOAP is a SOAP service. Similarly, the implementation of an API that is exposed as JSON over HTTP is a RESTful service.

Today, the topic, API vs. service, is debatable, as there are many overlapping areas. One popular definition is that an API is external facing, whereas a service is internal facing (see Figure 1-11). An enterprise uses an API whenever it wants to expose useful business functionality to the outside world through the firewall. This, of course, raises another question: why would a company want to expose its precious business assets to the outside world through an API? Twitter once again is the best example. It has a web site that allows users to log in and tweet from there. At the same time, anything that can be done through the web site can also be done via Twitter's API. As a result, third parties develop applications against the Twitter API; there are mobile apps, browser plug-ins, and desktop apps. This has drastically reduced traffic to the Twitter web site. Even today, the web site doesn't have a single advertisement (but as sponsored tweets on the usual twitter stream). If there was no public API, Twitter could easily have built an advertising platform around the web site, just as how Facebook did. However, having a public API helped to build a strong ecosystem around Twitter.

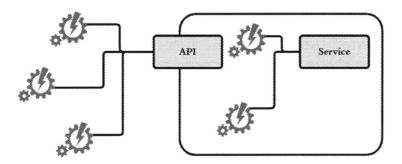

Figure 1-11. *API vs. service. An API is external facing*

Exposing corporate data via an API adds value. It gives access to the data, not just for corporate stakeholders but also for a larger audience. Limitless innovative ideas may pop up and, in the end, add value to the data. Say we have a pizza dealer with an API that returns the number of calories for a given pizza type and the size. You can develop an application to find out how many pizzas a person would have to eat per day to reach a body mass index (BMI) in the obesity range.

Even though APIs are known to be public, it's not a strict requirement. Most of the APIs started as public APIs and became the public face of the enterprise. At the same time, private APIs (not exposed to the public) proliferated within enterprises to share functionalities within it, between different components. In that case, the differentiator between an API and a service is not just its audience. In practice, most of the service implementations are exposed as APIs. In that case, API defines the contract between the service and the outside world (not necessarily public).

Microservices is the most trending buzzword at the time of this writing. Everyone talks about microservices, and everyone wants to have microservices implemented. The term "microservice" was first discussed at a software architects workshop in Venice, in May 2011. It's being used to explain a common architectural style they've been witnessing for some time. Later, after a year in May 2012, the same team agreed that the "microservice" is the best-suited term to call the previously discussed architectural style. At the same time, in March 2012, James Lewis went ahead and presented some of the ideas from the initial discussion in Venice at the 33rd Degree conference in Krakow, Poland.[37]

Note   The abstract of James Lewis' talk on "Microservices – Java, the Unix Way," which happened to be the very first public talk on Microservices, in March 2012:

"Write programs that do one thing and do it well. Write programs to work together" was accepted 40 years ago, yet we have spent the last decade building monolithic applications, communicating via bloated middleware and with our fingers crossed that Moore's Law keeps helping us out. There is a better way.

Microservices. In this talk, we will discover a consistent and reinforcing set of tools and practices rooted in the Unix philosophy of small and simple. Tiny applications, communicating via the web's uniform interface with single responsibilities and installed as well-behaved operating system services. So, are you sick of wading through tens of thousands of lines of code to make a simple one-line change? Of all that XML? Come along and check out what the cool kids are up to (and the cooler gray beards).

---

[37]Microservices – Java, the Unix Way, http://2012.33degree.org/talk/show/67

One can easily argue that a microservice is service-oriented architecture (SOA) done right. Most of the concepts we discussed today, related to microservices, are borrowed from SOA. SOA talks about an architectural style based on services. According to the Open Group definition, a service is a logical representation of a repeatable business activity that has a specified outcome and is self-contained, may be composed of other services; the implementation acts as a black box to the service consumers.[38] SOA brings the much-needed agility to business to scale and interoperate. However, over the past, SOA became a hugely overloaded term. Some people defined SOA under the context of SOAP-based web services, and others used to think SOA is all about an enterprise service bus (ESB). This led Netflix to call microservices as fine-grained SOA, at the initial stage.

> *I don't really care whether it's public or private. We used to call the things we were building on the cloud "cloud-native" or "fine-grained SOA," and then the ThoughtWorks people came up with the word "microservices." It's just another name for what we were doing anyways, so we just started calling it microservices, as well.*[39]

> —Adrian Cockcroft, former cloud architect at Netflix

NINE CHARACTERISTICS OF A MICROSERVICE

Martin Fowler and James Lewis, introducing microservices,[40] identify nine characteristics in a well-designed microservice, as briefly explained in the following:

Componentization via services: In microservices, the primary way of componentizing will be via services. This is a bit different from the traditional componentizing via libraries. A library in the Java world is a jar file, and in .NET world, it's a DLL file. A library can be defined as a component isolated to perform some specific task and plugged into the main program via in-memory function calls. In microservices world, these libraries mostly act as a proxy to a remote service running out of process.

---

[38]Service-Oriented Architecture Defined, `www.opengroup.org/soa/source-book/togaf/soadef.htm`

[39]Talking microservices with the man who made Netflix's cloud famous, `https://medium.com/s-c-a-l-e/talking-microservices-with-the-man-who-made-netflix-s-cloud-famous-1032689afed3`

[40]Microservices, `http://martinfowler.com/articles/microservices.html`

Organized around business capabilities: In most of the monolithic applications we see today, the layering is based on the technology not around the business capabilities. The user interface (UI) design team works on building the user interface for the application. They are the experts on HTML, JavaScript, Ajax, HCI (human-computer interaction), and many more. Then we have database experts who take care of database schema design and various application integration technologies, like JDBC, ADO.NET, and Hibernate. Then we have server-side logic team who write the actual business logic and also are the experts on Java, .NET, and many more server-side technologies. With the microservices approach, you build cross-functional, multidisciplined teams around business capabilities.

Products not projects: The objectives of a project team are to work according to a project plan, meet the set deadlines, and deliver the artifacts at the end of the project. Once the project is done, the maintenance team takes care of managing the project from there onward. It is estimated that 29% of an IT budget is spent on new system development, while 71% is spent on maintaining existing systems and adding capacity to those systems.[41] To avoid such wastage and to improve the efficiency throughout the product lifecycle, Amazon introduced the concept—*you build it, you own it*. The team, which builds the product, will own it forever. This brought in the product mentality and made the product team responsible for a given business functionality. Netflix, one of the very early promoters of microservices, treats each of their API as a product.

Smart endpoints and dumb pipes: Each microservice is developed for a well-defined scope. Once again, the best example is Netflix.[42] Netflix started with a single monolithic web application called netflix.war in 2008, and later in 2012, as a solution to address vertical scalability concerns, they moved into a microservices-based approach, where they have hundreds of fine-grained microservices today. The challenge here is how microservices talk to each other. Since the scope of each microservice is small (or micro), to accomplish a given business requirement, microservices have to talk to each other. Each microservice would be a smart endpoint, which exactly knows how to process an incoming request and generate the response. The communication channels between microservices act as dumb pipes. This is similar to the Unix pipes and filters architecture. For example, the `ps -ax` command in Unix will list out the status of currently running processes. The `grep` Unix command will search

---

[41]You build it, You run it, www.agilejourneyman.com/2012/05/you-build-it-you-run-it.html
[42]Microservice at Netflix, www.youtube.com/watch?v=LEcdWVfbHvc

any given input files, selecting lines that match one or more patterns. Each command is smart enough to do their job. We can combine both the commands with a pipe. For example, `ps -ax | grep 'apache'` will only list out the processes that matches the search criteria 'apache'. Here the pipe (|) acts as dumb—which basically takes the output from the first command and hands it over to the other. This is one of the main characteristics of a microservice design.

Decentralized governance: Most of the SOA deployments follow the concept of centralized governance. The design time governance and the runtime governance are managed and enforced centrally. The design time governance will look into the aspects such as whether the services passed all the unit tests, integration tests, and coding conventions, secured with accepted security policies and many more, before promoting from the developer phase to the QA (quality assurance) phase. In a similar way, one can enforce more appropriate checklists to be evaluated before the services are promoted from QA to staging and from staging to production. The runtime governance will worry about enforcing authentication policies, access control policies, and throttling policies in the runtime. With the microservices-based architecture, each service is designed with its own autonomy and highly decoupled from each other. The team behind each microservice can follow their own standards, tools, and protocols. This makes a decentralized governance model more meaningful for microservices architecture.

Decentralized data management: In a monolithic application, all the components in it talk to a single database. With the microservices design, where each distinguished functional component is developed into a microservice, based on their business capabilities, will have its own database—so each such service can scale end to end without having any dependency on other microservices. This approach can easily add overhead in distributed transaction management, as data resides in multiple heterogeneous database management systems.

Infrastructure automation: Continuous deployment and continuous delivery are two essential ingredients in infrastructure automation. Continuous deployment extends continuous delivery and results in every build that passes automated test gates being deployed into production, while with continuous delivery, the decision to deploy into the production setup is taken based on the business need.[43] Netflix, one of the pioneers in APIs and microservices, follows the former approach, the continuous deployment. With the continuous deployment, the new features need not be sitting on a shelf. Once they have gone through and passed all the

---

[43]Deploying the Netflix API, http://techblog.netflix.com/2013/08/deploying-netflix-api.html

tests, they are ready to be deployed in production. This also avoids deploying a large set of new features at one go, hence doing minimal changes to the current setup and the user experience. Infrastructure automation does not have a considerable difference between monolithic applications and microservices. Once the infrastructure is ready, it can be used across all the microservices.

Design for failure: The microservices-based approach is a highly distributed setup. In a distributed setup, failures are inevitable. No single component can guarantee 100% uptime. Any service call may fail due to various reasons: the transport channel between the services could be down, the server instance which hosts the service may be down, or even the service itself may be down. This is an extra overhead on microservices, compared to monolithic applications. Each microservice should be designed in a way to handle and tolerate these failures. In the entire microservices architecture, the failure of one service should ideally have zero or minimal impact on the rest of the running services. Netflix developed a set of tools called Simian Army,[44] based on the success of its Chaos Monkey, to simulate failure situations under a controlled environment to make sure the system can gracefully recover.

Evolutionary design: The microservices architecture inherently supports the evolutionary design. Unlike in monolithic applications, with microservices the cost of upgrading or replacing an individual component is extremely low, since they've been designed to function independently or in a loosely coupled manner.

Netflix is one of the pioneers in microservices adoption. Not just Netflix, General Electric (GE), Hewlett-Packard (HP), Equinox Inc, PayPal, Capital One Financial Corp, Goldman Sachs Group Inc, Airbnb, Medallia, Square, Xoom Corp, and many more are early adopters of microservices.[45] Even though microservices became a buzzword quite recently, some of the design principles brought forward by the microservices architecture were there for some time. It's widely believed that Google, Facebook, and Amazon were using microservices internally for several years—when you do a Google search, it calls out roughly 70 microservices before returning back the results.

Just like in the case of API vs. service, the differentiator between an API and a microservice also relies on the audience. APIs are known to be public facing, while microservices are used internally. Netflix, for example, has hundreds of microservices,

---

[44]The Netflix Simian Army, http://techblog.netflix.com/2011/07/netflix-simian-army.html
[45]Innovate or Die: The Rise of Microservices, http://blogs.wsj.com/cio/2015/10/05/
innovate-or-die-the-rise-of-microservices/

but none of them are exposed outside. The Netflix API still acts as their public-facing interface, and there is a one-to-many relationship between the Netflix API and its microservices. In other words, one API could talk to multiple microservices to cater a request generated by one of the devices supported by Netflix. Microservices have not substituted APIs—rather they work together.

Summary

- The API adoption has grown rapidly in the last few years, and almost all the cloud service providers today expose public managed APIs.

- In contrast to naked APIs, the managed APIs are secured, throttled, versioned, and monitored.

- An API store (or a developer portal), API publisher, and API gateway are the three key ingredients in building an API management solution.

- Lifecycle management is a key differentiator between a naked API and a managed API. A managed API has a lifecycle from its creation to its retirement. A typical API lifecycle might flow through Created, Published, Deprecated, and Retired stages.

- Microservices have not substituted APIs—rather they work together.

CHAPTER 2

Designing Security for APIs

Just a few days after everyone celebrated Thanksgiving Day in 2013, someone who fooled the Target defense system installed a malware in its security and payment system. It was the peak time in business for any retailer in the United States. While the customers were busy in getting ready for Christmas, the malware which was sitting in the Target payment system silently captured all the credit card information from the cashier's terminal and stored them in a server, which was under the control of the attacker. Forty million credit card numbers were stolen in this way from 1797 Target stores around the country.[1] It was a huge breach of trust and credibility from the retailer, and in March 2015 a federal judge in St. Paul, Minnesota, approved a $10 million offer by Target to settle the lawsuit against the data breach.[2]

Not just Target or the retail industry but as a whole, the cybercrime has gained a lot of momentum in the last few years. Figure 2-1 shows the annual number of data breaches and exposed records in the United States from 2005 to 2018. The attack on Dyn DNS in 2016 was one of the largest DDoS (distributed denial of service) attacks that took many large Internet services down for several hours. Then in February 2018, the largest recorded DDoS attack happened against GitHub. More than 1.35 terabits per second of traffic hit the developer platform GitHub all at once.[3]

---

[1]Target Credit Card Hack, `http://money.cnn.com/2013/12/22/news/companies/target-credit-card-hack/`

[2]Target Data Hack Settlement, `http://money.cnn.com/2015/03/19/technology/security/target-data-hack-settlement/`

[3]GitHub Survived the Biggest DDoS Attack Ever Recorded, `www.wired.com/story/github-ddos-memcached/`

© Prabath Siriwardena 2020
P. Siriwardena, *Advanced API Security*, https://doi.org/10.1007/978-1-4842-2050-4_2

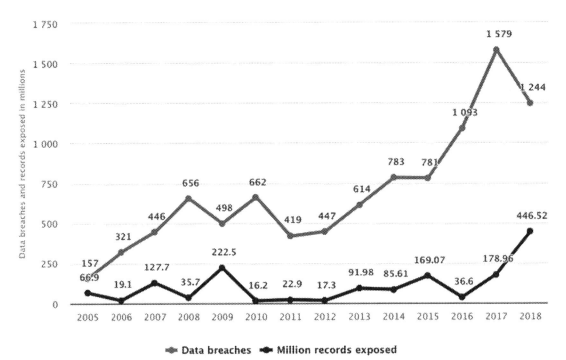

Figure 2-1. *Annual number of data breaches and exposed records in the United States from 2005 to 2018 (in millions), Statistica, 2019*

Identity Theft Resource Center[4] defines a data breach as the loss of information from computers or storage media that could potentially lead to identity theft, including social security numbers, bank account details, driving license numbers, and medical information. The most worrisome fact is that, according to an article[5] by *The Economist* magazine, the average time between an attacker breaching a network and its owner noticing the intrusion is 205 days.

Trinity of Trouble

Connectivity, extensibility, and complexity are the three trends behind the rise of data breaches around the globe in the last few years. Gary McGraw in his book, *Software Security*,[6] identifies these three trends as *the trinity of trouble.*

---

[4]Identity Theft Resource Center, www.idtheftcenter.org/

[5]The cost of immaturity, www.economist.com/news/business/21677639-business-protecting-against-computer-hacking-booming-cost-immaturity

[6]Gary McGraw, *Software Security: Building Security In*, Addison-Wesley Publisher

APIs play a major role in connectivity. As we discussed in detail, in Chapter 1, we live in a world today where almost everything is connected with each other. Connectivity exposes many paths of exploitation for attackers, which never existed before. Login to Yelp, Foursquare, Instagram, and many more via Facebook means an attacker only needs to worry about compromising one's Facebook account to get access to his/her all other connected accounts.

FACEBOOK DATA BREACH ~ SEPTEMBER 2018

In September 2018, Facebook team figured out an attack,[7] which put the personal information of more than 50 million Facebook users at risk. The attackers exploited multiple issues on Facebook code base around the View As feature and got hold of OAuth 2.0 access tokens that belong to more than 50 million users. Access token is some kind of a temporary token or a key, which one can use to access a resource on behalf of someone else. Say, for example, if I want to share my photos uploaded to Instagram on my Facebook wall, I would give an access token corresponding to my Facebook wall, which I obtained from Facebook, to Instagram. Now, at each time when I upload a photo to Instagram, it can use the access token to access my Facebook account and publish the same on my Facebook wall using the Facebook API. Even though Instagram can post photos on my Facebook wall using the provided access token, it cannot do anything else other than that. For example, it cannot see my friend list, cannot delete my wall posts, or read my messages. Also, this is usually what happens when you log in to a third-party application via Facebook; you simply share an access token corresponding to your Facebook account with the third-party web application, so the third-party web application can use the access token to access the Facebook API to know more about you.

In a connected enterprise, not just the applications developed with modern, bleeding edge technology get connected but also the legacy systems. These legacy systems may not support latest security protocols, even Transport Layer Security (TLS) for securing data in transit. Also, the libraries used in those systems could have many well-known security vulnerabilities, which are not fixed due to the complexities in upgrading to the latest versions. All in all, a connected system, not planned/designed quite well, could easily become a security graveyard.

---

[7]What Went Wrong?, https://medium.facilelogin.com/what-went-wrong-d09b0dc24de4

Most of the enterprise software are developed today with great extensibility. *Extensibility over modification* is a well-known design philosophy in the software industry. It talks about building software to evolve with new requirements, without changing or modifying the current source code, but having the ability to plug in new software components to the current system. Google Chrome extensions and Firefox add-ons all follow this concept. The Firefox add-on, Modify Headers, lets you add, modify, and filter the HTTP request headers sent to web servers. Another Firefox add-on, SSO Tracer, lets you track all the message flows between identity providers and service providers (web applications), via the browser. None of these are harmful—but, then again, if an attacker can fool you to install a malware as a browser plugin, it could easily bypass all your browser-level security protections, even the TLS, to get hold of your Facebook, Google, Amazon, or any other web site credentials. It's not just about an attacker installing a plugin into the user's browser, but also when there are many extensions installed in your browser, each one of them expands the attack surface. Attackers need not write new plugins; rather they can exploit security vulnerability in an already installed plugin.

THE STORY OF MAT HONAN

It was a day in August 2012. Mat Honan, a reporter for *Wired* magazine, San Francisco, returned home and was playing with his little daughter.[8] He had no clue what was going to happen next. Suddenly his iPhone was powered down. He was expecting a call—so he plugged it into a wall power socket and rebooted back. What he witnessed next blew him away. Instead of the iPhone home screen with all the apps, it asked for him to set up a new phone with a big Apple logo and a welcome screen. Honan thought his iPhone was misbehaving—but was not that worried since he backed up daily to the iCloud. Restoring everything from iCloud could simply fix this, he thought. Honan tried to log in to iCloud. Tried once—failed. Tried again—failed. Again—failed. Thought he was excited. Tried once again for the last time, and failed. Now he knew something weird has happened. His last hope was his MacBook. Thought at least he could restore everything from the local backup. Booted up the MacBook and found nothing in it—and it prompted him to enter a four-digit passcode that he has never set up before.

---

[8]How Apple and Amazon Security Flaws Led to My Epic Hacking, `www.wired.com/2012/08/apple-amazon-mat-honan-hacking`

Honan called Apple tech support to reclaim his iCloud account. Then he learned he has called Apple, 30 minutes before, to reset his iCloud password. The only information required at that time to reset an iCloud account was the billing address and the last four digits of the credit card. The billing address was readily available under the *whois* Internet domain record Honan had for his personal web site. The attacker was good enough to get the last four digits of Honan's credit card by talking to Amazon helpdesk; he already had Honan's email address and the full mailing address—those were more than enough for a social engineering attack.

Honan lost almost everything. The attacker was still desperate—next he broke into Honan's Gmail account. Then from there to his Twitter account. One by one—Honan's connected identity falls into the hands of the attacker.

The complexity of the source code or the system design is another well-known source of security vulnerabilities. According to a research, after some point, the number of defects in an application goes up as the square of the number of the lines of code.[9] At the time of this writing, the complete Google codebase to run all its Internet services was around 2 billion lines of code, while Microsoft Windows operating system had around 50 million lines of code.[10] As the number of lines of code goes high, the number of tests around the code should grow as well, to make sure that none of the existing functionalities are broken and the new code works in the expected way. At Nike, 1.5 million lines of test code is run against 400,000 lines of code.[11]

Design Challenges

Security isn't an afterthought. It has to be an integral part of any development project and also for APIs. It starts with requirements gathering and proceeds through the design, development, testing, deployment, and monitoring phases. Security brings a plethora of challenges into the system design. It's hard to build a 100% secured system. The only thing you can do is to make the attacker's job harder. This is in fact the philosophy followed while designing cryptographic algorithms. The following discusses some of the key challenges in a security design.

---

[9]Encapsulation and Optimal Module Size, `www.catb.org/esr/writings/taoup/html/ch04s01.html`

[10]Google Is 2 Billion Lines of Code, `www.catb.org/esr/writings/taoup/html/ch04s01.html`

[11]Nike's Journey to Microservices, `www.youtube.com/watch?v=h3OViSEZzWO`

MD5

MD5[12] algorithm (an algorithm for message hashing), which was designed in 1992, was accepted to be a strong hashing algorithm. One of key attributes of a hashing algorithm is, given the text, the hash corresponding to that text can be generated, but, given a hash, the text corresponding to the hash cannot be derived. In other words, hashes are not reversible. If the text can be derived from a given hash, then that hashing algorithm is broken.

The other key attribute of a hashing algorithm is that it should be collision-free. In other words, any two distinct text messages must not result in the same hash. The MD5 design preserved both of these two properties at the time of its design. With the available computational power, it was hard to break MD5 in the early 1990s. As the computational power increased and it was made available to many people via cloud-based infrastructure as a service (IaaS) providers, like Amazon, MD5 was proven to be insecure. On March 1, 2005, Arjen Lenstra, Xiaoyun Wang, and Benne de Weger demonstrated that MD5 is susceptible to hash collisions.[13]

User Experience

The most challenging thing in any security design is to find and maintain the right balance between security and the user comfort. Say you have the most complex password policy ever, which can never be broken by any brute-force attack. A password has to have more than 20 characters, with mandatory uppercase and lowercase letters, numbers, and special characters. Who on Earth is going to remember their passwords? Either you'll write it on a piece of paper and keep it in your wallet, or you'll add it as a note in your mobile device. Either way, you lose the ultimate objective of the strong password policy. Why would someone carry out a brute-force attack when the password is written down and kept in a wallet? The principle of psychological acceptability, discussed later in this chapter, states that security mechanisms should not make the resource more difficult to access than if the security mechanisms were not present. We have few good examples from the recent past, where user experience drastically improved while keeping security intact. Today, with the latest Apple Watch, you can unlock your MacBook, without retyping the password. Also the face recognition

---

[12]RFC 6156: The MD5 Message-Digest Algorithm, `https://tools.ietf.org/html/rfc1321`
[13]Colliding X.509 Certificates, `http://eprint.iacr.org/2005/067.pdf`

technology introduced in the latest iPhones lets you unlock the phone, just by looking at it. You never even notice that the phone was locked.

> *It is essential that the human interface be designed for ease of use, so that users routinely and automatically apply the protection mechanisms correctly. Also, to the extent that the user's mental image of his protection goals matches the mechanisms he must use, mistakes will be minimized. If he must translate his image of his protection needs into a radically different specification language, he will make errors.*

> —Jerome Saltzer and Michael Schroeder

Performance

Performance is another key criterion. What is the cost of the overhead you add to your business operations to protect them from intruders? Say you have an API secured with a key, and each API call must be digitally signed. If the key is compromised, an attacker can use it to access the API. How do you minimize the impact? You can make the key valid only for a very short period; so, whatever the attacker can do with the stolen key is limited to its lifetime. What kind of impact will this have on legitimate day-to-day business operations? Each client application should first check the validity period of the key (before doing the API call) and, if it has expired, make a call to the authorization server (the issuer of the key) to generate a new key. If you make the lifetime too short, then almost for each API call, there will be a call to the authorization server to generate a new key. That kills performance—but drastically reduces the impact of an intruder getting access to the API key.

The use of TLS for transport-level security is another good example. We will be discussing TLS in Appendix C, in detail. TLS provides protection for data in transit. When you pass your login credentials to Amazon or eBay, those are passed over a secured communication channel, or HTTP over TLS, which is in fact the HTTPS. No one in the middle will be able to see the data passed from your browser to the web server (assuming there is no room for a man-in-the-middle attack). But this comes at a cost. TLS adds more overhead over the plain HTTP communication channel, which would simply slow down things a bit. For the exact same reason, some enterprises follow the strategy where all of the communication channels open to the public are over HTTPS, while the communication between internal servers are over plain HTTP. They make sure no one can intercept any of those internal channels by enforcing strong network-level security. The other option is to use optimized hardware to carry out the encryption/decryption process in the TLS communication. Doing encryption/decryption process at the dedicated hardware level is far more cost-effective than doing the same at the application level, in terms of performance.

Even with TLS, the message is only protected while it is in transit. As soon as the message leaves the transport channel, it's in cleartext. In other words, the protection provided by TLS is point to point. When you log in to your banking web site from the browser, your credentials are only secured from your browser to the web server at your bank. If the web server talks to a Lightweight Directory Access Protocol (LDAP) server to validate the credentials, once again if this channel is not explicitly protected, then the credentials will be passed in cleartext. If anyone logs all the in and out messages to and from the bank's web server, then your credentials will be logged in plaintext. In a highly secured environment, this may not be acceptable. Using message-level security over transport-level security is the solution. With message-level security, as its name implies, the message is protected by itself and does not rely on the underlying transport for security. Since this has no dependency on the transport channel, the message will be still protected, even after it leaves the transport. This once again comes at a high performance cost. Using message-level protection is much costlier than simply using TLS. There is no clear-cut definition on making a choice between the security and the performance. Always there is a compromise, and the decision has to be taken based on the context.

Weakest Link

A proper security design should care about all the communication links in the system. Any system is no stronger than its weakest link. In 2010, it was discovered that since 2006, a gang of robbers equipped with a powerful vacuum cleaner had stolen more than 600,000 euros from the Monoprix supermarket chain in France.[14] The most interesting thing was the way they did it. They found out the weakest link in the system and attacked it. To transfer money directly into the store's cash coffers, cashiers slid tubes filled with

---

[14]"Vacuum Gang" Sucks Up $800,000 From Safeboxes, `https://gizmodo.com/vacuum-gang-sucks-up-800-000-from-safeboxes-5647047`

money through pneumatic suction pipes. The robbers realized that it was sufficient to drill a hole in the pipe near the trunk and then connect a vacuum cleaner to capture the money. They didn't have to deal with the coffer shield.

Not always, the weakest link in a system is either a communication channel or an application. There are many examples which show the humans have turned out to be the weakest link. The humans are the most underestimated or the overlooked entity in a security design. Most of the social engineering attacks target humans. In the famous Mat Honan's attack, calling to an Amazon helpdesk representative, the attacker was able to reset Mat Honan's Amazon credentials. The October 2015 attack on CIA Director John Brennan's private email account is another prime example of social engineering.[15] The teen who executed the attack said, he was able to fool a Verizon worker to get Brennan's personal information and duping AOL into resetting his password. The worst side of the story is that Brennan has used his private email account to hold officially sensitive information—which is again a prime example of a human being the weakest link of the CIA defense system. Threat modeling is one of the techniques to identify the weakest links in a security design.

Defense in Depth

A layered approach is preferred for any system being tightened for security. This is also known as *defense in depth*. Most international airports, which are at a high risk of terrorist attacks, follow a layered approach in their security design. On November 1, 2013, a man dressed in black walked into the Los Angeles International Airport, pulled a semi-automatic rifle out of his bag, and shot his way through a security checkpoint, killing a TSA screener and wounding at least two other officers.[16] This was the first layer of defense. In case someone got through it, there has to be another to prevent the gunman from entering a flight and taking control. If there had been a security layer before the TSA, maybe just to scan everyone who entered the airport, it would have detected the weapon and probably saved the life of the TSA officer.

NSA (National Security Agency of the United States) identifies *defense in depth* as a practical strategy for achieving information assurance in today's highly networked

---

[15]Teen says he hacked CIA director's AOL account, `http://nypost.com/2015/10/18/stoner-high-school-student-says-he-hacked-the-cia/`

[16]Gunman kills TSA screener at LAX airport, `https://wapo.st/2QBfNoI`

environments.[17] It further explains layered defense under five classes of attack: passive monitoring of communication channels, active network attacks, exploitation of insiders, close-in attacks, and attacks through various distribution channels. The link and network layer encryption and traffic flow security is proposed as the first line of defense for passive attacks, and the second line of defense is the security-enabled applications. For active attacks, the first line of defense is the enclave boundaries, while the second line of defense is the computing environment. The insider attacks are prevented by having physical and personnel security as the first line of defense and having authentication, authorization, and audits as the second line of defense. The close-in attacks are prevented by physical and personnel security as the first layer and having technical surveillance countermeasures as the second line of defense. Adhering to trusted software development and distribution practices and via runtime integrity controls prevents the attacks via multiple distributed channels.

The number of layers and the strength of each layer depend on which assets you want to protect and the threat level associated with them. Why would someone hire a security officer and also use a burglar alarm system to secure an empty garage?

Insider Attacks

Insider attacks are less complicated, but highly effective. From the confidential US diplomatic cables leaked by WikiLeaks to Edward Snowden's disclosure about the National Security Agency's secret operations, all are insider attacks. Both Snowden and Bradley Manning were insiders who had legitimate access to the information they disclosed. Most organizations spend the majority of their security budget to protect their systems from external intruders; but approximately 60% to 80% of network misuse incidents originate from inside the network, according to the Computer Security Institute (CSI) in San Francisco.

There are many prominent insider attacks listed down in the computer security literature. One of them was reported in March 2002 against the UBS Wealth Management firm in the United States. UBS is a global leader in wealth management having branches over 50 countries. Roger Duronio, one of the system administrators at UBS, found guilty of computer sabotage and securities fraud for writing, planting, and disseminating malicious code that took down up to 2000 servers. The US District Court in Newark,

---

[17]Defense in Depth, `www.nsa.gov/ia/_files/support/defenseindepth.pdf`

New Jersey, sentenced him for 97 months in jail.[18] The Target data breach that we discussed at the beginning of the chapter is another prime example for an insider attack. In that case, even the attackers were not insiders, they gained access to the Target internal system using the credentials of an insider, who is one of the company's refrigeration vendors.

According to an article by *Harvard Business Review* (HBR),[19] at least 80 million insider attacks take place in the United States each year. HBR further identifies three causes for the growth of insider attacks over the years:

- One is the dramatic increase in the size and the complexity of IT. As companies grow in size and business, a lot of isolated silos are being created inside. One department does not know what the other does. In 2005 call center staffers based in Pune, India, defrauded four Citibank account holders in New York of nearly $350,000, and later it was found those call center staffers are outsourced employees of Citibank itself and had legitimate access to customers' PINs and account numbers.

- The employees who use their own personal devices for work are another cause for the growing insider threats. According to a report released by Alcatel-Lucent in 2014, 11.6 million mobile devices worldwide are infected at any time.[20] An attacker can easily exploit an infected device of an insider to carry out an attack against the company.

- The third cause for the growth of insider threats, according to the HBR, is the social media explosion. Social media allow all sorts of information to leak from a company and spread worldwide, often without the company's knowledge.

Undoubtedly, insider attacks are one of the hardest problems to solve in a security design. These can be prevented to some extent by adopting robust insider policies, raising awareness, doing employee background checks at the point of hiring them,

---

[18]UBS insider attack, `www.informationweek.com/ex-ubs-systems-admin-sentenced-to-97-months-in-jail/d/d-id/1049873`

[19]The Danger from Within, `https://hbr.org/2014/09/the-danger-from-within`

[20]Surge in mobile network infections in 2013, `http://phys.org/news/2014-01-surge-mobile-network-infections.html`

enforcing strict processes and policies on subcontractors, and continuous monitoring of employees. In addition to these, SANS Institute also published a set of guidelines in 2009 to protect organizations from insider attacks.[21]

Note Insider attacks are identified as a growing threat in the military. To address this concern, the US Defense Advanced Research Projects Agency (DARPA) launched a project called Cyber Insider Threat (CINDER) in 2010. The objective of this project was to develop new ways to identify and mitigate insider threats as soon as possible.

Security by Obscurity

Kerckhoffs' principle[22] emphasizes that a system should be secured by its design, not because the design is unknown to an adversary. One common example of security by obscurity is how we share door keys between family members, when there is only a single key. Everyone locks the door and hides the key somewhere, which is known to all the other family members. The hiding place is a secret, and it is assumed only family members know about it. In case if someone can find the hiding place, the house is no more secured.

Another example for security by obscurity is Microsoft's NTLM (an authentication protocol) design. It was kept secret for some time, but at the point (to support interoperability between Unix and Windows) Samba engineers reverse-engineered it, they discovered security vulnerabilities caused by the protocol design itself. Security by obscurity is widely accepted as a bad practice in computer security industry. However, one can argue it as another layer of security before someone hits the real security layer. This can be further explained by extending our first example. Let's say instead of just hiding the door key somewhere, we put it to a lock box and hide it. Only the family members know the place where the lock box is hidden and also the key combination to

---

[21]Protecting Against Insider Attacks, `www.sans.org/reading-room/whitepapers/incident/protecting-insider-attacks-33168`

[22]In 1883, Auguste Kerckhoffs published two journal articles on *La Cryptographie Militaire* in which he emphasized six design principles for military ciphers. This resulted in the well-known Kerckhoffs' principle: *A cryptosystem should be secured even if everything about the system, except the key, is public knowledge.*

open the lock box. The first layer of defense is the location of the box, and the second layer is the key combination to open the lock box. In fact in this case, we do not mind anyone finding the lock box, because finding the lock box itself is not sufficient to open the door. But, anyone who finds the lock box can break it to get the key out, rather than trying out the key combination. In that case, security by obscurity adds some value as a layer of protection—but it's never good by its own.

Design Principles

Jerome Saltzer and Michael Schroeder produced one of the most widely cited research papers in the information security domain.[23] According to the paper, irrespective of the level of functionality provided, the effectiveness of a set of protection mechanisms depends upon the ability of a system to prevent security violations. In most of the cases, building a system at any level of functionality that prevents all unauthorized actions has proved to be extremely difficult. For an advanced user, it is not hard to find at least one way to crash a system, preventing other authorized users accessing the system. Penetration tests that involved a large number of different general-purpose systems have shown that users can build programs to obtain unauthorized access to information stored within. Even in systems designed and implemented with security as a top priority, design and implementation flaws could provide ways around the intended access restrictions. Even though the design and construction techniques that could systematically exclude flaws are the topic of much research activity, according to Jerome and Michael, no complete method applicable to the construction of large general-purpose systems existed during the early 1970s. In this paper, Jerome Saltzer and Michael Schroeder further highlight eight design principles for securing information in computer systems, as described in the following sections.

Least Privilege

The principle of least privilege states that an entity should only have the required set of permissions to perform the actions for which they are authorized, and no more. Permissions can be added as needed and should be revoked when no longer in use.

---

[23]The Protection of Information in Computer Systems, `http://web.mit.edu/Saltzer/www/`
  `publications/protection/`, October 11, 1974.

This limits the damage that can result from an accident or error. The *need to know* principle, which follows the least privilege philosophy, is popular in military security. This states that even if someone has all the necessary security clearance levels to access information, they should not be granted access unless there is a real/proven need.

Unfortunately, this principle didn't apply in the case of Edward Snowden,[24] or he was clever enough to work around it. Edward Snowden who worked for NSA (National Security Agency of the United States) as a contractor in Hawaii used unsophisticated techniques to access and copy an estimated 1.7 million classified NSA files. He was an employee of NSA and had legitimate access to all the information he downloaded. Snowden used a simple web crawler, similar to Google's Googlebot (which collects documents from the Web to build a searchable index for the Google Search engine), to crawl and scrape all the data from NSA's internal wiki pages. Being a system administrator, Snowden's role was to back up the computer systems and move information to local servers; he had no need to know the content of the data.

ISO 27002 (formerly known as ISO 17799) also emphasizes on the *least privilege* principle. ISO 27002 (*Information Technology - Code of Practice for Information Security Management*) standard is a well-known, widely used standard in the information security domain. It was originally developed by the British Standards Institution and called the BS7799 and subsequently accepted by the International Organization for Standardization (ISO) and published under their title in December 2000. According to ISO 27002, privileges should be allocated to individuals on a need-to-use basis and on an event-by-event basis, that is, the minimum requirement for their functional role only when needed. It further identifies the concept of "zero access" to start, which suggests that no access or virtually no access is the default, so that all subsequent access and the ultimate accumulation can be traced back through an approval process.[25]

Fail-Safe Defaults

The fail-safe defaults principle highlights the importance of making a system safe by default. A user's default access level to any resource in the system should be "denied" unless they've been granted a "permit" explicitly. A fail-safe design will not endanger the

---

[24]Snowden Used Low-Cost Tool to Best NSA, `www.nytimes.com/2014/02/09/us/snowden-used-low-cost-tool-to-best-nsa.html`

[25]Implementing Least Privilege at Your Enterprise, `www.sans.org/reading-room/whitepapers/bestprac/implementing-privilege-enterprise-1188`

system when it fails. The Java Security Manager implementation follows this principle—once engaged, none of the components in the system can perform any privileged operations unless explicitly permitted. Firewall rules are another example. Data packets are only allowed through a firewall when it's explicitly allowed; otherwise everything is denied by default.

Any complex system will have failure modes. Failures are unavoidable and should be planned for, to make sure that no security risks get immerged as part of a system failure. Possibility of failures is an assumption made under the security design philosophy, *defense in depth*. If no failures are expected, there is no point of having multiple layers of defense. Let's go through an example where every one of us is most probably familiar with: credit card verification. When you swipe your credit card at a retail store, the credit card machine there connects to the corresponding credit card service to verify the card details. The credit card verification service will verify the transaction after considering the available amount in the card, whether the card is reported as lost or blacklisted, and other context-sensitive information like the location where the transaction is initiated from, the time of the day, and many other factors. If the credit card machine fails to connect to the verification service, what would happen? In such case, the merchants are given a machine to get an imprint of your card manually. Getting an imprint of the card is not just sufficient, as it does not do any verification. The merchant also has to talk to his bank over the phone, authenticate by providing the merchant number, and then get the transaction verified. That's the fail-safe process for credit card verification, as the failure of the credit card transaction machine does not lead into any security risks. In case the merchant's phone line is also completely down, then according to the fail-safe defaults principle, the merchant should avoid accepting any credit card payments.

The failure to adhere to fail-safe defaults has resulted in many TLS (Transport Layer Security)/SSL (Secure Sockets Layer) vulnerabilities. Most of the TLS/SSL vulnerabilities are based on the TLS/SSL downgrade attack, where the attacker makes the server to use a cryptographically weak cipher suite (we discuss TLS in depth in Appendix C). In May 2015, a group from INRIA, Microsoft Research, Johns Hopkins, the University of Michigan, and the University of Pennsylvania published a deep analysis[26] of the Diffie-Hellman algorithm as used in TLS and other protocols. This analysis included a novel downgrade attack against the TLS protocol itself called Logjam, which exploits *export* cryptography. *Export* ciphers are weaker ciphers that were intentionally designed to be

---

[26]Imperfect Forward Secrecy: How Diffie-Hellman Fails in Practice, `https://weakdh.org/ imperfect-forward-secrecy-ccs15.pdf`

weaker to meet certain legal requirements enforced by the US government, in 1990s. Only weaker ciphers were legally possible to export into other countries outside the United States. Even though this legal requirement was lifted later on, most of the popular application servers still support *export* ciphers. The Logjam attack exploited the servers having support for *export* ciphers by altering the TLS handshake and forcing the servers to use a weaker cipher suite, which can be broken later on. According to the fail-safe defaults principle, in this scenario, the server should abort the TLS handshake when they see a cryptographically weaker algorithm is suggested by the client, rather than accepting and proceeding with it.

Economy of Mechanism

The economy of mechanism principle highlights the value of simplicity. The design should be as simple as possible. All the component interfaces and the interactions between them should be simple enough to understand. If the design and the implementation were simple, the possibility of bugs would be low, and at the same time, the effort on testing would be less. A simple and easy-to-understand design and implementation would also make it easy to modify and maintain, without introducing bugs exponentially. As discussed earlier in this chapter, Gary McGraw in his book, *Software Security*, highlights *complexity* in both the code and the system design as one attribute that is responsible for the high rate of data breaches.

The *keep it simple, stupid* (KISS) principle introduced by the US Navy in 1960 is quite close to what Jerome Saltzer and Michael Schroeder explained under the economy of mechanism principle. It states that most systems work best if they are kept simple rather than made complicated.[27] In practice, even though we want to adhere to the KISS principle, from operating systems to application code, everything is becoming more and more complex. Microsoft Windows 3.1 in 1990 started with a codebase slightly over 3 million lines of code. Over time, requirements got complex, and in 2001 Windows XP codebase crossed 40 million lines of code. As we discussed before in this chapter, at the time of this writing, the complete Google codebase to run all its Internet services was around 2 billion lines of code. Even though one can easily argue the increased number of lines of code will not directly reflect the code complexity, in most of the cases, sadly it's the case.

---

[27]KISS principle, https://en.wikipedia.org/wiki/KISS_principle

Complete Mediation

With complete mediation principle, a system should validate access rights to all its resources to ensure whether they're allowed to access or not. Most systems do access validation once at the entry point to build a cached permission matrix. Each subsequent operation will be validated against the cached permission matrix. This pattern is mostly followed to address performance concerns by reducing the time spent on policy evaluation, but could quite easily invite attackers to exploit the system. In practice, most systems cache user permissions and roles, but employ a mechanism to clear the cache in an event of a permission or role update.

Let's have a look at an example. When a process running under the UNIX operating system tries to read a file, the operating system itself determines whether the process has the appropriate rights to read the file. If that is the case, the process receives a file descriptor encoded with the allowed level of access. Each time the process reads the file, it presents the file descriptor to the kernel. The kernel examines the file descriptor and then allows the access. In case the owner of the file revokes the read permission from the process after the file descriptor is issued, the kernel still allows access, violating the principle of complete mediation. According to the principle of complete mediation, any permission update should immediately reflect in the application runtime (if cached, then in the cache).

Open Design

The open design principle highlights the importance of building a system in an open manner—with no secrets, confidential algorithms. This is the opposite of security by obscurity, discussed earlier in the section "Design Challenges." Most of the strong cryptographic algorithms in use today are designed and implemented openly. One good example is the AES (Advanced Encryption Standard) symmetric key algorithm. NIST (National Institute of Standards and Technology, United States) followed an open process, which expanded from 1997 to 2000 to pick the best cryptographically strong algorithm for AES, to replace DES (Data Encryption Standard), which by then was susceptible to brute-force attacks. On January 2, 1997, the initial announcement was made by NIST regarding the competition to build an algorithm to replace DES. During the first nine months, after the competition began, there were 15 different proposals from several countries. All the designs were open, and each one of them was subjected to thorough cryptanalysis. NIST also held two open conferences to discuss the proposals, in August 1998 and March 1999, and then narrowed down all 15 proposals into 5. After another round of intense analysis during the April 2000 AES conference, the winner was announced in October 2000, and they picked Rijndael as the AES algorithm. More than the final outcome, everyone (even the losers of the competition) appreciated NIST for the open process they carried throughout the AES selection phase.

The open design principle further highlights that the architects or developers of a particular application should not rely on the design or coding secrets of the application to make it secure. If you rely on open source software, then this is not even possible at all. There are no secrets in open source development. Under the open source philosophy from the design decisions to feature development, all happens openly. One can easily argue, due to the exact same reason, open source software is bad in security. This is a very popular argument against open source software, but facts prove otherwise. According to a report[28] by Netcraft published in January 2015, almost 51% of all active sites in the Internet are hosted on web servers powered by the open source Apache web server. The OpenSSL library, which is another open source project implementing the SSL (Secure Sockets Layer) and TLS (Transport Layer Security) protocols, is used by more than 5.5 million web sites in the Internet, by November 2015.[29] If anyone seriously worries about the security aspects of open source, it's highly recommended for him or her to read the white paper published by SANS Institute, under the topic *Security Concerns in Using Open Source Software for Enterprise Requirements*.[30]

Note   Gartner predicts, by 2020, 98% of IT organizations will leverage open source software technology in their mission-critical IT portfolios, including many cases where they will be unaware of it.[31]

---

[28]Netcraft January 2015 Web Server Survey, http://news.netcraft.com/archives/2015/01/15/january-2015-web-server-survey.html

[29]OpenSSL Usage Statistics, http://trends.builtwith.com/Server/OpenSSL

[30]Security Concerns in Using Open Source Software for Enterprise Requirements, www.sans.org/reading-room/whitepapers/awareness/security-concerns-open-source-software-enterprise-requirements-1305

[31]Middleware Technologies—Enabling Digital Business, www.gartner.com/doc/3163926/hightech-tuesday-webinar-middleware-technologies

Separation of Privilege

The principle of separation of privilege states that a system should not grant permissions based on a single condition. The same principle is also known as segregation of duties, and one can look into it from multiple aspects. For example, say a reimbursement claim can be submitted by any employee but can only be approved by the manager. What if the manager wants to submit a reimbursement? According to the principle of separation of privilege, the manager should not be granted the right to approve his or her own reimbursement claims.

It is interesting to see how Amazon follows the separation of privilege principle in securing AWS (Amazon Web Services) infrastructure. According to the security white paper[32] published by Amazon, the AWS production network is segregated from the Amazon Corporate network by means of a complex set of network security/segregation devices. AWS developers and administrators on the corporate network who need to access AWS cloud components in order to maintain them must explicitly request access through the AWS ticketing system. All requests are reviewed and approved by the applicable service owner. Approved AWS personnel then connect to the AWS network through a bastion host that restricts access to network devices and other cloud components, logging all activity for security review. Access to bastion hosts require SSH public key authentication for all user accounts on the host.

NSA (National Security Agency, United States) too follows a similar strategy. In a fact sheet[33] published by NSA, it highlights the importance of implementing the separation of privilege principle at the network level. Networks are composed of interconnected devices with varying functions, purposes, and sensitivity levels. Networks can consist of multiple segments that may include web servers, database servers, development environments, and the infrastructure that binds them together. Because these segments have different purposes as well as different security concerns, segregating them appropriately is paramount in securing a network from exploitation and malicious intent.

---

[32]AWS security white paper, `https://d0.awsstatic.com/whitepapers/aws-security-whitepaper.pdf`

[33]Segregating networks and functions, `www.nsa.gov/ia/_files/factsheets/I43V_Slick_Sheets/Slicksheet_SegregatingNetworksAndFunctions_Web.pdf`

Least Common Mechanism

The principle of least common mechanism concerns the risk of sharing state information among different components. In other words, it says that mechanisms used to access resources should not be shared. This principle can be interpreted in multiple angles. One good example is to see how Amazon Web Services (AWS) works as an infrastructure as a service (IaaS) provider. Elastic Compute Cloud, or EC2, is one of the key services provided by AWS. Netflix, Reddit, *Newsweek*, and many other companies run their services on EC2. EC2 provides a cloud environment to spin up and down server instances of your choice based on the load you get. With this approach, you do not need to plan before for the highest expected load and let the resources idle most of the time when there is low load. Even though in this case, each EC2 user gets his own isolated server instance running its own guest operating system (Linux, Windows, etc.), ultimately all the servers are running on top of a shared platform maintained by AWS. This shared platform includes a networking infrastructure, a hardware infrastructure, and storage. On top of the infrastructure, there runs a special software called hypervisor. All the guest operating systems are running on top of the hypervisor. Hypervisor provides a virtualized environment over the hardware infrastructure. Xen and KVM are two popular hypervisors, and AWS is using Xen internally. Even though a given virtual server instance running for one customer does not have access to another virtual server instance running for another customer, if someone can find a security hole in the hypervisor, then he can get the control of all the virtual server instances running on EC2. Even though this sounds like nearly impossible, in the past there were many security vulnerabilities reported against the Xen hypervisor.[34]

The principle of least common mechanism encourages minimizing common, shared usage of resources. Even though the usage of common infrastructure cannot be completely eliminated, its usage can be minimized based on business requirements. AWS Virtual Private Cloud (VPC) provides a logically isolated infrastructure for each of its users. Optionally, one can also select to launch dedicated instances, which run on hardware dedicated to each customer for additional isolation.

The principle of least common mechanism can also be applied to a scenario where you store and manage data in a shared multitenanted environment. If we follow the strategy shared everything, then the data from different customers can be stored in

---

[34]Xen Security Advisories, `http://xenbits.xen.org/xsa/`

the same table of the same database, isolating each customer data by the customer id. The application, which accesses the database, will make sure that a given customer can only access his own data. With this approach, if someone finds a security hole in the application logic, he can access all customer data. The other approach could be to have an isolated database for each customer. This is a more expensive but much secure option. With this we can minimize what is being shared between customers.

Psychological Acceptability

The principle of psychological acceptability states that security mechanisms should not make the resource more difficult to access than if the security mechanisms were not present. Accessibility to resources should not be made difficult by security mechanisms. If security mechanisms kill the usability or accessibility of resources, then users may find ways to turn off those mechanisms. Wherever possible, security mechanisms should be transparent to the users of the system or at most introduce minimal distractions. Security mechanisms should be user-friendly to encourage the users to occupy them more frequently.

Microsoft introduced information cards in 2005 as a new paradigm for authentication to fight against phishing. But the user experience was bad, with a high setup cost, for people who were used to username/password-based authentication. It went down in history as another unsuccessful initiative from Microsoft.

Most of the web sites out there use CAPTCHA as a way to differentiate human beings from automated scripts. CAPTCHA is in fact an acronym, which stands for Completely Automated Public Turing test to tell Computers and Humans Apart. CAPTCHA is based on a challenge-response model and mostly used along with user registration and password recovery functions to avoid any automated brute-force attacks. Even though this tightens up security, this also could easily kill the user experience. Some of the challenges provided by certain CAPTCHA implementations are not even readable to humans. Google tries to address this concern with Google reCAPTCHA.[35] With reCAPTCHA users can attest they are humans without having to solve a CAPTCHA. Instead, with just a single click, one can confirm that he is not a robot. This is also known as No CAPTCHA reCAPTCHA experience.

---

[35]Google reCAPTCHA, `www.google.com/recaptcha/intro/index.html`

Security Triad

Confidentiality, integrity, and availability (CIA), widely known as the triad of information security, are three key factors used in benchmarking information systems security. This is also known as CIA triad or AIC triad. The CIA triad helps in both designing a security model and assessing the strength of an existing security model. In the following sections, we discuss the three key attributes of the CIA triad in detail.

Confidentiality

Confidentiality attribute of the CIA triad worries about how to protect data from unintended recipients, both at rest and in transit. You achieve confidentiality by protecting transport channels and storage with encryption. For APIs, where the transport channel is HTTP (most of the time), you can use Transport Layer Security (TLS), which is in fact known as HTTPS. For storage, you can use disk-level encryption or application-level encryption. Channel encryption or transport-level encryption only protects a message while it's in transit. As soon as the message leaves the transport channel, it's no more secure. In other words, transport-level encryption only provides point-to-point protection and truncates from where the connection ends. In contrast, there is message-level encryption, which happens at the application level and has no dependency on the transport channel. In other words, with message-level encryption, the application itself has to worry about how to encrypt the message, prior to sending it over the wire, and it's also known as end-to-end encryption. If you secure data with message-level encryption, then you can use even an insecure channel (like HTTP) to transport the message.

A TLS connection, when going through a proxy, from the client to the server can be established in two ways: either with TLS bridging or with TLS tunneling. Almost all proxy servers support both modes. For a highly secured deployment, TLS tunneling is recommended. In TLS bridging, the initial connection truncates from the proxy server, and a new connection to the gateway (or the server) is established from there. That means the data is in cleartext while inside the proxy server. Any intruder who can plant malware in the proxy server can intercept traffic that passes through. With TLS tunneling, the proxy server facilitates creating a direct channel between the client machine and the gateway (or the server). The data flow through this channel is invisible to the proxy server.

Message-level encryption, on the other hand, is independent from the underlying transport. It's the application developers' responsibility to encrypt and decrypt messages. Because this is application specific, it hurts interoperability and builds tight couplings between the sender and the receiver. Each has to know how to encrypt/ decrypt data beforehand—which will not scale well in a largely distributed system. To overcome this challenge, there have been some concentrated efforts to build standards around message-level security. XML Encryption is one such effort, led by the W3C. It standardizes how to encrypt an XML payload. Similarly, the IETF JavaScript Object Signing and Encryption (JOSE) working group has built a set of standards for JSON payloads. In Chapters 7 and 8, we discuss JSON Web Signature and JSON Web Encryption, respectively—which are two prominent standards in securing JSON messages.

Note   Secure Sockets Layer (SSL) and Transport Layer Security (TLS) are often used interchangeably, but in pure technical terms, they aren't the same. TLS is the successor of SSL 3.0. TLS 1.0, which is defined under the IETF RFC 2246, is based on the SSL 3.0 protocol specification, which was published by Netscape. The differences between TLS 1.0 and SSL 3.0 aren't dramatic, but they're significant enough that TLS 1.0 and SSL 3.0 don't interoperate.

There are few more key differences between transport-level security and message-level security, in addition to what were discussed before.

- Transport-level security being point to point, it encrypts the entire message while in transit.

- Since transport-level relies on the underlying channel for protection, application developers have no control over which part of the data to encrypt and which part not to.

- Partial encryption isn't supported by transport-level security, but it is supported by message-level security.

- Performance is a key factor, which differentiates message-level security from transport-level security. Message-level encryption is far more expensive than transport-level encryption, in terms of resource consumption.

- Message-level encryption happens at the application layer, and it has to take into consideration the type and the structure of the message to carry out the encryption process. If it's an XML message, then the process defined in the XML Encryption standard has to be followed.

Integrity

Integrity is a guarantee of data's correctness and trustworthiness and the ability to detect any unauthorized modifications. It ensures that data is protected from unauthorized or unintentional alteration, modification, or deletion. The way to achieve integrity is twofold: preventive measures and detective measures. Both measures have to take care of data in transit as well as data at rest.

To prevent data from alteration while in transit, you should use a secure channel that only intended parties can read or do message-level encryption. TLS (Transport Layer Security) is the recommended approach for transport-level encryption. TLS itself has a way of detecting data modifications. It sends a message authentication code in each message from the first handshake, which can be verified by the receiving party to make sure the data has not been modified while in transit. If you use message-level encryption to prevent data alteration, then to detect any modification in the message at the recipient, the sender has to sign the message, and with the public key of the sender, the recipient can verify the signature. Similar to what we discussed in the previous section, there are standards based on the message type and the structure, which define the process of signing. If it's an XML message, then the XML Signature standard by W3C defines the process.

For data at rest, you can calculate the message digest periodically and keep it in a secured place. The audit logs, which can be altered by an intruder to hide suspicious activities, need to be protected for integrity. Also with the advent of network storage and new technology trends, which have resulted in new failure modes for storage, interesting challenges arise in ensuring data integrity. A paper[36] published by Gopalan Sivathanu, Charles P. Wright, and Erez Zadok of Stony Brook University highlights the causes of integrity violations in storage and presents a survey of integrity assurance techniques that exist today. It describes several interesting applications of storage integrity checking, apart from security, and discusses the implementation issues associated with those techniques.

---

[36]Ensuring Data Integrity in Storage: Techniques and Applications, `www.fsl.cs.sunysb.edu/docs/integrity-storagess05/integrity.html`

Note   HTTP Digest authentication with the quality of protection (qop) value set to `auth-int` can be used to protect messages for integrity. Appendix F discusses HTTP Digest authentication in depth.

Availability

Making a system available for legitimate users to access all the time is the ultimate goal of any system design. Security isn't the only aspect to look into, but it plays a major role in keeping the system up and running. The goal of the security design should be to make the system highly available by protecting it from illegal access attempts. Doing so is extremely challenging. Attacks, especially on a public API, can vary from an attacker planting malware in the system to a highly organized distributed denial of service (DDoS) attack.

DDoS attacks are hard to eliminate fully, but with a careful design, they can be minimized to reduce their impact. In most cases, DDoS attacks must be detected at the network perimeter level—so, the application code doesn't need to worry too much. But vulnerabilities in the application code can be exploited to bring a system down. A paper[37] published by Christian Mainka, Juraj Somorovsky, Jorg Schwenk, and Andreas Falkenberg discusses eight types of DoS attacks that can be carried out against SOAP-based APIs with XML payloads:

- *Coercive parsing attack*: The attacker sends an XML document with a deeply nested XML structure. When a DOM-based parser processes the XML document, an out-of-memory exception or a high CPU load can occur.

- *SOAP array attack*: Forces the attacked web service to declare a very large SOAP array. This can exhaust the web service's memory.

- *XML element count attack*: Attacks the server by sending a SOAP message with a high number of non-nested elements.

---

[37]A New Approach towards DoS Penetration Testing on Web Services, `www.nds.rub.de/media/nds/veroeffentlichungen/2013/07/19/ICWS_DoS.pdf`

- *XML attribute count attack*: Attacks the server by sending a SOAP message with a high attribute count.

- *XML entity expansion attack*: Causes a system failure by forcing the server to recursively resolve entities defined in a document type definition (DTD). This attack is also known as an *XML bomb* or a *billion laughs attack.*

- *XML external entity DoS attack*: Causes a system failure by forcing the server to resolve a large external entity defined in a DTD. If an attacker is able to execute the external entity attack, an additional attack surface may appear.

- *XML overlong name attack*: Injects overlong XML nodes in the XML document. Overlong nodes can be overlong element names, attribute names, attribute values, or namespace definitions.

- *Hash collision attack (HashDoS)*: Different keys result in the same bucket assignments, causing a collision. A collision leads to resource-intensive computations in the bucket. When a weak hash function is used, an attacker can intentionally create hash collisions that lead to a system failure.

Most of these attacks can be prevented at the application level. For CPU- or memory-intensive operations, you can keep threshold values. For example, to prevent a coercive parsing attack, the XML parser can enforce a limit on the number of elements. Similarly, if your application executes a thread for a longer time, you can set a threshold and kill it. Aborting any further processing of a message as soon as it's found to be not legitimate is the best way to fight against DoS attacks. This also highlights the importance of having authentication/authorization checks closest to the entry point of the flow.

Note   According to eSecurity Planet, one of the largest DDoS attacks hit the Internet in March 2013 and targeted the Cloudflare network with 120 Gbps. The upstream providers were hit by 300 Gbps DDoS at the peak of the attack.

There are also DoS attacks carried out against JSON vulnerabilities. CVE-2013-0269[38] explains a scenario in which a carefully crafted JSON message can be used to trigger the creation of arbitrary Ruby symbols or certain internal objects, to result in a DoS attack.

Security Control

The CIA triad (confidentiality, integrity, and availability), which we discussed in detail in the previous section of this chapter, is one of the core principles of information security. In achieving CIA, *authentication*, *authorization*, *nonrepudiation*, and *auditing* are four prominent controls, which play a vital role. In the following sections, we discuss these four security controls in detail.

Authentication

Authentication is the process of identifying a user, a system, or a thing in a unique manner to prove that it is the one who it claims to be. Authentication can be direct or brokered, based on how you bring your authentication assertions. If you directly log in to a system just providing your username and password, it falls under direct authentication. In other words, under direct authentication, the entity which wants to authenticate itself presents the authentication assertions to the service it wants to access. Under brokered authentication, there is a third party involved. This third party is commonly known as an *identity provider*. When you log in to your Yelp account via Facebook, it falls under brokered authentication, and Facebook is the identity provider. With brokered authentication, the service provider (or the website you want to log in, or the API you want to access) does not trust you directly. It only trusts an identity provider. You can access the service only if the trusted identity provider (by the service provider) passes a positive assertion to the service provider.

Authentication can be done in a single factor or in multiple factors (also known as multifactor authentication). *Something you know*, *something you are*, and *something you have* are the well-known three factors of authentication. For multifactor authentication, a system should use a combination of at least two factors. Combining two techniques

---

[38]CVE-2013-0269, https://nvd.nist.gov/vuln/detail/CVE-2013-0269

that fall under the same category isn't considered multifactor authentication. For example, entering a username and a password and then a PIN number isn't considered multifactor authentication, because both fall under the *something you know* category.

Note   Google two-step verification falls under multifactor authentication. First you need to provide a username and a password (something you know), and then a PIN is sent to your mobile phone. Knowing the PIN verifies that the registered mobile phone is under your possession: it's something you have. Then again one can argue this is not multifactor authentication, because you only need to know the PIN, having the phone with you to get the PIN is not mandatory. This sounds bit weird, but Grant Blakeman's incident proved exactly the same thing.[39] An attacker was able to set a call forwarding number into Grant's cell phone and was able to receive Google password reset information to the new number (via call forwarding).

Something You Know

Passwords, passphrases, and PIN numbers belong to the category of *something you know*. This has been the most popular form of authentication not just for decades but also for centuries. It goes back to the eighteenth century. In the Arabian folktale *Ali Baba and the Forty Thieves* from *One Thousand and One Nights*, Ali Baba uses the passphrase "open sesame" to open the door to a hidden cave. Since then, this has become the most popular form of authentication. Unfortunately, it's also the weakest form of authentication. Password-protected systems can be broken in several ways. Going back to Ali Baba's story, his brother-in-law got stuck in the same cave without knowing the password and tried shouting all the words he knew. This, in modern days, is known as a *brute-force attack*. The first known brute-force attack took place in the 18th century. Since then, it has become a popular way of breaking password-secured systems.

---

[39]The value of a name, https://ello.co/gb/post/knOWk-qeTqfSpJ6f8-arCQ

Note   In April 2013, WordPress was hit with a brute-force attack of massive scale. The average scans per day in April were more than 100,000.[40] There are different forms of brute-force attacks. The dictionary attack is one of them, where the brute-force attack is carried out with a limited set of inputs based on a dictionary of commonly used words. This is why you should have a corporate password policy that should enforce strong passwords with mixed alphanumeric characters that aren't found in dictionaries. Most public web sites enforce a CAPTCHA after few failed login attempts. This makes automated/tool-based brute-force attacks harder to execute.

Something You Have

Certificates and smart card–based authentication fall into the category of *something you have*. This is a much stronger form of authentication than something you know. TLS mutual authentication is the most popular way of securing APIs with client certificates; this is covered in detail in Chapter 3.

FIDO (Fast IDentity Online) authentication also falls under the *something you have* category. FIDO alliance[41] has published three open specifications to address certain concerns in strong authentication: FIDO Universal Second Factor (FIDO U2F), FIDO Universal Authentication Framework (FIDO UAF) and the Client to Authenticator Protocol (CTAP). FIDO U2F protocol allows online services to augment the security of their existing password infrastructure by adding a strong second factor to user login. The largest deployment of FIDO U2F–based authentication is at Google. Google has been using FIDO U2F internally for some time to secure its internal services, and in October 2014 Google made FIDO U2F enabled to all its users publicly.[42]

---

[40]The WordPress Brute Force Attack Timeline, http://blog.sucuri.net/2013/04/the-wordpress-brute-force-attack-timeline.html

[41]FIDO Alliance, https://fidoalliance.org/specifications/overview/

[42]Strengthening 2-Step Verification with Security Key, https://googleonlinesecurity.blogspot.com/2014/10/strengthening-2-step-verification-with.html

Something You Are

Fingerprints, eye retina, facial recognition, and all other biometric-based authentication techniques fall into the category of *something you are*. This is the strongest form of authentication. In most of the cases, biometric authentication is not done on its own, rather used with another factor to further improve the security.

With the wide adoption of mobile devices, most of the retailers, financial institutes, and many others have chosen fingerprint-based authentication for their mobile apps. In the iOS platform, all these applications associate their username- and password-based authentication with Apple Touch ID (or face recognition). Once the initial association is done, a user can log in to all the associated applications just by scanning his fingerprint. Further iPhone also associates Touch ID with App Store login and to authorize Apple Pay transactions.

Authorization

Authorization is the process of validating what actions an authenticated user, a system, or a thing can perform within a well-defined system boundary. Authorization happens with the assumption that the user is already authenticated. Discretionary Access Control (DAC) and Mandatory Access Control (MAC) are two prominent models to control access in a system.

With Discretionary Access Control (DAC), the user who owns the data, at their discretion, can transfer rights to another user. Most operating systems support DAC, including Unix, Linux, and Windows. When you create a file in Linux, you can decide who should be able to read, write to, and execute it. Nothing prevents you from sharing it with any user or a group of users. There is no centralized control—which can easily bring security flaws into the system.

With Mandatory Access Control (MAC), only designated users are allowed to grant rights. Once rights are granted, users can't transfer them. SELinux, Trusted Solaris, and TrustedBSD are some of the operating systems that support MAC.

Note   SELinux is an NSA research project that added the Mandatory Access Control (MAC) architecture to the Linux kernel, which was then merged into the mainstream version of Linux in August 2003. It utilizes a Linux 2.6 kernel feature called the Linux Security Modules (LSM) interface.

The difference between DAC and MAC lies in who owns the right to delegate. In either case, you need to have a way to represent access control rules or the access matrix. Authorization tables, access control lists (see Figure 2-2), and capabilities are three ways of representing access control rules. An authorization table is a three-column table with subject, action, and resource. The subject can be an individual user or a group. With access control lists, each resource is associated with a list, indicating, for each subject, the actions that the subject can exercise on the resource. With capabilities, each subject has an associated list called a capability list, indicating, for each resource, the actions that the user is allowed to exercise on the resource. A bank locker key can be considered a capability: the locker is the resource, and the user holds the key to the resource. At the time the user tries to open the locker with the key, you only have to worry about the capabilities of the key—not the capabilities of its owner. An access control list is resource driven, whereas capabilities are subject driven.

Authorization tables, access control lists and capabilities are very coarse grained. One alternative is to use policy-based access control. With policy-based access control, you can have authorization policies with fine granularity. In addition, capabilities and access control lists can be dynamically derived from policies. eXtensible Access Control Markup Language (XACML) is one of the OASIS standards for policy-based access control.

	File-1	File-2	File-3
Tom	Read	Write	Read
Peter	Write	Write	Read
Jene	Read	Read	Write

Figure 2-2. *Access control list*

Note   XACML is an XML-based open standard for policy-based access control developed under the OASIS XACML Technical Committee. XACML 3.0, the latest XACML specification, was standardized in January 2013.[43] Then again XACML is little too complex in defining access control policies, irrespective of how powerful it is. You can also check the Open Policy Agent (OPA) project, which has become quite popular recently in building fine-grained access control policies.

Nonrepudiation

Whenever you do a business transaction via an API by proving your identity, later you should not be able to reject it or repudiate it. The property that ensures the inability to repudiate is known as *nonrepudiation*. You do it once—you own it forever. Nonrepudiation should provide proof of the origin and the integrity of data, both in an unforgeable manner, which a third party can verify at any time. Once a transaction is initiated, none of its content—including the user identity, date and time, and transaction details—should be altered to maintain the transaction integrity and allow future verifications. One has to ensure that the transaction is unaltered and logged after it's committed and confirmed. Logs must be archived and properly secured to prevent unauthorized modifications. Whenever there is a repudiation dispute, transaction logs along with other logs or data can be retrieved to verify the initiator, date and time, transaction history, and so on.

Note   TLS ensures authentication (by verifying the certificates), confidentiality (by encrypting the data with a secret key), and integrity (by digesting the data), but not nonrepudiation. In TLS, the Message Authentication Code (MAC) value of the data transmitted is calculated with a shared secret key, known to both the client and the server. Shared keys can't be used for nonrepudiation.

---

[43]XACML 3.0 specification, `http://docs.oasis-open.org/xacml/3.0/xacml-3.0-core-spec-os-en.pdf`

Digital signatures provide a strong binding between the user (who initiates the transaction) and the transaction the user performs. A key known only to the user should sign the complete transaction, and the server (or the service) should be able to verify the signature through a trusted broker that vouches for the legitimacy of the user's key. This trusted broker can be a certificate authority (CA). Once the signature is verified, the server knows the identity of the user and can guarantee the integrity of the data. For nonrepudiation purposes, the data must be stored securely for any future verification.

Note   The paper[44] *Non-Repudiation in Practice*, by Chii-Ren Tsai of Citigroup, discusses two potential nonrepudiation architectures for financial transactions using challenge-response one-time password tokens and digital signatures.

Auditing

There are two aspects of auditing: keeping track of all legitimate access attempts to facilitate nonrepudiation, and keeping track of all illegal access attempts to identify possible threats. There can be cases where you're permitted to access a resource, but it should be with a valid purpose. For example, a mobile operator is allowed to access a user's call history, but he should not do so without a request from the corresponding user. If someone frequently accesses a user's call history, you can detect it with proper audit trails. Audit trails also play a vital role in fraud detection. An administrator can define fraud-detection patterns, and the audit logs can be evaluated in near real time to find any matches.

Summary

- Security isn't an afterthought. It has to be an integral part of any development project and also for APIs. It starts with requirements gathering and proceeds through the design, development, testing, deployment, and monitoring phases.

---

[44]*Non-Repudiation in Practice*, `www.researchgate.net/publication/240926842_Non-Repudiation_In_Practice`

- Connectivity, extensibility, and complexity are the three trends behind the rise of data breaches around the globe in the last few years.

- The most challenging thing in any security design is to find and maintain the right balance between security and the user comfort.

- A proper security design should care about all the communication links in the system. Any system is no stronger than its weakest link.

- A layered approach is preferred for any system being tightened for security. This is also known as defense in depth.

- Insider attacks are less complicated, but highly effective.

- Kerckhoffs' principle emphasizes that a system should be secured by its design, not because the design is unknown to an adversary.

- The principle of least privilege states that an entity should only have the required set of permissions to perform the actions for which they are authorized, and no more.

- The fail-safe defaults principle highlights the importance of making a system safe by default.

- The economy of mechanism principle highlights the value of simplicity. The design should be as simple as possible.

- With complete mediation principle, a system should validate access rights to all its resources to ensure whether they're allowed to access or not.

- The open design principle highlights the importance of building a system in an open manner—with no secrets, confidential algorithms.

- The principle of separation of privilege states that a system should not grant permissions based on a single condition.

- The principle of least common mechanism concerns the risk of sharing state information among different components.

- The principle of psychological acceptability states that security mechanisms should not make the resource more difficult to access than if the security mechanisms were not present.

- Confidentiality, integrity, and availability (CIA), widely known as the triad of information security, are three key factors used in benchmarking information systems security.

CHAPTER 3

Securing APIs with Transport Layer Security (TLS)

Securing APIs with Transport Layer Security (TLS) is the most common form of protection we see in any API deployment. If you are new to TLS, please check Appendix C first, which explains TLS in detail and how it works. In securing APIs, we use TLS to secure or encrypt the communication—or protect the data in transit—and also we use TLS mutual authentication to make sure only the legitimate clients can access the APIs.

In this chapter, we discuss how to deploy an API implemented in Java Spring Boot, enable TLS, and protect an API with mutual TLS.

Setting Up the Environment

In this section, we'll see how we can develop an API using Spring Boot from scratch. Spring Boot (https://projects.spring.io/spring-boot/) is the most popular microservices development framework for Java developers. To be precise, Spring Boot offers an opinionated[1] runtime for Spring, which takes out a lot of complexities. Even though Spring Boot is opinionated, it also gives developers to override many of its default picks. Due to the fact that many Java developers are familiar with Spring, and the ease of development is a key success factor in the microservices world, many adopted Spring Boot. Even for Java developers who are not using Spring, still it is a household name. If you have worked on Spring, you surely would have worried how painful it was

---

[1]An opinionated framework locks or guides its developers into its own way of doing things.

© Prabath Siriwardena 2020
P. Siriwardena, *Advanced API Security*, https://doi.org/10.1007/978-1-4842-2050-4_3

to deal with large, chunky XML configuration files. Unlike Spring, Spring Boot believes in convention over configuration—no more XML hell! In this book, we use Spring Boot to implement our APIs. Even if you are not familiar with Java, you will be able to get started with no major learning curve, as we provide all the code examples.

To run the samples, you will need `Java 8` or latest, `Maven 3.2` or latest, and a `git` client. Once you are successfully done with the installation, run the following two commands in the command line to make sure everything is working fine. If you'd like some help in setting up Java or Maven, there are plenty of online resources out there.

```
\>java -version
java version "1.8.0_121" Java(TM) SE Runtime Environment
(build 1.8.0_121-b13)
Java HotSpot(TM) 64-Bit Server VM (build 25.121-b13, mixed mode)
\>mvn -version
Apache Maven 3.5.0 (ff8f5e7444045639af65f6095c62210b5713f426; 2017-04-
03T12:39:06-07:00)
Maven home: /usr/local/Cellar/maven/3.5.0/libexec
Java version: 1.8.0_121, vendor: Oracle Corporation
Java home: /Library/Java/JavaVirtualMachines/jdk1.8.0_121.jdk/Contents/
Home/jre Default locale: en_US, platform encoding: UTF-8 OS name: "mac os
x", version: "10.12.6", arch: "x86_64", family: "mac
```

All the samples used in this book are available in the `https://github.com/apisecurity/samples.git` git repository. Use the following git command to clone it. All the samples related to this chapter are inside the directory `ch03`.

```
\> git clone https://github.com/apisecurity/samples.git
\> cd samples/ch03
```

To anyone who loves Maven, the best way to get started with a Spring Boot project would be with a Maven archetype. Unfortunately, it is no more supported. One option we have is to create a template project via `https://start.spring.io/` –which is known as the *Spring Initializer*. There you can pick which type of project you want to create, project dependencies, give a name, and download a maven project as a zip file. The other option is to use the Spring Tool Suite (STS).[2] It's an IDE (integrated development

---

[2]`https://spring.io/tools`

environment) built on top of the Eclipse platform, with many useful plugins to create Spring projects. However, in this book, we provide you all the fully coded samples in the preceding git repository.

Note   If you find any issues in building or running the samples given in this book, please refer to the README file under the corresponding chapter in the git repository: `https://github.com/apisecurity/samples.git`. We will update the samples and the corresponding README files in the git repository, to reflect any changes happening, related to the tools, libraries, and frameworks used in this book.

Deploying Order API

This is the simplest API ever. You can find the code inside the directory `ch03/sample01`. To build the project with Maven, use the following command:

```
\> cd sample01
\> mvn clean install
```

Before we delve deep into the code, let's have a look at some of the notable Maven dependencies and plugins added into `ch03/sample01/pom.xml`.

Spring Boot comes with different `starter` dependencies to integrate with different Spring modules. The `spring-boot-starter-web` dependency brings in Tomcat and Spring MVC and, does all the wiring between the components, making the developer's work to a minimum. The `spring-boot-starter-actuator` dependency helps you monitor and manage your application.

```
<dependency>
      <groupId>org.springframework.boot</groupId>
      <artifactId>spring-boot-starter-web</artifactId>
</dependency>
<dependency>
      <groupId>org.springframework.boot</groupId>
      <artifactId>spring-boot-starter-actuator</artifactId>
</dependency>
```

In the pom.xml file, we also have the spring-boot-maven-plugin plugin, which lets you start the Spring Boot API from Maven itself.

```
<plugin>
    <groupId>org.springframework.boot</groupId>
    <artifactId>spring-boot-maven-plugin</artifactId>
</plugin>
```

Now let's have a look at the checkOrderStatus method in the class file src/main/java/com/apress/ch03/sample01/service/OrderProcessing.java. This method accepts an order id and returns back the status of the order. There are three notable annotations used in the following code. The @RestController is a class-level annotation that marks the corresponding class as a REST endpoint, which accepts and produces JSON payloads. The @RequestMapping annotation can be defined both at the class level and the method level. The value attribute at the class-level annotation defines the path under which the corresponding endpoint is registered. The same at the method level appends to the class-level path. Anything defined within curly braces is a placeholder for any variable value in the path. For example, a GET request on /order/101 and /order/102 (where 101 and 102 are the order ids), both hit the method checkOrderStatus. In fact, the value of the value attribute is a URI template.[3] The annotation @PathVariable extracts the provided variable from the URI template defined under the value attribute of the @RequestMapping annotation and binds it to the variable defined in the method signature.

```
@RestController
@RequestMapping(value = "/order")
public class OrderProcessing {
  @RequestMapping(value = "/{id}", method = RequestMethod.GET)
  public String checkOrderStatus(@PathVariable("id") String orderId)
  {
    return ResponseEntity.ok("{'status' : 'shipped'}");
  }
}
```

---

[3]https://tools.ietf.org/html/rfc6570

There is another important class file at src/main/java/com/apress/ch03/sample01/ OrderProcessingApp.java worth having a look at. This is the class which spins up our API in its own application server, in this case the embedded Tomcat. By default the API starts on port 8080, and you can change the port by adding, say, for example, server.port=9000 to the sample01/src/main/resources/application.properties file. This will set the server port to 9000. The following shows the code snippet from OrderProcessingApp class, which spins up our API. The @SpringBootApplication annotation, which is defined at the class level, is being used as a shortcut for four other annotations defined in Spring: @Configuration, @EnableAutoConfiguration, @EnableWebMvc, and @ComponentScan.

```
@SpringBootApplication
public class OrderProcessingApp {
    public static void main(String[] args) {
            SpringApplication.run(OrderProcessingApp.class, args);
    }
}
```

Now, let's see how to run our API and talk to it with a cURL client. The following command executed from ch03/sample01 directory shows how to start our Spring Boot application with Maven.

```
\> mvn spring-boot:run
```

To test the API with a cURL client, use the following command from a different command console. It will print the output as shown in the following, after the initial command.

```
\> curl http://localhost:8080/order/11
{"customer_id":"101021","order_id":"11","payment_method":{"card_type":"V
ISA","expiration":"01/22","name":"John Doe","billing_address":"201, 1st
Street, San Jose, CA"},"items": [{"code":"101","qty":1},{"code":"103","qty"
:5}],"shipping_address":"201, 1st Street, San Jose, CA"}
```

Securing Order API with Transport Layer Security (TLS)

To enable Transport Layer Security (TLS), first we need to create a public/private key pair. The following command uses keytool that comes with the default Java distribution to generate a key pair and stores it in keystore.jks file. This file is also known as a keystore, and it can be in different formats. Two most popular formats are Java KeyStore (JKS) and PKCS#12. JKS is specific to Java, while PKCS#12 is a standard, which belongs to the family of standards defined under Public Key Cryptography Standards (PKCS). In the following command, we specify the keystore type with the storetype argument, which is set to JKS.

```
\> keytool -genkey -alias spring -keyalg RSA -keysize 4096 -validity 3650
-dname "CN=foo,OU=bar,O=zee,L=sjc,S=ca,C=us" -keypass springboot -keystore
keystore.jks -storeType jks -storepass springboot
```

The alias argument in the preceding command specifies how to identify the generated keys stored in the keystore. There can be multiple keys stored in a given keystore, and the value of the corresponding alias must be unique. Here we use spring as the alias. The validity argument specifies that the generated keys are only valid for 10 years or 3650 days. The keysize and keystore arguments specify the length of the generated key and the name of the keystore, where the keys are stored. The genkey is the option, which instructs the keytool to generate new keys; instead of genkey, you can also use genkeypair option. Once the preceding command is executed, it will create a keystore file called keystore.jks, which is protected with the password springboot.

The certificate created in this example is known as a self-signed certificate. In other words, there is no external certificate authority (CA). Typically, in a production deployment, either you will use a public certificate authority or an enterprise-level certificate authority to sign the public certificate, so any client, who trusts the certificate authority, can verify it. If you are using certificates to secure service-to-service communications in a microservices deployment or for an internal API deployment, then you need not worry about having a public certificate authority; you can have your own certificate authority. But for APIs, which you expose to external client applications, you would need to get your certificates signed by a public certificate authority.

To enable TLS for the Spring Boot API, copy the keystore file (keystore.jks), which we created earlier, to the home directory of the sample (e.g., ch03/sample01/) and add the following to the `sample01/src/main/resources/application.properties` file. The samples that you download from the `samples` git repository already have these values (and you only need to uncomment them), and we are using `springboot` as the password for both the keystore and the private key.

```
server.ssl.key-store: keystore.jks
server.ssl.key-store-password: springboot
server.ssl.keyAlias: spring
```

To validate that everything works fine, use the following command from `ch03/sample01/` directory to spin up the `Order` API and notice the line which prints the HTTPS port.

```
\> mvn spring-boot:run
Tomcat started on port(s): 8080 (https) with context path "
```

To test the API with a cURL client, use the following command from a different command console. It will print the output as shown in the following, after the initial command. Instead of HTTP, we are using HTTPS here.

```
\> curl -k https://localhost:8080/order/11
{"customer_id":"101021","order_id":"11","payment_method":{"card_type":"V
ISA","expiration":"01/22","name":"John Doe","billing_address":"201, 1st
Street, San Jose, CA"},"items": [{"code":"101","qty":1},{"code":"103","qty"
:5}],"shipping_address":"201, 1st Street, San Jose, CA"}
```

We used the `-k` option in the preceding cURL command. Since we have a self-signed (untrusted) certificate to secure our HTTPS endpoint, we need to pass the –k parameter to advise cURL to ignore the trust validation. In a production deployment with proper certificate authority–signed certificates, you do not need to do that. Also, if you have a self-signed certificate, you can still avoid using –k, by pointing cURL to the corresponding public certificate.

```
\> curl --cacert ca.crt https://localhost:8080/order/11
```

You can use the following keytool command from `ch03/sample01/` to export the public certificate of the Order API to ca.crt file in PEM (with the `-rfc` argument) format.

```
\> keytool -export -file ca.crt -alias spring –rfc -keystore keystore.jks
-storePass springboot
```

75

The preceding curl command with the `ca.crt` will result in the following error. It complains that the common name in the public certificate of the Order API, which is foo, does not match with the hostname (localhost) in the cURL command.

```
curl: (51) SSL: certificate subject name 'foo' does not match target host
name 'localhost'
```

Ideally in a production deployment when you create a certificate, its common name should match the hostname. In this case, since we do not have a Domain Name Service (DNS) entry for the foo hostname, you can use the following workaround, with cURL.

```
\> curl --cacert ca.crt https://foo:8080/order/11 --resolve
foo:8080:127.0.0.1
```

Protecting Order API with Mutual TLS

In this section, we'll see how to enable TLS mutual authentication between the Order API and the cURL client. In most of the cases, TLS mutual authentication is used to enable system-to-system authentication. First make sure that we have the keystore at `sample01/keystore.jks`, and then to enable TLS mutual authentication, uncomment the following property in the `sample01/src/main/resources/application.properties` file.

```
server.ssl.client-auth:need
```

Now we can test the flow by invoking the Order API using cURL. First, use the following command from `ch03/sample01/` directory to spin up the Order API and notice the line which prints the HTTPS port.

```
\> mvn spring-boot:run
Tomcat started on port(s): 8080 (https) with context path ''
```

To test the API with a cURL client, use the following command from a different command console.

```
\> curl –k https://localhost:8080/order/11
```

Since we have protected the API with TLS mutual authentication, the preceding command will result in the following error message, which means the API (or the server) has refused to connect with the cURL client, because it didn't present a valid client certificate.

```
curl: (35) error:1401E412:SSL routines:CONNECT_CR_FINISHED:sslv3 alert bad
certificate
```

To fix this, we need to create a key pair (a public key and a private key) for the cURL client and configure Order API to trust the public key. Then we can use the key pair we generated along with the cURL command to access the API, which is protected with mutual TLS.

To generate a private key and a public key for the cURL client, we use the following OpenSSL command. OpenSSL is a commercial-grade toolkit and cryptographic library for TLS and available for multiple platforms. You can download and set up the distribution that fits your platform from www.openssl.org/source. If not, the easiest way is to use an OpenSSL Docker image. In the next section, we discuss how to run OpenSSL as a Docker container.

```
\> openssl genrsa -out privkey.pem 4096
```

Now, to generate a self-signed certificate, corresponding to the preceding private key (privkey.pem), use the following OpenSSL command.

```
\> openssl req -key privkey.pem -new -x509 -sha256 -nodes -out client.crt
-subj "/C=us/ST=ca/L=sjc/O=zee/OU=bar/CN=client"
```

Let's take down the Order API, if it is still running, and import the public certificate (client.crt) we created in the preceding step to sample01/keystore.jks, using the following command.

```
\> keytool -import -file client.crt -alias client -keystore keystore.jks
-storepass springboot
```

Now we can test the flow by invoking the Order API using cURL. First, use the following command from ch03/sample01/ directory to spin up the Order API.

```
\> mvn spring-boot:run
Tomcat started on port(s): 8080 (https) with context path ''
```

To test the API with a cURL client, use the following command from a different command console.

```
\> curl -k --key privkey.pem --cert client.crt https://localhost:8080/
order/11
```

In case we use a key pair, which is not known to the Order API, or in other words not imported into the sample01/keystore.jks file, you will see the following error, when you execute the preceding cURL command.

```
curl: (35) error:1401E416:SSL routines:CONNECT_CR_FINISHED:sslv3 alert
certificate unknown
```

Running OpenSSL on Docker

In the last few years, Docker revolutionized the way we distribute software. Docker provides a containerized environment to run software in self-contained manner. A complete overview of Docker is out of the scope of this book—and if you are interested in learning more, we recommend you check out the book *Docker in Action* (Manning Publications, 2019) by Jeff Nickoloff and Stephen Kuenzli.

Setting up Docker in your local machine is quite straightforward, following the steps in Docker documentation available at https://docs.docker.com/install/. Once you get Docker installed, run the following command to verify the installation, and it will show the version of Docker engine client and server.

```
\> docker version
```

To start OpenSSL as a Docker container, use the following command from the ch03/ sample01 directory.

```
\> docker run -it -v $(pwd):/export prabath/openssl
#
```

When you run the preceding command for the first time, it will take a couple of minutes to execute and ends with a command prompt, where you can execute your OpenSSL commands to create the keys, which we used toward the end of the previous sections. The preceding docker run command starts OpenSSL in a Docker container, with a volume mount, which maps ch03/sample01 (or the current directory, which is indicated by $(pwd) in the preceding command) directory from the host file system to the /export directory of the container file system. This volume mount helps you to share part of the host file system with the container file system. When the OpenSSL container generates certificates, those are written to the /export directory of the container file system. Since we have a volume mount, everything inside the /export directory of the container file system is also accessible from the ch03/sample01 directory of the host file system.

To generate a private key and a public key for the cURL client, we use the following OpenSSL command.

```
# openssl genrsa -out /export/privkey.pem 4096
```

Now, to generate a self-signed certificate, corresponding to the preceding private key (privkey.pem), use the following OpenSSL command.

```
# openssl req -key /export/privkey.pem -new -x509 -sha256 -nodes -out
client.crt -subj "/C=us/ST=ca/L=sjc/O=zee/OU=bar/CN=client"
```

Summary

- Transport Layer Security (TLS) is fundamental in securing any API.

- Securing APIs with TLS is the most common form of protection we see in any API deployment.

- TLS protects data in transit for confidentiality and integrity, and mutual TLS (mTLS) protects your APIs from intruders by enforcing client authentication.

- OpenSSL is a commercial-grade toolkit and cryptographic library for TLS and available for multiple platforms.

CHAPTER 4

OAuth 2.0 Fundamentals

OAuth 2.0 is a major breakthrough in identity delegation. It has its roots in OAuth 1.0 (see Appendix B), but OAuth Web Resource Authorization Profiles (see Appendix B) primarily influenced it. The main difference between OAuth 1.0 and 2.0 is that OAuth 1.0 is a standard protocol for identity delegation, whereas OAuth 2.0 is a highly extensible authorization framework. OAuth 2.0 is already the de facto standard for securing APIs and is widely used by Facebook, Google, LinkedIn, Microsoft (MSN, Live), PayPal, Instagram, Foursquare, GitHub, Yammer, Meetup, and many more. There is one popular exception: Twitter still uses OAuth 1.0.

Understanding OAuth 2.0

OAuth 2.0 primarily solves the access delegation problem. Let's say you want a third-party application to read your status messages on your Facebook wall. In other words, you want to delegate the third-party application the access to your Facebook wall. One way to do that is by sharing your Facebook credentials with the third-party application, so it can directly access your Facebook wall. This is called access delegation by credential sharing. Even though this solves the access delegation problem, once you share your Facebook credentials with the third-party application, it can use your credentials to do anything it wants, which in turns creates more problems! OAuth 2.0 solves this problem in a way you do not need to share your credentials with third-party applications, but only share a time-bound temporary token that is only good enough for a well-defined

© Prabath Siriwardena 2020
P. Siriwardena, *Advanced API Security*, https://doi.org/10.1007/978-1-4842-2050-4_4

purpose. Figure 4-1 shows at a high level how access delegation works with OAuth 2.0, and the following explains each step in Figure 4-1:

1. The user visits the third-party web application and wants to let the web application publish messages to his/her Facebook wall. To do that, the web application needs a token from Facebook, and to get the token, it redirects the user to Facebook.

2. Facebook prompts the user to authenticate (if not authenticated already) and requests the consent from the user to give permissions to the third-party web application to publish messages to his/her Facebook wall.

3. User authenticates and provides his/her consent to Facebook, so that Facebook can share a token with the third-party web application. This token is only good enough to publish messages to the Facebook wall for a limited period and cannot do anything else. For example, the third-party web application cannot send friend requests, delete status messages, upload photos, and so on with the token.

4. The third-party web application gets a token from Facebook. To explain what exactly happens in this step, first we need to understand how OAuth 2.0 grant types work, and we discuss that later in the chapter.

5. The third-party web application accesses the Facebook API with the token provided to it by Facebook in step 4. Facebook API makes sure only requests that come along with a valid token can access it. Then again later in the chapter, we will explain in detail what happens in this step.

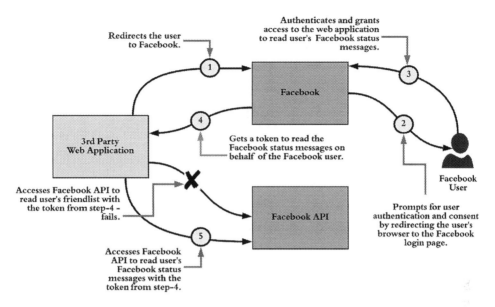

Figure 4-1. OAuth 2.0 solves the access delegation problem by issuing a temporary time-bound token to a third-party web application that is only good enough for a well-defined purpose

OAuth 2.0 Actors

OAuth 2.0 introduces four actors in a typical OAuth flow. The following explains the role of each of them with respect to Figure 4-1:

1. *Resource owner*: One who owns the resources. In our example earlier, the third-party web application wants to access the Facebook wall of a Facebook user via the Facebook API and publish messages on behalf of him/her. In that case, the Facebook user who owns the Facebook wall is the resource owner.

2. *Resource server*: This is the place which hosts protected resources. In the preceding scenario, the server that hosts the Facebook API is the resource server, where Facebook API is the resource.

3. *Client*: This is the application which wants to access a resource on behalf of the resource owner. In the preceding use case, the third-party web application is the client.

4.   *Authorization server*: This is the entity which acts as a security token service to issue OAuth 2.0 access tokens to client applications. In the preceding use case, Facebook itself acts as the authorization server.

Grant Types

A grant type in OAuth 2.0 defines how a client can obtain an authorization grant from a resource owner to access a resource on his/her behalf. The origin of the word grant comes from the French word granter which carries the meaning consent to support. In other words, a grant type defines a well-defined process to get the consent from the resource owner to access a resource on his/her behalf for a well-defined purpose. In OAuth 2.0, this well-defined purpose is also called **scope**. Also you can interpret scope as a permission, or in other words, scope defines what actions the client application can do on a given resource. In Figure 4-1, the token issued from the Facebook authorization server is bound to a scope, where the client application can only use the token to post messages to the corresponding user's Facebook wall.

The grant types in OAuth 2.0 are very similar to the OAuth profiles in WRAP (see Appendix B). The OAuth 2.0 core specification introduces four core grant types: the authorization code grant type, the implicit grant type, the resource owner password credentials grant type, and the client credentials grant type. Table 4-1 shows how OAuth 2.0 grant types match with WRAP profiles.

Table 4-1. *OAuth 2.0 Grant Types vs. OAuth WRAP Profiles*

OAuth 2.0	OAuth WRAP
Authorization code grant type	Web App Profile/Rich App Profile
Implicit grant type	–
Resource owner password credentials grant type	Username and Password Profile
Client credentials grant type	Client Account and Password Profile

Authorization Code Grant Type

The authorization code grant type in OAuth 2.0 is very similar to the Web App Profile in WRAP. It's mostly recommended for applications—either web applications or native mobile applications—that have the capability to spin up a web browser (see Figure 4-2). The resource owner who visits the client application initiates the authorization code grant type. The client application, which must be a registered application at the authorization server, as shown in step 1 in Figure 4-2, redirects the resource owner to the authorization server to get the approval. The following shows an HTTP request the client application generates while redirecting the user to the authorize endpoint of the authorization server:

```
https://authz.example.com/oauth2/authorize?
                response_type=code&
                client_id=OrhQErXIX49svVYoXJGtODWBuFca&
                redirect_uri=https%3A%2F%2Fmycallback
```

The authorize endpoint is a well-known, published endpoint of an OAuth 2.0 authorization server. The value of `response_type` parameter must be `code`. This indicates to the authorization server that the request is for an authorization code (under the authorization code grant type). `client_id` is an identifier for the client application. Once the client application is registered with the authorization server, the client gets a `client_id` and a `client_secret`. During the client registration phase, the client application must provide a URL under its control as the `redirect_uri`, and in the initial request, the value of the `redirect_uri` parameter should match with the one registered with the authorization server. We also call the `redirect_uri` the callback URL. The URL-encoded value of the callback URL is added to the request as the `redirect_uri` parameter. In addition to these parameters, a client application can also include the `scope` parameter. The value of the `scope` parameter is shown to the resource owner on the approval screen: it indicates to the authorization server the level of access the client needs on the target resource/API.

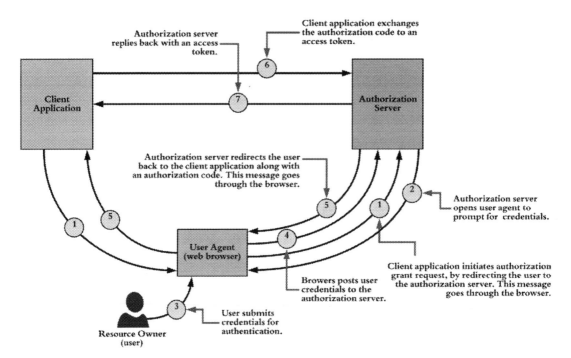

Figure 4-2. *Authorization code grant type*

In step 5 in Figure 4-2, the authorization server returns the requested code to the registered callback URL (also known as `redirect_uri`) of the client application. This code is called the authorization code. Each authorization code should have a lifetime. A lifetime longer than 1 minute isn't recommended:

`https://callback.example.com/?code=9142d4cad58c66d0a5edfad8952192`

The value of the authorization code is delivered to the client application via an HTTP redirect and is visible to the resource owner. In the next step (step 6), the client must exchange the authorization code for an OAuth access token by talking to the OAuth token endpoint exposed by the authorization server.

Note   The ultimate goal of any OAuth 2.0 grant type is to provide a token (which is known as access token) to the client application. The client application can use this token to access a resource. An access token is bound to the resource owner, client application, and one or more scopes. Given an access token, the authorization server knows who the corresponding resource owner and client application and also what the attached scopes are.

The token endpoint in most of the cases is a secured endpoint. The client application can generate the token request along with the corresponding client_id (OrhQErXIX49s vVYoXJGtODWBuFca) and the client_secret (eYOFkL756W8usQaVNgCNkz9C2DOa), which will go in the HTTP Authorization header. In most of the cases, the token endpoint is secured with HTTP Basic authentication, but it is not a must. For stronger security, one may use mutual TLS as well, and if you are using the authorization code grant type from a single-page app or a mobile app, then you may not use any credentials at all. The following shows a sample request (step 6) to the token endpoint. The value of the grant_type parameter there must be the authorization_code, and the value of the code should be the one returned from the previous step (step 5). If the client application sent a value in the redirect_uri parameter in the previous request (step 1), then it must include the same value in the token request as well. In case the client application does not authenticate to the token endpoint, you need to send the corresponding client_id as a parameter in the HTTP body:

Note   The authorization code returned from the authorization server acts as an intermediate code. This code is used to map the end user or resource owner to the OAuth client. The OAuth client may authenticate itself to the token endpoint of the authorization server. The authorization server should check whether the code is issued to the authenticated OAuth client prior to exchanging it for an access token.

```
\> curl -v -k -X POST --basic
    -u OrhQErXIX49svVYoXJGtODWBuFca:eYOFkL756W8usQaVNgCNkz9C2DOa
    -H "Content-Type:application/x-www-form-urlencoded;charset=UTF-8"
    -d "grant_type=authorization_code&
        code=9142d4cad58c66d0a5edfad8952192&
        redirect_uri=https://mycallback"
        https://authz.example.com/oauth2/token
```

Note   The authorization code should be used only once by the client. If the authorization server detects that it's been used more than once, it must revoke all the tokens issued for that particular authorization code.

The preceding cURL command returns the following response from the authorization server (step 7). The token_type parameter in the response indicates the type of the token. (The section "OAuth 2.0 Token Types" talks more about token types.) In addition to the access token, the authorization server also returns a refresh token, which is optional. The refresh token can be used by the client application to obtain a new access token before the refresh token expires. The expires_in parameter indicates the lifetime of the access token in seconds.

```
{
    "token_type":"bearer",
    "expires_in":3600,
    "refresh_token":"22b157546b26c2d6c0165c4ef6b3f736",
    "access_token":"cac93e1d29e45bf6d84073dbfb460"
}
```

Note   Each refresh token has its own lifetime. Compared to the lifetime of the access token, the refresh token's is longer: the lifetime of an access token is in minutes, whereas the lifetime of a refresh token is in days.

Implicit Grant Type

The implicit grant type to acquire an access token is mostly used by JavaScript clients running in the web browser (see Figure 4-3). Even for JavaScript clients now, we do not recommend using implicit grant type, rather use authorization code grant type with no client authentication. This is mostly due to the inherent security issues in the implicit grant type, which we discuss in Chapter 14. The following discussion on implicit grant type will help you understand how it works, but never use it in a production deployment.

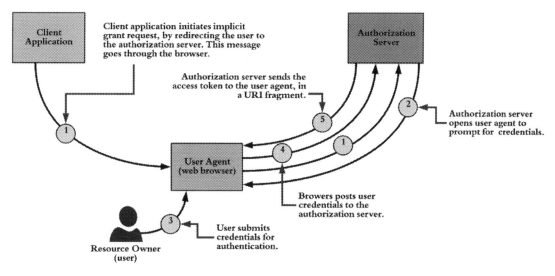

Figure 4-3. *Implicit grant type*

Unlike the authorization code grant type, the implicit grant type doesn't have any
equivalent profiles in OAuth WRAP. The JavaScript client initiates the implicit grant flow
by redirecting the user to the authorization server. The response_type parameter in the
request indicates to the authorization server that the client expects a token, not a code. The
implicit grant type doesn't require the authorization server to authenticate the JavaScript
client; it only has to send the client_id in the request. This is for logging and auditing
purposes and also to find out the corresponding redirect_uri. The redirect_uri in the
request is optional; if it's present, it must match what is provided at the client registration:

```
https://authz.example.com/oauth2/authorize?
               response_type=token&
               client_id=OrhQErXIX49svVYoXJGtoDWBuFca&
               redirect_uri=https%3A%2F%2Fmycallback
```

This returns the following response. The implicit grant type sends the access token as
a URI fragment and doesn't provide any refreshing mechanism:

```
https://callback.example.com/#access_token=cac93e1d29e45bf6d84073dbfb460&ex
pires_in=3600
```

Unlike the authorization code grant type, the implicit grant type client receives
the access token in the response to the grant request. When we have something in the
URI fragment of a URL, the browser never sends it to the back end. It only stays on the
browser. So when authorization server sends a redirect to the callback URL of the client

application, the request first comes to the browser, and the browser does an HTTP GET to the web server that hosts the client application. But in that HTTP GET, you will not find the URI fragment, and the web server will never see it. To process the access token that comes in the URI fragment, as a response to HTTP GET from the browser, the web server of the client application will return back an HTML page with a JavaScript, which knows how to extract the access_token from the URI fragment, which still remains in the browser address bar. In general this is how single-page applications work.

Note   The authorization server must treat the authorization code, access token, refresh token, and client secret key as sensitive data. They should never be sent over HTTP—the authorization server must use Transport Layer Security (TLS). These tokens should be stored securely, possibly by encrypting or hashing them.

Resource Owner Password Credentials Grant Type

Under the resource owner password credentials grant type, the resource owner must trust the client application. This is equivalent to the Username and Password Profile in OAuth WRAP. The resource owner has to give his/her credentials directly to the client application (see Figure 4-4).

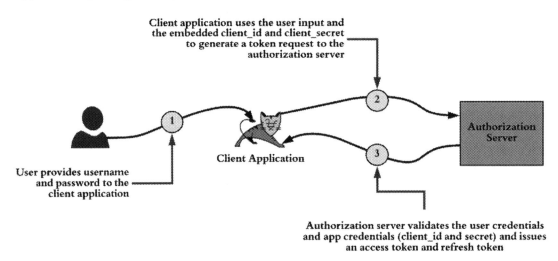

Figure 4-4. *Resource owner password credentials grant type*

The following cURL command talks to the token endpoint of the authorization server, passing the resource owner's username and password as parameters. In addition, the client application proves its identity. In most of the cases, the token endpoint is secured with HTTP Basic authentication (but not a must), and the client application passes its client_id (OrhQErXIX49svVYoXJGtODWBuFca) and client_secret (eYOFkL756W8usQaVNgCNkz9C2DOa) in the HTTP Authorization header. The value of the grant_type parameter must be set to password:

```
\> curl -v -k -X POST --basic
      -u OrhQErXIX49svVYoXJGtODWBuFca:eYOFkL756W8usQaVNgCNkz9C2DOa
      -H "Content-Type:application/x-www-form-urlencoded;charset=UTF-8"
      -d "grant_type=password&
          username=admin&password=admin"
          https://authz.example.com/oauth2/token
```

This returns the following response, which includes an access token along with a refresh token:

```
{
    "token_type":"bearer",
    "expires_in":685,"
    "refresh_token":"22b157546b26c2d6c0165c4ef6b3f736",
    "access_token":"cac93e1d29e45bf6d84073dbfb460"
}
```

Note   If using the authorization code grant type is an option, it should be used over the resource owner password credentials grant type. The resource owner password credentials grant type was introduced to aid migration from HTTP Basic authentication and Digest authentication to OAuth 2.0.

Client Credentials Grant Type

The client credentials grant type is equivalent to the Client Account and Password Profile in OAuth WRAP and to two-legged OAuth in OAuth 1.0 (see Appendix B). With this grant type, the client itself becomes the resource owner (see Figure 4-5). The following cURL command talks to the token endpoint of the authorization server, passing the client application's client_id (OrhQErXIX49svVYoXJGtODWBuFca) and client_secret (eYOFkL756W8usQaVNgCNkz9C2DOa).

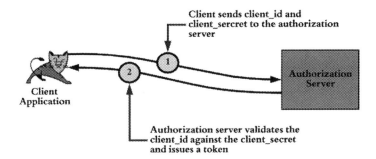

Figure 4-5. *Client credentials grant type*

```
\> curl -v -k -X POST --basic
      -u OrhQErXIX49svVYoXJGtODWBuFca:eYOFkL756W8usQaVNgCNkz9C2DOa
      -H "Content-Type: application/x-www-form-urlencoded;charset=UTF-8"
      -d "grant_type=client_credentials"
      https://authz.example.com/oauth2/token
```

This returns the following response, which includes an access token. Unlike the resource owner password credentials grant type, the client credentials grant type doesn't return a refresh token:

```
{       "token_type":"bearer",
        "expires_in":3600,
        "access_token":"4c9a9ae7463ff9bb93ae7f169bd6a"
}
```

This client credential grant type is mostly used for system-to-system interactions with no end user. For example, a web application needs to access an OAuth secured API to get some metadata.

Refresh Grant Type

Although it's not the case with the implicit grant type and the client credentials grant type, with the other two grant types, the OAuth access token comes with a refresh token. This refresh token can be used to extend the validity of the access token without the involvement of the resource owner. The following cURL command shows how to get a new access token from the refresh token:

```
\> curl -v -X POST --basic
    -u OrhQErXIX49svVYoXJGtODWBuFca:eYOFkL756W8usQaVNgCNkz9C2DOa
    -H "Content-Type: application/x-www-form-urlencoded;charset=UTF-8"
    -k -d "grant_type=refresh_token&
          refresh_token=22b157546b26c2d6c0165c4ef6b3f736"
    https://authz.example.com/oauth2/token
```

This returns the following response:

```
{
    "token_type":"bearer",
    "expires_in":3600,
    "refresh_token":"9ecc381836fa5e3baf5a9e86081",
    "access_token":"b574d1ba554c26148f5fca3cceb05e2"
}
```

Note   The refresh token has a much longer lifetime than the access token. If the lifetime of the refresh token expires, then the client must initiate the OAuth token flow from the start and get a new access token and refresh token. The authorization server also has the option to return a new refresh token each time the client refreshes the access token. In such cases, the client has to discard the previously obtained refresh token and begin using the new one.

How to Pick the Right Grant Type?

As we discussed at the very beginning of the chapter, OAuth 2.0 is an authorization framework. The nature of a framework is to provide multiple options, and it's up to the application developers to pick the best out of those options, based on their use cases. OAuth can be used with any kind of application. It can be a web application, single-page application, desktop application, or a native mobile application.

To pick the right grant type for those applications, first we need to think how the client application is going to invoke the OAuth secured API: whether it is going to access the API by itself or on behalf of an end user. If the application wants to access the API just being itself, then we should use client credentials grant type and, if not, should use authorization code grant type. Both the implicit and password grant types are now obsolete.

OAuth 2.0 Token Types

Neither OAuth 1.0 nor WRAP could support custom token types. OAuth 1.0 always used signature-based tokens, and OAuth WRAP always used bearer tokens over TLS. OAuth 2.0 isn't coupled into any token type. In OAuth 2.0, you can introduce your own token type if needed. Regardless of the token_type returned in the OAuth token response from the authorization server, the client must understand it before using it. Based on the token_ type, the authorization server can add additional attributes/parameters to the response.

OAuth 2.0 has two main token profiles: OAuth 2.0 Bearer Token Profile and OAuth 2.0 MAC Token Profile. The most popular OAuth token profile is Bearer; almost all OAuth 2.0 deployments today are based on the OAuth 2.0 Bearer Token Profile. The next section talks about the Bearer Token Profile in detail, and Appendix G discusses the MAC Token Profile.

OAuth 2.0 Bearer Token Profile

The OAuth 2.0 Bearer Token Profile was influenced by OAuth WRAP, which only supported bearer tokens. As its name implies, anyone who bears the token can use it—don't lose it! Bearer tokens must always be used over Transport Layer Security (TLS) to avoid losing them in transit. Once the bearer access token is obtained from the authorization server, the client can use it in three ways to talk to the resource server. These three ways are defined in the RFC 6750. The most popular way is to include the access token in the HTTP Authorization header:

Note   An OAuth 2.0 bearer token can be a reference token or self-contained token. A reference token is an arbitrary string. An attacker can carry out a brute-force attack to guess the token. The authorization server must pick the right length and use other possible measures to prevent brute forcing. A self-contained access token is a JSON Web Token (JWT), which we discuss in Chapter 7. When the resource server gets an access token, which is a reference token, then to validate the token, it has to talk to the authorization server (or the token issuer). When the access token is a JWT, the resource server can validate the token by itself, by verifying the signature of the JWT.

```
GET /resource HTTP/1.1
Host: rs.example.com
Authorization: Bearer JGjhgyuyibGGjgjkjdlsjkjdsd
```

The access token can also be included as a query parameter. This approach is mostly used by the client applications developed in JavaScript:

```
GET /resource?access_token=JGjhgyuyibGGjgjkjdlsjkjdsd
Host: rs.example.com
```

Note When the value of the OAuth access token is sent as a query parameter, the name of the parameter must be `access_token`. Both Facebook and Google use the correct parameter name, but LinkedIn uses `oauth2_access_token` and Salesforce uses `oauth_token`.

It's also possible to send the access token as a form-encoded body parameter. An authorization server supporting the Bearer Token Profile should be able to handle any of these patterns:

```
POST /resource HTTP/1.1
Host: server.example.com
Content-Type: application/x-www-form-urlencoded
access_token=JGjhgyuyibGGjgjkjdlsjkjdsd
```

Note The value of the OAuth bearer token is only meaningful to the authorization server. The client application should not try to interpret what it says. To make the processing logic efficient, the authorization server may include some meaningful but nonconfidential data in the access token. For example, if the authorization server supports multiple domains with multitenancy, it may include the tenant domain in the access token and then base64-encode (see Appendix E) it or simply use a JSON Web Token (JWT).

OAuth 2.0 Client Types

OAuth 2.0 identifies two types of clients: confidential clients and public clients. Confidential clients are capable of protecting their own credentials (the client key and the client secret), whereas public clients can't. The OAuth 2.0 specification is built around three types of client profiles: web applications, user agent–based applications, and native applications. Web applications are considered to be confidential clients, running on a web server: end users or resource owners access such applications via a web browser. User agent–based applications are considered to be public clients: they download the code from a web server and run it on the user agent, such as JavaScript running in the browser. These clients are incapable of protecting their credentials—the end user can see anything in the JavaScript. Native applications are also considered as public clients: these clients are under the control of the end user, and any confidential data stored in those applications can be extracted out. Android and iOS native applications are a couple of examples.

Note   All four grant types defined in the OAuth 2.0 core specification require the client to preregister with the authorization server, and in return it gets a client identifier. Under the implicit grant type, the client doesn't get a client secret. At the same time, even under other grant types, it's an option whether to use the client secret or not.

Table 4-2 lists the key differences between OAuth 1.0 and OAuth 2.0 Bearer Token Profile.

Table 4-2.   *OAuth 1.0 vs. OAuth 2.0*

OAuth 1.0	OAuth 2.0 Bearer Token Profile
An access delegation protocol	An authorization framework for access delegation
Signature based: HMAC-SHA256/RSA-SHA256	Nonsignature-based, Bearer Token Profile
Less extensibility	Highly extensible via grant types and token types
Less developer-friendly	More developer-friendly
TLS required only during the initial handshake	Bearer Token Profile mandates using TLS during
Secret key never passed on the wire	the entire flow
	Secret key goes on the wire (Bearer Token Profile)

> **Note**   OAuth 2.0 introduces a clear separation between the client, the resource owner, the authorization server, and the resource server. But the core OAuth 2.0 specification doesn't talk about how the resource server validates an access token. Most OAuth implementations started doing this by talking to a proprietary API exposed by the authorization server. The OAuth 2.0 Token Introspection profile standardized this to some extent, and in Chapter 9, we talk more about it.

JWT Secured Authorization Request (JAR)

In an OAuth 2.0 request to the authorize endpoint of the authorization server, all the request parameters flow via the browser as query parameters. The following is an example of an OAuth 2.0 authorization code grant request:

```
https://authz.example.com/oauth2/authorize?
                    response_type=token&
                    client_id=OrhQErXIX49svVYoXJGtoDWBuFca&
                    redirect_uri=https%3A%2F%2Fmycallback
```

There are a couple of issues with this approach. Since these parameters flow via the browser, the end user or anyone on the browser can change the input parameters that could result in some unexpected outcomes at the authorization server. At the same time, since the request is not integrity protected, the authorization server has no means to validate who initiated the request. With JSON Web Token (JWT) secured authorization requests, we can overcome these two issues. If you are new to JWT, please check Chapters 7 and 8. JSON Web Token (JWT) defines a container to transport data between interested parties in a cryptographically safe manner. The JSON Web Signature (JWS) specification developed under the IETF JOSE working group, represents a message or a payload, which is digitally signed or MACed (when a hashing algorithm is used with HMAC), while the JSON Web Encryption (JWE) specification standardizes a way to represent an encrypted payload.

One of the draft proposals[1] to the IETF OAuth working group suggests to introduce the ability to send request parameters in a JWT, which allows the request to be signed

---

[1]The OAuth 2.0 Authorization Framework: JWT Secured Authorization Request (JAR).

with JWS and encrypted with JWE so that the integrity, source authentication, and confidentiality properties of the authorization request are preserved. At the time of writing, this proposal is in its very early stage—and if you are familiar with Security Assertion Markup Language (SAML) Single Sign-On, this is quite analogous to the signed authentication requests in SAML. The following shows the decoded payload of a sample authorization request, which ideally goes within a JWT:

```
{
  "iss": "s6BhdRkqt3",
  "aud": "https://server.example.com",
  "response_type": "code id_token",
  "client_id": "s6BhdRkqt3",
  "redirect_uri": "https://client.example.org/cb",
  "scope": "openid",
  "state": "af0ifjsldkj",
  "nonce": "n-0S6_WzA2Mj",
  "max_age": 86400
}
```

Once the client application constructs the JWT (a JWS or a JWE—please see Chapters 7 and 8 for the details), it can send the authorization request to the OAuth authorization server in two ways. One way is called passing by value, and the other is passing by reference. The following shows an example of passing by value, where the client application sends the JWT in a query parameter called request. The [jwt_assertion] in the following request represents either the actual JWS or JWE.

```
https://server.example.com/authorize?request=[jwt_assertion]
```

The draft proposal for JWT authorization request introduces the pass by reference method to overcome some of the limitations in the pass by value method, as listed here:

- Many mobile phones in the market as of this writing still do not accept large payloads. The payload restriction is typically either 512 or 1024 ASCII characters.

- The maximum URL length supported by older versions of the Internet Explorer is 2083 ASCII characters.

- On a slow connection such as a 2G mobile connection, a large URL would cause a slow response. Therefore the use of such is not advisable from the user experience point of view.

The following shows an example of pass by reference, where the client application sends a link in the request, which can be used by the authorization server to fetch the JWT. This is a typical OAuth 2.0 authorization code request, along with the new `request_uri` query parameter. The value of the `request_uri` parameter carries a link pointing to the corresponding JWS or JWE.

```
https://server.example.com/authorize?
        response_type=code&
        client_id=s6BhdRkqt3&
        request_uri=https://tfp.example.org/request.jwt/Schjwew&
        state=af0ifjsldkj
```

Pushed Authorization Requests (PAR)

This is another draft proposal being discussed under the IETF OAuth working group at the moment, which complements the JWT Secured Authorization Request (JAR) approach we discussed in the previous section. One issue with JAR is each client has to expose an endpoint directly to the authorization server. This is the endpoint that hosts the corresponding JWT, which is used by the authorization server. With Pushed Authorization Requests (PAR) draft proposal, this requirement goes a way. PAR defines an endpoint at the authorization server end, where each client can directly push (without going through the browser) all the parameters in a typical OAuth 2.0 authorization request and then use the normal authorization flow via the browser to pass a reference to the pushed request. Following is an example, where the client application pushes authorization request parameters to an endpoint hosted at the authorization server. This push endpoint on the authorization server can be secured either with mutual Transport Layer Security (TLS) or with OAuth 2.0 itself (client credentials) or with any other means as agreed between the client application and the authorization server.

```
POST /as/par HTTP/1.1
Host: server.example.com
Content-Type: application/x-www-form-urlencoded
Authorization: Basic czZCaGRSa3F0FOMzo3RmpmcDBaQnIxS3REUmJuZlZlZkbUl3
```

```
response_type=code&
state=af0ifjsldkj&
client_id=s6BhdRkqt3&
redirect_uri=https%3A%2F%2Fclient.example.org%2Fcb&
scope=ais
```

If the client follows the JAR specification which, we discussed in the previous section, it can also send a JWS or a JWE to the push endpoint in the following way.

```
POST /as/par HTTP/1.1
Host: server.example.com
Content-Type: application/x-www-form-urlencoded
Authorization: Basic czZCaGRSa3FOMzo3RmpmcDBaQnIxS3REUmJuJuZlZkbUl3

request=[jwt_assertion]
```

Once the push endpoint at the authorization server receives the preceding request, it has to carry out all the validation checks against the request that it usually performs against a typical authorization request. If it all looks good, the authorization server responds with the following. The value of the request_uri parameter in the response is bound to the client_id in the request and acts as a reference to the authorization request.

```
HTTP/1.1 201 Created
Date: Tue, 2 Oct 2019 15:22:31 GMT
Content-Type: application/json

{
  "request_uri": "urn:example:bwc4JK-ESC0w8acc191e-Y1LTC2",
  "expires_in": 3600
}
```

Upon receiving the push response from the authorization server, the client application can construct the following request with the request_uri parameter from the response to redirect the user to the authorization server.

```
https://server.example.com/authorize?
        request_uri=urn:example:bwc4JK-ESC0w8acc191e-Y1LTC2
```

Summary

- OAuth 2.0 is the de facto standard for securing APIs, and it primarily solves the access delegation problem.

- A grant type in OAuth 2.0 defines how a client can obtain an authorization grant from a resource owner to access a resource on his/her behalf.

- OAuth 2.0 core specification defines five grant types: authorization code, implicit, password, client credentials, and refresh.

- Refresh grant type is a special grant type, which is used by an OAuth 2.0 client application to renew an expired or closer to expiry access token.

- Implicit grant type and client credentials grant types do not return back any refresh tokens.

- Implicit grant type is obsolete and is not recommended to use due to its own inherent security issues.

- OAuth 2.0 supports two types of client applications: public clients and confidential clients. Single-page applications and native mobile applications fall under public clients, while web applications fall under confidential clients.

- The OAuth 2.0 Authorization Framework: JWT Secured Authorization Request (JAR) draft proposal suggests to introduce the ability to send request parameters in a JWT.

- The Pushed Authorization Requests (PAR) draft proposal suggests to introduce a push endpoint at the authorization server end, so the client applications can securely push all the authorization request parameters and then initiate the browser-based login flow.

CHAPTER 5

Edge Security with an API Gateway

The API gateway is the most common pattern in securing APIs in a production deployment. In other words, it's the entry point to your API deployment. There are many open source and proprietary products out there, which implement the API gateway pattern, which we commonly identify as API gateways. An API gateway is a policy enforcement point (PEP), which centrally enforces authentication, authorization, and throttling policies. Further we can use an API gateway to centrally gather all the analytics related to APIs and publish those to an analytics product for further analysis and presentation.

Setting Up Zuul API Gateway

Zuul[1] is an API gateway (see Figure 5-1) that provides dynamic routing, monitoring, resiliency, security, and more. It is acting as the front door to Netflix's server infrastructure, handling traffic from all Netflix users around the world. It also routes requests, supports developers' testing and debugging, provides deep insight into Netflix's overall service health, protects the Netflix deployment from attacks, and channels traffic to other cloud regions when an Amazon Web Services (AWS) region is in trouble. In this section, we are going to set up Zuul as an API gateway to front the Order API, which we developed in Chapter 3.

---

[1]https://github.com/Netflix/zuul

© Prabath Siriwardena 2020
P. Siriwardena, *Advanced API Security*, https://doi.org/10.1007/978-1-4842-2050-4_5

All the samples used in this book are available in the `https://github.com/apisecurity/samples.git` git repository. Use the following git command to clone it. All the samples related to this chapter are inside the directory ch05. To run the samples in the book, we assumed you have installed Java (JDK 1.8+) and Apache Maven 3.2.0+.

```
\> git clone https://github.com/apisecurity/samples.git
\> cd samples/ch05
```

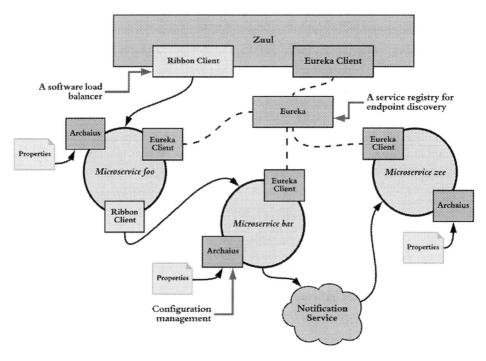

Figure 5-1. *A typical Zuul API gateway deployment at Netflix. All the Netflix microservices are fronted by an API gateway*

Running the Order API

This is the simplest API implementation ever, which is developed with Java Spring Boot. In fact one can call it as a microservice as well. You can find the code inside the directory, ch05/sample01. To build the project with Maven, use the following command from the sample01 directory:

```
\> cd sample01
\> mvn clean install
```

Now, let's see how to run our Spring Boot service and talk to it with a cURL client. Execute the following command from `ch05/sample01` directory to start the Spring Boot service with Maven.

```
\> mvn spring-boot:run
```

To test the API with a cURL client, use the following command from a different command console. It will print the output as shown in the following, after the initial command.

```
\> curl http://localhost:8080/order/11
{"customer_id":"101021","order_id":"11","payment_method":{"card_type":
"VISA","expiration":"01/22","name":"John Doe","billing_address":"201, 1st
Street, San Jose, CA"},"items": [{"code":"101","qty":1},{"code":"103","qty"
:5}],"shipping_address":"201, 1st Street, San Jose, CA"}
```

Running the Zuul API Gateway

In this section, we are going to build the Zuul API gateway as a Spring Boot project and run it against the Order service. Or in other words, the Zuul gateway will proxy all the requests to the Order service. You can find the code inside `ch05/sample02` directory. To build the project with Maven, use the following commands:

```
\> cd sample02
\> mvn clean install
```

Before we delve deep into the code, let's have a look at some of the notable Maven dependencies and plugins added into `ch05/sample02/pom.xml`. Spring Boot comes with different `starter` dependencies to integrate with different Spring modules. The `spring-cloud-starter-zuul` dependency (as shown in the following) brings in Zuul API gateway dependencies and does all the wiring between the components, making the developer's work to a minimum.

```
<dependency>
  <groupId>org.springframework.cloud</groupId>
  <artifactId>spring-cloud-starter-zuul</artifactId>
</dependency>
```

It is important to have a look at the class file src/main/java/com/apress/ch05/ sample02/GatewayApplication.java. This is the class which spins up the Zuul API gateway. By default it starts on port 8080, and you can change the port by adding, say, for example, server.port=9000 to the src/main/resources/application.properties file. This will set the API gateway port to 9000. The following shows the code snippet from GatewayApplication class, which spins up the API gateway. The @EnableZuulProxy annotation instructs the Spring framework to start the Spring application as a Zuul proxy.

```
@EnableZuulProxy
@SpringBootApplication
public class GatewayApplication {
    public static void main(String[] args) {
        SpringApplication.run(GatewayApplication.class, args);
    }
}
```

Now, let's see how to start the API gateway and talk to it with a cURL client. The following command executed from ch05/sample02 directory shows how to start the API gateway with Maven. Since the Zuul API gateway is also another Spring Boot application, the way you start it is the same as how we did before with the Order service.

```
\> mvn spring-boot:run
```

To test the Order API, which is now proxied through the Zuul API gateway, let's use the following cURL. It will print the output as shown in the following. Also make sure that the Order service is still up and running on port 8080. Here we add a new context called retail (which we didn't see in the direct API call) and talk to the port 9090, where the API gateway is running.

```
\> curl http://localhost:9090/retail/order/11
{"customer_id":"101021","order_id":"11","payment_method":{"card_type":
"VISA","expiration":"01/22","name":"John Doe","billing_address":"201, 1st
Street, San Jose, CA"},"items": [{"code":"101","qty":1},{"code":"103","qty"
:5}],"shipping_address":"201, 1st Street, San Jose, CA"}
```

What Happens Underneath?

When the API gateway receives a request to the retail context, it routes the request to the back-end API. These routing instructions are set in the src/main/resources/application.properties file, as shown in the following. If you want to use some other context, instead of retail, then you need to change the property key appropriately.

```
zuul.routes.retail.url=http://localhost:8080
```

Enabling TLS for the Zuul API Gateway

In the previous section, the communication between the cURL client and the Zuul API gateway happened over HTTP, which is not secure. In this section, let's see how to enable Transport Layer Security (TLS) at the Zuul API gateway. In Chapter 3, we discussed how to secure the Order service with TLS. There the Order service is a Java Spring Boot application, and we follow the same process here to secure the Zuul API gateway with TLS, as Zuul is also another Java Spring Boot application.

To enable TLS, first we need to create a public/private key pair. The following command uses keytool that comes with the default Java distribution to generate a key pair and stores it in keystore.jks file. If you are to use the keystore.jks file as it is, which is inside sample02 directory, you can possibly skip this step. Chapter 3 explains in detail what each parameter in the following command means.

```
\> keytool -genkey -alias spring -keyalg RSA -keysize 4096 -validity 3650
-dname "CN=zool,OU=bar,O=zee,L=sjc,S=ca,C=us" -keypass springboot -keystore
keystore.jks -storeType jks -storepass springboot
```

To enable TLS for the Zuul API gateway, copy the keystore file (keystore.jks), which we created earlier, to the home directory of the gateway (e.g., ch05/sample02/) and add the following to the [SAMPLE_HOME]/src/main/resources/application.properties file. The samples that you download from the samples git repository already have these values (and you only need to uncomment them), and we are using springboot as the password for both the keystore and the private key.

```
server.ssl.key-store: keystore.jks
server.ssl.key-store-password: springboot
server.ssl.keyAlias: spring
```

To validate that everything works fine, use the following command from ch05/sample02/ directory to spin up the Zuul API gateway and notice the line, which prints the HTTPS port. If you already have the Zuul gateway running from the previous exercise, please shut it down first.

```
\> mvn spring-boot:run
Tomcat started on port(s): 9090 (https) with context path "
```

Assuming you already have the Order service still running from the previous section, run the following cURL command to access the Order service via the Zuul gateway, over HTTPS.

```
\> curl -k https://localhost:9090/retail/order/11
{"customer_id":"101021","order_id":"11","payment_method":{"card_type":"V
ISA","expiration":"01/22","name":"John Doe","billing_address":"201, 1st
Street, San Jose, CA"},"items": [{"code":"101","qty":1},{"code":"103","qty"
:5}],"shipping_address":"201, 1st Street, San Jose, CA"}
```

We used the -k option in the preceding cURL command. Since we have self-signed (untrusted) certificates to secure our HTTPS endpoint, we need to pass the –k parameter to advise cURL to ignore the trust validation. In a production deployment with proper certificate authority–signed certificates, you do not need to do that. Also, if you have self-signed certificates, you can still avoid using –k, by pointing cURL to the corresponding public certificate.

```
\> curl --cacert ca.crt https://localhost:9090/retail/order/11
```

You can use the following keytool command from ch05/sample02/ to export the public certificate of the Zuul gateway to ca.crt file in PEM (with the -rfc argument) format.

```
\> keytool -export -file ca.crt -alias spring –rfc -keystore keystore.jks
-storePass springboot
```

The preceding command will result in the following error. This complains that the common name in certificate, which is zool, does not match with the hostname (localhost) in the cURL command.

```
curl: (51) SSL: certificate subject name 'zool' does not match target host
name 'localhost'
```

Ideally, in a production deployment when you create a certificate, its common name should match the hostname. In this case, since we do not have Domain Name Service (DNS) entry for the zool hostname, you can use the following workaround, with cURL.

```
\> curl --cacert ca.crt https://zool:9090/retail/order/11 --resolve
zool:9090:127.0.0.1
```

Enforcing OAuth 2.0 Token Validation at the Zuul API Gateway

In the previous section, we explained how to proxy requests to an API, via the Zuul API gateway. There we didn't worry about enforcing security. In this section, we will discuss how to enforce OAuth 2.0 token validation at the Zuul API gateway. There are two parts in doing that. First we need to have an OAuth 2.0 authorization server (also we can call it a security token service) to issue tokens, and then we need to enforce OAuth token validation at the Zuul API gateway (see Figure 5-2).

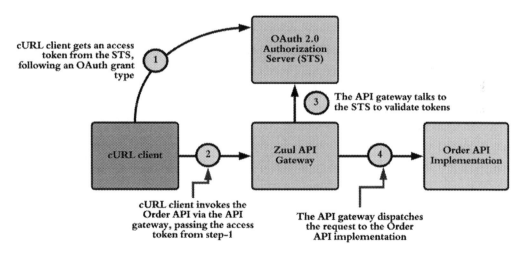

Figure 5-2. *The Zuul API gateway intercepts all the requests going to the Order API and validates OAuth 2.0 access tokens against the authorization server (STS)*

Setting Up an OAuth 2.0 Security Token Service (STS)

The responsibility of the security token service (STS) is to issue tokens to its clients and respond to the validation requests from the API gateway. There are many open source OAuth 2.0 authorization servers out there: WSO2 Identity Server, Keycloak, Gluu, and many more. In a production deployment, you may use one of them, but for this example, we are setting up a simple OAuth 2.0 authorization server with Spring Boot. It is another microservice and quite useful in developer testing. The code corresponding to the authorization server is under ch05/sample03 directory.

Let's have a look at ch05/sample03/pom.xml for notable Maven dependencies. These dependencies introduce a new set of annotations (@EnableAuthorizationServer annotation and @EnableResourceServer annotation), to turn a Spring Boot application to an OAuth 2.0 authorization server.

```
<dependency>
  <groupId>org.springframework.boot</groupId>
  <artifactId>spring-boot-starter-security</artifactId>
</dependency>
<dependency>
  <groupId>org.springframework.security.oauth</groupId>
  <artifactId>spring-security-oauth2</artifactId>
</dependency>
```

The class sample03/src/main/java/com/apress/ch05/sample03/TokenServiceApp. java carries the @EnableAuthorizationServer annotation, which turns the project into an OAuth 2.0 authorization server. We've added @EnableResourceServer annotation to the same class, as it also has to act as a resource server, to validate access tokens and return back the user information. It's understandable that the terminology here is a little confusing, but that's the easiest way to implement the token validation endpoint (in fact the user info endpoint, which also indirectly does the token validation) in Spring Boot. When you use self-contained access tokens (JWTs), this token validation endpoint is not required. If you are new to JWT, please check Chapter 7 for details.

The registration of clients with the Spring Boot authorization server can be done in multiple ways. This example registers clients in the code itself, in sample03/src/ main/java/com/apress/ch05/sample03/config/AuthorizationServerConfig. java file. The AuthorizationServerConfig class extends the AuthorizationServerConfigurerAdapter class to override its default behavior. Here we set the value of client id to 10101010, client secret to 11110000, available scope values to foo and/or bar, authorized grant types to client_credentials, password, and refresh_token, and the validity period of an access token to 6000 seconds. Most of the terms we use here are from OAuth 2.0 and explained in Chapter 4.

```
@Override
public void configure(ClientDetailsServiceConfigurer clients) throws
Exception {
    clients.inMemory().withClient("10101010")
            .secret("11110000").scopes("foo", "bar")
            .authorizedGrantTypes("client_credentials", "password",
                              "refresh_token")
            .accessTokenValiditySeconds(6000);
}
```

To support password grant type, the authorization server has to connect to a user store. A user store can be a database or an LDAP server, which stores user credentials and attributes. Spring Boot supports integration with multiple user stores, but once again, the most convenient one, which is just good enough for this example, is an in-memory user store. The following code from sample03/src/main/java/com/apress/ch05/sample03/config/WebSecurityConfiguration.java file adds a user to the system, with the role USER.

```
@Override
public void configure(AuthenticationManagerBuilder auth) throws
Exception {
    auth.inMemoryAuthentication()
        .withUser("peter").password("peter123").roles("USER");
}
```

Once we define the in-memory user store in Spring Boot, we also need to engage that with the OAuth 2.0 authorization flow, as shown in the following, in the code sample03/src/main/java/com/apress/ch05/sample03/config/AuthorizationServerConfig.java.

```
@Autowired
private AuthenticationManager authenticationManager;
@Override
```

```
public void configure(AuthorizationServerEndpointsConfigurer endpoints)
throws Exception {
       endpoints.authenticationManager(authenticationManager);
}
```

To start the authorization server, use the following command from ch05/sample03/ directory to spin up the TokenService microservice, and it starts running on HTTPS port 8443.

```
\> mvn spring-boot:run
```

Testing OAuth 2.0 Security Token Service (STS)

To get an access token using the OAuth 2.0 client credentials grant type, use the following command. Make sure to replace the values of $CLIENTID and $CLIENTSECRET appropriately. The hard-coded values for client id and client secret used in our example are 10101010 and 11110000, respectively. Also you might have noticed already, the STS endpoint is protected with Transport Layer Security (TLS). To protect STS with TLS, we followed the same process we did before while protecting the Zuul API gateway with TLS.

```
\> curl -v -X POST --basic -u $CLIENTID:$CLIENTSECRET -H "Content-Type:
application/x-www-form-urlencoded;charset=UTF-8" -k -d "grant_type=client_
credentials&scope=foo" https://localhost:8443/oauth/token
{"access_token":"81aad8c4-b021-4742-93a9-e25920587c94","token_
type":"bearer","expires_in":43199,"scope":"foo"}
```

Note   We use the –k option in the preceding cURL command. Since we have self-signed (untrusted) certificates to secure our HTTPS endpoint, we need to pass the –k parameter to advise cURL to ignore the trust validation. You can find more details regarding the parameters used here from the OAuth 2.0 6749 RFC: https://tools.ietf.org/html/rfc6749 and also explained in Chapter 4.

To get an access token using the password OAuth 2.0 grant type, use the following command. Make sure to replace the values of $CLIENTID, $CLIENTSECRET, $USERNAME, and $PASSWORD appropriately. The hard-coded values for client id and client secret used in our example are 10101010 and 11110000, respectively; and for username and password, we use peter and peter123, respectively.

```
\> curl -v -X POST --basic -u $CLIENTID:$CLIENTSECRET -H "Content-Type:
application/x-www-form-urlencoded;charset=UTF-8" -k -d "grant_type=passwor
d&username=$USERNAME&password=$PASSWORD&scope=foo" https://localhost:8443/
oauth/token
{"access_token":"69ff86a8-eaa2-4490-adda-6ce0f10b9f8b","token_
type":"bearer","refresh_token":"ab3c797b-72e2-4a9a-a1c5-
c550b2775f93","expires_in":43199,"scope":"foo"}
```

Note   If you carefully observe the two responses we got for the OAuth 2.0 client credentials grant type and the password grant type, you might have noticed that there is no refresh token in the client credentials grant type flow. In OAuth 2.0, the refresh token is used to obtain a new access token, when the access token has expired or is closer to expire. This is quite useful, when the user is offline and the client application has no access to his/her credentials to get a new access token and the only way is to use a refresh token. For the client credentials grant type, there is no user involved, and it always has access to its own credentials, so can be used any time it wants to get a new access token. Hence, a refresh token is not required.

Now let's see how to validate an access token, by talking to the authorization server. The resource server usually does this. An interceptor running on the resource server intercepts the request, extracts out the access token, and then talks to the authorization server. In a typical API deployment, this validation happens over a standard endpoint exposed by the OAuth authorization server. This is called the introspection endpoint, and in Chapter 9, we discuss OAuth token introspection in detail. However, in this example, we have not implemented the standard introspection endpoint at the authorization server (or the STS), but rather use a custom endpoint for token validation.

The following command shows how to directly talk to the authorization server to validate the access token obtained in the previous command. Make sure to replace the value of $TOKEN with the corresponding access token appropriately.

```
\> curl -k -X POST -H "Authorization: Bearer $TOKEN" -H "Content-Type:
application/json"   https://localhost:8443/user
{"details":{"remoteAddress":"0:0:0:0:0:0:0:1","sessionId":null,"tokenValue":
"9f3319a1-c6c4-4487-ac3b-51e9e479b4ff","tokenType":"Bearer","decodedDetails":
null},"authorities":[],"authenticated":true,"userAuthentication":null,
"credentials":"","oauth2Request":{"clientId":"10101010","scope":["bar"],
"requestParameters":{"grant_type":"client_credentials","scope":"bar"},
"resourceIds":[],"authorities":[],"approved":true,"refresh":false,"redirect
Uri":null,"responseTypes":[],"extensions":{},"grantType":"client_credentials",
"refreshTokenRequest":null},"clientOnly":true,"principal":"10101010",
"name":"10101010"}
```

The preceding command returns back the metadata associated with the access token, if the token is valid. The response is built inside the user() method of sample03/ src/main/java/com/apress/ch05/sample03/TokenServiceApp.java class, as shown in the following code snippet. With the @RequestMapping annotation, we map the /user context (from the request) to the user() method.

```
@RequestMapping("/user")
public Principal user(Principal user) {
     return user;
}
```

Note   By default, with no extensions, Spring Boot stores issued tokens in memory. If you restart the server after issuing a token, and then validate it, it will result in an error response.

Setting Up Zuul API Gateway for OAuth 2.0 Token Validation

To enforce token validation at the API gateway, we need to uncomment the following property in sample02/src/main/resources/application.properties file, as shown in the following. The value of the security.oauth2.resource.user-info-uri property carries the endpoint of the OAuth 2.0 security token service, which is used to validate tokens.

```
security.oauth2.resource.user-info-uri=https://localhost:8443/user
```

The preceding property points to an HTTPs endpoint on the authorization server. To support the HTTPS connection between the Zuul gateway and the authorization server, there is one more change we need to do at the Zuul gateway end. When we have a TLS connection between the Zuul gateway and the authorization server, the Zuul gateway has to trust the certificate authority associated with the public certificate of the authorization server. Since we are using self-signed certificate, we need to export authorization server's public certificate and import it to Zuul gateway's keystore. Let's use the following keytool command from ch05/sample03 directory to export authorization server's public certificate and copy it to ch05/sample02 directory. If you are using keystores from the samples git repo, then you may skip the following two keytool commands.

```
\> keytool -export -alias spring -keystore keystore.jks -storePass
springboot -file sts.crt
Certificate stored in file <sts.crt>
\> cp sts.crt ../sample02
```

Let's use the following keytool command from ch05/sample02 directory to import security token service's public certificate to Zuul gateway's keystore.

```
\> keytool -import -alias sts -keystore keystore.jks -storePass springboot
-file sts.crt
Trust this certificate? [no]:yes
Certificate was added to keystore
```

We also need to uncomment the following two dependencies in the sample02/pom.xml file. These dependencies do the autowiring between Spring Boot components to enforce OAuth 2.0 token validation at the Zuul gateway.

```
<dependency>
 <groupId>org.springframework.security</groupId>
 <artifactId>spring-security-jwt</artifactId>
</dependency>
<dependency>
 <groupId>org.springframework.security.oauth</groupId>
 <artifactId>spring-security-oauth2</artifactId>
</dependency>
```

Finally, we need to uncomment the @EnableResourceServer annotation and the corresponding package import on the GatewayApplication (ch05/sample02/ GatewayApplication.java) class.

Let's run the following command from the ch05/sample02 directory to start the Zuul API gateway. In case it is running already, you need to stop it first. Also, please make sure sample01 (Order service) and sample03 (STS) are still up and running.

```
\> mvn spring-boot:run
```

To test the API, which is now proxied through the Zuul API gateway and secured with OAuth 2.0, let's use the following cURL. It should fail, because we do not pass an OAuth 2.0 token.

```
\> curl -k https://localhost:9090/retail/order/11
```

Now let's see how to invoke the API properly with a valid access token. First we need to talk to the security token service and get an access token. Make sure to replace the values of $CLIENTID, $CLIENTSECRET, $USERNAME, and $PASSWORD appropriately in the following command. The hard-coded values for client id and client secret used in our example are 10101010 and 11110000, respectively; and for username and password, we used peter and peter123, respectively.

```
\> curl -v -X POST --basic -u $CLIENTID:$CLIENTSECRET -H "Content-Type:
application/x-www-form-urlencoded;charset=UTF-8" -k -d "grant_type=passwor
d&username=$USERNAME&password=$PASSWORD&scope=foo" https://localhost:8443/
oauth/token
{"access_token":"69ff86a8-eaa2-4490-adda-6ce0f10b9f8b","token_
type":"bearer","refresh_token":"ab3c797b-72e2-4a9a-a1c5-
c550b2775f93","expires_in":43199,"scope":"foo"}
```

Now let's use the access token from the preceding response to invoke the Order API. Make sure to replace the value of $TOKEN with the corresponding access token appropriately.

```
\> curl -k -H "Authorization: Bearer $TOKEN" -H "Content-Type: application/
json"   https://localhost:9090/retail/order/11
{"customer_id":"101021","order_id":"11","payment_method":{"card_type":
"VISA","expiration":"01/22","name":"John Doe","billing_address":"201, 1st
```

Street, San Jose, CA"},"items": [{"code":"101","qty":1},{"code":"103","qty" :5}],"shipping_address":"201, 1st Street, San Jose, CA"}

Enabling Mutual TLS Between Zuul API Gateway and Order Service

So far in this chapter, we have protected the communication between the cURL client and STS, cURL client and Zuul API gateway, and Zuul API gateway and STS over TLS. Still we have a weak link in our deployment (see Figure 5-3). The communication between the Zuul gateway and Order service is neither protected with TLS nor authentication. In other words, if someone can bypass the gateway, they can reach the Order server with no authentication. To fix this, we need to secure the communication between the gateway and the Order service over mutual TLS. Then, no other request can reach the Order service without going through the gateway. Or in other words, the Order service only accepts requests generated from the gateway.

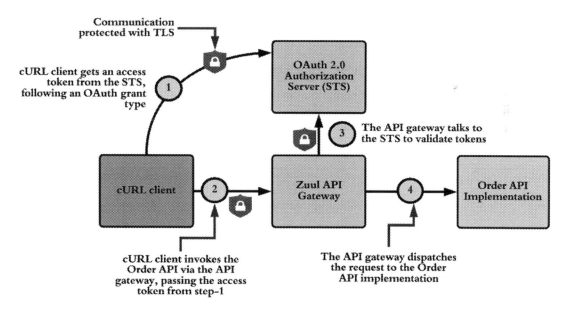

Figure 5-3. *The Zuul API gateway intercepts all the requests going to the Order API and validates OAuth 2.0 access tokens against the authorization server (STS)*

To enable mutual TLS between the gateway and the Order service, first we need to create a public/private key pair. The following command uses `keytool` that comes with the default Java distribution to generate a key pair and stores it in `keystore.jks` file. Chapter 3 explains in detail what each parameter in the following command means. If you are using keystores from the `samples` git repo, then you may skip the following keytool commands.

```
\> keytool -genkey -alias spring -keyalg RSA -keysize 4096 -validity
3650 -dname "CN=order,OU=bar,O=zee,L=sjc,S=ca,C=us" -keypass springboot
-keystore keystore.jks -storeType jks -storepass springboot
```

To enable mutual TLS for the Order service, copy the keystore file (`keystore.jks`), which we created earlier, to the home directory of the Order service (e.g., `ch05/sample01/`) and add the following to the `[SAMPLE_HOME]/src/main/resources/application.properties` file. The samples that you download from the `samples` git repository already have these values (and you only need to uncomment them), and we are using `springboot` as the password for both the keystore and the private key. The `server.ssl.client-auth` parameter is used to enforce mutual TLS at the Order service.

```
server.ssl.key-store: keystore.jks
server.ssl.key-store-password: springboot
server.ssl.keyAlias: spring
server.ssl.client-auth:need
```

There are two more changes we need to do at the Order service end. When we enforce mutual TLS at the Order service, the Zuul gateway (which acts as a client to the Order service) has to authenticate itself with an X.509 certificate—and the Order service must trust the certificate authority associated with Zuul gateway's X.509 certificate. Since we are using self-signed certificate, we need to export Zuul gateway's public certificate and import it to the Order service's keystore. Let's use the following keytool command from `ch05/sample02` directory to export Zuul gateway's public certificate and copy it to `ch05/sample01` directory.

```
\> keytool -export -alias spring -keystore keystore.jks -storePass
springboot -file zuul.crt
Certificate stored in file <zuul.crt>
\> cp zuul.crt ../sample01
```

Let's use the following keytool command from ch05/sample01 directory to import Zuul gateway's public certificate to Order service's keystore.

```
\> keytool -import -alias zuul -keystore keystore.jks -storePass springboot
-file zuul.crt
Trust this certificate? [no]:yes
Certificate was added to keystore
```

Finally, when we have a TLS connection between the Zuul gateway and the Order service, the Zuul gateway has to trust the certificate authority associated with the public certificate of the Order service. Even though we do not enable mutual TLS between these two parties, we still need to satisfy this requirement to enable just TLS. Since we are using self-signed certificate, we need to export Order service's public certificate and import it to Zuul gateway's keystore. Let's use the following keytool command from ch05/sample01 directory to export Order service's public certificate and copy it to ch05/sample02 directory.

```
\> keytool -export -alias spring -keystore keystore.jks -storePass
springboot -file order.crt
Certificate stored in file <order.crt>
\> cp order.crt ../sample02
```

Let's use the following keytool command from ch05/sample02 directory to import Order service's public certificate to Zuul gateway's keystore.

```
\> keytool -import -alias order -keystore keystore.jks -storePass
springboot -file order.crt
Trust this certificate? [no]:yes
Certificate was added to keystore
```

To validate that TLS works fine with the Order service, use the following command from ch05/sample01/ directory to spin up the Order service and notice the line, which prints the HTTPS port. If you already have the Order service running from the previous exercise, please shut it down first.

```
\> mvn spring-boot:run
Tomcat started on port(s): 8080 (https) with context path "
```

Since we updated the Order service endpoint to use HTTPS instead of HTTP, we also need to update the Zuul gateway to use the new HTTPS endpoint. These routing instructions are set in the ch05/sample02/src/main/resources/application.

119

properties file, as shown in the following. Just update it to use HTTPS instead of HTTP. Also we need to uncomment the `zuul.sslHostnameValidationEnabled` property in the same file and set it to false. This is to ask Spring Boot to ignore hostname verification. Or in other words, now Spring Boot won't check whether the hostname of the Order service matches the common name of the corresponding public certificate.

```
zuul.routes.retail.url=https://localhost:8080
zuul.sslHostnameValidationEnabled=false
```

Restart the Zuul gateway with the following command from `ch05/sample02`.

```
\> mvn spring-boot:run
```

Assuming you have authorization server up and running, on HTTPS port 8443, run the following command to test the end-to-end flow. First we need to talk to the security token service and get an access token. Make sure to replace the values of $CLIENTID, $CLIENTSECRET, $USERNAME, and $PASSWORD appropriately in the following command. The hard-coded values for client id and client secret used in our example are 10101010 and 11110000, respectively; and for `username` and `password`, we used `peter` and `peter123`, respectively.

```
\> curl -v -X POST --basic -u $CLIENTID:$CLIENTSECRET -H "Content-Type:
application/x-www-form-urlencoded;charset=UTF-8" -k -d "grant_type=passwor
d&username=$USERNAME&password=$PASSWORD&scope=foo" https://localhost:8443/
oauth/token
{"access_token":"69ff86a8-eaa2-4490-adda-6ce0f10b9f8b","token_
type":"bearer","refresh_token":"ab3c797b-72e2-4a9a-a1c5-
c550b2775f93","expires_in":43199,"scope":"foo"}
```

Now let's use the access token from the preceding response to invoke the Order API. Make sure to replace the value of $TOKEN with the corresponding access token appropriately.

```
\> curl -k -H "Authorization: Bearer $TOKEN" -H "Content-Type: application/
json"   https://localhost:9090/retail/order/11
{"customer_id":"101021","order_id":"11","payment_method":{"card_type":"V
ISA","expiration":"01/22","name":"John Doe","billing_address":"201, 1st
Street, San Jose, CA"},"items": [{"code":"101","qty":1},{"code":"103","qty"
:5}],"shipping_address":"201, 1st Street, San Jose, CA"}
```

Securing Order API with Self-Contained Access Tokens

An OAuth 2.0 bearer token can be a reference token or self-contained token. A reference token is an arbitrary string. An attacker can carry out a brute-force attack to guess the token. The authorization server must pick the right length and use other possible measures to prevent brute forcing. A self-contained access token is a JSON Web Token (JWT), which we discuss in Chapter 7. When the resource server gets an access token, which is a reference token, then to validate the token, it has to talk to the authorization server (or the token issuer). When the access token is a JWT, the resource server can validate the token by itself, by verifying the signature of the JWT. In this section, we discuss how to obtain a JWT access token from the authorization server and use it to access the Order service through the Zuul API gateway.

Setting Up an Authorization Server to Issue JWT

In this section, we'll see how to extend the authorization server we used in the previous section (ch05/sample03/) to support self-contained access tokens or JWTs. The first step is to create a new key pair along with a keystore. This key is used to sign the JWTs issued from our authorization server. The following keytool command will create a new keystore with a key pair.

```
\> keytool -genkey -alias jwtkey -keyalg RSA -keysize 2048 -dname
"CN=localhost" -keypass springboot -keystore jwt.jks -storepass springboot
```

The preceding command creates a keystore with the name jwt.jks, protected with the password springboot. We need to copy this keystore to sample03/src/main/resources/. Now to generate self-contained access tokens, we need to set the values of the following properties in sample03/src/main/resources/application.properties file.

```
spring.security.oauth.jwt: true
spring.security.oauth.jwt.keystore.password: springboot
spring.security.oauth.jwt.keystore.alias: jwtkey
spring.security.oauth.jwt.keystore.name: jwt.jks
```

The value of spring.security.oauth.jwt is set to false by default, and it has to be changed to true to issue JWTs. The other three properties are self-explanatory, and you need to set them appropriately based on the values you used in creating the keystore.

Let's go through the notable changes in the source code to support JWTs. First, in the pom.xml, we need to add the following dependency, which takes care of building JWTs.

```
<dependency>
  <groupId>org.springframework.security</groupId>
  <artifactId>spring-security-jwt</artifactId>
</dependency>
```

In sample03/src/main/java/com/apress/ch05/sample03/config/ AuthorizationServerConfig.java class, we have added the following method, which takes care of injecting the details about how to retrieve the private key from the jwt.jks keystore, which we created earlier. This private key is used to sign the JWT.

```
@Bean
protected JwtAccessTokenConverter jwtConeverter() {
    String pwd = environment.getProperty("spring.security.oauth.jwt.
    keystore.password");
    String alias = environment.getProperty("spring.security.oauth.jwt.
    keystore.alias");
    String keystore = environment.getProperty("spring.security.oauth.jwt.
    keystore.name");
    String path = System.getProperty("user.dir");

    KeyStoreKeyFactory keyStoreKeyFactory = new KeyStoreKeyFactory(
            new FileSystemResource(new File(path + File.separator +
            keystore)), pwd.toCharArray());
    JwtAccessTokenConverter converter = new JwtAccessTokenConverter();
    converter.setKeyPair(keyStoreKeyFactory.getKeyPair(alias));
    return converter;
}
```

In the same class file, we also set JwtTokenStore as the token store. The following function does it in a way, we only set the JwtTokenStore as the token store only if spring.security.oauth.jwt property is set to true in the application.properties file.

```
@Bean
public TokenStore tokenStore() {
    String useJwt = environment.getProperty("spring.security.oauth.jwt");
    if (useJwt != null && "true".equalsIgnoreCase(useJwt.trim())) {
        return new JwtTokenStore(jwtConeverter());
    } else {
        return new InMemoryTokenStore();
    }
}
```

Finally, we need to set the token store to `AuthorizationServerEndpointsConfigurer`, which is done in the following method, and once again, only if we want to use JWTs.

```
@Autowired
private AuthenticationManager authenticationManager;

@Override
public void configure(AuthorizationServerEndpointsConfigurer endpoints)
throws Exception {
    String useJwt = environment.getProperty("spring.security.oauth.jwt");
    if (useJwt != null && "true".equalsIgnoreCase(useJwt.trim())) {
        endpoints.tokenStore(tokenStore()).tokenEnhancer(jwtConeverter())
                        .authenticationManager(authenticationManager);
    } else {
        endpoints.authenticationManager(authenticationManager);
    }
}
```

To start the authorization server, use the following command from `ch05/sample03/` directory, which now issues self-contained access tokens (JWTs).

```
\> mvn spring-boot:run
```

To get an access token using the OAuth 2.0 client credentials grant type, use the following command. Make sure to replace the values of $CLIENTID and $CLIENTSECRET appropriately. The hard-coded values for client id and client secret used in our example are 10101010 and 11110000, respectively.

```
\> curl -v -X POST --basic -u $CLIENTID:$CLIENTSECRET -H "Content-Type:
application/x-www-form-urlencoded;charset=UTF-8" -k -d "grant_type=client_
credentials&scope=foo" https://localhost:8443/oauth/token
```

The preceding command will return back a base64-url-encoded JWT, and the following shows the decoded version.

```
{ "alg": "RS256", "typ": "JWT" }
{ "scope": [ "foo" ], "exp": 1524793284, "jti": "6e55840e-886c-46b2-bef7-
1a14b813dd0a", "client_id": "10101010" }
```

Only the decoded header and the payload are shown in the output, skipping the signature (which is the third part of the JWT). Since we used `client_credentials` grant type, the JWT does not include a subject or username. It also includes the scope value(s) associated with the token.

Protecting Zuul API Gateway with JWT

In this section, we'll see how to enforce self-issued access token or JWT-based token validation at the Zuul API gateway. We only need to comment out `security.oauth2.resource.user-info-uri` property and uncomment `security.oauth2.resource.jwt.keyUri` property in `sample02/src/main/resources/application.properties` file. The updated `application.properties` file will look like the following.

```
#security.oauth2.resource.user-info-uri:https://localhost:8443/user
security.oauth2.resource.jwt.keyUri: https://localhost:8443/oauth/token_key
```

Here the value of `security.oauth2.resource.jwt.keyUri` points to the public key corresponding to the private key, which is used to sign the JWT by the authorization server. It's an endpoint hosted under the authorization server. If you just type `https://localhost:8443/oauth/token_key` on the browser, you will find the public key, as shown in the following. This is the key the API gateway uses to verify the signature of the JWT included in the request.

```
{
    "alg":"SHA256withRSA",
    "value":"-----BEGIN PUBLIC KEY-----\nMIIBIjANBgkqhkiG9w0BAQEFAAOCAQ8AMI
IBCgKCAQEA+WcBjPsrFvGOwqVJd8vpV+gNx5onTyLjYx864mtIvUxO8D4mwAaYpjXJgsre2dc
XjQo3BOLJdcjY5Nc9Kclea09nhFIEJDG3obwxm9gQw5Op1TShCP3OXqf8b7I738EHDFT6
```

qABul7itIxSrz+AqUvj9LSUKEw/cdXrJeu6b71qHd/YiElUIAOfjVwlFctbw7REbi3Sy3nWdm
9yk7M3GIKka77jxw1MwIBg2klfDJgnE72fPkPi3FmaJTJA4+9sKgfniFqdMNfkyLVbOi9E3Dla
oGxEit6fKTI9GR1SWX40FhhgLdTyWdu2z9RS2BOp+3d9WFMTddab8+fd4L2mYCQIDAQ
AB\n-----END PUBLIC KEY-----"
}

Once the changes are made as highlighted earlier, let's restart the Zuul gateway with the following command from the sample02 directory.

```
\> mvn spring-boot:run
```

Once we have a JWT access token obtained from the OAuth 2.0 authorization server, in the same way as we did before, with the following cURL command, we can access the protected resource. Make sure the value of $TOKEN is replaced appropriately with a valid JWT access token.

```
\> curl -k -H "Authorization: Bearer $TOKEN" https://localhost:9443/
order/11
{"customer_id":"101021","order_id":"11","payment_method":{"card_type":"VISA",
"expiration":"01/22","name":"John Doe","billing_address":"201, 1st Street,
San Jose, CA"},"items":[{"code":"101","qty":1},{"code":"103","qty":5}],"
shipping_address":"201, 1st Street, San Jose, CA"}
```

The Role of a Web Application Firewall (WAF)

As we discussed before, an API gateway is a policy enforcement point (PEP), which centrally enforces authentication, authorization, and throttling policies. In a public-facing API deployment, an API gateway is not just sufficient. We also need a web application firewall (WAF) sitting in front of the API gateway (see Figure 5-4). The primary role of a WAF is to protect your API deployment from distributed denial of service (DDoS) attacks—do threat detection and message validation against OpenAPI Specification (OAS) along with known threats identified by Open Web Application Security Project (OWASP). Gartner (one of the leading analyst firms) predicts that by 2020, more than 50% of public-facing web applications will be protected by cloud-based WAF service platforms such Akamai, Imperva, Cloudflare, Amazon Web Services, and so on, up from less than 20% in December 2018.

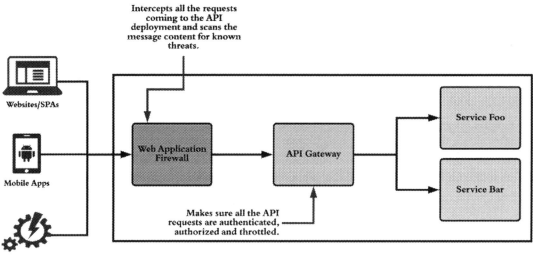

Figure 5-4. *A web application firewall (WAF) intercepts all the traffic coming into an API deployment*

Summary

- OAuth 2.0 is the de facto standard for securing APIs.

- The API gateway is the most common pattern in securing APIs in a production deployment. In other words, it's the entry point to your API deployment.

- There are many open source and proprietary products out there, which implement the API gateway pattern, which we commonly identify as API gateways.

- An OAuth 2.0 bearer token can be a reference token or self-contained token. A reference token is an arbitrary string. An attacker can carry out a brute-force attack to guess the token. The authorization server must pick the right length and use other possible measures to prevent brute forcing.

- When the resource server gets an access token, which is a reference token, then to validate the token, it has to talk to the authorization server (or the token issuer). When the access token is a JWT, the resource server can validate the token by itself, by verifying the signature of the JWT.

- Zuul is an API gateway that provides dynamic routing, monitoring, resiliency, security, and more. It is acting as the front door to Netflix's server infrastructure, handling traffic from all Netflix users around the world.

- In a public-facing API deployment, an API gateway is not just sufficient. We also need a web application firewall (WAF) sitting in front of the API gateway.

CHAPTER 6

OpenID Connect (OIDC)

OpenID Connect provides a lightweight framework for identity interactions in a RESTful manner and was ratified as a standard by its membership on February 26, 2014.[1] It was developed under the OpenID Foundation and has its roots in OpenID, but was greatly affected by OAuth 2.0. OpenID Connect is the most popular Identity Federation protocol at the time of this writing. Most of the applications developed in the last few years are supporting OpenID Connect. Ninety-two percent of the 8 billion+ authentication requests Microsoft Azure AD handled in May 2018 were from OpenID Connect–enabled applications.

From OpenID to OIDC

OpenID, which followed in the footsteps of Security Assertion Markup Language (SAML) in 2005, revolutionized web authentication. Brad Fitzpatrick, the founder of LiveJournal, came up with the initial idea of OpenID. The basic principle behind both OpenID and SAML (discussed in Chapter 12) is the same. Both can be used to facilitate web single sign-on (SSO) and cross-domain identity federation. OpenID is more community-friendly, user centric, and decentralized. Yahoo! added OpenID support in January 2008, MySpace announced its support for OpenID in July of the same year, and Google joined the party in October. By December 2009, there were more than 1 billion OpenID-enabled accounts. It was a huge success as a web SSO protocol.

OpenID and OAuth 1.0 address two different concerns. OpenID is about authentication, whereas OAuth 1.0 is about delegated authorization. As both of these standards were gaining popularity in their respective domains, there was an interest in

---

[1]The announcement by the OpenID Foundation regarding the launch of the OpenID Connect standard is available at `http://bit.ly/31PowsS`

© Prabath Siriwardena 2020
P. Siriwardena, *Advanced API Security*, https://doi.org/10.1007/978-1-4842-2050-4_6

combining them, so that it would be possible to authenticate a user and also get a token to access resources on his or her behalf in a single step.

The Google Step 2 project was the first serious effort in this direction. It introduced an OpenID extension for OAuth, which basically takes OAuth-related parameters in the OpenID request/response. The same people who initiated the Google Step 2 project later brought it into the OpenID Foundation.

OpenID has gone through three generations to date. OpenID 1.0/1.1/2.0 was the first generation, and the OpenID extension for OAuth is the second. OpenID Connect (OIDC) is the third generation of OpenID. Yahoo!, Google, and many other OpenID providers discontinued their support for OpenID around mid-2015 and migrated to OpenID Connect.

OPENID CONNECT IS NOT OPENID, THIS IS HOW OPENID WORKS!

How many profiles do you maintain today at different web sites? Perhaps you have one on Yahoo!, one on Facebook, one on Google, and so on. Each time you update your mobile number or home address, either you have to update all your profiles or you risk outdating most of your profiles. OpenID solves the problem of scattered profiles on different websites. With OpenID, you maintain your profile only at your OpenID provider, and all the other sites become OpenID relying parties. These relying parties communicate with your OpenID provider to obtain your information.

Each time you try to log in to a relying party website, you're redirected to your OpenID provider. At the OpenID provider, you have to authenticate and approve the request from the relying party for your attributes. Upon approval, you're redirected back to the relying party with the requested attributes. This goes beyond simple attribute sharing to facilitate decentralized SSO.

With SSO, you only log in once at the OpenID provider. That is, when a relying party redirects you to the OpenID provider for the first time. After that, for the subsequent redirects by other relying parties, your OpenID provider doesn't ask for credentials but uses the authenticated session you created before at the OpenID provider. This authenticated session is maintained either by a cookie until the browser is closed or with persistent cookies. Figure 6-1 illustrates how OpenID works.

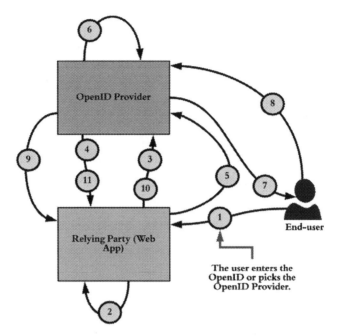

Figure 6-1. *OpenID protocol flow*

The end user initiates the OpenID flow by typing his or her OpenID on the relying party web site (step 1). An OpenID is a unique URL or an XRI (Extensible Resource Identifier). For example, `http://prabath.myopenid.com` is an OpenID. Once the user types his or her OpenID, the relying party has to do a discovery based on it to find out the corresponding OpenID provider (step 2). The relying party performs an HTTP GET on the OpenID (which is a URL) to get back the HTML text behind it. For example, if you view the source that is behind `http://prabath.myopenid.com`, you'll see the following tag (MyOpenID was taken down some years back). This is exactly what the relying party sees during the discovery phase. This tag indicates which OpenID provider is behind the provided OpenID:

```
<link rel="openid2.provider" href="http://www.myopenid.com/server" />
```

OpenID has another way of identifying the OpenID provider, other than asking for an OpenID from the end user. This is known as *directed identity*, and Yahoo!, Google, and many other OpenID providers used it. If a relying party uses directed identity, it already knows who the OpenID provider is, so a discovery phase isn't needed. The relying party lists the set of OpenID providers it supports, and the user has to pick which one it wants to authenticate against.

Once the OpenID provider is discovered, the next step depends on the type of the relying party. If it's a smart relying party, then it executes step 3 in Figure 6-1 to create an association with the OpenID provider. During the association, a shared secret key is established between the OpenID provider and the relying party. If a key is already established between the two parties, this step is skipped, even for a smart relying party. A dumb relying party always ignores step 3.

In step 5, the user is redirected to the discovered OpenID provider. In step 6, the user has to authenticate and approve the attribute request from the relying party (steps 6 and 7). Upon approval, the user is redirected back to the relying party (step 9). A key only known to the OpenID provider and the corresponding relying party signs this response from the OpenID provider. Once the relying party receives the response, if it's a smart relying party, it validates the signature itself. The key shared during the association phase should sign the message. If it's a dumb relying party, it directly talks to the OpenID provider in step 10 (not a browser redirect) and asks to validate the signature. The decision is passed back to the relying party in step 11, and that concludes the OpenID protocol flow.

Amazon Still Uses OpenID 2.0

Few have noticed that Amazon still uses (at the time of this writing) OpenID for user authentication. Check it out yourself: go to www.amazon.com, and click the Sign In button. Then observe the browser address bar. You see something similar to the following, which is an OpenID authentication request:

```
https://www.amazon.com/ap/signin?_encoding=UTF8
    &openid.assoc_handle=usflex
    &openid.claimed_id=
            http://specs.openid.net/auth/2.0/identifier_select
    &openid.identity=
            http://specs.openid.net/auth/2.0/identifier_select
    &openid.mode=checkid_setup
    &openid.ns=http://specs.openid.net/auth/2.0
    &openid.ns.pape=
            http://specs.openid.net/extensions/pape/1.0
    &openid.pape.max_auth_age=0
    &openid.return_to=https://www.amazon.com/gp/yourstore/home
```

Understanding OpenID Connect

OpenID Connect was built on top of OAuth 2.0. It introduces an identity layer on top of OAuth 2.0. This identity layer is abstracted into an ID token, which is JSON Web Token (JWT), and we talk about JWT in detail in Chapter 7. An OAuth 2.0 authorization server that supports OpenID Connect returns an ID token along with the access token.

OpenID Connect is a profile built on top of OAuth 2.0. OAuth talks about access delegation, while OpenID Connect talks about authentication. In other words, OpenID Connect builds an identity layer on top of OAuth 2.0.

Authentication is the act of confirming the truth of an attribute of a datum or entity. If I say I am Peter, I need to prove that. I can prove that with something I know, something I have, or with something I am. Once proven who I claim I am, then the system can trust me. Sometimes systems do not just want to identify end users just by the name. Name could help to identify uniquely—but how about other attributes? Before you get through the border control, you need to identify yourself—by name, by picture, and also by fingerprints and eye retina. Those are validated in real time against the data from the VISA office, which issued the VISA for you. That check will make sure it's the same person who claimed to have the VISA that enters into the country.

That is proving your identity. Proving your identity is authentication. Authorization is about what you can do or your capabilities.

You could prove your identity at the border control by name, by picture, and also by fingerprints and eye retina—but it's your visa that decides what you can do. To enter into the country, you need to have a valid visa that has not expired. A valid visa is not a part of your identity, but a part of what you can do. What you can do inside the country depends on the visa type. What you do with a B1 or B2 visa differs from what you can do with an L1 or L2 visa. That is authorization.

OAuth 2.0 is about authorization—not about authentication. With OAuth 2.0, the client does not know about the end user (only exception is resource owner password credentials grant type, which we discussed in Chapter 4). It simply gets an access token to access a resource on behalf of the user. With OpenID Connect, the client will get an ID token along with the access token. ID token is a representation of the end user's identity. What does it mean by securing an API with OpenID Connect? Or is it totally meaningless? OpenID Connect is at the application level or at the client level—not at the API level or at the resource server level. OpenID Connect helps client or the application to find out who the end user is, but for the API that is meaningless. The only thing API expects is the access token. If the resource owner or the API wants to find who the end user is, it has to query the authorization server or rely on a self-contained access token (which is a JWT).

Anatomy of the ID Token

The ID token is the primary add-on to OAuth 2.0 to support OpenID Connect. It's a JSON Web Token (JWT) that transports authenticated user information from the authorization server to the client application. Chapter 7 delves deeper into JWT. The structure of the ID token is defined by the OpenID Connect specification. The following shows a sample ID token:

```
{
    "iss":"https://auth.server.com",
    "sub":"prabath@apache.org",
    "aud":"67jjuyuy7JHk12",
    "nonce":"88797jgjg32332",
    "exp":1416283970,
    "iat":1416281970,
    "auth_time":1311280969,
    "acr":"urn:mace:incommon:iap:silver",
    "amr":"password",
    "azp":"67jjuyuy7JHk12"
}
```

Let's examine the definition of each attribute:

- iss: The token issuer's (authorization server or identity provider) identifier in the format of an HTTPS URL with no query parameters or URL fragments. In practice, most of the OpenID Provider implementations or products let you configure an issuer you want— and also this is mostly being used as an identifier, rather than a URL. This is a required attribute in the ID token.

- sub: The token issuer or the asserting party issues the ID token for a particular entity, and the claims set embedded into the ID token normally represents this entity, which is identified by the sub parameter. The value of the sub parameter is a case-sensitive string value and is a required attribute in the ID token.

- aud: The audience of the token. This can be an array of identifiers, but it must have the OAuth client ID in it; otherwise, the client ID should be added to the azp parameter, which we discuss later in this section. Prior to any validation check, the OpenID client must first see whether the particular ID token is issued for its use and if not should reject immediately. In other words, you need to check whether the value of the aud attribute matches with the OpenID client's identifier. The value of the aud parameter can be a case-sensitive string value or an array of strings. This is a required attribute in the ID token.

- nonce: A new parameter introduced by the OpenID Connect specification to the initial authorization grant request. In addition to the parameters defined in OAuth 2.0, the client application can optionally include the nonce parameter. This parameter was introduced to mitigate replay attacks. The authorization server must reject any request if it finds two requests with the same nonce value. If a nonce is present in the authorization grant request, then the authorization server must include the same value in the ID token. The client application must validate the value of the nonce once it receives the ID token from the authorization server.

- exp: Each ID token carries an expiration time. The recipient of the ID token must reject it, if that token has expired. The issuer can decide the value of the expiration time. The value of the exp parameter is calculated by adding the expiration time (from the token issued time) in seconds to the time elapsed from 1970-01-01T00:00:00Z UTC to the current time. If the token issuer's clock is out of sync with the recipient's clock (irrespective of their time zone), then the expiration time validation could fail. To fix that, each recipient can add a couple of minutes as the clock skew during the validation process. This is a required attribute in the ID token.

- iat: The iat parameter in the ID token indicates the issued time of the ID token as calculated by the token issuer. The value of the iat parameter is the number of seconds elapsed from 1970-01-01T00:00:00Z UTC to the current time, when the token is issued. This is a required attribute in the ID token.

- `auth_time`: The time at which the end user authenticates with the authorization server. If the user is already authenticated, then the authorization server won't ask the user to authenticate back. How a given authorization server authenticates the user, and how it manages the authenticated session, is outside the scope of OpenID Connect. A user can create an authenticated session with the authorization server in the first login attempt from a different application, other than the OpenID client application. In such cases, the authorization server must maintain the authenticated time and include it in the parameter `auth_time`. This is an optional parameter.

- `acr`: Stands for *authentication context class reference*. The value of this parameter must be understood by both the authorization server and the client application. It gives an indication of the level of authentication. For example, if the user authenticates with a long-lived browser cookie, it is considered as level 0. OpenID Connect specification does not recommend using an authentication level of 0 to access any resource of any monetary value. This is an optional parameter.

- `amr`: Stands for *authentication method references*. It indicates how the authorization server authenticates the user. It may consist of an array of values. Both the authorization server and the client application must understand the value of this parameter. For example, if the user authenticates at the authorization server with username/password and with one-time passcode over SMS, the value of `amr` parameter must indicate that. This is an optional parameter.

- `azp`: Stands for *authorized party*. It's needed when there is one audience (aud) and its value is different from the OAuth client ID. The value of `azp` must be set to the OAuth client ID. This is an optional parameter.

Note   The authorization server must sign the ID token, as defined in JSON Web Signature (JWS) specification. Optionally, it can also be encrypted. Token encryption should follow the rules defined in the JSON Web Encryption (JWE) specification. If the ID token is encrypted, it must be signed first and then encrypted. This is because signing the encrypted text is questionable in many legal entities. Chapters 7 and 8 talk about JWT, JWS, and JWE.

OPENID CONNECT WITH WSO2 IDENTITY SERVER

In this exercise, you see how to obtain an OpenID Connect ID token along with an OAuth 2.0 access token. Here we run the WSO2 Identity Server as the OAuth 2.0 authorization server.

Note   WSO2 Identity Server is a free, open source identity and entitlement management server, released under the Apache 2.0 license. At the time of this writing, the latest released version is 5.9.0 and runs on Java 8.

Follow these steps to register your application as a service provider in WSO2 Identity Server and then log in to your application via OpenID Connect:

1. Download WSO2 Identity Server 5.9.0 from `http://wso2.com/products/ identity-server/`, set up the JAVA_HOME environment variable, and start the server from the `wso2server.sh/wso2server.bat` file in the WSO2_IS_HOME/ bin directory. If the WSO2 Identity Server 5.9.0 isn't available from the main download page, you can find it at `http://wso2.com/more-downloads/ identity-server/`.

2. By default, the WSO2 Identity Server starts on HTTPS port 9443.

3. Log in to the Identity Server running at `https://localhost:9443` with its default username and password (`admin/admin`).

4. To get an OAuth 2.0 client ID and a client secret for a client application, you need to register it as a service provider on the OAuth 2.0 authorization server. Choose Main ➤ Service Providers ➤ Add. Enter a name, say, `oidc-app`, and click Register.

5. Choose Inbound Authentication Configuration ➤ OAuth and OpenID Connect Configuration ➤ Configure.

6. Uncheck all the grant types except Code. Make sure the OAuth version is set to 2.0.

7. Provide a value for the Callback Url text box—say, `https://localhost/ callback`—and click Add.

8. Copy the values of OAuth Client Key and the OAuth Client Secret.

9. You use cURL here instead of a full-blown web application. First you need to
    get an authorization code. Copy the following URL, and paste it into a browser.
    Replace the values of `client_id` and `redirect_uri` appropriately. Note that
    here we are passing the `openid` as the value of the `scope` parameter in the
    request. This is a must to use OpenID Connect. You're directed to a login page
    where you can authenticate with `admin/admin` and then approve the request
    by the client:

    ```
    https://localhost:9443/oauth2/authorize?
            response_type=code&scope=openid&
            client_id=NJOLXcfdOW2OEvD6DUOlOpO1u_Ya&
            redirect_uri=https://localhost/callback
    ```

10. Once approved, you're redirected back to the `redirect_uri` with the
    authorization code, as shown here. Copy the value of the authorization code:

    ```
    https://localhost/callback?code=577fc84a51c2aceac2a9e2f723f0f47f
    ```

11. Now you can exchange the authorization code from the previous step
    for an ID token and an access token. Replace the value of `client_id`,
    `client_secret`, code, and `redirect_uri` appropriately. The value of –u is
    constructed as `client_id:client_secret`:

    ```
    curl -v -X POST --basic
        -u NJOLXcfdOW2...:EsSP5GfYliU96MQ6...
        -H "Content-Type: application/x-www-form-urlencoded;
        charset=UTF-8" -k
        -d "client_id=NJOLXcfdOW2OEvD6DUOlOpO1u_Ya&
            grant_type=authorization_code&
            code=577fc84a51c2aceac2a9e2f723f0f47f&
            redirect_uri=https://localhost/callback"
            https://localhost:9443/oauth2/token
    ```

    This results in the following JSON response:

    ```
    {
        "scope":"openid",
        "token_type":"bearer",
        "expires_in":3299,
        "refresh_token":"1caf88a1351d2d74093f6b84b8751bb",
    ```

```
    "id_token":"eyJhbGciOiJub25......",
    "access_token":"6cc611211a941cc95c0c5caf1385295"
}
```

12. The value of id_token is base64url-encoded. Once it's base64url-decoded, it looks like the following. Also you can use an online tool like https://jwt.io to decode the ID token:

```
{
    "alg":"none",
    "typ":"JWT"
}.
{
    "exp":1667236118,
    "azp":"NJOLXcfdOW2OEvD6DUOlOp01u_Ya",
    "sub":"admin@carbon.super",
    "aud":"NJOLXcfdOW2OEvD6DUOlOp01u_Ya",
    "iss":"https://localhost:9443/oauth2endpoints/token",
    "iat":1663636118
}
```

OpenID Connect Request

The ID token is the heart of OpenID Connect, but that isn't the only place where it deviates from OAuth 2.0. OpenID Connect introduced some optional parameters to the OAuth 2.0 authorization grant request. The previous exercise didn't use any of those parameters. Let's examine a sample authorization grant request with all the optional parameters:

```
https://localhost:9443/oauth2/authorize?response_type=code&
    scope=openid&
    client_id=NJOLXcfdOW2OEvD6DUOlOp01u_Ya&
    redirect_uri= https://localhost/callback&
    response_mode=.....&
    nonce=.....&
    display=....&
    prompt=....&
    max_age=.....&
    ui_locales=.....&
```

```
id_token_hint=.....&
login_hint=.....&
acr_value=.....
```

Let's review the definition of each attribute:

- `response_mode`: Determines how the authorization server sends back the parameters in the response. This is different from the `response_type` parameter, defined in the OAuth 2.0 core specification. With the `response_type` parameter in the request, the client indicates whether it expects a code or a token. In the case of an authorization code grant type, the value of `response_type` is set to `code`, whereas with an implicit grant type, the value of `response_type` is set to `token`. The `response_mode` parameter addresses a different concern. If the value of `response_mode` is set to `query`, the response parameters are sent back to the client as query parameters appended to the `redirect_uri`; and if the value is set to fragment, then the response parameters are appended to the `redirect_uri` as a URI fragment.

- `nonce`: Mitigates replay attacks. The authorization server must reject any request if it finds two requests with the same `nonce` value. If a nonce is present in the authorization grant request, then the authorization server must include the same value in the ID token. The client application must validate the value of the nonce once it receives the ID token from the authorization server.

- `display`: Indicates how the client application expects the authorization server to display the login page and the user consent page. Possible values are `page`, `popup`, `touch`, and `wap`.

- `prompt`: Indicates whether to display the login or the user consent page at the authorization server. If the value is `none`, then neither the login page nor the user consent page should be presented to the user. In other words, it expects the user to have an authenticated session at the authorization server and a preconfigured user consent. If the value is `login`, the authorization server must reauthenticate the user. If the value is `consent`, the authorization server must display the user consent page to the end user. The `select_account` option can be used if the user has multiple accounts on the authorization server. The authorization server must then give the user an option to select from which account he or she requires attributes.

- max_age: In the ID token there is a parameter that indicates the time of user authentication (auth_time). The max_age parameter asks the authorization server to compare that value with max_age. If it's less than the gap between the current time and max_age (current time-max_age), the authorization server must reauthenticate the user. When the client includes the max_age parameter in the request, the authorization server must include the auth_time parameter in the ID token.

- ui_locales: Expresses the end user's preferred language for the user interface.

- id_token_hint: An ID token itself. This could be an ID token previously obtained by the client application. If the token is encrypted, it has to be decrypted first and then encrypted back by the public key of the authorization server and then placed into the authentication request. If the value of the parameter prompt is set to none, then the id_token_hint could be present in the request, but it isn't a requirement.

- login_hint: This is an indication of the login identifier that the end user may use at the authorization server. For example, if the client application already knows the email address or phone number of the end user, this could be set as the value of the login_hint. This helps provide a better user experience.

- acr_values: Stands for *authentication context reference values*. It includes a space-separated set of values that indicates the level of authentication required at the authorization server. The authorization server may or may not respect these values.

Note   All OpenID Connect authentication requests must have a *scope* parameter with the value *openid*.

Requesting User Attributes

OpenID Connect defines two ways to request user attributes. The client application can either use the initial OpenID Connect authentication request to request attributes or else later talk to a UserInfo endpoint hosted by the authorization server. If it uses the initial authentication request, then the client application must include the requested claims in the claims parameter as a JSON message. The following authorization grant request asks to include the user's email address and the given name in the ID token:

```
https://localhost:9443/oauth2/authorize?
        response_type=code&
        scope=openid&
        client_id=NJOLXcfdOW2OEvD6DUOlOp01u_Ya&
        redirect_uri=https://localhost/callback&
        claims={ "id_token":
                {
                    "email": {"essential": true},
                    "given_name": {"essential": true},
                }
        }
```

Note   The OpenID Connect core specification defines 20 standard user claims. These identifiers should be understood by all of the authorization servers and client applications that support OpenID Connect. The complete set of OpenID Connect standard claims is defined in Section 5.1 of the OpenID Connect core specification, available at `http://openid.net/specs/openid-connect-core-1_0.html`.

The other approach to request user attributes is via the UserInfo endpoint. The UserInfo endpoint is an OAuth 2.0-protected resource on the authorization server. Any request to this endpoint must carry a valid OAuth 2.0 token. Once again, there are two ways to get user attributes from the UserInfo endpoint. The first approach is to use the OAuth access token. With this approach, the client must specify the corresponding attribute scope in the authorization grant request. The OpenID Connect specification defines four scope values to request attributes: profile, email, address, and phone. If the scope value is set to profile, that implies that the client requests access to a set of attributes, which includes name, family_name, given_name, middle_name, nickname, preferred_username, profile, picture, website, gender, birthdate, zoneinfo, locale, and updated_at.

The following authorization grant request asks permission to access a user's email address and phone number:

Note   The `UserInfo` endpoint must support both HTTP GET and POST. All communication with the `UserInfo` endpoint must be over Transport Layer Security (TLS).

```
https://localhost:9443/oauth2/authorize?
        response_type=code
        &scope=openid phone email
        &client_id=NJOLXcfdOW2OEvD6DUOlOpO1u_Ya
        &redirect_uri=https://localhost/callback
```

This results in an authorization code response. Once the client application has exchanged the authorization code for an access token, by talking to the token endpoint of the authorization server, it can use the access token it received to talk to the UserInfo endpoint and get the user attributes corresponding to the access token:

```
GET /userinfo HTTP/1.1
Host: auth.server.com
Authorization: Bearer SJHkhew87Ohooi9O
```

The preceding request to the UserInfo endpoint results in the following JSON message, which includes the user's email address and phone number:

```
HTTP/1.1 200 OK
Content-Type: application/json
  {
    "phone": "94712841302",
    "email": "joe@authserver.com",
  }
```

The other way to retrieve user attributes from the UserInfo endpoint is through the claims parameter. The following example shows how to retrieve the email address of the user by talking to the OAuth-protected UserInfo endpoint:

```
POST /userinfo HTTP/1.1
Host: auth.server.com
Authorization: Bearer SJHkhew870hooi9o
claims={ "userinfo":
            {
                "email": {"essential": true}
            }
        }
```

> **Note**   Signing or encrypting the response message from the `UserInfo` endpoint isn't a requirement. If it's signed or encrypted, then the response should be wrapped in a JWT, and the `Content-Type` of the response should be set to `application/jwt`.

OpenID Connect Flows

All the examples in this chapter so far have used an authorization code grant type to request an ID token—but it isn't a requirement. In fact OpenID Connect, independent of OAuth 2.0 grant types, defined a set of flows: code flow, implicit flow, and hybrid flow. Each of the flows defines the value of the response_type parameter. The response_type parameter always goes with the request to the authorize endpoint (in contrast the grant_type parameter always goes to the token endpoint), and it defines the expected type of response from the authorize endpoint. If it is set to code, the authorize endpoint of the authorization server must return a code, and this flow is identified as the authorization code flow in OpenID Connect.

For implicit flow under the context of OpenID Connect, the value of response_type can be either id_token or id_token token (separated by a space). If it's just id_token, then the authorization server returns an ID token from the authorize endpoint; if it includes both, then both the ID token and the access token are included in the response.

The hybrid flow can use different combinations. If the value of `response_type` is set to `code id_token` (separated by a space), then the response from the authorize endpoint includes the authorization code as well as the `id_token`. If it's `code token` (separated by a space), then it returns the authorization code along with an access token (for the UserInfo endpoint). If `response_type` includes all three (`code token id_token`), then the response includes an `id_token`, an access token, and the authorization code. Table 6-1 summarizes this discussion.

Table 6-1. *OpenID Connect Flows*

Type of Flow	response_type	Tokens Returned
Authorization code	`code`	Authorization code
Implicit	`id_token`	ID token
Implicit	`id_token token`	ID token and access token
Hybrid	`code id_token`	ID token and authorization code
Hybrid	`code id_token token`	ID token, authorization code, and access token
Hybrid	`code token`	Access token and authorization code

Note When `id_token` is being used as the `response_type` in an OpenID Connect flow, the client application never has access to an access token. In such a scenario, the client application can use the `scope` parameter to request attributes, and those are added to the `id_token`.

Requesting Custom User Attributes

As discussed before, OpenID Connect defines 20 standard claims. These claims can be requested via the scope parameter or through the claims parameter. The only way to request custom-defined claims is through the claims parameter. The following is a sample OpenID Connect request that asks for custom-defined claims:

```
https://localhost:9443/oauth2/authorize?response_type=code
       &scope=openid
       &client_id=NJOLXcfdOW2OEvD6DUOlopO1u_Ya
```

```
&redirect_uri=https://localhost/callback
&claims=
  { "id_token":
   {
    "http://apress.com/claims/email": {"essential": true},
    "http://apress.com/claims/phone": {"essential": true},
   }
  }
```

OpenID Connect Discovery

At the beginning of the chapter, we discussed how OpenID relying parties discover OpenID providers through the user-provided OpenID (which is a URL). OpenID Connect Discovery addresses the same concern, but in a different way (see Figure 6-2). In order to authenticate users via OpenID Connect, the OpenID Connect relying party first needs to figure out what authorization server is behind the end user. OpenID Connect utilizes the WebFinger (RFC 7033) protocol for this discovery.

Note   The OpenID Connect Discovery specification is available at `http://openid.net/specs/openid-connect-discovery-1_0.html`. If a given OpenID Connect relying party already knows who the authorization server is, it can simply ignore the discovery phase.

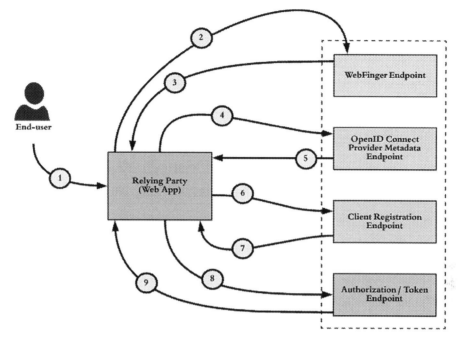

Figure 6-2. *OpenID Connect Discovery*

Let's assume a user called Peter visits an OpenID Connect relying party and wants to log in (see Figure 6-2). To authenticate Peter, the OpenID Connect relying party should know the authorization server corresponding to Peter. To discover this, Peter has to provide to the relying party some unique identifier that relates to him. Using this identifier, the relying party should be able to find the WebFinger endpoint corresponding to Peter.

Let's say that the identifier Peter provides is his email address, peter@apress.com (step 1). The relying party should be able to find enough detail about the WebFinger endpoint using Peter's email address. In fact, the relying party should be able to derive the WebFinger endpoint from the email address. The relying party can then send a query to the WebFinger endpoint to find out which authorization server (or the identity provider) corresponds to Peter (steps 2 and 3). This query is made according to the WebFinger specification. The following shows a sample WebFinger request for peter@apress.com:

```
GET /.well-known/webfinger?resource=acct:peter@apress.com
&rel=http://openid.net/specs/connect/1.0/issuer HTTP/1.1
Host: apress.com
```

The WebFinger request has two key parameters: resource and rel. The resource parameter should uniquely identify the end user, whereas the value of rel is fixed for OpenID Connect and must be equal to `http://openid.net/specs/connect/1.0/issuer`. The rel (relation-type) parameter acts as a filter to determine the OpenID Connect issuer corresponding to the given resource.

A WebFinger endpoint can accept many other discovery requests for different services. If it finds a matching entry, the following response is returned to the OpenID Connect relying party. The value of the OpenID identity provider or the authorization server endpoint is included in the response:

```
HTTP/1.1 200 OK
Access-Control-Allow-Origin: *
Content-Type: application/jrd+json
{
    "subject":"acct:peter@apress.com",
    "links":[
            {
                "rel":"http://openid.net/specs/connect/1.0/issuer",
                "href":"https://auth.apress.com"
            }
        ]
}
```

Note   Neither the WebFinger nor the OpenID Connect Discovery specification mandates the use of the email address as the resource or the end user identifier. It must be a URI that conforms to the URI definition in RFC 3986, which can be used to derive the WebFinger endpoint. If the resource identifier is an email address, then it must be prefixed with `acct`.

The `acct` is a URI scheme as defined in `http://tools.ietf.org/html/draft-ietf-appsawg-acct-uri-07`. When the `acct` URI scheme is being used, everything after the @ sign is treated as the hostname. The WebFinger hostname is derived from an email address as per the `acct` URI scheme, which is the part after the @ sign.

If a URL is being used as the resource identifier, the hostname (and port number) of the URL is treated as the WebFinger hostname. If the resource identifier is `https://auth.server.com:9443/prabath`, then the WebFinger hostname is `auth.server.com:9443`.

Once the endpoint of the identity provider is discovered, that concludes the role of WebFinger. Yet you don't have enough data to initiate an OpenID Connect authentication request with the corresponding identity provider. You can find more information about the identity provider by talking to its metadata endpoint, which must be a well-known endpoint (steps 4 and 5 in Figure 6-2). After that, for the client application to talk to the authorization server, it must be a registered client application. The client application can talk to the client registration endpoint of the authorization server (steps 6 and 7) to register itself—and then can access the authorize and token endpoints (steps 8 and 9).

Note   Both the WebFinger and OpenID Connect Discovery specifications use the Defining Well-Known URIs (`http://tools.ietf.org/html/rfc5785`) specification to define endpoint locations. The RFC 5785 specification introduces a path prefix called `/.well-known/` to identify well-known locations. Most of the time, these locations are metadata endpoints or policy endpoints.

The WebFinger specification has the well-known endpoint `/.well-known/webfinger`. The OpenID Connect Discovery specification has the well-known endpoint for OpenID provider configuration metadata, `/.well-known/openid-configuration`.

OpenID Connect Identity Provider Metadata

An OpenID Connect identity provider, which supports metadata discovery, should host its configuration at the endpoint /.well-known/openid-configuration. In most cases, this is a nonsecured endpoint, which can be accessed by anyone. An OpenID Connect relying party can send an HTTP GET to the metadata endpoint to retrieve the OpenID provider configuration details as follows:

```
GET /.well-known/openid-configuration HTTP/1.1
Host: auth.server.com
```

This results in the following JSON response, which includes everything an OpenID Connect relying party needs to know to talk to the OpenID provider or the OAuth authorization server:

```
HTTP/1.1 200 OK
Content-Type: application/json
{
  "issuer":"https://auth.server.com",
  "authorization_endpoint":"https://auth.server.com/connect/authorize",
  "token_endpoint":"https://auth.server.com/connect/token",
  "token_endpoint_auth_methods_supported":["client_secret_basic", "private_
  key_jwt"],
  "token_endpoint_auth_signing_alg_values_supported":["RS256", "ES256"],
  "userinfo_endpoint":"https://auth.sever.com/connect/userinfo",
  "check_session_iframe":"https://auth.server.com/connect/check_session",
  "end_session_endpoint":"https://auth.server.com/connect/end_session",
  "jwks_uri":"https://auth.server.com/jwks.json",
  "registration_endpoint":"https://auth.server.com/connect/register",
  "scopes_supported":["openid", "profile", "email", "address", "phone",
  "offline_access"],
  "response_types_supported":["code", "code id_token", "id_token", "token
  id_token"],
  "acr_values_supported":["urn:mace:incommon:iap:silver", "urn:mace:incommo
  n:iap:bronze"],
  "subject_types_supported":["public", "pairwise"],
  "userinfo_signing_alg_values_supported":["RS256", "ES256", "HS256"],
  "userinfo_encryption_alg_values_supported":["RSA1_5", "A128KW"],
  "userinfo_encryption_enc_values_supported":["A128CBC-HS256", "A128GCM"],
  "id_token_signing_alg_values_supported":["RS256", "ES256", "HS256"],
  "id_token_encryption_alg_values_supported":["RSA1_5", "A128KW"],
  "id_token_encryption_enc_values_supported":["A128CBC-HS256", "A128GCM"],
  "request_object_signing_alg_values_supported":["none", "RS256", "ES256"],
  "display_values_supported":["page", "popup"],
  "claim_types_supported":["normal", "distributed"],
  "claims_supported":["sub", "iss", "auth_time", "acr",
                      "name", "given_name", "family_name", "nickname",
```

```
                    "profile", "picture", "website","email",
                    "email_verified",
                    "locale", "zoneinfo",
                    "http://example.info/claims/groups"],
  "claims_parameter_supported":true,
  "service_documentation":"http://auth.server.com/connect/service_
  documentation.html",
  "ui_locales_supported":["en-US", "fr-CA"]
}
```

Note   If the endpoint of the discovered identity provider is `https://auth.server.com`, then the OpenID provider metadata should be available at `https://auth.server.com/.well-known/openid-configuration`. If the endpoint is `https://auth.server.com/openid`, then the metadata endpoint is `https://auth.server.com/openid/.well-known/openid-configuration`.

Dynamic Client Registration

Once the OpenID provider endpoint is discovered via WebFinger (and all the metadata related to it through OpenID Connect Discovery), the OpenID Connect relying party still needs to have a client ID and a client secret (not under the implicit grant type) registered at the OpenID provider to initiate the authorization grant request or the OpenID Connect authentication request. The OpenID Connect Dynamic Client Registration specification[2] facilitates a mechanism to register dynamically OpenID Connect relying parties at the OpenID provider.

The response from the OpenID provider metadata endpoint includes the endpoint for client registration under the parameter `registration_endpoint`. To support dynamic client registrations, this endpoint should accept open registration requests, with no authentication requirements.

---

[2]http://openid.net/specs/openid-connect-registration-1_0.html

To fight against denial of service (DoS) attacks, the endpoint can be protected with rate limits or with a web application firewall (WAF). To initiate client registration, the OpenID relying party sends an HTTP POST message to the registration endpoint with its own metadata.

The following is a sample client registration request:

```
POST /connect/register HTTP/1.1
Content-Type: application/json
Accept: application/json
Host: auth.server.com
{
"application_type":"web",
"redirect_uris":["https://app.client.org/callback","https://app.client.org/
callback2"],
"client_name":"Foo",
"logo_uri":"https://app.client.org/logo.png",
"subject_type":"pairwise",
"sector_identifier_uri":"https://other.client.org /file_of_redirect_uris.
json",
"token_endpoint_auth_method":"client_secret_basic",
"jwks_uri":"https://app.client.org/public_keys.jwks",
"userinfo_encrypted_response_alg":"RSA1_5",
"userinfo_encrypted_response_enc":"A128CBC-HS256",
"contacts":["prabath@wso2.com", "prabath@apache.org"],
"request_uris":["https://app.client.org/rf.txt#qpXaRLh_
n93TTR9F252ValdatUQvQiJi5BDub2BeznA"]
}
```

In response, the OpenID Connect provider or the authorization server sends back the following JSON message. It includes a client_id and a client_secret:

```
HTTP/1.1 201 Created
Content-Type: application/json
Cache-Control: no-store
Pragma: no-cache
{
"client_id":"Gjjhj678jhkh89789ew",
```

```
"client_secret":"IUi989jkjo_989klkjuk89080kjkuoikjkUIl",
"client_secret_expires_at":2590858900,
"registration_access_token":"this.is.an.access.token.value.ffx83",
"registration_client_uri":"https://auth.server.com/connect/register?client_
id=Gjjhj678jhkh89789ew ",
"token_endpoint_auth_method":"client_secret_basic",
"application_type": "web",
"redirect_uris":["https://app.client.org/callback","https://app.client.org/
callback2"],
"client_name":"Foo",
"logo_uri":"https://client.example.org/logo.png",
"subject_type":"pairwise",
"sector_identifier_uri":"https://other.client.org/file_of_redirect_uris.
json",
"jwks_uri":"https://app.client.org/public_keys.jwks",
"userinfo_encrypted_response_alg":"RSA1_5",
"userinfo_encrypted_response_enc":"A128CBC-HS256",
"contacts":["prabath@wso2.com", "prabath@apache.org"],
"request_uris":["https://app.client.org/rf.txt#qpXaRLh_
n93TTR9F252ValdatUQvQiJi5BDub2BeznA"]
}
```

Once the OpenID Connect relying party obtains a client ID and a client secret, it concludes the OpenID Connect Discovery phase. The relying party can now initiate the OpenID Connect authentication request.

Note   Section 2.0 of the OpenID Connect Dynamic Client Registration specification lists all the attributes that can be included in an OpenID Connect client registration request: `http://openid.net/specs/openid-connect-registration-1_0.html`.

OpenID Connect for Securing APIs

So far, you have seen a detailed discussion about OpenID Connect. But in reality, how will it help you in securing APIs? The end users can use OpenID Connect to authenticate into web applications, mobile applications, and much more. Nonetheless, why would you need OpenID Connect to secure a headless API? At the end of the day, all the APIs are secured with OAuth 2.0, and you need to present an access token to talk to the API. The API (or the policy enforcement component) validates the access token by talking to the authorization server. Why would you need to pass an ID token to an API?

OAuth is about delegated authorization, whereas OpenID Connect is about authentication. An ID token is an assertion about your identity, that is, a proof of your identity. It can be used to authenticate into an API. As of this writing, no HTTP binding is defined for JWT.

The following example suggests passing the JWT assertion (or the ID token) to a protected API as an access token in the HTTP Authorization header. The ID token, or the signed JWT, is base64-url-encoded in three parts. Each part is separated by a dot (.). The first part up to the first dot is the JWT header. The second part is the JWT body. The third part is the signature. Once the JWT is obtained by the client application, it can place it in the HTTP Authorization header in the manner shown here:

```
POST /employee HTTP/1.1
Content-Type: application/json
Accept: application/json
Host: resource.server.com
Authorization: Bearer eyJhbGciOiljiuo98kljlk2KJl.
IUojlkoiaos298jkkdksdosiduIUiopo.oioYJ21sajds
{
    "empl_no":"109082",
    "emp_name":"Peter John",
    "emp_address":"Mountain View, CA, USA"
}
```

To validate the JWT, the API (or the policy enforcement component) has to extract the JWT assertion from the HTTP Authorization header, base64-url-decode it, and validate the signature to see whether it's signed by a trusted issuer. In addition, the claims in the JWT can be used for authentication and authorization.

Note   When an OpenID Connect identity provider issues an ID token, it adds the aud parameter to the token to indicate the audience of the token. This can be an array of identifiers.

When using ID tokens to access APIs, a URI known to the API should also be added to the aud parameter. Currently this can't be requested in the OpenID Connect authentication request, so it must be set out of band at the OpenID Connect identity provider.

Summary

- OpenID Connect was built on top of OAuth 2.0. It introduces an identity layer on top of OAuth 2.0. This identity layer is abstracted into an ID token, which is a JSON Web Token (JWT).

- OpenID Connect evolved from OpenID to an OAuth 2.0 profile.

- The OpenID Connect Dynamic Client Registration specification facilitates a mechanism to register dynamically OpenID Connect relying parties at the OpenID provider.

- OpenID Connect defines two ways to request user attributes. The client application can either use the initial OpenID Connect authentication request to request attributes or else later talk to the UserInfo endpoint hosted by the authorization server.

- OpenID Connect utilizes the WebFinger protocol in its discovery process along with OpenID Connect dynamic client registration and identity provider metadata configuration.

- An OpenID Connect identity provider, which supports metadata discovery, should host its configuration at the endpoint /.well-known/openid-configuration.

CHAPTER 7

Message-Level Security with JSON Web Signature

JavaScript Object Notation (JSON) provides a way of exchanging data in a language-neutral, text-based, and lightweight manner. It was originally derived from the ECMAScript programming language. JSON and XML are the most commonly used data exchange formats for APIs. Observing the trend over the last few years, it's quite obvious that JSON is replacing XML. Most of the APIs out there have support for JSON, and some support both JSON and XML. XML-only APIs are quite rare.

Understanding JSON Web Token (JWT)

JSON Web Token (JWT) defines a container to transport data between interested parties in JSON. It became an IETF standard in May 2015 with the RFC 7519. The OpenID Connect specification, which we discussed in Chapter 6, uses a JWT to represent the ID token. Let's examine an OpenID Connect ID token returned from the Google API, as an example (to understand JWT, you do not need to know about OpenID Connect):

eyJhbGciOiJSUzI1NiIsImtpZCI6Ijc4YjRjZjIzNjU2ZGMzOTUzNjRmMWI2YzAyOTA3
NjkxZjJjZGZmZTEifQ.eyJpc3MiOiJhY2NvdW50cy5nb29nbGUuY29tIiwic3ViIjoiMT
EwNTAyMjUxMTU4OTIwMTQ3NzMyIiwiYXpwIjoiODI1MjQ5ODM1NjU5LXRlOHF
nbDcwMWtnb25ub21ucDRzcXY3ZXJodGEyMTFzLmFwcHMuZ29vZ2xldXNlcmNvb
nRlbnQuY29tIiwiZW1haWwiOiJwcmFiYXRoQHdzbzIuY29tIiwiYXRfaGFzaCI6InpmO
DZ2TnVsc0xxCOGdGYXFSd2R6R6WWciLCJlbWFpbF92ZXJpZmllZCI6dHJ1ZSwiYXVkI
joiODI1MjQ5ODM1NjU5LXRlOHFnbDcwMWtnb25ub21ucDRzcXY3ZXJodEyMTFz
LmFwcHMuZ29vZ2xldXNlcmNvbnRlbnQuY29tIiwiaGQiOiJ3c28yLmNvbSIsImlhdCI6
MTQwMTkwODI3MSwiZXhwIjoxNDAxOTEyMTcxfQ.TVKv-pdyvk2gW8sGsCbsnkq

© Prabath Siriwardena 2020
P. Siriwardena, *Advanced API Security*, https://doi.org/10.1007/978-1-4842-2050-4_7

srSoT-HOOxnY6ETkIfgIxfotvFn5IwKm3xyBMpyOFFeORb5Ht8AEJV6PdWyxz8rMgX
2HROWqSo_RfEfUpBb4iOsq4W28KftW5HOIA44VmNZ6zU4YTqPSt4TPhyFC9fP2D
_Hg7JQozpQRUfbWTJI

Note   Way before JWT, in 2009, Microsoft introduced Simple Web Token (SWT).[1] It is neither JSON nor XML. It defined its own token format to carry out a set of HTML form–encoded name/value pairs. Both JWTs and SWTs define a way to carry claims between applications. In SWT, both the claim names and claim values are strings, while in JWT claim names are strings, but claim values can be any JSON type. Both of these token types offer cryptographic protection for their content: SWTs with HMAC SHA256 and JWTs with a choice of algorithms, including signature, MAC, and encryption algorithms. Even though SWT was developed as a proposal for IETF, it never became an IETF proposed standard. Dick Hardt was the editor of the SWT specification, who also played a major role later in building the OAuth WRAP specification, which we discuss in Appendix B.

JOSE Header

The preceding JWT has three main elements. Each element is base64url-encoded and separated by a period (.). Appendix E explains how base64url encoding works in detail. Let's identify each individual element in the JWT. The first element of the JWT is called the *JavaScript Object Signing and Encryption (JOSE)* header. The JOSE header lists out the properties related to the cryptographic operations applied on the JWT claims set (which we explain later in this chapter). The following is the base64url-encoded JOSE header of the preceding JWT:

eyJhbGciOiJSUzI1NiIsImtpZCI6Ijc4YjRjZjIzNjU2ZGMzOTUzNjRmMWI2YzAyOTA3
NjkxZjJjZGZmZTEifQ

To make the JOSE header readable, we need to base64url-decode it. The following shows the base64url-decoded JOSE header, which defines two attributes, the algorithm (alg) and key identifier (kid).

```
{"alg":"RS256","kid":"78b4cf23656dc395364f1b6c02907691f2cdffe1"}
```

---

[1]Simple Web Token, http://msdn.microsoft.com/en-us/library/hh781551.aspx

Both the `alg` and `kid` parameters are not defined in the JWT specification, but in the JSON Web Signature (JWS) specification. Let's briefly identify here what these parameters mean and will discuss in detail when we explain JWS. The JWT specification is not bound to any specific algorithm. All applicable algorithms are defined under the JSON Web Algorithms (JWA) specification, which is the RFC 7518. Section 3.1 of RFC 7518 defines all possible `alg` parameter values for a JWS token. The value of the `kid` parameter provides an indication or a hint about the key, which is used to sign the message. Looking at the `kid`, the recipient of the message should know where to look up for the key and find it. The JWT specification only defines two parameters in the JOSE header; the following lists out those:

- `typ` *(type)*: The `typ` parameter is used to define the media type of the complete JWT. A media type is an identifier, which defines the format of the content, transmitted over the Internet. There are two types of components that process a JWT: the JWT implementations and JWT applications. Nimbus[2] is a JWT implementation in Java. The Nimbus library knows how to build and parse a JWT. A JWT application can be anything, which uses JWTs internally. A JWT application uses a JWT implementation to build or parse a JWT. The `typ` parameter is just another parameter for the JWT implementation. It will not try to interpret the value of it, but the JWT application would. The `typ` parameter helps JWT applications to differentiate the content of the JWT when the values that are not JWTs could also be present in an application data structure along with a JWT object. This is an optional parameter, and if present for a JWT, it is recommended to use JWT as the media type.

- `cty` *(content type)*: The `cty` parameter is used to define the structural information about the JWT. It is only recommended to use this parameter in the case of a nested JWT. The nested JWTs are discussed in Chapter 8, and the definition of the `cty` parameter is further explained there.

---

[2]Nimbus JWT Java implementation, `http://connect2id.com/products/nimbus-jose-jwt`

JWT Claims Set

The second element of the JWT is known as either the *JWT payload* or the *JWT claims set*. It is a JSON object, which carries the business data. The following is the base64url-encoded JWT claims set of the preceding JWT (which is returned from the Google API); it includes information about the authenticated user:

eyJpc3MiOiJhY2NvdW50cy5nb29nbGUuY29tIiwic3ViIjoiMTEwNTAyMjUxMTU4OT
IwMTQ3NzMyIiwiYXpwIjoiODI1MjQ5ODM1NjU5LXRlOHFnbDcwMWtnb25ub21uuc
DRzcXY3ZXJodTEyMTFzLmFwcHMuZ29vZ2xldXNlcmNvbnRlbnQuY29tIiwiZW1ha
WwiOiJwcmFiYXRoQHdzbzIuY29tIiwiYXRfaGFzaCI6InpmODZ2TnVsc0xCOGdGYX
FSd2R6WWciLCJlbWFpbF92ZXJpZmllZCI6dHJ1ZSwiYXVkIjoiODI1MjQ5ODM1NjU
5LXRlOHFnbDcwMWtnb25ub21uuc DRzcXY3ZXJodTEyMTFzLmFwcHMuZ29vZ2xld
XNlcmNvbnRlbnQuY29tIiwiaGQiOiJ3c28yLmNvbSIsImlhdCI6MTQwMTkwODI3MS
wiZXhwIjoxNDAxOTEyMTcxfQ

To make the JWT claims set readable, we need to base64url-decode it. The following shows the base64url-decoded JWT claims set. Whitespaces can be explicitly retained while building the JWT claims set—no canonicalization is required before base64url-encoding. *Canonicalization* is the process of converting different forms of a message into a single standard form. This is used mostly before signing XML messages. In XML, the same message can be represented in different forms to carry the same meaning. For example, <vehicles><car></car></vehicles> and <vehicles><car/></vehicles> are equivalent in meaning, but have two different canonical forms. Before signing an XML message, you should follow a canonicalization algorithm to build a standard form.

```
{
    "iss":"accounts.google.com",
    "sub":"110502251158920147732",
    "azp":"825249835659-te8qgl701kgonnomnp4sqv7erhu1211s.apps.
    googleusercontent.com",
    "email":"prabath@wso2.com",
    "at_hash":"zf86vNulsLB8gFaqRwdzYg",
    "email_verified":true,
    "aud":"825249835659-te8qgl701kgonnomnp4sqv7erhu1211s.apps.
    googleusercontent.com",
```

```
    "hd":"wso2.com",
    "iat":1401908271,
    "exp":1401912171
}
```

The JWT claims set represents a JSON object whose members are the claims asserted by the JWT issuer. Each claim name within a JWT must be unique. If there are duplicate claim names, then the JWT parser could either return a parsing error or just return back the claims set with the very last duplicate claim. JWT specification does not explicitly define what claims are mandatory and what are optional. It's up to each application of JWT to define mandatory and optional claims. For example, the OpenID Connect specification, which we discussed in detail in Chapter 6, defines the mandatory and optional claims.

The JWT specification defines three classes of claims: *registered claims*, *public claims*, and *private claims*. The registered claims are registered in the Internet Assigned Numbers Authority (IANA) JSON Web Token Claims registry. Even though these claims are treated as registered claims, the JWT specification doesn't mandate their usage. It's totally up to the other specifications which are built on top of JWT to decide which are mandatory and which aren't. For example, in OpenID Connect specification, iss is a mandatory claim. The following lists out the registered claims set as defined by the JWT specification:

- iss *(issuer)*: The issuer of the JWT. This is treated as a case-sensitive string value. Ideally, this represents the asserting party of the claims set. If Google issues the JWT, then the value of iss would be accounts.google.com. This is an indication to the receiving party who the issuer of the JWT is.

- sub *(subject)*: The token issuer or the asserting party issues the JWT for a particular entity, and the claims set embedded into the JWT normally represents this entity, which is identified by the sub parameter. The value of the sub parameter is a case-sensitive string value.

- aud *(audience)*: The token issuer issues the JWT to an intended recipient or a list of recipients, which is represented by the aud parameter. The recipient or the recipient list should know how to parse the JWT and validate it. Prior to any validation check, it must first see whether the particular JWT is issued for its use and if not should reject immediately. The value of the aud parameter can be a case-sensitive string value or an array of strings. The token issuer should know, prior to issuing the token, who the intended recipient (or the recipients) of the token is, and the value of the aud parameter must be a pre-agreed value between the token issuer and the recipient. In practice, one can also use a regular expression to validate the audience of the token. For example, the value of the aud in the token can be *.apress.com, while each recipient under the apress.com domain can have its own aud values: foo.apress. com, bar.apress.com likewise. Instead of finding an exact match for the aud value, each recipient can just check whether the aud value matches the regular expression: (?:[a-zA-Z0-9]*|*).apress.com. This will make sure that any recipient can use a JWT, which is having any subdomain of apress.com.

- exp *(expiration time)*: Each JWT carries an expiration time. The recipient of the JWT token must reject it, if that token has expired. The issuer can decide the value of the expiration time. The JWT specification does not recommend or provide any guidelines on how to decide the best token expiration time. It's a responsibility of the other specifications, which use JWT internally to provide such recommendations. The value of the exp parameter is calculated by adding the expiration time (from the token issued time) in seconds to the time elapsed from 1970-01-01T00:00:00Z UTC to the current time. If the token issuer's clock is out of sync with the recipient's clock (irrespective of their time zone), then the expiration time validation could fail. To fix that, each recipient can add a couple of minutes as the clock skew during the validation process.

- nbf *(not before)*: The recipient of the token should reject it, if the value of the nbf parameter is greater than the current time. The JWT is not good enough to use prior to the value indicated in the nbf parameter. The value of the nbf parameter is the number of seconds elapsed from 1970-01-01T00:00:00Z UTC to the not before time.

- iat *(issued at)*: The iat parameter in the JWT indicates the issued time of the JWT as calculated by the token issuer. The value of the iat parameter is the number of seconds elapsed from 1970-01-01T00:00:00Z UTC to the current time, when the token is issued.

- jti *(JWT ID)*: The jti parameter in the JWT is a unique token identifier generated by the token issuer. If the token recipient accepts JWTs from multiple token issuers, then this value may not be unique across all the issuers. In that case, the token recipient can maintain the token uniqueness by maintaining the tokens under the token issuer. The combination of the token issuer identifier + the jti should produce a unique token identifier.

The public claims are defined by the other specifications, which are built on top of JWT. To avoid any collisions in such cases, names should either be registered in the IANA JSON Web Token Claims registry or defined in a collision-resistant manner with a proper namespace. For example, the OpenID Connect specification defines its own set of claims, which are included inside the ID token (the ID token itself is a JWT), and those claims are registered in the IANA JSON Web Token Claims registry.

The private claims should indeed be private and shared only between a given token issuer and a selected set of recipients. These claims should be used with caution, because there is a chance for collision. If a given recipient accepts tokens from multiple token issuers, then the semantics of the same claim may be different from one issuer to another, if it is a private claim.

JWT Signature

The third part of the JWT is the signature, which is also base64url-encoded. The cryptographic parameters related to the signature are defined in the JOSE header. In this particular example, Google uses RSASSA-PKCS1-V1_5[3] with the SHA256 hashing algorithm, which is expressed by value of the alg parameter in the JOSE header: RS256. The following shows the signature element of the JWT returned back from Google. The signature itself is not human readable—so there is no point of trying to base64url-decode the following:

```
TVKv-pdyvk2gW8sGsCbsnkqsrSOTHOOxnY6ETkIfgIxfotvFn5IwKm3xyBMpyO
FFeORb5Ht8AEJV6PdWyxz8rMgX2HROWqSo_RfEfUpBb4iOsq4W28KftW5
HOIA44VmNZ6zU4YTqPSt4TPhyFC-9fP2D_Hg7JQozpQRUfbWTJI
```

---

[3]RSASSA-PKCS1-V1_5 is defined in RFC 3447: www.ietf.org/rfc/rfc3447.txt. It uses the signer's RSA private key to sign the message in the way defined by PKCS#1.

GENERATING A PLAINTEXT JWT

The plaintext JWT doesn't have a signature. It has only two parts. The value of the `alg` parameter in the JOSE header must be set to none. The following Java code generates a plaintext JWT. You can download the complete Java sample as a Maven project from `https://github.com/apisecurity/samples/tree/master/ch07/sample01`.

```
public static String buildPlainJWT() {

// build audience restriction list.
List<String> aud = new ArrayList<String>();
aud.add("https://app1.foo.com");
aud.add("https://app2.foo.com");

Date currentTime = new Date();

// create a claims set.
JWTClaimsSet jwtClaims = new JWTClaimsSet.Builder().
                         // set the value of the issuer.
                         issuer("https://apress.com").
                         // set the subject value - JWT belongs to
                         // this subject.
                         subject("john").
                         // set values for audience restriction.
                         audience(aud).
                         // expiration time set to 10 minutes.
                         expirationTime(new Date(new Date().getTime()
                         + 1000 * 60 * 10)).
                         // set the valid from time to current time.
                         notBeforeTime(currentTime).
                         // set issued time to current time.
                         issueTime(currentTime).
                         // set a generated UUID as the JWT
                         // identifier.
                         jwtID(UUID.randomUUID().toString()).
                         build();
```

```java
// create plaintext JWT with the JWT claims.
PlainJWT plainJwt = new PlainJWT(jwtClaims);

// serialize into string.
String jwtInText = plainJwt.serialize();

// print the value of the JWT.
System.out.println(jwtInText);

return jwtInText;
}
```

To build and run the program, execute the following Maven command from the ch07/ sample01 directory.

```
\> mvn test -Psample01
```

The preceding code produces the following output, which is a JWT. If you run the code again and again, you may not get the same output as the value of the currentTime variable changes every time you run the program:

eyJhbGciOiJub25lIn0.eyJleHAiOjE0MDIwMzcxNDEsInN1YiI6ImpvaG4iLCJuYm
YiOjE0MDIwMzY1NDEsImF1ZCI6WyJodHRwczpcL1wvYXBwMS5mb28uY29tIi
wiaHR0cHM6XC9cL2FwcDIuZm9vLmNvbSJdLCJpc3MiOiJodHRwczpcL1wvYX
ByZXNzLmNvbSIsImp0aSI6IjVmMmQzM2RmLTEyNDktNGIwMS04MmYxLWJl
MjliM2NhOTY0OSIsImlhdCI6MTQwMjAzNjU0MX0.

The following Java code shows how to parse a base64url-encoded JWT. This code would ideally run at the JWT recipient end:

```java
public static PlainJWT parsePlainJWT() throws ParseException {
        // get JWT in base64url-encoded text.
        String jwtInText = buildPlainJWT();
        // build a plain JWT from the bade64url-encoded text.
        PlainJWT plainJwt  = PlainJWT.parse(jwtInText);
        // print the JOSE header in JSON.
        System.out.println(plainJwt.getHeader().toString());
        // print JWT body in JSON.
        System.out.println(plainJwt.getPayload().toString());
        return plainJwt;
}
```

This code produces the following output, which includes the parsed JOSE header and the payload:

```
{"alg":"none"}
{
    "exp":1402038339,
    "sub":"john",
    "nbf":1402037739,
    "aud":["https:\/\/app1.foo.com","https:\/\/app2.foo.com"],
    "iss":"https:\/\/apress.com",
    "jti":"1e41881f-7472-4030-8132-856ccf4cbb25",
    "iat":1402037739
}
```

JOSE WORKING GROUP

Many working groups within the IETF work directly with JSON, including the OAuth working group and the System for Cross-domain Identity Management (SCIM) working group. The SCIM working group is building a provisioning standard based on JSON. Outside the IETF, the OASIS XACML working group is working on building a JSON profile for XACML 3.0.

The OpenID Connect specification, which is developed under the OpenID Foundation, is also heavily based on JSON. Due to the rise of standards built around JSON and the heavy usage of JSON for data exchange in APIs, it has become absolutely necessary to define how to secure JSON messages at the message level. The use of Transport Layer Security (TLS) only provides confidentiality and integrity at the transport layer. The JOSE working group, formed under the IETF, has the goal of standardizing integrity protection and confidentiality as well as the format for keys and algorithm identifiers to support interoperability of security services for protocols that use JSON. JSON Web Signature (RFC 7515), JSON Web Encryption (RFC 7516), JSON Web Key (RFC 7517), and JSON Web Algorithms (RFC 7518) are four IETF proposed standards, which were developed under the JOSE working group.

JSON Web Signature (JWS)

The JSON Web Signature (JWS) specification, developed under the IETF JOSE working group, represents a message or a payload, which is digitally signed or MACed (when a hashing algorithm is used with HMAC). A signed message can be serialized in two ways by following the JWS specification: the *JWS compact serialization* and the *JWS JSON serialization*. The Google OpenID Connect example discussed at the beginning of this chapter uses JWS compact serialization. In fact, the OpenID Connect specification mandates to use JWS compact serialization and JWE compact serialization whenever necessary (we discuss JWE in Chapter 8). The term *JWS token* is used to refer to the serialized form of a payload, following any of the serialization techniques defined in the JWS specification.

Note   JSON Web Tokens (JWTs) are always serialized with the JWS compact serialization or the JWE compact serialization. We discuss JWE (JSON Web Encryption) in Chapter 8.

JWS Compact Serialization

JWS compact serialization represents a signed JSON payload as a compact URL-safe string. This compact string has three main elements separated by periods (.): the JOSE header, the JWS payload, and the JWS signature (see Figure 7-1). If you use compact serialization against a JSON payload, then you can have only a single signature, which is computed over the complete JOSE header and JWS payload.

Figure 7-1. *A JWS token with compact serialization*

JOSE Header

The JWS specification introduces 11 parameters to the JOSE header. The following lists out the parameters carried in a JOSE header, which are related to the message signature. Out of all those parameters, the JWT specification only defines the typ and cty parameters (as we discussed before); the rest is defined by the JWS specification. The JOSE header in a JWS token carries all the parameters required by the JWS token recipient to properly validate its signature:

- alg *(algorithm)*: The name of the algorithm, which is used to sign the JSON payload. This is a required attribute in the JOSE header. Failure to include this in the header will result in a token parsing error. The value of the alg parameter is a string, which is picked from the JSON Web Signature and Encryption Algorithms registry defined by the JSON Web Algorithms (JWA) specification. If the value of the alg parameter is not picked from the preceding registry, then it should be defined in a collision-resistant manner, but that won't give any guarantee that the particular algorithm is identified by all JWS implementations. It's always better to stick to the algorithms defined in the JWA specification.

- jku: The jku parameter in the JOSE header carries a URL, which points to a JSON Web Key (JWK) set. This JWK set represents a collection of JSON-encoded public keys, where one of the keys is used to sign the JSON payload. Whatever the protocol used to retrieve the key set should provide the integrity protection. If keys are retrieved over HTTP, then instead of plain HTTP, HTTPS (or HTTP over TLS) should be used. We discuss Transport Layer Security (TLS) in detail in Appendix C. The jku is an optional parameter.

- jwk: The jwk parameter in JOSE header represents the public key corresponding to the key that is used to sign the JSON payload. The key is encoded as per the JSON Web Key (JWK) specification. The jku parameter, which we discussed before, points to a link that holds a set of JWKs, while the jwk parameter embeds the key into the JOSE header itself. The jwk is an optional parameter.

- kid: The kid parameter of the JOSE header represents an identifier for the key that is used to sign the JSON payload. Using this identifier, the recipient of the JWS should be able locate the key. If the token issuer uses the kid parameter in the JOSE header to let the recipient know about the signing key, then the corresponding key should be exchanged "somehow" between the token issuer and the recipient beforehand. How this key exchange happens is out of the scope of the JWS specification. If the value of the kid parameter refers to a JWK, then the value of this parameter should match the value of the kid parameter in the JWK. The kid is an optional parameter in the JOSE header.

- x5u: The x5u parameter in the JOSE header is very much similar to the jku parameter, which we discussed before. Instead of pointing to a JWK set, the URL here points to an X.509 certificate or a chain of X.509 certificates. The resource pointed by the URL must hold the certificate or the chain of certificates in the PEM-encoded form. Each certificate in the chain must appear between the delimiters[4]: -----BEGIN CERTIFICATE----- and -----END CERTIFICATE-----. The public key corresponding to the key used to sign the JSON payload should be the very first entry in the certificate chain, and the rest is the certificates of intermediate CAs (certificate authority) and the root CA. The x5u is an optional parameter in the JOSE header.

- x5c: The x5c parameter in the JOSE header represents the X.509 certificate (or the certificate chain), which corresponds to the private key, which is used to sign the JSON payload. This is similar to the jwk parameter we discussed before, but in this case, instead of a JWK, it's an X.509 certificate (or a chain of certificates). The certificate or the certificate chain is represented in a JSON array of certificate value strings. Each element in the array should be a base64-encoded DER PKIX certificate value. The public key corresponding to the key used to sign the JSON payload should be the very first entry in the JSON array, and the rest is the certificates of intermediate CAs (certificate authority) and the root CA. The x5c is an optional parameter in the JOSE header.

---

[4]The Internet IP Security PKI Profile of IKEv1/ISAKMP, IKEv2, and PKIX (RFC 4945) defines the delimiters for X.509 certificates under Section 6.1, https://tools.ietf.org/html/rfc4945

- x5t: The x5t parameter in the JOSE header represents the base64url-encoded SHA-1 thumbprint of the X.509 certificate corresponding to the key used to sign the JSON payload. This is similar to the kid parameter we discussed before. Both these parameters are used to locate the key. If the token issuer uses the x5t parameter in the JOSE header to let the recipient know about the signing key, then the corresponding key should be exchanged "somehow" between the token issuer and the recipient beforehand. How this key exchange happens is out of the scope of the JWS specification. The x5t is an optional parameter in the JOSE header.

- x5t#s256: The x5t#s256 parameter in the JOSE header represents the base64url-encoded SHA256 thumbprint of the X.509 certificate corresponding to the key used to sign the JSON payload. The only difference between x5t#s256 and the x5t is the hashing algorithm. The x5t#s256 is an optional parameter in the JOSE header.

- typ: The typ parameter in the JOSE header is used to define the media type of the complete JWS. There are two types of components that process a JWS: JWS implementations and JWS applications. Nimbus[5] is a JWS implementation in Java. The Nimbus library knows how to build and parse a JWS. A JWS application can be anything, which uses JWS internally. A JWS application uses a JWS implementation to build or parse a JWS. In this case, the typ parameter is just another parameter for the JWS implementation. It will not try to interpret the value of it, but the JWS application would. The typ parameter will help JWS applications to differentiate the content when multiple types of objects are present. For a JWS token using JWS compact serialization and for a JWE token using JWE compact serialization, the value of the typ parameter is JOSE, and for a JWS token using JWS JSON serialization and for a JWE token using JWE JSON serialization, the value is JOSE+JSON. (JWS serialization is discussed later in this chapter, and JWE serialization is discussed in Chapter 8). The typ is an optional parameter in the JOSE header.

---

[5]Nimbus JWT Java implementation, http://connect2id.com/products/nimbus-jose-jwt

- cty: The cty parameter in the JOSE header is used to represent the media type of the secured content in the JWS. It is only recommended to use this parameter in the case of a nested JWT. The nested JWT is discussed later in Chapter 8, and the definition of the cty parameter is further explained there. The cty is an optional parameter in the JOSE header.

- crit: The crit parameter in the JOSE header is used to indicate the recipient of the JWS that the presence of custom parameters, which neither defined by the JWS or JWA specifications, in the JOSE header. If these custom parameters are not understood by the recipient, then the JWS token will be treated as invalid. The value of the crit parameter is a JSON array of names, where each entry represents a custom parameter. The crit is an optional parameter in the JOSE header.

Out of all the 11 parameters defined earlier, 7 talk about how to reference the public key corresponding to the key, which is used to sign the JSON payload. There are three ways of referencing a key: external reference, embedded, and key identifier. The jku and x5u parameters fall under the external reference category. Both of them reference the key through a URI. The jwk and x5c parameters fall under embedded reference category. Each one of them defines how to embed the key to the JOSE header itself. The kid, x5t, and x5t#s256 parameters fall under the key identifier reference category. All three of them define how to locate the key using an identifier. Then again all the seven parameters can further divide into two categories based on the representation of the key: JSON Web Key (JWK) and X.509. The jku, jwk, and kid fall under the JWK category, while x5u, x5c, x5t, and x5t#s256 fall under the X.509 category. In the JOSE header of a given JWS token, at a given time, we only need to have one from the preceding parameters.

Note   If any of the jku, jwk, kid, x5u, x5c, x5t, and x5t#s256 are present in the JOSE header, those must be integrity protected. Failure to do so will let an attacker modify the key used to sign the message and change the content of the message payload. After validating the signature of a JWS token, the recipient application must check whether the key associated with the signature is trusted. Checking whether the recipient knows the corresponding key can do the trust validation.

The JWS specification does not restrict applications only to use 11 header parameters defined earlier. There are two ways to introduce new header parameters: public header names and private header names. Any header parameter that is intended to use in the public space should be introduced in a collision-resistant manner. It is recommended to register such public header parameters in the IANA JSON Web Signature and Encryption Header Parameters registry. The private header parameters are mostly used in a restricted environment, where both the token issuer and the recipients are well aware of each other. These parameters should be used with caution, because there is a chance for collision. If a given recipient accepts tokens from multiple token issuers, then the semantics of the same parameter may be different from one issuer to another, if it is a private header. In either case, whether it's a public or a private header parameter, if it is not defined in the JWS or the JWA specification, the header name should be included in the `crit` header parameter, which we discussed before.

JWS Payload

The JWS payload is the message that needs to be signed. The message can be anything—need not be a JSON payload. If it is a JSON payload, then it could contain whitespaces and/or line breaks before or after any JSON value. The second element of the serialized JWS token carries the base64url-encoded value of the JWS payload.

JWS Signature

The JWS signature is the digital signature or the MAC, which is calculated over the JWS payload and the JOSE header. The third element of the serialized JWS token carries the base64url-encoded value of the JWS signature.

The Process of Signing (Compact Serialization)

We discussed about all the ingredients that are required to build a JWS token under compact serialization. The following discusses the steps involved in building a JWS token. There are three elements in a JWS token; the first element is produced by step 2, the second element is produced by step 4, and the third element is produced by step 7.

1. Build a JSON object including all the header parameters, which express the cryptographic properties of the JWS token—this is known as the JOSE header. As discussed before in this chapter, under the section "JOSE Header," the token issuer should advertise in the JOSE header the public key corresponding to the key used to sign the message. This can be expressed via any of these header parameters: jku, jwk, kid, x5u, x5c, x5t, and x5t#s256.

2. Compute the base64url-encoded value against the UTF-8 encoded JOSE header from step 1 to produce the first element of the JWS token.

3. Construct the payload or the content to be signed—this is known as the JWS payload. The payload is not necessarily JSON—it can be any content.

4. Compute the base64url-encoded value of the JWS payload from step 3 to produce the second element of the JWS token.

5. Build the message to compute the digital signature or the MAC. The message is constructed as ASCII(BASE64URL-ENCODE(UTF8(JOSE Header)) . BASE64URL-ENCODE(JWS Payload)).

6. Compute the signature over the message constructed in step 5, following the signature algorithm defined by the JOSE header parameter alg. The message is signed using the private key corresponding to the public key advertised in the JOSE header.

7. Compute the base64url-encoded value of the JWS signature produced in step 6, which is the third element of the serialized JWS token.

8. Now we have all the elements to build the JWS token in the following manner. The line breaks are introduced only for clarity.

   BASE64URL(UTF8(JWS Protected Header)).

   BASE64URL(JWS Payload).

   BASE64URL(JWS Signature)

JWS JSON Serialization

In contrast to the JWS compact serialization, the JWS JSON serialization can produce multiple signatures over the same JWS payload along with different JOSE header parameters. The ultimate serialized form under JWS JSON serialization wraps the signed payload in a JSON object, with all related metadata. This JSON object includes two top-level elements, payload and signatures, and three subelements under the signatures element: protected, header, and signature. The following is an example of a JWS token, which is serialized with JWS JSON serialization. This is neither URL safe nor optimized for compactness. It carries two signatures over the same payload, and each signature and the metadata around it are stored as an element in the JSON array, under the signatures top-level element. Each signature uses a different key to sign, represented by the corresponding kid header parameter. The JSON serialization is also useful in selectively signing JOSE header parameters. In contrast, JWS compact serialization signs the complete JOSE header:

```
{
"payload":"eyJpc3MiOiJqb2UiLA0KICJleHAiOjEzMDA4MTkzOD",
"signatures":[
            {
                "protected":"eyJhbGciOiJSUzI1NiJ9",
                "header":{"kid":"2014-06-29"},
                "signature":"cC4hiUPoj9Eetdgtv3hF80EGrhuB"
            },
            {
                "protected":"eyJhbGciOiJFUzI1NiJ9",
                "header":{"kid":"e909097a-ce81-4036-9562-d21d2992db0d"},
                "signature":"DtEhU3ljbEg8L38VWAfUAqOyKAM"
            }
        ]
}
```

JWS Payload

The payload top-level element of the JSON object includes the base64url-encoded value of the complete JWS payload. The JWS payload necessarily need not be a JSON payload, it can be of any content type. The payload is a required element in the serialized JWS token.

JWS Protected Header

The *JWS Protected Header* is a JSON object that includes the header parameters that have to be integrity protected by the signing or MAC algorithm. The `protected` parameter in the serialized JSON form represents the base64url-encoded value of the *JWS Protected Header*. The `protected` is not a top-level element of the serialized JWS token. It is used to define elements in the `signatures` JSON array and includes the base64url-encoded header elements, which should be signed. If you base64url-decode the value of the first `protected` element in the preceding code snippet, you will see `{"alg":"RS256"}`. The `protected` parameter must be present, if there are any protected header parameters. There is one `protected` element for each entry of the `signatures` JSON array.

JWS Unprotected Header

The *JWS Unprotected Header* is a JSON object that includes the header parameters that are not integrity protected by the signing or MAC algorithm. The `header` parameter in the serialized JSON form represents the base64url-encoded value of the *JWS Unprotected Header*. The `header` is not a top-level parameter of the JSON object. It is used to define elements in the `signatures` JSON array. The `header` parameter includes unprotected header elements related to the corresponding signature, and these elements are not signed. Combining both the protected headers and unprotected headers ultimately derives the JOSE header corresponding to the signature. In the preceding code snippet, the complete JOSE header corresponding to the first entry in the `signatures` JSON array would be `{"alg":"RS256", "kid":"2010-12-29"}`. The `header` element is represented as a JSON object and must be present if there are any unprotected header parameters. There is one `header` element for each entry of the `signatures` JSON array.

JWS Signature

The `signatures` parameter of the JSON object includes an array of JSON objects, where each element includes a signature or MAC (over the JWS payload and JWS protected header) and the associated metadata. This is a required parameter. The `signature` subelement, which is inside each entry of the `signatures` array, carries the base64url-encoded value of the signature computed over the protected header elements (represented by the `protected` parameter) and the JWS payload. Both the `signatures` and `signature` are required parameters.

Note   Even though JSON serialization provides a way to selectively sign JOSE header parameters, it does not provide a direct way to selectively sign the parameters in the JWS payload. Both forms of serialization mentioned in the JWS specification sign the complete JWS payload. There is a workaround for this using JSON serialization. You can replicate the payload parameters that need to be signed selectively in the JOSE header. Then with JSON serialization, header parameters can be selectively signed.

The Process of Signing (JSON Serialization)

We discussed about all the ingredients that are required to build a JWS token under JSON serialization. The following discusses the steps involved in building the JWS token.

1. Construct the payload or the content to be signed—this is known as the JWS payload. The payload is not necessarily JSON—it can be any content. The payload element in the serialized JWS token carries the base64url-encoded value of the content.

2. Decide how many signatures you would need against the payload and for each case which header parameters must be signed and which are not.

3. Build a JSON object including all the header parameters that are to be integrity protected or to be signed. In other words, construct the *JWS Protected Header* for each signature. The base64url-encoded value of the UTF-8 encoded *JWS Protected Header* will produce the value of the protected subelement inside the signatures top-level element of the serialized JWS token.

4. Build a JSON object including all the header parameters that need not be integrity protected or not be signed. In other words, construct the *JWS Unprotected Header* for each signature. This will produce the header subelement inside the signatures top-level element of the serialized JWS token.

5. Both the *JWS Protected Header* and the *JWS Unprotected Header* express the cryptographic properties of the corresponding signature (there can be more than one `signature` element)— this is known as the JOSE header. As discussed before in this chapter, under the section "JOSE Header," the token issuer should advertise in the JOSE header the public key corresponding to the key used to sign the message. This can be expressed via any of these header parameters: `jku`, `jwk`, `kid,` `x5u`, `x5c`, `x5t`, and `x5t#s256.`

6. Build the message to compute the digital signature or the MAC against each entry in the signatures JSON array of the serialized JWS token. The message is constructed as ASCII(BASE64URL-ENCODE(UTF8(JWS Protected Header)). BASE64URL-ENCODE(JWS Payload)).

7. Compute the signature over the message constructed in step 6, following the signature algorithm defined by the header parameter `alg`. This parameter can be either inside the *JWS Protected Header* or the *JWS Unprotected Header*. The message is signed using the private key corresponding to the public key advertised in the header.

8. Compute the base64url-encoded value of the JWS signature produced in step 7, which will produce the value of the `signature` subelement inside the `signatures` top-level element of the serialized JWS token.

9. Once all the signatures are computed, the `signatures` top-level element can be constructed and will complete the JWS JSON serialization.

SIGNATURE TYPES

The XML Signature specification, which was developed under W3C, proposes three types of signatures: enveloping, enveloped, and detached. These three kinds of signatures are only discussed under the context of XML.

With the enveloping signature, the XML content to be signed is inside the signature itself. That is, inside the <ds:Signature xmlns:ds="http://www.w3.org/2000/09/xmldsig#"> element.

With the enveloped signature, the signature is inside the XML content to be signed. In other words, the <ds:Signature xmlns:ds="http://www.w3.org/2000/09/xmldsig#"> element is inside the parent element of the XML payload to be signed.

With the detached signature, there is no parent-child relationship between the XML content to be signed and the corresponding signature. They are detached from each other.

For anyone who is familiar with XML Signature, all the signatures defined in the JWS specification can be treated as detached signatures.

Note   The XML Signature specification by W3C only talks about signing an XML payload. If you have to sign any content, then first you need to embed that within an XML payload and then sign. In contrast, the JWS specification is not just limited to JSON. You can sign any content with JWS without wrapping it inside a JSON payload.

GENERATING A JWS TOKEN WITH HMAC-SHA256 WITH A JSON PAYLOAD

The following Java code generates a JWS token with HMAC-SHA256. You can download the complete Java sample as a Maven project from https://github.com/apisecurity/samples/tree/master/ch07/sample02.

The method buildHmacSha256SignedJWT() in the code should be invoked by passing a secret value that is used as the shared key to sign. The length of the secret value must be at least 256 bits:

```java
public static String buildHmacSha256SignedJSON(String sharedSecretString)
throws JOSEException {

// build audience restriction list.
List<String> aud = new ArrayList<String>();
aud.add("https://app1.foo.com");
aud.add("https://app2.foo.com");
```

```java
Date currentTime = new Date();

// create a claims set.
JWTClaimsSet jwtClaims = new JWTClaimsSet.Builder().
                            // set the value of the issuer.
                            issuer("https://apress.com").
                            // set the subject value - JWT belongs to
                            // this subject.
                            subject("john").
                            // set values for audience restriction.
                            audience(aud).
                            // expiration time set to 10 minutes.
                            expirationTime(new Date(new Date().getTime()
                            + 1000 * 60 * 10)).
                            // set the valid from time to current time.
                            notBeforeTime(currentTime).
                            // set issued time to current time.
                            issueTime(currentTime).
                            // set a generated UUID as the JWT
                            // identifier.
                            jwtID(UUID.randomUUID().toString()).
                            build();

// create JWS header with HMAC-SHA256 algorithm.
JWSHeader jswHeader = new JWSHeader(JWSAlgorithm.HS256);
// create signer with the provider shared secret.
JWSSigner signer = new MACSigner(sharedSecretString);
// create the signed JWT with the JWS header and the JWT body.
SignedJWT signedJWT = new SignedJWT(jswHeader, jwtClaims);
// sign the JWT with HMAC-SHA256.
signedJWT.sign(signer);
// serialize into base64url-encoded text.
String jwtInText = signedJWT.serialize();
// print the value of the JWT.
System.out.println(jwtInText);
return jwtInText;
}
```

To build and run the program, execute the following Maven command from the ch07/ sample02 directory.

\> mvn test -Psample02

The preceding code produces the following output, which is a signed JSON payload (a JWS). If you run the code again and again, you may not get the same output as the value of the currentTime variable changes every time you run the program:

eyJhbGciOiJIUzI1NiJ9.eyJleHAiOjEOMDIwMzkyOTIsInN1YiI6ImpvaG4iLCJuYm
YiOjEOMDIwMzg2OTIsImF1ZCI6WyJodHRwczpcL1wvYXBwMS5mb28uY29tIiw
iaHROcHM6XC9cL2FwcDIuZm9vLmNvbSJdLCJpc3MiOiJodHRwczpcL1wvYXBy
ZXNzLmNvbSIsImpoaSI6ImVkNjkwN2YwLWRlOGEtNDMyYi1hZDU2LWE5ZmE
5NjA2YTVhOCIsImlhdCI6MTQwMjAzODY5Mn0.3v_pa-QFCRwoKUORaP7pLOox
T57okVuZMe_AOUcqQ8

The following Java code shows how to validate the signature of a signed JSON message with HMAC-SHA256. To do that, you need to know the shared secret used to sign the JSON payload:

```
public static boolean isValidHmacSha256Signature()
                                    throws JOSEException, ParseException {
        String sharedSecretString = "ea9566bd-590d-4fe2-a441-d5f240050dbc";
        // get signed JWT in base64url-encoded text.
        String jwtInText = buildHmacSha256SignedJWT(sharedSecretString);
        // create verifier with the provider shared secret.
        JWSVerifier verifier = new MACVerifier(sharedSecretString);
        // create the signed JWS token with the base64url-encoded text.
        SignedJWT signedJWT = SignedJWT.parse(jwtInText);
        // verify the signature of the JWS token.
        boolean isValid = signedJWT.verify(verifier);

        if (isValid) {
            System.out.println("valid JWT signature");
        } else {
            System.out.println("invalid JWT signature");
        }
        return isValid;
}
```

GENERATING A JWS TOKEN WITH RSA-SHA256 WITH A JSON PAYLOAD

The following Java code generates a JWS token with RSA-SHA256. You can download the complete Java sample as a Maven project from `https://github.com/apisecurity/samples/tree/master/ch07/sample03`. First you need to invoke the method generateKeyPair() and pass the PrivateKey(generateKeyPair(). getPrivateKey()) into the method buildRsaSha256SignedJSON():

```java
public static KeyPair generateKeyPair()
                                throws NoSuchAlgorithmException {
    // instantiate KeyPairGenerate with RSA algorithm.
    KeyPairGenerator keyGenerator = KeyPairGenerator.getInstance("RSA");
    // set the key size to 1024 bits.
    keyGenerator.initialize(1024);
    // generate and return private/public key pair.
    return keyGenerator.genKeyPair();
}

public static String buildRsaSha256SignedJSON(PrivateKey privateKey)
                                    throws JOSEException {
    // build audience restriction list.
    List<String> aud = new ArrayList<String>();
    aud.add("https://app1.foo.com");
    aud.add("https://app2.foo.com");

    Date currentTime = new Date();

    // create a claims set.
    JWTClaimsSet jwtClaims = new JWTClaimsSet.Builder().
                        // set the value of the issuer.
                        issuer("https://apress.com").
                        // set the subject value - JWT belongs to
                        // this subject.
                        subject("john").
                        // set values for audience restriction.
                        audience(aud).
                        // expiration time set to 10 minutes.
                        expirationTime(new Date(new Date().getTime()
                        + 1000 * 60 * 10)).
```

181

```
                              // set the valid from time to current time.
                              notBeforeTime(currentTime).
                              // set issued time to current time.
                              issueTime(currentTime).
                              // set a generated UUID as the JWT identifier.
                              jwtID(UUID.randomUUID().toString()).
                              build();

        // create JWS header with RSA-SHA256 algorithm.
        JWSHeader jswHeader = new JWSHeader(JWSAlgorithm.RS256);
        // create signer with the RSA private key..
        JWSSigner signer = new RSASSASigner((RSAPrivateKey)privateKey);
        // create the signed JWT with the JWS header and the JWT body.
        SignedJWT signedJWT = new SignedJWT(jswHeader, jwtClaims);
        // sign the JWT with HMAC-SHA256.
        signedJWT.sign(signer);
        // serialize into base64-encoded text.
        String jwtInText = signedJWT.serialize();
        // print the value of the JWT.
        System.out.println(jwtInText);
        return jwtInText;
}
```

The following Java code shows how to invoke the previous two methods:

```
KeyPair keyPair = generateKeyPair();
buildRsaSha256SignedJSON(keyPair.getPrivate());
```

To build and run the program, execute the following Maven command from the ch07/ sample03 directory.

\> mvn test -Psample03

Let's examine how to validate a JWS token signed by RSA-SHA256. You need to know the PublicKey corresponding to the PrivateKey used to sign the message:

```
public static boolean isValidRsaSha256Signature()
                                        throws NoSuchAlgorithmException,
                                               JOSEException,
                                               ParseException {
        // generate private/public key pair.
```

```
    KeyPair keyPair = generateKeyPair();
    // get the private key - used to sign the message.
    PrivateKey privateKey = keyPair.getPrivate();
    // get public key - used to verify the message signature.
    PublicKey publicKey = keyPair.getPublic();
    // get signed JWT in base64url-encoded text.
    String jwtInText = buildRsaSha256SignedJWT(privateKey);
    // create verifier with the provider shared secret.
    JWSVerifier verifier = new RSASSAVerifier((RSAPublicKey) publicKey);
    // create the signed JWT with the base64url-encoded text.
    SignedJWT signedJWT = SignedJWT.parse(jwtInText);
    // verify the signature of the JWT.
    boolean isValid = signedJWT.verify(verifier);

    if (isValid) {
        System.out.println("valid JWT signature");
    } else {
        System.out.println("invalid JWT signature");
    }
    return isValid;
}
```

GENERATING A JWS TOKEN WITH HMAC-SHA256 WITH A NON-JSON PAYLOAD

The following Java code generates a JWS token with HMAC-SHA256. You can download the complete Java sample as a Maven project from https://github.com/apisecurity/ samples/tree/master/ch07/sample04. The method buildHmacSha256Signed NonJSON() in the code should be invoked by passing a secret value that is used as the shared key to sign. The length of the secret value must be at least 256 bits:

```
public static String buildHmacSha256SignedJWT(String sharedSecretString)
                                              throws JOSEException {

// create an HMAC-protected JWS object with a non-JSON payload
JWSObject jwsObject = new JWSObject(new JWSHeader(JWSAlgorithm.HS256),
                           new Payload("Hello world!"));
```

```
// create JWS header with HMAC-SHA256 algorithm.
jwsObject.sign(new MACSigner(sharedSecretString));

// serialize into base64-encoded text.
String jwtInText = jwsObject.serialize();

// print the value of the serialzied JWS token.
System.out.println(jwtInText);

return jwtInText;
}
```

To build and run the program, execute the following Maven command from the ch07/ sample04 directory.

```
\> mvn test -Psample04
```

The preceding code uses the JWS compact serialization and will produce the following output:

eyJhbGciOiJIUzI1NiJ9.SGVsbG8gd29ybGQh.zub7JGOFOh7EIKAgWMzx95w-nFpJdRMvUh_pMwd6wnA

Summary

- JSON has already become the de facto message exchange format for APIs.

- Understanding JSON security plays a key role in securing APIs.

- JSON Web Token (JWT) defines a container to transport data between interested parties in a cryptographically safe manner. It became an IETF standard in May 2015 with the RFC 7519.

- Both JWS (JSON Web Signature) and JWE (JSON Web Encryption) standards are built on top of JWT.

- There are two types of serialization techniques defined by the JWS specification: compact serialization and JSON serialization.

- The JWS specification is not just limited to JSON. You can sign any content with JWS without wrapping it inside a JSON payload.

CHAPTER 8

Message-Level Security with JSON Web Encryption

In Chapter 7, we discussed in detail the JWT (JSON Web Token) and JWS (JSON Web Signature) specifications. Both of these specifications are developed under the IETF JOSE working group. This chapter focuses on another prominent standard developed by the same IETF working group for encrypting messages (not necessarily JSON payloads): JSON Web Encryption (JWE). Like in JWS, JWT is the foundation for JWE. The JWE specification standardizes the way to represent an encrypted content in a JSON-based data structure. The JWE[1] specification defines two serialized forms to represent the encrypted payload: the JWE compact serialization and JWE JSON serialization. Both of these two serialization techniques are discussed in detail in the sections to follow. Like in JWS, the message to be encrypted using JWE standard need not be a JSON payload, it can be any content. The term *JWE token* is used to refer to the serialized form of an encrypted message (any message, not just JSON), following any of the serialization techniques defined in the JWE specification.

JWE Compact Serialization

With the JWE compact serialization, a JWE token is built with five key components, each separated by periods (.): JOSE header, JWE Encrypted Key, JWE Initialization Vector, JWE Ciphertext, and JWE Authentication Tag. Figure 8-1 shows the structure of a JWE token formed by JWE compact serialization.

---

[1]The JSON Web Encryption specification, `https://tools.ietf.org/html/rfc7516`

© Prabath Siriwardena 2020
P. Siriwardena, *Advanced API Security*, https://doi.org/10.1007/978-1-4842-2050-4_8

Figure 8-1. *A JWE token with compact serialization*

JOSE Header

The JOSE header is the very first element of the JWE token produced under compact serialization. The structure of the JOSE header is the same, as we discussed in Chapter 7, other than few exceptions. The JWE specification introduces two new parameters (`enc` and `zip`), which are included in the JOSE header of a JWE token, in addition to those introduced by the JSON Web Signature (JWS) specification. The following lists out all the JOSE header parameters, which are defined by the JWE specification:

- `alg` *(algorithm)*: The name of the algorithm, which is used to encrypt the Content Encryption Key (CEK). The CEK is a symmetric key, which encrypts the plaintext JSON payload. Once the plaintext is encrypted with the CEK, the CEK itself will be encrypted with another key following the algorithm identified by the value of the `alg` parameter. The encrypted CEK will then be included in the JWE Encrypted Key section of the JWE token. This is a required attribute in the JOSE header. Failure to include this in the header will result in a token parsing error. The value of the alg parameter is a string, which is picked from the JSON Web Signature and Encryption Algorithms registry defined by the JSON Web Algorithms[2] (JWA) specification. If the value of the alg parameter is not picked from the preceding registry, then it should be defined in a collision-resistant manner, but that won't give any guarantee that the particular algorithm is identified by all JWE implementations. It's always better to stick to the algorithms defined in the JWA specification.

- `enc`: The enc parameter in the JOSE header represents the name of the algorithm, which is used for content encryption. This algorithm should be a symmetric Authenticated Encryption with Associated

---

[2]JWS algorithms are defined and explained in the JSON Web Algorithms (JWA) specification, `https://tools.ietf.org/html/rfc7518`.

Data (AEAD) algorithm. This is a required attribute in the JOSE header. Failure to include this in the header will result in a token parsing error. The value of the enc parameter is a string, which is picked from the JSON Web Signature and Encryption Algorithms registry defined by the JSON Web Algorithms (JWA) specification. If the value of the enc parameter is not picked from the preceding registry, then it should be defined in a collision-resistant manner, but that won't give any guarantee that the particular algorithm is identified by all JWE implementations. It's always better to stick to the algorithms defined in the JWA specification.

- `zip:` The zip parameter in the JOSE header defines the name of the compression algorithm. The plaintext JSON payload gets compressed before the encryption, if the token issuer decides to use compression. The compression is not a must. The JWE specification defines DEF as the compression algorithm, but it's not a must to use it. The token issuers can define their own compression algorithms. The default value of the compression algorithm is defined in the JSON Web Encryption Compression Algorithms registry under the JSON Web Algorithms (JWA) specification. This is an optional parameter.

- jku: The jku parameter in the JOSE header carries a URL, which points to a JSON Web Key (JWK)[3] set. This JWK set represents a collection of JSON-encoded public keys, where one of the keys is used to encrypt the Content Encryption Key (CEK). Whatever the protocol used to retrieve the key set should provide the integrity protection. If keys are retrieved over HTTP, then instead of plain HTTP, HTTPS (or HTTP over TLS) should be used. We discuss Transport Layer Security (TLS) in detail in Appendix C. The jku is an optional parameter.

- jwk: The jwk parameter in JOSE header represents the public key corresponding to the key that is used to encrypt the Content Encryption Key (CEK). The key is encoded as per the JSON Web Key (JWK) specification.[3] The jku parameter, which we discussed before,

---

[3]A JSON Web Key (JWK) is a JSON data structure that represents a cryptographic key, `https://tools.ietf.org/html/rfc7517`

points to a link that holds a set of JWKs, while the `jwk` parameter embeds the key into the JOSE header itself. The `jwk` is an optional parameter.

- `kid`: The `kid` parameter of the JOSE header represents an identifier for the key that is used to encrypt the Content Encryption Key (CEK). Using this identifier, the recipient of the JWE should be able to locate the key. If the token issuer uses the `kid` parameter in the JOSE header to let the recipient know about the signing key, then the corresponding key should be exchanged "somehow" between the token issuer and the recipient beforehand. How this key exchange happens is out of the scope of the JWE specification. If the value of the `kid` parameter refers to a JWK, then the value of this parameter should match the value of the `kid` parameter in the JWK. The `kid` is an optional parameter in the JOSE header.

- `x5u`: The `x5u` parameter in the JOSE header is very much similar to the `jku` parameter, which we discussed before. Instead of pointing to a JWK set, the URL here points to an X.509 certificate or a chain of X.509 certificates. The resource pointed by the URL must hold the certificate or the chain of certificates in the PEM-encoded form. Each certificate in the chain must appear between the delimiters[4]: -----BEGIN CERTIFICATE----- and -----END CERTIFICATE-----. The public key corresponding to the key used to encrypt the Content Encryption Key (CEK) should be the very first entry in the certificate chain, and the rest is the certificates of intermediate CAs (certificate authority) and the root CA. The `x5u` is an optional parameter in the JOSE header.

- `x5c`: The `x5c` parameter in the JOSE header represents the X.509 certificate (or the certificate chain), which corresponds to the public key, which is used to encrypt the Content Encryption Key (CEK). This is similar to the `jwk` parameter we discussed before, but in this case instead of a JWK, it's an X.509 certificate (or a chain of certificates). The certificate or the certificate chain is represented in a JSON

---

[4]The Internet IP Security PKI Profile of IKEv1/ISAKMP, IKEv2, and PKIX (RFC 4945) defines the delimiters for X.509 certificates under Section 6.1, `https://tools.ietf.org/html/rfc4945`

array of certificate value strings. Each element in the array should be a base64-encoded DER PKIX certificate value. The public key corresponding to the key used to encrypt the Content Encryption Key (CEK) should be the very first entry in the JSON array, and the rest is the certificates of intermediate CAs (certificate authority) and the root CA. The x5c is an optional parameter in the JOSE header.

- x5t: The x5t parameter in the JOSE header represents the base64url-encoded SHA-1 thumbprint of the X.509 certificate corresponding to the key used to encrypt the Content Encryption Key (CEK). This is similar to the kid parameter we discussed before. Both these parameters are used to locate the key. If the token issuer uses the x5t parameter in the JOSE header to let the recipient know about the signing key, then the corresponding key should be exchanged "somehow" between the token issuer and the recipient beforehand. How this key exchange happens is out of the scope of the JWE specification. The x5t is an optional parameter in the JOSE header.

- x5t#s256: The x5t#s256 parameter in the JOSE header represents the base64url-encoded SHA256 thumbprint of the X.509 certificate corresponding to the key used to encrypt the Content Encryption Key (CEK). The only difference between x5t#s256 and the x5t is the hashing algorithm. The x5t#s256 is an optional parameter in the JOSE header.

- typ: The typ parameter in the JOSE header is used to define the media type of the complete JWE. There are two types of components that process a JWE: JWE implementations and JWE applications. Nimbus[5] is a JWE implementation in Java. The Nimbus library knows how to build and parse a JWE. A JWE application can be anything, which uses JWE internally. A JWE application uses a JWE implementation to build or parse a JWE. In this case, the typ parameter is just another parameter for the JWE implementation. It will not try to interpret the value of it, but the JWE application would. The typ parameter will help JWE applications to differentiate the

---

[5]Nimbus JWT Java implementation, http://connect2id.com/products/nimbus-jose-jwt

content when multiple types of objects are present. For a JWS token using JWS compact serialization and for a JWE token using JWE compact serialization, the value of the typ parameter is JOSE, and for a JWS token using JWS JSON serialization and for a JWE token using JWE JSON serialization, the value is JOSE+JSON. (JWS serialization was discussed in Chapter 7 and JWE serialization is discussed later in this chapter). The typ is an optional parameter in the JOSE header.

- cty: The cty parameter in the JOSE header is used to represent the media type of the secured content in the JWE. It is only recommended to use this parameter in the case of a nested JWT. The nested JWT is discussed later in this chapter, and the definition of the cty parameter is further explained there. The cty is an optional parameter in the JOSE header.

- crit: The crit parameter in the JOSE header is used to indicate to the recipient of the JWE that the presence of custom parameters, which neither defined by the JWE or JWA specifications, in the JOSE header. If these custom parameters are not understood by the recipient, then the JWE token will be treated as invalid. The value of the crit parameter is a JSON array of names, where each entry represents a custom parameter. The crit is an optional parameter in the JOSE header.

Out of all the 13 parameters defined earlier, 7 talk about how to reference the public key, which is used to encrypt the Content Encryption Key (CEK). There are three ways of referencing a key: external reference, embedded, and key identifier. The jku and x5u parameters fall under the external reference category. Both of them reference the key through a URI. The jwk and x5c parameters fall under embedded reference category. Each one of them defines how to embed the key to the JOSE header itself. The kid, x5t, and x5t#s256 parameters fall under the key identifier reference category. All three of them define how to locate the key using an identifier. Then again all the seven parameters can further divide into two categories based on the representation of the key: JSON Web Key (JWK) and X.509. The jku, jwk, and kid fall under the JWK category, while x5u, x5c, x5t, and x5t#s256 fall under the X.509 category. In the JOSE header of a given JWE token, at a given time, we only need to have one from the preceding parameters.

Note   The JSON payload, which is subject to encryption, could contain whitespaces and/or line breaks before or after any JSON value.

The JWE specification does not restrict applications only to use 13 header parameters defined earlier. There are two ways to introduce new header parameters: public header names and private header names. Any header parameter that is intended to use in the public space should be introduced in a collision-resistant manner. It is recommended to register such public header parameters in the IANA JSON Web Signature and Encryption Header Parameters registry. The private header parameters are mostly used in a restricted environment, where both the token issuer and the recipients are well aware of each other. These parameters should be used with caution, because there is a chance for collision. If a given recipient accepts tokens from multiple token issuers, then the semantics of the same parameter may be different from one issuer to another, if it is a private header. In either case, whether it's a public or a private header parameter, if it is not defined in the JWE or the JWA specification, the header name should be included in the `crit` header parameter, which we discussed before.

JWE Encrypted Key

To understand JWE Encrypted Key section of the JWE, we first need to understand how a JSON payload gets encrypted. The `enc` parameter of the JOSE header defines the content encryption algorithm, and it should be a symmetric Authenticated Encryption with Associated Data (AEAD) algorithm. The `alg` parameter of the JOSE header defines the encryption algorithm to encrypt the Content Encryption Key (CEK). We can also call this algorithm a key wrapping algorithm, as it wraps the CEK.

AUTHENTICATED ENCRYPTION

Encryption alone only provides the data confidentiality. Only the intended recipient can decrypt and view the encrypted data. Even though data is not visible to everyone, anyone having access to the encrypted data can change the bit stream of it to reflect a different message. For example, if Alice transfers US $100 from her bank account to Bob's account and if that message is encrypted, then Eve in the middle can't see what's inside it. But, Eve can modify the bit stream of the encrypted data to change the message, let's say from US $100 to US

$150. The bank which controls the transaction would not detect this change done by Eve in the middle and will treat it as a legitimate transaction. This is why encryption itself is not always safe, and in the 1970s, this was identified as an issue in the banking industry.

Unlike just encryption, the *Authenticated Encryption* simultaneously provides a confidentiality, integrity, and authenticity guarantee for data. ISO/IEC 19772:2009 has standardized six different authenticated encryption modes: GCM, OCB 2.0, CCM, Key Wrap, EAX, and Encrypt-then-MAC. *Authenticated Encryption with Associated Data (AEAD)* extends this model to add the ability to preserve the integrity and authenticity of *Additional Authenticated Data* (AAD) that isn't encrypted. AAD is also known as *Associated Data* (AD). AEAD algorithms take two inputs, plaintext to be encrypted and the Additional Authentication Data (AAD), and result in two outputs: the ciphertext and the authentication tag. The AAD represents the data to be authenticated, but not encrypted. The authentication tag ensures the integrity of the ciphertext and the AAD.

Let's look at the following JOSE header. For content encryption, it uses A256GCM algorithm, and for key wrapping, RSA-OAEP:

```
{"alg":"RSA-OAEP","enc":"A256GCM"}
```

A256GCM is defined in the JWA specification. It uses the Advanced Encryption Standard (AES) in Galois/Counter Mode (GCM) algorithm with a 256-bit long key, and it's a symmetric key algorithm used for AEAD. Symmetric keys are mostly used for content encryption. Symmetric key encryption is much faster than asymmetric key encryption. At the same time, asymmetric key encryption can't be used to encrypt large messages. RSA-OAEP is too defined in the JWA specification. During the encryption process, the token issuer generates a random key, which is 256 bits in size, and encrypts the message using that key following the AES GCM algorithm. Next, the key used to encrypt the message is encrypted using RSA-OAEP,[6] which is an asymmetric encryption scheme. The RSA-OAEP encryption scheme uses RSA algorithm with the Optimal Asymmetric Encryption Padding (OAEP) method. Finally, the encrypted symmetric key is placed in the JWE Encrypted Header section of the JWE.

---

[6]RSA-OAEP is a public key encryption scheme, which uses the RSA algorithm with the Optimal Asymmetric Encryption Padding (OAEP) method.

KEY MANAGEMENT MODES

The key management mode defines the method to derive or compute a value to the Content Encryption Key (CEK). The JWE specification employs five key management modes, as listed in the following, and the appropriate key management mode is decided based on the `alg` parameter, which is defined in the JOSE header:

1. *Key encryption:* With the key encryption mode, the value of the CEK is encrypted using an asymmetric encryption algorithm. For example, if the value of the `alg` parameter in the JOSE header is RSA-OAEP, then the corresponding key management algorithm is the RSAES OAEP using the default parameters. This relationship between the `alg` parameter and the key management algorithm is defined in the JWA specification. The RSAES OAEP algorithm occupies the *key encryption* as the key management mode to derive the value of the CEK.

2. *Key wrapping:* With the key wrapping mode, the value of the CEK is encrypted using a symmetric key wrapping algorithm. For example, if the value of the `alg` parameter in the JOSE header is A128KW, then the corresponding key management algorithm is the AES Key Wrap with the default initial value, which uses a 128-bit key. The AES Key Wrap algorithm occupies *the key wrapping* as the key management mode to derive the value of the CEK.

3. *Direct key agreement:* With the direct key agreement mode, the value of the CEK is decided based upon a key agreement algorithm. For example, if the value of the `alg` parameter in the JOSE header is ECDH-ES, then the corresponding key management algorithm is the Elliptic Curve Diffie-Hellman Ephemeral Static key agreement using Concat KDF. This algorithm occupies the *direct key agreement* as the key management mode to derive the value of the CEK.

4. *Key agreement with key wrapping:* With the direct key agreement with key wrapping mode, the value of the CEK is decided based upon a key agreement algorithm, and it is encrypted using a symmetric key wrapping algorithm. For example, if the value of the `alg` parameter in the JOSE header is ECDH-ES+A128KW, then the corresponding key management algorithm is the ECDH-ES using Concat KDF and CEK rapped with A128KW. This algorithm occupies the *direct key agreement with key wrapping* as the key management mode to derive the value of the CEK.

5. *Direct encryption*: With the direct encryption mode, the value of the CEK is the same as the symmetric key value, which is already shared between the token issuer and the recipient. For example, if the value of the `alg` parameter in the JOSE header is `dir`, then the *direct encryption* is occupied as the key management mode to derive the value of the CEK.

JWE Initialization Vector

Some encryption algorithms, which are used for content encryption, require an initialization vector, during the encryption process. Initialization vector is a randomly generated number, which is used along with a secret key to encrypt data. This will add randomness to the encrypted data, which will prevent repetition even if the same data gets encrypted using the same secret key again and again. To decrypt the message at the token recipient end, it has to know the initialization vector, hence included in the JWE token, under the JWE Initialization Vector element. If the content encryption algorithm does not require an initialization vector, then the value of this element should be kept empty.

JWE Ciphertext

The fourth element of the JWE token is the base64url-encoded value of the JWE ciphertext. The JWE ciphertext is computed by encrypting the plaintext JSON payload using the CEK, the JWE Initialization Vector, and the Additional Authentication Data (AAD) value, with the encryption algorithm defined by the header parameter enc. The algorithm defined by the enc header parameter should be a symmetric Authenticated Encryption with Associated Data (AEAD) algorithm. The AEAD algorithm, which is used to encrypt the plaintext payload, also allows specifying Additional Authenticated Data (AAD).

JWE Authentication Tag

The base64url-encoded value of the JWE Authentication Tag is the final element of the JWE token. The value of the authentication tag is produced during the AEAD encryption process, along with the ciphertext. The authentication tag ensures the integrity of the ciphertext and the Additional Authenticated Data (AAD).

The Process of Encryption (Compact Serialization)

We have discussed about all the ingredients that are required to build a JWE token under compact serialization. The following discusses the steps involved in building the JWE token. There are five elements in a JWE token; the first element is produced by step 6, the second element is produced by step 3, the third element is produced by step 4, the fourth element is produced by step 10, and the fifth element is produced by step 11.

1. Figure out the key management mode by the algorithm used to determine the Content Encryption Key (CEK) value. This algorithm is defined by the alg parameter in the JOSE header. There is only one alg parameter per JWE token.

2. Compute the CEK and calculate the JWE Encrypted Key based on the key management mode, picked in step 1. The CEK is later used to encrypt the JSON payload. There is only one JWE Encrypted Key element in the JWE token.

3. Compute the base64url-encoded value of the *JWE Encrypted Key*, which is produced by step 2. This is the second element of the JWE token.

4. Generate a random value for the JWE Initialization Vector. Irrespective of the serialization technique, the JWE token carries the value of the base64url-encoded value of the JWE Initialization Vector. This is the third element of the JWE token.

5. If token compression is needed, the JSON payload in plaintext must be compressed following the compression algorithm defined under the zip header parameter.

6. Construct the JSON representation of the JOSE header and find the base64url-encoded value of the JOSE header with UTF-8 encoding. This is the first element of the JWE token.

7. To encrypt the JSON payload, we need the CEK (which we already have), the JWE Initialization Vector (which we already have), and the Additional Authenticated Data (AAD). Compute ASCII value of the encoded JOSE header (step 6) and use it as the AAD.

8. Encrypt the compressed JSON payload (from step 5) using the CEK, the JWE Initialization Vector, and the Additional Authenticated Data (AAD), following the content encryption algorithm defined by the enc header parameter.

9. The algorithm defined by the enc header parameter is an AEAD algorithm, and after the encryption process, it produces the ciphertext and the Authentication Tag.

10. Compute the base64url-encoded value of the ciphertext, which is produced by step 9. This is the fourth element of the JWE token.

11. Compute the base64url-encoded value of the Authentication Tag, which is produced by step 9. This is the fifth element of the JWE token.

12. Now we have all the elements to build the JWE token in the following manner. The line breaks are introduced only for clarity.

    BASE64URL-ENCODE(UTF8(JWE Protected Header)).

    BASE64URL-ENCODE(JWE Encrypted Key).

    BASE64URL-ENCODE(JWE Initialization Vector).

    BASE64URL-ENCODE(JWE Ciphertext).

    BASE64URL-ENCODE(JWE Authentication Tag)

JWE JSON Serialization

Unlike the JWE compact serialization, the JWE JSON serialization can produce encrypted data targeting at multiple recipients over the same JSON payload. The ultimate serialized form under JWE JSON serialization represents an encrypted JSON payload as a JSON object. This JSON object includes six top-level elements: protected, unprotected, recipients, iv, ciphertext, and tag. The following is an example of a JWE token, which is serialized with JWE JSON serialization:

```
{
    "protected":"eyJlbmMiOiJBMTI4Q0JDLUhTMjU2In0",
    "unprotected":{"jku":"https://server.example.com/keys.jwks"},
    "recipients":[
       {
        "header":{"alg":"RSA1_5","kid":"2011-04-29"},
        "encrypted_key":"UGhIOguC7IuEvf_NPVaXsGMoLOmwvc1GyqlIK..."
       },
       {
        "header":{"alg":"A128KW","kid":"7"},
        "encrypted_key":"6KB707dM9YTIgHtLvtgWQ8mKwb..."
       }
    ],
    "iv":"AxY8DCtDaGlsbGljb3RoZQ",
    "ciphertext":"KDlTtXchhZTGufMYmOYGS4HffxPSUrfmqCHXaI9wOGY",
    "tag":"Mz-VPPyU4RlcuYv1IwIvzw"
}
```

JWE Protected Header

The *JWE Protected Header* is a JSON object that includes the header parameters that have to be integrity protected by the AEAD algorithm. The parameters inside the *JWE Protected Header* are applicable to all the recipients of the JWE token. The protected parameter in the serialized JSON form represents the base64url-encoded value of the *JWE Protected Header*. There is only one protected element in a JWE token at the root level, and any header parameter that we discussed before under the JOSE header can also be used under the *JWE Protected Header*.

JWE Shared Unprotected Header

The *JWE Shared Unprotected Header* is a JSON object that includes the header parameters that are not integrity protected. The unprotected parameter in the serialized JSON form represents the *JWE Shared Unprotected Header*. There is only one unprotected element in a JWE token at the root level, and any header parameter that we discussed before under the JOSE header can also be used under the *JWE Shared Unprotected Header*.

JWE Per-Recipient Unprotected Header

The *JWE Per-Recipient Unprotected Header* is a JSON object that includes the header parameters that are not integrity protected. The parameters inside the *JWE Per-Recipient Unprotected Header* are applicable only to a particular recipient of the JWE token. In the JWE token, these header parameters are grouped under the parameter `recipients`. The `recipients` parameter represents an array of recipients of the JWE token. Each member consists of a `header` parameter and an `encryptedkey` parameter.

- `header`: The `header` parameter, which is inside the `recipients` parameter, represents the value of the JWE header elements that aren't protected for integrity by authenticated encryption for each recipient.

- `encryptedkey`: The `encryptedkey` parameter represents the base64url-encoded value of the encrypted key. This is the key used to encrypt the message payload. The key can be encrypted in different ways for each recipient.

Any header parameter that we discussed before under the JOSE header can also be used under the *JWE Per-Recipient Unprotected Header.*

JWE Initialization Vector

This carries the same meaning as explained under JWE compact serialization previously in this chapter. The `iv` parameter in the JWE token represents the value of the initialization vector used for encryption.

JWE Ciphertext

This carries the same meaning as explained under JWE compact serialization previously in this chapter. The `ciphertext` parameter in the JWE token carries the base64url-encoded value of the JWE ciphertext.

JWE Authentication Tag

This carries the same meaning as explained under JWE compact serialization previously in this chapter. The tag parameter in the JWE token carries the base64url-encoded value of the JWE Authentication Tag, which is an outcome of the encryption process using an AEAD algorithm.

The Process of Encryption (JSON Serialization)

We have discussed about all the ingredients that are required to build a JWE token under JSON serialization. The following discusses the steps involved in building the JWE token.

1. Figure out the key management mode by the algorithm used to determine the Content Encryption Key (CEK) value. This algorithm is defined by the alg parameter in the JOSE header. Under JWE JSON serialization, the JOSE header is built by the union of all the parameters defined under the JWE Protected Header, JWE Shared Unprotected Header, and Per-Recipient Unprotected Header. Once included in the Per-Recipient Unprotected Header, the alg parameter can be defined per recipient.

2. Compute the CEK and calculate the JWE Encrypted Key based on the key management mode, picked in step 1. The CEK is later used to encrypt the JSON payload.

3. Compute the base64url-encoded value of the *JWE Encrypted Key*, which is produced by step 2. Once again, this is computed per recipient, and the resultant value is included in the *Per-Recipient Unprotected Header* parameter, encryptedkey.

4. Perform steps 1–3 for each recipient of the JWE token. Each iteration will produce an element in the recipients JSON array of the JWE token.

5. Generate a random value for the JWE Initialization Vector. Irrespective of the serialization technique, the JWE token carries the value of the base64url-encoded value of the JWE Initialization Vector.

6. If token compression is needed, the JSON payload in plaintext must be compressed following the compression algorithm defined under the `zip` header parameter. The value of the `zip` header parameter can be defined either in the *JWE Protected Header* or *JWE Shared Unprotected Header.*

7. Construct the JSON representation of the *JWE Protected Header, JWE Shared Unprotected Header,* and *Per-Recipient Unprotected Headers.*

8. Compute the base64url-encoded value of the *JWE Protected Header* with UTF-8 encoding. This value is represented by the `protected` element in the serialized JWE token. The JWE Protected Header is optional, and if present there can be only one header. If no JWE header is present, then the value of the `protected` element will be empty.

9. Generate a value for the Additional Authenticated Data (AAD) and compute the base64url-encoded value of it. This is an optional step, and if it's there, then the base64url-encoded AAD value will be used as an input parameter to encrypt the JSON payload, as in step 10.

10. To encrypt the JSON payload, we need the CEK (which we already have), the JWE Initialization Vector (which we already have), and the Additional Authenticated Data (AAD). Compute ASCII value of the encoded *JWE Protected Header* (step 8) and use it as the AAD. In case step 9 is done and then the value of AAD is computed as ASCII(encoded *JWE Protected Header.* BASE64URL-ENCODE(AAD)).

11. Encrypt the compressed JSON payload (from step 6) using the CEK, the JWE Initialization Vector, and the Additional Authenticated Data (AAD from step 10), following the content encryption algorithm defined by the `enc` header parameter.

12. The algorithm defined by the enc header parameter is an AEAD algorithm, and after the encryption process, it produces the ciphertext and the Authentication Tag.

13. Compute the base64url-encoded value of the ciphertext, which is produced by step 12.

14. Compute the base64url-encoded value of the Authentication Tag, which is produced by step 12.

Now we have all the elements to build the JWE token under JSON serialization.

Note   The XML Encryption specification by W3C only talks about encrypting an XML payload. If you have to encrypt any content, then first you need to embed that within an XML payload and then encrypt. In contrast, the JWE specification is not just limited to JSON. You can encrypt any content with JWE without wrapping it inside a JSON payload.

Nested JWTs

Both in a JWS token and a JWE token, the payload can be of any content. It can be JSON, XML, or anything. In a *Nested JWT*, the payload must be a JWT itself. In other words, a JWT, which is enclosed in another JWS or JWE token, builds a *Nested JWT*. A *Nested JWT* is used to perform nested signing and encryption. The cty header parameter must be present and set to the value JWT, in the case of a *Nested JWT*. The following lists out the steps in building a *Nested JWT*, which signs a payload first using JWS and then encrypts the JWS token using JWE:

1. Build the JWS token with the payload or the content of your choice.

2. Based on the JWS serialization technique you use, step 1 will produce either a JSON object with JSON serialization or a three-element string where each element is separated out by a period (.)—with compact serialization.

3. Base64url-encode the output from step 2 and use it as the payload to be encrypted for the JWE token.

4.   Set the value of the cty header parameter of the JWE JOSE header
     to JWT.

5.   Build the JWE following any of the two serialization techniques
     defined in the JWE specification.

Note   Sign first and then encrypt is the preferred approach in building a nested
JWT, instead of sign and then encrypt. The signature binds the ownership of the
content to the signer or the token issuer. It is an industry accepted best practice to
sign the original content, rather than the encrypted content. Also, when sign first
and encrypt the signed payload, the signature itself gets encrypted too, preventing
an attacker in the middle stripping off the signature. Since the signature and all its
related metadata are encrypted, an attacker cannot derive any details about the
token issuer looking at the message. When encrypt first and sign the encrypted
payload, then the signature is visible to anyone and also an attacker can strip it off
from the message.

JWE VS. JWS

From an application developer's point of view, it may be quite important to identify whether
a given message is a JWE token or a JWS token and start processing based on that. The
following lists out a few techniques that can be used to differentiate a JWS token from a JWE
token:

1.   When compact serialization is used, a JWS token has three base64url-encoded
     elements separated by periods (.), while a JWE token has five base64url-
     encoded elements separated by periods (.).

2.   When JSON serialization is used, the elements of the JSON object produced
     are different in JWS token and JWE token. For example, the JWS token has a
     top-level element called payload, which is not in the JWE token, and the JWE
     token has a top-level element called ciphertext, which is not in the JWS
     token.

3.   The JOSE header of a JWE token has the enc header parameter, while it is not
     present in the JOSE header of a JWS token.

4. The value of the alg parameter in the JOSE header of a JWS token carries a digital signature or a MAC algorithm or none, while the same parameter in the JOSE header of a JWE token carries a key encryption, key wrapping, direct key agreement, key agreement with key wrapping, or direct encryption algorithm.

GENERATING A JWE TOKEN WITH RSA-OAEP AND AES WITH A JSON PAYLOAD

The following Java code generates a JWE token with RSA-OAEP and AES. You can download the complete Java sample as a Maven project from https://github.com/apisecurity/samples/tree/master/ch08/sample01—and it runs on Java 8+. First you need to invoke the method generateKeyPair() and pass the PublicKey(generateKeyPair(). getPublicKey()) into the method buildEncryptedJWT():

```java
// this method generates a key pair and the corresponding public key is used
// to encrypt the message.
public static KeyPair generateKeyPair() throws NoSuchAlgorithmException {
    // instantiate KeyPairGenerate with RSA algorithm.
    KeyPairGenerator keyGenerator = KeyPairGenerator.getInstance("RSA");
    // set the key size to 1024 bits.
    keyGenerator.initialize(1024);
    // generate and return private/public key pair.
    return keyGenerator.genKeyPair();
}
// this method is used to encrypt a JWT claims set using the provided public
// key.
public static String buildEncryptedJWT(PublicKey publicKey) throws
JOSEException {
    // build audience restriction list.
    List<String> aud = new ArrayList<String>();
    aud.add("https://app1.foo.com");
    aud.add("https://app2.foo.com");
    Date currentTime = new Date();
    // create a claims set.
    JWTClaimsSet jwtClaims = new JWTClaimsSet.Builder().
                // set the value of the issuer.
                issuer("https://apress.com").
                // set the subject value - JWT belongs to this subject.
```

203

```
                subject("john").
                // set values for audience restriction.
                audience(aud).
                // expiration time set to 10 minutes.
                expirationTime(new Date(new Date().getTime() + 1000 *
                60 * 10)).
                // set the valid from time to current time.
                notBeforeTime(currentTime).
                // set issued time to current time.
                issueTime(currentTime).
                // set a generated UUID as the JWT identifier.
                jwtID(UUID.randomUUID().toString()).build();
        // create JWE header with RSA-OAEP and AES/GCM.
        JWEHeader jweHeader = new JWEHeader(JWEAlgorithm.RSA_OAEP,
        EncryptionMethod.A128GCM);
        // create encrypter with the RSA public key.
        JWEEncrypter encrypter = new RSAEncrypter((RSAPublicKey) publicKey);
        // create the encrypted JWT with the JWE header and the JWT payload.
        EncryptedJWT encryptedJWT = new EncryptedJWT(jweHeader, jwtClaims);
        // encrypt the JWT.
        encryptedJWT.encrypt(encrypter);
        // serialize into base64-encoded text.
        String jwtInText = encryptedJWT.serialize();
        // print the value of the JWT.
        System.out.println(jwtInText);
        return jwtInText;
    }
```

The following Java code shows how to invoke the previous two methods:

```
KeyPair keyPair = generateKeyPair();
buildEncryptedJWT(keyPair.getPublic());
```

To build and run the program, execute the following Maven command from the ch08/ sample01 directory.

\> mvn test -Psample01

Let's see how to decrypt a JWT encrypted by RSA-OAEP. You need to know the `PrivateKey` corresponding to the `PublicKey` used to encrypt the message:

```
public static void decryptJWT() throws NoSuchAlgorithmException,
                            JOSEException, ParseException {
// generate private/public key pair.
KeyPair keyPair = generateKeyPair();
// get the private key - used to decrypt the message.
PrivateKey privateKey = keyPair.getPrivate();
// get the public key - used to encrypt the message.
PublicKey publicKey = keyPair.getPublic();
// get encrypted JWT in base64-encoded text.
String jwtInText = buildEncryptedJWT(publicKey);
// create a decrypter.
JWEDecrypter decrypter = new RSADecrypter((RSAPrivateKey) privateKey);
// create the encrypted JWT with the base64-encoded text.
EncryptedJWT encryptedJWT = EncryptedJWT.parse(jwtInText);
// decrypt the JWT.
encryptedJWT.decrypt(decrypter);
// print the value of JOSE header.
System.out.println("JWE Header:" + encryptedJWT.getHeader());
// JWE content encryption key.
System.out.println("JWE Content Encryption Key: " + encryptedJWT.
getEncryptedKey());
// initialization vector.
System.out.println("Initialization Vector: " + encryptedJWT.getIV());
// ciphertext.
System.out.println("Ciphertext : " + encryptedJWT.getCipherText());
// authentication tag.
System.out.println("Authentication Tag: " + encryptedJWT.getAuthTag());
// print the value of JWT body
System.out.println("Decrypted Payload: " + encryptedJWT.getPayload());
}
```

The preceding code produces something similar to the following output:

```
JWE Header: {"alg":"RSA-OAEP","enc":"A128GCM"}
JWE Content Encryption Key: NbIuAjnNBwmwlbKiIpEzffU1duaQfxJpJaodkxDj
SC2s3tO76ZdUZ6YfPrwSZ6DU8F51pbEw2f2MK_C7kLpgWUl8hMHP7g2_Eh3y
```

Th5iK6Agx72o8IPwpD4woY7CVvIB_iJqz-cngZgNAikHjHzOC6JF748MwtgSiiyrI
9BsmU
Initialization Vector: JPPFsk6yimrkohJf
Ciphertext: XF2kAcBrAX_4LSOGejsegoxEfb8kV58yFJSQO_WOONP5wQo7HG
mMLTyR713ufXwannitR6d2eTDMFe1xkTFfF9ZskYj5qJ36rOvhGGhNqNdGEpsB
YK5wmPiRlk3tbUtd_DulQWEUKHqPc_VszWKFOlLQW5UgMeHndVi3JOZgiwN
gy9bvzacWazK8lTpxSQVf-NrD_zu_qPYJRisvbKI8dudv7ayKoE4mnQW_fUY-U1o
AMy-7Bg4WQE4j6dfxMlQGoPOo
Authentication Tag: pZWfYyt2kO-VpHSW7btznA
Decrypted Payload:
{
    "exp":1402116034,
    "sub":"john",
    "nbf":1402115434,
    "aud":["https:\/\/app1.foo.com "," https:\/\/app2.foo.com"],
    "iss":"https:\/\/apress.com",
    "jti":"a1b41dd4-ba4a-4584-b06d-8988e8f995bf",
    "iat":1402115434
}

GENERATING A JWE TOKEN WITH RSA-OAEP AND AES WITH A NON-JSON PAYLOAD

The following Java code generates a JWE token with RSA-OAEP and AES for a non-JSON payload. You can download the complete Java sample as a Maven project from https://github.com/apisecurity/samples/tree/master/ch08/sample02—and it runs on Java 8+. First you need to invoke the method generateKeyPair() and pass the PublicKey(generateKeyPair().getPublicKey()) into the method buildEncryptedJWT():

```
// this method generates a key pair and the corresponding public key is used
// to encrypt the message.
public static KeyPair generateKeyPair() throws NoSuchAlgorithmException,
JOSEException {
    // instantiate KeyPairGenerate with RSA algorithm.
    KeyPairGenerator keyGenerator = KeyPairGenerator.getInstance("RSA");
    // set the key size to 1024 bits.
    keyGenerator.initialize(1024);
```

```
    // generate and return private/public key pair.
    return keyGenerator.genKeyPair();
}
// this method is used to encrypt a non-JSON payload using the provided
// public key.
public static String buildEncryptedJWT(PublicKey publicKey) throws
JOSEException {
    // create JWE header with RSA-OAEP and AES/GCM.
    JWEHeader jweHeader = new JWEHeader(JWEAlgorithm.RSA_OAEP,
EncryptionMethod.A128GCM);
    // create encrypter with the RSA public key.
    JWEEncrypter encrypter = new RSAEncrypter((RSAPublicKey) publicKey);
    // create a JWE object with a non-JSON payload
    JWEObject jweObject = new JWEObject(jweHeader, new Payload("Hello
world!"));
    // encrypt the JWT.
    jweObject.encrypt(encrypter);
    // serialize into base64-encoded text.
    String jwtInText = jweObject.serialize();
    // print the value of the JWT.
    System.out.println(jwtInText);
    return jwtInText;
}
```

To build and run the program, execute the following Maven command from the ch08/
sample02 directory.

```
\> mvn test -Psample02
```

GENERATING A NESTED JWT

The following Java code generates a nested JWT with RSA-OAEP and AES for encryption and
HMAC-SHA256 for signing. The nested JWT is constructed by encrypting the signed JWT. You
can download the complete Java sample as a Maven project from https://github.com/
apisecurity/samples/tree/master/ch08/sample03—and it runs on Java 8+. First
you need to invoke the method buildHmacSha256SignedJWT() with a shared secret and

pass its output along with the generateKeyPair().getPublicKey() into the method buildNestedJWT():

```
// this method generates a key pair and the corresponding public key is used
// to encrypt the message.
public static KeyPair generateKeyPair() throws NoSuchAlgorithmException {
    // instantiate KeyPairGenerate with RSA algorithm.
    KeyPairGenerator keyGenerator = KeyPairGenerator.getInstance("RSA");
    // set the key size to 1024 bits.
    keyGenerator.initialize(1024);
    // generate and return private/public key pair.
    return keyGenerator.genKeyPair();
}
// this method is used to sign a JWT claims set using the provided shared
// secret.
public static SignedJWT buildHmacSha256SignedJWT(String sharedSecretString)
throws JOSEException {
    // build audience restriction list.
    List<String> aud = new ArrayList<String>();
    aud.add("https://app1.foo.com");
    aud.add("https://app2.foo.com");
    Date currentTime = new Date();
    // create a claims set.
    JWTClaimsSet jwtClaims = new JWTClaimsSet.Builder().
    // set the value of the issuer.
    issuer("https://apress.com").
    // set the subject value - JWT belongs to this subject.
    subject("john").
    // set values for audience restriction.
    audience(aud).
    // expiration time set to 10 minutes.
    expirationTime(new Date(new Date().getTime() + 1000 * 60 * 10)).
    // set the valid from time to current time.
    notBeforeTime(currentTime).
    // set issued time to current time.
    issueTime(currentTime).
    // set a generated UUID as the JWT identifier.
    jwtID(UUID.randomUUID().toString()).build();
```

```java
    // create JWS header with HMAC-SHA256 algorithm.
    JWSHeader jswHeader = new JWSHeader(JWSAlgorithm.HS256);
    // create signer with the provider shared secret.
    JWSSigner signer = new MACSigner(sharedSecretString);
    // create the signed JWT with the JWS header and the JWT body.
    SignedJWT signedJWT = new SignedJWT(jswHeader, jwtClaims);
    // sign the JWT with HMAC-SHA256.
    signedJWT.sign(signer);
    // serialize into base64-encoded text.
    String jwtInText = signedJWT.serialize();
    // print the value of the JWT.
    System.out.println(jwtInText);
    return signedJWT;
}
// this method is used to encrypt the provided signed JWT or the JWS using
// the provided public key.
public static String buildNestedJWT(PublicKey publicKey, SignedJWT signedJwt)
throws JOSEException {
    // create JWE header with RSA-OAEP and AES/GCM.
    JWEHeader jweHeader = new JWEHeader(JWEAlgorithm.RSA_OAEP,
    EncryptionMethod.A128GCM);
    // create encrypter with the RSA public key.
    JWEEncrypter encrypter = new RSAEncrypter((RSAPublicKey) publicKey);
    // create a JWE object with the passed SignedJWT as the payload.
    JWEObject jweObject = new JWEObject(jweHeader, new Payload(signedJwt));
    // encrypt the JWT.
    jweObject.encrypt(encrypter);
    // serialize into base64-encoded text.
    String jwtInText = jweObject.serialize();
    // print the value of the JWT.
    System.out.println(jwtInText);
    return jwtInText;
}
```

To build and run the program, execute the following Maven command from the ch08/ sample03 directory.

```
\> mvn test -Psample03
```

Summary

- The JWE specification standardizes the way to represent encrypted content in a cryptographically safe manner.

- JWE defines two serialized forms to represent the encrypted payload: the JWE compact serialization and JWE JSON serialization.

- In the JWE compact serialization, a JWE token is built with five components, each separated by a period (.): JOSE header, JWE Encrypted Key, JWE Initialization Vector, JWE Ciphertext, and JWE Authentication Tag.

- The JWE JSON serialization can produce encrypted data targeting at multiple recipients over the same payload.

- In a Nested JWT, the payload must be a JWT itself. In other words, a JWT, which is enclosed in another JWS or JWE token, builds a Nested JWT.

- A Nested JWT is used to perform nested signing and encryption.

CHAPTER 9

OAuth 2.0 Profiles

OAuth 2.0 is a framework for delegated authorization. It doesn't address all specific enterprise API security use cases. The OAuth 2.0 profiles built on top of the core framework build a security ecosystem to make OAuth 2.0 ready for enterprise grade deployments. OAuth 2.0 introduced two extension points via grant types and token types. The profiles for OAuth 2.0 are built on top of this extensibility. This chapter talks about five key OAuth 2.0 profiles for token introspection, chained API invocation, dynamic client registration, and token revocation.

Token Introspection

OAuth 2.0 doesn't define a standard API for communication between the resource server and the authorization server. As a result, vendor-specific, proprietary APIs have crept in to couple the resource server to the authorization server. The Token Introspection profile[1] for OAuth 2.0 fills this gap by proposing a standard API to be exposed by the authorization server (Figure 9-1), allowing the resource server to talk to it and retrieve token metadata.

---

[1]`https://tools.ietf.org/html/rfc7662`

© Prabath Siriwardena 2020
P. Siriwardena, *Advanced API Security*, https://doi.org/10.1007/978-1-4842-2050-4_9

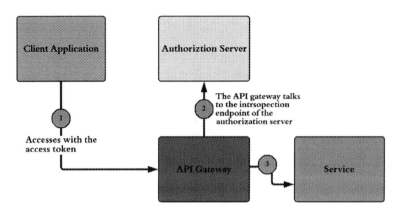

Figure 9-1. *OAuth 2.0 Token Introspection*

Any party in possession of the access token can generate a token introspection request. The introspection endpoint can be secured and the popular options are mutual Transport Layer Security (mTLS) and OAuth 2.0 client credentials.

```
POST /introspection HTTP/1.1
Accept: application/x-www-form-urlencoded
Host: authz.server.com
Authorization: Basic czZCaGRSa3FOMzo3RmpmcDBaQnIxS3REUmJuZlZkbUl3Ul3
                token=X3241Affw.423399JXJ&
                token_type_hint=access_token&
```

Let's examine the definition of each parameter:

- token: The value of the access_token or the refresh_token. This is the token where we need to get metadata about.

- token_type_hint: The type of the token (either the access_token or the refresh_token). This is optional and the value passed here could optimize the authorization server's operations in generating the introspection response.

This request returns the following JSON response. The following response does not show all possible parameters that an introspection response could include:

```
HTTP/1.1 200 OK
Content-Type: application/json
Cache-Control: no-store
```

```
{
        "active": true,
        "client_id":"s6BhdRkqt3",
        "scope": "read write dolphin",
        "sub": "2309fj32kl",
        "aud": "http://my-resource/*"
}
```

Let's examine the definition of the key parameters that you could expect in an introspection response:

- active: Indicates whether the token is active. To be active, the token should not be expired or revoked. The authorization server can define its own criteria for how to define active. This is the only required parameter the introspection response must include. All the others are optional.

- client_id: The identifier of the client to which the authorization server issued this token.

- scope: Approved scopes associated with the token. The resource server must validate that the scopes required to access the API are at least a subset of scopes attached to the token.

- sub: The subject identifier of the user who approved the authorization grant or in other words an identifier for the user who this token represents. This identifier is not necessarily a human-readable identifier, but it must carry a unique value all the time. The authorization server may produce a unique subject for each authorization server/resource server combination. This is implementation specific, and to support this, the authorization server must uniquely identify the resource server. In terms of privacy, it is essential that the authorization server maintains different subject identifiers by resource server, and this kind of an identifier is known as a persistence pseudonym. Since the authorization server issues different pseudonyms for different resource servers, for a given user, these resource servers together won't be able to identify what other services this user accesses.

- `username`: Carries a human-readable identifier of the user who approved the authorization grant or in other words a human-readable identifier for the user who this token represents. If you are to persist anything at the resource server end, with respect to the user, username is not the right identifier. The value of the username can change time to time, based on how it is implemented at the authorization server end.

- `aud`: The allowed audience for the token. Ideally, this should carry an identifier that represents the corresponding resource server. If it does not match with your identifier, the resource server must immediately reject the token. This aud element can carry more than one identifier, and in that case you need to see whether your resource server's one is part of it. Also in some implementations, rather than doing one-to-one string match, you can also match against a regular expression. For example, `http://*.my-resource.com` will find a match for both the resource servers carrying the identifiers `http://foo.my-resource.com` and `http://bar.my-resource.com`.

Note   The audience (aud) parameter is defined in the OAuth 2.0: Audience Information Internet draft available at `http://tools.ietf.org/html/draft-tschofenig-oauth-audience-00`. This is a new parameter introduced into the OAuth token request flow and is independent of the token type.

- `exp`: Defines in seconds from January 1, 1970, in UTC, the expiration time of the token. This looks like redundant, as the active parameter is already there in the response. But resource server can utilize this parameter to optimize how frequently it wants to talk to the introspection endpoint of the authorization server. Since the call to the introspection endpoint is remote, there can be performance issues, and also it can be down due to some reason. In that case, the resource server can have a cache to carry the introspection responses, and when it gets the same token again and again, it can check the cache, and if the token has not expired, it can accept the token as valid. Also there should be a valid cache expiration time;

otherwise, even if the token is revoked at the authorization server, the resource server will not know about it.

- `iat`: Defines in seconds from January 1, 1970, in UTC, the issued time of the token.

- `nbf`: Defines in seconds from January 1, 1970, in UTC, the time before the token should not be used.

- `token_type`: Indicates the type of the token. It can be a bearer token, a MAC token (see Appendix G), or any other type.

- `iss`: Carries an identifier that represents the issuer of the token. A resource server can accept tokens from multiple issuers (or authorization servers). If you store the subject of the token at the resource server end, it becomes unique only with the issuer. So you need to store it along with the issuer. There can be a case where the resource server connects to a multitenanted authorization server. In that case, your introspection endpoint will be the same, but it will be different issuers who issue tokens under different tenants.

- `jti`: This is a unique identifier for the token, issued by the authorization server. The `jti` is mostly used when the access token the authorization server issues is a JWT or a self-contained access token. This is useful to avoid replaying access tokens.

While validating the response from the introspection endpoint, the resource server should first check whether the value of active is set to true. Then it should check whether the value of aud in the response matches the aud URI associated with the resource server or the resource. Finally, it can validate the scope. The required scope to access the resource should be a subset of the scope values returned in the introspection response. If the resource server wants to do further access control based on the client or the resource owner, it can do so with respect to the values of sub and client_id.

Chain Grant Type

Once the audience restriction is enforced on OAuth tokens, they can only be used against the intended audience. You can access an API with an access token that has an audience restriction corresponding to that API. If this API wants to talk to another protected API to form the response to the client, the first API must authenticate to the second API. When it does so, the first API can't just pass the access token it received initially from the client. That will fail the audience restriction validation at the second API. The Chain Grant Type OAuth 2.0 profile defines a standard way to address this concern.

According to the OAuth Chain Grant Type profile, the API hosted in the first resource server must talk to the authorization server and exchange the OAuth access token it received from the client for a new one that can be used to talk to the other API hosted in the second resource server.

Note   The Chain Grant Type for OAuth 2.0 profile is available at `https://datatracker.ietf.org/doc/draft-hunt-oauth-chain`.

The chain grant type request must be generated from the first resource server to the authorization server. The value of the grant type must be set to `http://oauth.net/grant_type/chain` and should include the OAuth access token received from the client. The scope parameter should express the required scopes for the second resource in space-delimited strings. Ideally, the scope should be the same as or a subset of the scopes associated with the original access token. If there is any difference, then the authorization server can decide whether to issue an access token or not. This decision can be based on an out-of-band agreement with the resource owner:

```
POST /token HTTP/1.1
Host: authz.server.net
Content-Type: application/x-www-form-urlencoded
grant_type=http://oauth.net/grant_type/chain
oauth_token=dsddDLJkuiiuieqjhk238khjh
scope=read
```

This returns the following JSON response. The response includes an access token with a limited lifetime, but it should not have a refresh token. To get a new access token, the first resource server once again must present the original access token:

```
HTTP/1.1 200 OK
Content-Type: application/json;charset=UTF-8
Cache-Control: no-store
```

```
Pragma: no-cache
{

        "access_token":"2YotnFZFEjr1zCsicMWpAA",
        "token_type":"Bearer",
        "expires_in":1800,

}
```

The first resource server can use the access token from this response to talk to the second resource server. Then the second resource server talks to the authorization server to validate the access token (see Figure 9-2).

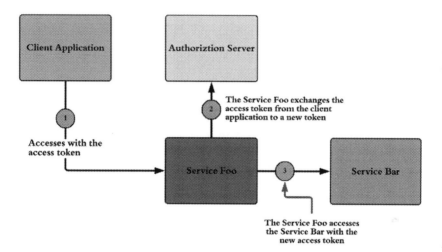

Figure 9-2. *OAuth 2.0 Token Exchange*

We talked about the chain grant type in the first edition of the book as well. But since then this specification didn't make any progress. If you are using the chain grant type already, you should migrate to the OAuth 2.0 Token Exchange specification, which is still at the draft stage, but closer to being an RFC. In the next section, we talk about OAuth 2.0 Token Exchange draft RFC.

Token Exchange

The OAuth 2.0 Token Exchange is a draft proposal discussed under the IETF working group at the moment. It solves a similar problem, which was addressed by the Chain Grant Type proposal we discussed in the previous section, with some improvements. Like in the chain grant type, when the first resource server receives an access token from the client application, and when it wants to talk to another resource server, the first resource server generates the following request to talk to the authorization server—and exchanges the access token it got from the client application to a new one.

```
POST /token HTTP/1.1
Host: authz.server.net
Content-Type: application/x-www-form-urlencoded
grant_type=urn:ietf:params:oauth:grant-type:token-exchange
subject_token=dsddDLJkuiiuieqjhk238khjh
subject_token_type=urn:ietf:params:oauth:token-type:access_token
requested_token_type=urn:ietf:params:oauth:token-type:access_token
resource=https://bar.example.com
scope=read
```

The preceding sample request does not include all possible parameters. Let's have a look at the key parameters that you could expect in a token exchange request:

- grant_type: Indicates to the token endpoint that, this is a request related to token exchange and must carry the value urn:ietf:params:oauth:grant-type:token-exchange. This is a required parameter.

- resource: The value of this parameter carries a reference to the target resource. For example, if the initial request comes to foo API, and it wants to talk to the bar API, then the value of the resource parameter carries the endpoint of the bar API. This is also quite useful in a microservices deployment, where one microservice has to authenticate to another microservice. The OAuth 2.0 authorization server can enforce access control policies against this request to check whether the foo API can access the bar API. This is an optional parameter.

- audience: The value of this parameter serves the same purpose as the resource parameter, but in this case the value of the audience parameter is a reference of the target resource, not an absolute URL. If you intend to use the same token against multiple target resources, you can include a list of audience values under the audience parameter. This is an optional parameter.

- `scope`: Indicates the scope values with respect to the new token. This parameter can carry a list of space-delimited, case-sensitive strings. This is an optional parameter.

- `requested_token_type`: Indicates the type of request token, which can be any of `urn:ietf:params:oauth:token-type:access_token`, `urn:ietf:params:oauth:token-type:refresh_token`, `urn:ietf:params:oauth:token-type:id_token`, `urn:ietf:params:oauth:token-type:saml1`, and `urn:ietf:params:oauth:token-type:saml2`. This is an optional parameter, and if it is missing, the token endpoint can decide the type of the token to return. If you use a different token type, which is not in the above list, then you can have your own URI as the `requested_token_type`.

- `subject_token`: Carries the initial token the first API receives. This carries the identity of the entity that initially invokes the first API. This is a required parameter.

- `subject_token_type`: Indicates the type of `subject_token`, which can be any of `urn:ietf:params:oauth:token-type:access_token`, `urn:ietf:params:oauth:token-type:refresh_token`, `urn:ietf:params:oauth:token-type:id_token`, `urn:ietf:params:oauth:token-type:saml1`, and `urn:ietf:params:oauth:token-type:saml2`. This is a required parameter. If you use a different token type, which is not in the above list, then you can have your own URI as the `subject_token_type`.

- `actor_token`: Carries a security token, which represents the identity of the entity that intends to use the requested token. In our case, when `foo` API wants to talk to the `bar` API, `actor_token` represents the `foo` API. This is an optional parameter.

- `actor_token_type`: Indicates the type of `actor_token`, which can be any of `urn:ietf:params:oauth:token-type:access_token`, `urn:ietf:params:oauth:token-type:refresh_token`, `urn:ietf:params:oauth:token-type:id_token`, `urn:ietf:params:oauth:token-type:saml1`, and `urn:ietf:params:oauth:token-type:saml2`. This is a required parameter when the `actor_token` is present in the request.

If you use a different token type, which is not in the above list, then
you can have your own URI as the `actor_token_type`.

The preceding request returns the following JSON response. The `access_token`
parameter in the response carries the requested token, while the `issued_token_type`
indicates its type. The other parameters in the response, `token_type`, `expires_in`, `scope`,
and `refresh_token`, carry the same meaning as in a typical OAuth 2.0 token response,
which we discussed in Chapter 4.

```
HTTP/1.1 200 OK
Content-Type: application/json
Cache-Control: no-cache, no-store

{
 "access_token":"eyJhbGciOiJFUzI1NiIsImtpZCI6IjllciJ9 ",
 "issued_token_type":
        "urn:ietf:params:oauth:token-type:access_token",
 "token_type":"Bearer",
 "expires_in":60
}
```

Dynamic Client Registration Profile

According to the OAuth 2.0 core specification, all OAuth clients must be registered with
the OAuth authorization server and obtain a client identifier before any interactions. The
aim of the Dynamic Client Registration OAuth 2.0 profile[2] is to expose an endpoint for
client registration in a standard manner to facilitate on-the-fly registrations.

The dynamic registration endpoint exposed by the authorization server can be
secured or not. If it's secured, it can be secured with OAuth, HTTP Basic authentication,
Mutual Transport Layer Security (mTLS), or any other security protocol as desired by
the authorization server. The Dynamic Client Registration profile doesn't enforce any
authentication protocols over the registration endpoint, but it must be secured with
TLS. If the authorization server decides that it should allow the endpoint to be public
and let anyone be registered, it can do so. For the registration, the client application must
pass all its metadata to the registration endpoint:

---

[2]`https://tools.ietf.org/html/rfc7591`

```
POST /register HTTP/1.1
Content-Type: application/json
Accept: application/json
Host: authz.server.com
{
"redirect_uris":["https://client.org/callback","https://client.org/
callback2"],
"token_endpoint_auth_method":"client_secret_basic",
"grant_types": ["authorization_code" , "implicit"],
"response_types": ["code" , "token"],
}
```

Let's examine the definition of some of the important parameters in the client registration request:

- redirect_uris: An array of URIs under the control of the client. The user is redirected to one of these redirect_uris after the authorization grant. These redirect URIs must be over Transport Layer Security (TLS).

- token_endpoint_auth_method: The supported authentication scheme when talking to the token endpoint. If the value is client_ secret_basic, the client sends its client ID and the client secret in the HTTP Basic Authorization header. If it's client_secret_post, the client ID and the client secret are in the HTTP POST body. If the value is none, the client doesn't want to authenticate, which means it's a public client (as in the case of the OAuth implicit grant type or when you use authorization code grant type with a single-page application). Even though this RFC only supports three client authentication methods, the other OAuth profiles can introduce their own. For example, OAuth 2.0 Mutual-TLS Client Authentication and Certificate-Bound Access Tokens, a draft RFC which is being discussed under the IETF OAuth working group at the moment, introduces a new authentication method called tls_client_auth. This indicates that client authentication to the token endpoint happens with mutual TLS.

- `grant_types`: An array of grant types supported by the client. It is always better to limit your client application only to use the grant types it needs and no more. For example, if your client application is a single-page application, then you must only use `authorization_code` grant type.

- `response_types`: An array of expected response types from the authorization server. In most of the cases, there is a correlation between the `grant_types` and `response_types`—and if you pick something inconsistent, the authorization server will reject the registration request.

- `client_name`: A human-readable name that represents the client application. The authorization server will display the client name to the end users during the login flow. This must be informative enough so that the end users will be able to figure out the client application, during the login flow.

- `client_uri`: A URL that points to the client application. The authorization server will display this URL to the end users, during the login flow in a clickable manner.

- `logo_uri`: A URL pointing to the logo of the client application. The authorization server will display the logo to the end users, during the login flow.

- `scope`: A string containing a space-separated list of scope values where the client intends to request from the authorization server.

- `contacts`: A list of representatives from the client application end.

- `tos_uri`: A URL pointing to the terms of service document of the client application. The authorization server will display this link to the end users, during the login flow.

- `policy_uri`: A URL pointing to the privacy policy document of the client application. The authorization server will display this link to the end users, during the login flow.

- `jwks_uri`: Points to the endpoint, which carries the JSON Web Key (JWK) Set document with the client's public key. Authorization server uses this public key to validate the signature of any of the requests signed by the client application. If the client application cannot host its public key via an endpoint, it can share the JWKS document under the parameter `jwks` instead of `jwks_uri`. Both the parameters must not be present in a single request.

- `software_id`: This is similar to `client_id`, but there is a major difference. The `client_id` is generated by the authorization server and mostly used to identify the application. But the `client_id` can change during the lifetime of an application. In contrast, the `software_id` is unique to the application across its lifecycle and uniquely represents all the metadata associated with it throughout the application lifecycle.

- `software_version`: The version of the client application, identified by the `software_id`.

- `software_statement`: This is a special parameter in the registration request, which carries a JSON Web Token (JWT). This JWT includes all the metadata defined earlier with respect to the client. In case the same parameter is defined in JWT and also in the request outside the `software_statement` parameter, then the parameter within the `software_statement` will take the precedence.

Based on the policies of the authorization server, it can decide whether it should proceed with the registration or not. Even if it decides to go ahead with the registration, the authorization server need not accept all the suggested parameters from the client. For example, the client may suggest using both authorization_code and implicit as grant types, but the authorization server can decide what to allow. The same is true for the token_endpoint_auth_method: the authorization server can decide what to support. The following is a sample response from the authorization server:

```
HTTP/1.1 200 OK
Content-Type: application/json
Cache-Control: no-store
Pragma: no-cache
```

```
{
"client_id":"iuyiSgfgfhffgfh",
"client_secret":"hkjhkiiu89hknhkjhuyjhk",
"client_id_issued_at":2343276600,
"client_secret_expires_at":2503286900,
"redirect_uris":["https://client.org/callback","https://client.org/callback2"],
"grant_types":"authorization_code",
"token_endpoint_auth_method":"client_secret_basic",
}
```

Let's examine the definition of each parameter:

- client_id: The generated unique identifier for the client.

- client_secret: The generated client secret corresponding to the client_id. This is optional. For example, for public clients the client_secret isn't required.

- client_id_issued_at: The number of seconds since January 1, 1970.

- client_secret_expires_at: The number of seconds since January 1, 1970 or 0 if it does not expire.

- redirect_uris: Accepted redirect_uris.

- token_endpoint_auth_method: The accepted authentication method for the token endpoint.

Note   The Dynamic Client Registration OAuth 2.0 profile is quite useful in mobile applications. Mobile client applications secured with OAuth have the client ID and the client secret baked into the application. These are the same for all the installations of a given application. If a given client secret is compromised, that will affect all the installations, and rogue client applications can be developed using the stolen keys. These rogue client applications can generate more traffic on the server and exceed the legitimate throttling limit, hence causing a denial of service attack. With dynamic client registration, you need not set the same client ID and client secret for all the installations of a give application. During the installation process, the application can talk to the authorization server's registration endpoint and generate a client ID and a client secret per installation.

Token Revocation Profile

Two parties can perform OAuth token revocation. The resource owner should be able to revoke an access token issued to a client, and the client should be able to revoke an access token or a refresh token it has acquired. The Token Revocation OAuth 2.0 profile[3] addresses the latter. It introduces a standard token-revoke endpoint at the authorization server end. To revoke an access token or a refresh token, the client must notify the revoke endpoint.

Note   In October 2013, there was an attack against Buffer (a social media management service that can be used to cross-post between Facebook, Twitter, etc.). Buffer was using OAuth to access user profiles in Facebook and Twitter. Once Buffer detected that it was under attack, it revoked all its access keys from Facebook, Twitter, and other social media sites, which prevented attackers from getting access to users' Facebook and Twitter accounts.

The client must initiate the token revocation request. The client can authenticate to the authorization server via HTTP Basic authentication (with its client ID and client secret), with mutual TLS or with any other authentication mechanism proposed by the authorization server and then talk to the revoke endpoint. The request should consist of either the access token or the refresh token and then a token_type_hint that informs the authorization server about the type of the token (access_token or refresh_token). This parameter may not be required, but the authorization server can optimize its search criteria using it.

Here is a sample request:

```
POST /revoke HTTP/1.1
Host: server.example.com
Content-Type: application/x-www-form-urlencoded
Authorization: Basic czZCaGRSdadsdI9iuiaHk99kjkh
token=dsd0lkjkkljkkllkdsdds&token_type_hint=access_token
```

---

[3]https://tools.ietf.org/html/rfc7009

In response to this request, the authorization server first must validate the client credentials and then proceed with the token revocation. If the token is a refresh token, the authorization server must invalidate all the access tokens issued for the authorization grant associated with that refresh token. If it's an access token, it's up to the authorization server to decide whether to revoke the refresh token or not. In most cases, it's ideal to revoke the refresh token, too. Once the token revocation is completed successfully, the authorization server must send an HTTP 200 status code back to the client.

Summary

- The OAuth 2.0 profiles built on top of the core framework build a security ecosystem to make OAuth 2.0 ready for enterprise grade deployments.

- OAuth 2.0 introduced two extension points via grant types and token types.

- The Token Introspection profile for OAuth 2.0 introduces a standard API at the authorization server, allowing the resource server to talk to it and retrieve token metadata.

- According to the OAuth Chain Grant Type profile, the API hosted in the first resource server must talk to the authorization server and exchange the OAuth access token it received from the client for a new one that can be used to talk to another API hosted in a second resource server.

- The OAuth 2.0 Token Exchange is a draft proposal discussed under the IETF working group at the moment, which solves a similar problem as the Chain Grant Type proposal with some improvements.

- The aim of the Dynamic Client Registration OAuth 2.0 profile is to expose an endpoint for client registration in a standard manner to facilitate on-the-fly registrations.

- The Token Revocation OAuth 2.0 profile introduces a standard token-revoke endpoint at the authorization server to revoke an access token or a refresh token by the client.

CHAPTER 10

Accessing APIs via Native Mobile Apps

The adoption of native mobile apps has increased heavily in the last few years. Within the first decade of the 21st century, the Internet users worldwide increased from 350 million to more than 2 billion and mobile phone subscribers from 750 million to 5 billion—and today it hits 6 billion, where the world population is around 7 billion. Most of the mobile devices out there–even the cheapest ones—could be used to access the Internet.

We treat a native mobile application as an untrusted or a public client. A client application, which is not capable of protecting its own keys or credentials, is identified as a public client under OAuth terminology. Since the native mobile apps run on a device owned by the user, the user who is having complete access to the mobile device can figure out any keys the application hides. This is a hard challenge we face in accessing secured APIs from a native mobile application.

In this chapter, we discuss the best practices in using OAuth 2.0 for native apps, Proof Key for Code Exchange (PKCE), which is an approach for protecting native apps from code interception attack and protecting native apps in a browser-less environment.

Mobile Single Sign-On (SSO)

It takes an average of 20 seconds for a user to log in to an application. Not having to enter a password each time a user needs to access a resource saves time and makes users more productive and also reduces the frustration of multiple login events and forgotten passwords. When we have single sign-on, the users will only have one password to remember and update and only one set of password rules to remember. Their initial login provides them with access to all the resources, typically for the entire day or the week.

© Prabath Siriwardena 2020
P. Siriwardena, *Advanced API Security*, https://doi.org/10.1007/978-1-4842-2050-4_10

If you provide multiple mobile applications for your corporate employees to access from their mobile devices, it's a pain to ask them to re-login to each application independently. Possibly all of them may be sharing the same credential store. This is analogous to a case where Facebook users log in to multiple third-party mobile applications with their Facebook credentials. With Facebook login, you only login once to Facebook and will automatically log into the other applications rely on Facebook login.

In mobile world, login to native apps is done in three different ways: directly asking for user credentials, using a WebView, and using the system browser.

Login with Direct Credentials

With this approach, the user directly provides the credentials to the native app itself (see Figure 10-1). And the app will use an API (or OAuth 2.0 password grant type) to authenticate the user. This approach assumes the native app is trusted. In case your native app uses a third-party identity provider for login, we must not use this. Even this approach may not be possible, unless the third-party identity provider provides a login API or supports OAuth 2.0 password grant type. Also this approach can make the users vulnerable for phishing attacks. An attacker can plant a phishing attack by fooling the user to install a native app with the same look and feel as the original app and then mislead the user to share his or her credentials with it. In addition to this risk, login with direct credentials does not help in building a single sign-on experience, when you have multiple native apps. You need to use your credentials to log in to each individual application.

Figure 10-1. *The Chase bank's mobile app, which users directly provide credentials for login*

Login with WebView

The native app developers use a WebView in a native app to embed the browser, so that the app can use web technologies such as HTML, JavaScript, and CSS. During the login flow, the native app loads the system browser into a WebView and uses HTTP redirects to get the user to the corresponding identity provider. For example, if you want to authenticate users with Facebook, to your native app, you load the system browser into a WebView first and then redirect the user to Facebook. What's happening in the browser loaded into the WebView is no different from the flow you see when you log in to a web app via Facebook using a browser.

The WebView-based approach was popular in building hybrid native apps, because it provides better user experience. The users won't notice the browser being loaded into the WebView. It looks like everything happens in the same native app.

It also has some major disadvantages. The web session under the browser loaded into a WebView of a native app is not shared between multiple native apps. For example, if you do login with Facebook to one native app, by redirecting the user to facebook.com via a browser loaded into a WebView, the user has to log in to Facebook again and again, when multiple native apps follow the same approach. That is because the web session created under facebook.com in one WebView is not shared with another WebView of a different native app. So the single sign-on (SSO) between native apps will not work with the WebView approach.

WebView-based native apps also make the users more vulnerable to phishing attacks. In the same example we discussed before, when a user gets redirected to facebook.com via the system browser loaded into a WebView, he or she won't be able to figure out whether they are visiting something outside the native app. So, the native app developer can trick the user by presenting something very similar to facebook.com and steal user's Facebook credentials. Due to this reason, most of the developers are now moving away from using a WebView for login.

Login with a System Browser

This approach for login into a native app is similar to what we discussed in the previous section, but instead of the WebView, the native app spins up the system browser (see Figure 10-2). System browser itself is another native app. User experience in this approach is not as smooth as with the WebView approach, as the user has to switch between two native apps during the login process, but in terms of security, this is the best approach. Also, this is the only approach we can have single sign-on experience in a mobile environment. Unlike WebView approach, when you use the system browser, it manages a single web session for the user. Say, for example, when there are multiple native apps using Facebook login via the same system browser, the users only need to log in to Facebook once. Once a web session is created under facebook.com domain with the system browser, for the subsequent login requests from other native apps, users will be logged in automatically. In the next section, we see how we can use OAuth 2.0 securely to build this use case.

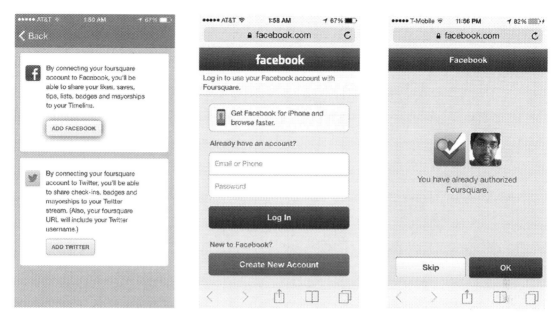

Figure 10-2. *Login to Foursquare native app using Facebook*

Using OAuth 2.0 in Native Mobile Apps

OAuth 2.0 has become the de facto standard for mobile application authentication. In our security design, we need to treat a native app a dumb application. It is very much similar to a single-page application. The following lists out the sequence of events that happen in using OAuth 2.0 to log in to a native mobile app.

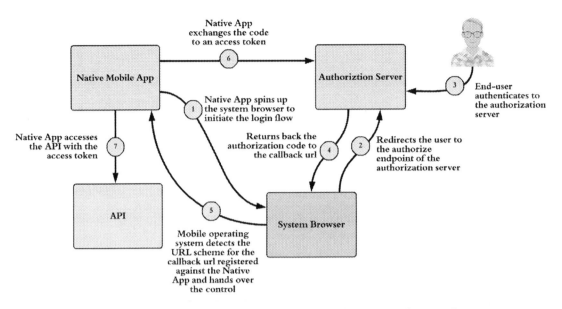

Figure 10-3. *A typical login flow for a native mobile app with OAuth 2.0*

1. Mobile app developer has to register the application with the corresponding identity provider or the OAuth 2.0 authorization server and obtain a client_id. The recommendation is to use OAuth 2.0 authorization code grant type, without a client secret. Since the native app is an untrusted client, there is no point of having a client secret. Some were using implicit grant type for native apps, but it has its own inherent security issues and not recommended any more.

2. Instead of WebView, use SFSafariViewController with iOS9+ or Chrome Custom Tabs for Android. This web controller provides all the benefits of the native system browser in a control that can be placed within an application. Then you can embed the client_id obtained from step 1 into the application. When you embed a client_id into an app, it will be the same for all the instances of that native app. If you want to differentiate each instance of the app (installed in different devices), then we can dynamically generate a client_id for each instance at the start of the app, following the protocol defined in OAuth 2.0 Dynamic Client Registration profile, which we explained in detail in Chapter 9.

3.   During the installation of the app, we need to register an app-specific custom URL scheme with the mobile operating system. This URL scheme must match the callback URL or redirect URI you used in step 1, at the time of app registration. A custom URL scheme lets the mobile operating system to pass back the control to your app from another external application, for example from the system browser. If you send some parameters to the app-specific custom URI scheme on the browser, the mobile operating system will track that and invoke the corresponding native app with those parameters.

4.   Once the user clicks login, on the native app, we need to spin up the system browser and follow the protocol defined in OAuth 2.0 authorization code grant type (see Figure 10-3), which we discussed in detail in Chapter 4.

5.   After the user authenticates to the identity provider, the browser redirects the user back to the registered redirect URI, which is in fact a custom URL scheme registered with the mobile operating system.

6.   Upon receiving the authorization code to the custom URL scheme on the system browser, the mobile operating system spins up the corresponding native app and passes over the control.

7.   The native app will talk to the token endpoint of the authorization server and exchange the authorization code to an access token.

8.   The native app uses the access token to access APIs.

Inter-app Communication

The system browser itself is another native app. We used a custom URL scheme as a way of inter-app communication to receive the authorization code from the authorization server. There are multiple ways for inter-app communication available in a mobile environment: private-use URI scheme (also known as custom URL scheme), claimed HTTPS URL scheme, and loopback URI scheme.

Private URI Schemes

In the previous section, we already discussed how a private URI scheme works. When the browser hits with a private URI scheme, it invokes the corresponding native app, registered for that URI scheme, and hands over the control. The RFC 7595[1] defines guidelines and registration procedures for URI schemes, and according to that, it is recommended to use a domain name that is under your control, in its reverse order as the private URI scheme. For example, if you own app.foo.com, then the private URI scheme should be com.foo.app. The complete private URI scheme may look like *com.foo.app:/oauth2/redirect*, and there is only one slash that appears right after the scheme component.

In the same mobile environment, the private URI schemes can collide with each other. For example, there can be two apps registered for the same URI scheme. Ideally, this should not happen if you follow the convention we discussed before while choosing an identifier. But still there is an opportunity that an attacker can use this technique to carry out a code interception attack. To prevent such attacks, we must use Proof Key for Code Exchange (PKCE) along with private URI schemes. We discuss PKCE in a later section.

Claimed HTTPS URI Scheme

Just like the private URI scheme, which we discussed in the previous section, when a browser sees a claimed HTTPS URI scheme, instead of loading the corresponding page, it hands over the control to the corresponding native app. In supported mobile operating systems, you can claim an HTTPS domain, which you have control. The complete claimed HTTPS URI scheme may look like `https://app.foo.com/oauth2/redirect`. Unlike in private URI scheme, the browser verifies the identity of the claimed HTTPS URI before redirection, and for the same reason, it is recommended to use claimed HTTPS URI scheme over others where possible.

Loopback Interface

With this approach, your native app will listen on a given port in the device itself. In other words, your native app acts as a simple web server. For example, your redirect URI will look like *http://127.0.0.1:5000/oauth2/redirect*. Since we are using the

---

[1]https://tools.ietf.org/html/rfc7595#section-3.8

loopback interface (127.0.0.1), when the browser sees this URL, it will hand over the control to the service listening on the mobile device on port 5000. The challenge with this approach is that your app may not be able to run on the same port on all the devices, if there are any other apps on the mobile device already using the same port.

Proof Key for Code Exchange (PKCE)

Proof Key for Code Exchange (PKCE) is defined in the RFC 7636 as a way to mitigate code interception attack (more details in Chapter 14) in a mobile environment. As we discussed in the previous section, when you use a custom URL scheme to retrieve the authorization code from the OAuth authorization server, there can be a case where it goes to a different app, which is also registered with the mobile device for the same custom URL scheme as the original app. An attacker can possibly do this with the intention of stealing the code.

When the authorization code gets to the wrong app, it can exchange it to an access token and then gets access to the corresponding APIs. Since we use authorization code with no client secret in mobile environments, and the client id of the original app is public, the attacker has no issue in exchanging the code to an access token by talking to the token endpoint of the authorization server.

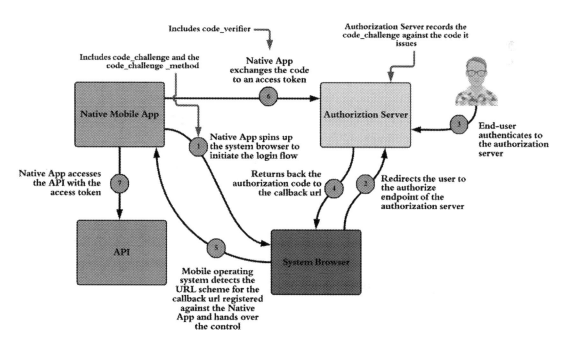

Figure 10-4. *A typical login flow for a native mobile app with OAuth 2.0 and PKCE*

Let's see how PKCE solves the code interception attack (see Figure 10-4):

1. The native mobile app, before redirecting the user to the authorization server, generates a random value, which is called the code_verifier. The value of the code_verifier must have a minimum length of 43 characters and a maximum of 128 characters.

2. Next the app has to calculate the SHA256 of the code_verifier and find its base64-url-encoded (see Appendix E) representation, with no padding. Since SHA256 hashing algorithm always results in a hash of 256 bits, when you base64-url-encode it, there will be a padding all the time, which is represented by the = sign. According to the PKCE RFC, we need to remove that padding— and that value, which is the SHA256-hashed, base64-url-encoded, unpadded code_verifier, is known as the code_challenge.

3. Now, when the native app initiates the authorization code request and redirects the user to the authorization server, it has to construct the request URL in the following manner, along with the code_challenge and the code_challenge_method query parameters. The code_challenge_method carries the name of the hashing algorithm.

   ```
   https://idp.foo.com/authorization?client_id=FFGFGOIPI7898778&s
   copeopenid&redirect_uri=com.foo.app:/oauth2/redirect&response_
   type=code&code_challenge=YzfcdAoRg7rAfj9_Fllh7XZ6BBl4PIHC-
   xoMrfqvWUc&code_challenge_method=S256"
   ```

4. At the time of issuing the authorization code, the authorization server must record the provided code_challenge against the issued authorization code. Some authorization servers may embed the code_challenge into the code itself.

5. Once the native app gets the authorization code, it can exchange the code to an access token by talking to the authorization server's token endpoint. But, when you follow PKCE, you must send the code_verifier (which is corresponding to the code_challenge) along with the token request.

```
curl -k --user "XDFHKKJURJSHJD" -d "code=XDFHKKJURJSHJD&grant_
type=authorization_code&client_id=FFGFGOIPI7898778
&redirect_uri=com.foo.app:/oauth2/redirect&code_
verifier=ewewewoiuojslkdjsd9sadoidjalskdjsdsdewewewoiuojslkd
jsd9sadoidjalskdjsdsd" https://idp.foo.com/token
```

6. If the attacker's app gets the authorization code, it still cannot
    exchange it to an access token, because only the original app
    knows the code_verifier.

7. Once the authorization server receives the code_verifier along with the
    token request, it will find the SHA256-hashed, base64-url-encoded,
    unpadded value of it and compare it with the recorded code_challenge. If
    those two match, then it will issue the access token.

Browser-less Apps

So far in this chapter, we only discussed about mobile devices, which are capable of
spinning up a web browser. There is another growing requirement to use OAuth secured
APIs from applications running on devices with input constraints and no web browser,
such as smart TVs, smart speakers, printers, and so on. In this section, we discuss how
to access OAuth 2.0 protected APIs from browser-less apps using the OAuth 2.0 device
authorization grant. In any case, the device authorization grant does not replace any
of the approaches we discussed earlier with respect to native apps running on capable
mobile devices.

OAuth 2.0 Device Authorization Grant

The OAuth 2.0 device authorization grant[2] is the RFC 8628, which is published by
the IETF OAuth working group. According to this RFC, a device to use the device
authorization grant type must satisfy the following requirements:

- The device is already connected to the Internet or to the network,
  which has access to the authorization server.

- The device is able to make outbound HTTPS requests.

---

[2]https://tools.ietf.org/html/rfc8628

- The device is able to display or otherwise communicate a URI and code sequence to the user.

- The user has a secondary device (e.g., personal computer or smartphone) from which they can process a request.

Let's see how device authorization grant works, with an example. Say we have a YouTube app running on a smart TV, and we need the smart TV to access our YouTube account on behalf of us. In this case, YouTube acts as both the OAuth authorization server and the resource server, and the YouTube app running on the smart TV is the OAuth client application.

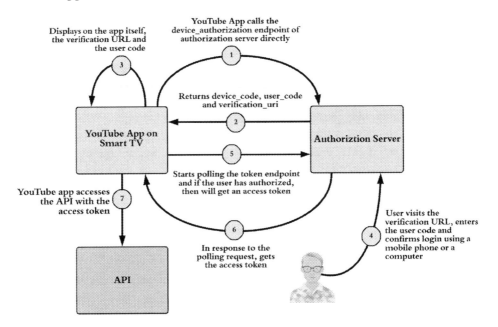

Figure 10-5. *A typical login flow for a browser-less app with OAuth 2.0*

1. The user takes the TV remote and clicks the YouTube app to associate his/her YouTube account with the app.

2. The YouTube app running on the smart TV has an embedded client ID and sends a direct HTTP request over HTTPS to the authorization server.

   ```
   POST /device_authorization HTTP/1.1
   Host: idp.youtube.com
   Content-Type: application/x-www-form-urlencoded

   client_id=XDFHKKJURJSHJD
   ```

3. In response to the preceding request, the authorization server
    returns back a device_code, a user_code, and a verification
    URI. Both the device_code and the user_code have an expiration
    time associated with them, which is communicated to the client
    app via expires_in parameter (in seconds).

```
HTTP/1.1 200 OK
Content-Type: application/json
Cache-Control: no-store
{
    "device_code": "GmRhmhcxhwAzkoEqiMEg_DnyEysNkuNhszIySk9eS",
    "user_code": "WDJB-MJHT",
    "verification_uri": "https://youtube.com/device",
    "verification_uri_complete":
                "https://youtube.com/device?user_code=WDJB-MJHT",
    "expires_in": 1800,
    "interval": 5
}
```

4. The YouTube client app instructs the user to visit the provided
    verification URI (from the preceding response) and confirm the
    authorization request with the provided user code (from the
    preceding response).

5. Now the user has to use a secondary device (a laptop or mobile
    phone) to visit the verification URI. While that action is in
    progress, the YouTube app will keep polling the authorization
    server to see whether the user has confirmed the authorization
    request. The minimum amount of time the client should wait
    before polling or the time between polling is specified by the
    authorization server in the preceding response under the
    interval parameter. The poll request to the token endpoint of the
    authorization server includes three parameters. The grant_type
    parameter must carry the value urn:ietf:params:oauth:grant-
    type:device_code, so the authorization server knows how to

process this request. The device_code parameter carries the
device code issued by the authorization server in its first response,
and the client_id parameter carries the client identifier of the
YouTube app.

```
POST /token HTTP/1.1
Host: idp.youtube.com
Content-Type: application/x-www-form-urlencoded

grant_type=urn%3Aietf%3Aparams%3Aoauth%3Agrant-type%3Adevice_code
&device_code=GmRhmhcxhwAzkoEqiMEg_DnyEysNkuNhszIySk9eS
&client_id=459691054427
```

6. The user visits the provided verification URI, enters the user code,
    and confirms the authorization request.

7. Once the user confirms the authorization request, the
    authorization server issues the following response to the request
    in step 5. This is the standard response from an OAuth 2.0
    authorization server token endpoint.

```
HTTP/1.1 200 OK
Content-Type: application/json;charset=UTF-8
Cache-Control: no-store
Pragma: no-cache
{
        "access_token":"2YotnFZFEjr1zCsicMWpAA",
        "token_type":"Bearer",
        "expires_in":3600,
        "refresh_token":"tGzv3JOkF0XG5Qx2TlKWIA",
 }
```

8. Now the YouTube app can use this access token to access the
    YouTube API on behalf of the user.

Summary

- There are multiple grant types in OAuth 2.0; however, while using OAuth 2.0 to access APIs from a native mobile app, it is recommended to use authorization code grant type, along with Proof Key for Code Exchange (PKCE).

- PKCE protects the native apps from code interception attack.

- The use of browser-less devices such as smart TVs, smart speakers, printers, and so on is gaining popularity.

- The OAuth 2.0 device authorization grant defines a standard flow to use OAuth 2.0 from a browser-less device and gain access to APIs.

CHAPTER 11

OAuth 2.0 Token Binding

Most of the OAuth 2.0 deployments do rely upon bearer tokens. A bearer token is like "cash." If I steal 10 bucks from you, I can use it at a Starbucks to buy a cup of coffee—no questions asked. I do not need to prove that I own the ten-dollar note. Unlike cash, if I use my credit card, I need to prove the possession. I need to prove I own it. I need to sign to authorize the transaction, and it's validated against the signature on the card. The bearer tokens are like cash—once stolen, an attacker can use it to impersonate the original owner. Credit cards are like proof of possession (PoP) tokens.

OAuth 2.0 recommends using Transport Layer Security (TLS) for all the interactions between the client, authorization server, and resource server. This makes the OAuth 2.0 model quite simple with no complex cryptography involved—but at the same time, it carries all the risks associated with a bearer token. There is no second level of defense. Also not everyone is fully bought into the idea of using OAuth 2.0 bearer tokens—just trusting the underlying TLS communication. I've met several people—mostly from the financial domain—who are reluctant to use OAuth 2.0, just because of the bearer tokens.

An attacker may attempt to eavesdrop authorization code/access token/refresh token (see Chapter 4 for details) in transit from the authorization server to the client, using any of the following means:

- Malware installed in the browser (public clients).

- Browser history (public clients/URI fragments).

- Intercept the TLS communication between the client and the authorization server or the resource server (exploiting the vulnerabilities in the TLS layer like Heartbleed and Logjam).

© Prabath Siriwardena 2020
P. Siriwardena, *Advanced API Security*, https://doi.org/10.1007/978-1-4842-2050-4_11

- TLS is point to point (not end to end)—an attacker having access to a proxy server could simply log all the tokens. Also, in many production deployments, the TLS connection is terminated at the edge, and from there onward, it's either a new TLS connection or a plain HTTP connection. In either case, as soon as a token leaves the channel, it's no more secure.

Understanding Token Binding

OAuth 2.0 token binding proposal cryptographically binds security tokens to the TLS layer, preventing token export and replay attacks. It relies on TLS—and since it binds the tokens to the TLS connection itself, anyone who steals a token cannot use it over a different channel.

We can break down the token binding protocol into three main phases (see Figure 11-1).

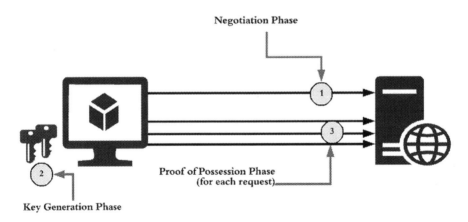

Figure 11-1. *Three main phases in the token binding protocol*

Token Binding Negotiation

During the negotiation phase, the client and the server negotiate a set of parameters to use for token binding between them. This is independent of the application layer protocols—as it happens during the TLS handshake (see Appendix C). We discuss more about this in the next section. The token binding negotiation is defined in the RFC 8472. Keep in mind we do not negotiate any keys in this phase, only the metadata.

Key Generation

During the key generation phase, the client generates a key pair according to the parameters negotiated in the negotiation phase. The client will have a key pair for each host it talks to (in most of the cases).

Proof of Possession

During the proof of possession phase, the client uses the keys generated in the key generation phase to prove the possession. Once the keys are agreed upon, in the key generation phase, the client proves the possession of the key by signing the exported keying material (EKM) from the TLS connection. The RFC 5705 allows an application to get additional application-specific keying material derived from the TLS master secret (see Appendix C). The RFC 8471 defines the structure of the token binding message, which includes the signature and other key materials, but it does not define how to carry the token binding message from the client to the server. It's up to the higher-level protocols to define it. The RFC 8473 defines how to carry the token binding message over an HTTP connection (see Figure 11-2).

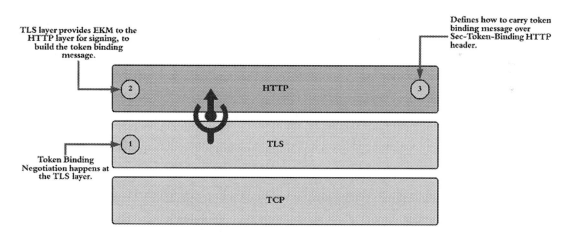

Figure 11-2. *The responsibilities of each layer in a token binding flow*

TLS Extension for Token Binding Protocol Negotiation

To bind security tokens to the TLS connection, the client and the server need to first agree upon the token binding protocol (we'll discuss about this later) version and the parameters (signature algorithm, length) related to the token binding key. This is accomplished by a new TLS extension without introducing additional network roundtrips in TLS 1.2 and earlier versions.

The token binding protocol version reflects the protocol version defined by the Token Binding Protocol (RFC 8471)—and the key parameters are defined by the same specification itself.

The client uses the Token Binding TLS extension to indicate the highest supported token binding protocol version and key parameters. This happens with the Client Hello message in the TLS handshake. To support the token binding specification, both the client and the server should support the token binding protocol negotiation extension.

The server uses the Token Binding TLS extension to indicate the support for the token binding protocol and to select the protocol version and key parameters. The server that supports token binding and receives a Client Hello message containing the Token Binding extension will include the Token Binding extension in the Server Hello if the required conditions are satisfied.

If the Token Binding extension is included in the Server Hello and the client supports the token binding protocol version selected by the server, it means that the version and key parameters have been negotiated between the client and the server and shall be definitive for the TLS connection. If the client does not support the token binding protocol version selected by the server, then the connection proceeds without token binding.

Every time a new TLS connection is negotiated (TLS handshake) between the client and the server, a token binding negotiation happens too. Even though the negotiation happens repeatedly by the TLS connection, the token bindings (you will learn more about this later) are long-lived; they encompass multiple TLS connections and TLS sessions between a given client and server.

In practice, Nginx (`https://github.com/google/ngx_token_binding`) and Apache (`https://github.com/zmartzone/mod_token_binding`) have support for token binding. An implementation of Token Binding Protocol Negotiation TLS Extension in Java is available here: `https://github.com/pingidentity/java10-token-binding-negotiation`.

Key Generation

The Token Binding Protocol specification (RFC 8471) defines the parameters related to key generation. These are the ones agreed upon during the negotiation phase.

- If *rsa2048_pkcs1.5* key parameter is used during the negotiation phase, then the signature is generated using the RSASSA-PKCS1-v1_5 signature scheme as defined in RFC 3447 with SHA256 as the hash function.

- If *rsa2048_pss* key parameter is used during the negotiation phase, then the signature is generated using the RSASSA-PSS signature scheme as defined in RFC 3447 with SHA256 as the hash function.

- If ecdsap256 key parameter is used during the negotiation phase, the signature is generated with ECDSA using Curve P-256 and SHA256 as defined in ANSI.X9–62.2005 and FIPS.186–4.2013.

In case a browser acts as the client, then the browser itself has to generate the keys and maintain them against the hostname of the server. You can find the status of this feature development for Chrome from here (`www.chromestatus.com/feature/5097603234529280`). Then again the token binding is not only for a browser, it's useful in all the interactions between a client and a server—irrespective of the client being thin or thick.

Proof of Possession

A token binding is established by a user agent (or the client) generating a private/public key pair (possibly, within a secure hardware module, such as trusted platform module (TPM)) per target server, providing the public key to the server, and proving the possession of the corresponding private key, on every TLS connection to the server. The generated public key is reflected in the token binding ID between the client and the server. At the server end, the verification happens in two steps.

First, the server receiving the token binding message needs to verify that the key parameters in the message match with the token binding parameters negotiated and then validate the signature contained in the token binding message. All the key parameters and the signature are embedded into the token binding message.

247

The structure of the token binding message is defined in the Token Binding Protocol specification (RFC 8471). A token binding message can have multiple token bindings (see Figure 11-3). A given token binding includes the token binding ID, the type of the token binding (provided or referred—we'll talk about this later), extensions, and the signature over the concatenation of exported keying material (EKM) from the TLS layer, token binding type, and key parameters. The token binding ID reflects the derived public key along with the key parameters agreed upon the token binding negotiation.

Once the TLS connection is established between a client and a server, the EKM will be the same—both at the client end and at the server end. So, to verify the signature, the server can extract the EKM from the underneath TLS connection and use the token binding type and key parameters embedded into the token binding message itself. The signature is validated against the embedded public key (see Figure 11-3).

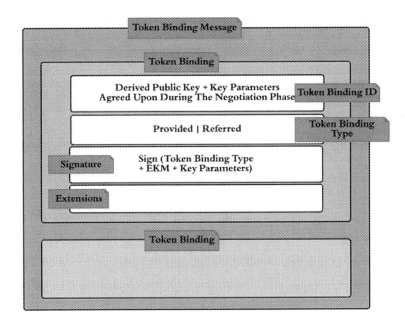

Figure 11-3. *The structure of the token binding message*

How to carry the token binding message from the client to the server is not defined in the Token Binding Protocol specification, but in the Token Binding for HTTP specification or the RFC 8473. In other words, the core token binding specification lets the higher-level protocols make the decision on that. The Token Binding for HTTP specification introduces a new HTTP header called *Sec-Token-Binding*—and it carries the base64url-encoded value of the token binding message. The *Sec-Token-Binding* header field MUST NOT be included in HTTP responses—MUST include only once in an HTTP request.

Once the token binding message is accepted as valid, the next step is to make sure that the security tokens carried in the corresponding HTTP connection are bound to it. Different security tokens can be transported over HTTP—for example, cookies and OAuth 2.0 tokens. In the case of OAuth 2.0, how the authorization code, access token, and refresh token are bound to the HTTP connection is defined in the OAuth 2.0 Token Binding specification (`https://tools.ietf.org/html/draft-ietf-oauth-token-binding-08`).

Token Binding for OAuth 2.0 Refresh Token

Let's see how the token binding works for OAuth 2.0 refresh tokens. A refresh token, unlike authorization code and access token, is only used between the client and the authorization server. Under the OAuth 2.0 authorization code grant type, the client first gets the authorization code and then exchanges it to an access token and a refresh token by talking to the token endpoint of the OAuth 2.0 authorization server (see Chapter 4 for details). The following flow assumes the client has already got the authorization code (see Figure 11-4).

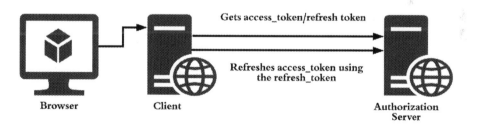

Figure 11-4. *OAuth 2.0 refresh grant type*

1. The connection between the client and the authorization server must be on TLS.

2. The client which supports OAuth 2.0 token binding, during the TLS handshake itself, negotiates the required parameters with the authorization server, which too supports OAuth 2.0 token binding.

3.   Once the TLS handshake is completed, the OAuth 2.0 client will
     generate a private key and a public key and will sign the exported
     keying material (EKM) from the underlying TLS connection
     with the private key—and builds the token binding message. (To
     be precise, the client will sign EKM + token binding type + key
     parameters.)

4.   The base64url-encoded token binding message will be added
     as the value to the Sec-Token-Binding HTTP header to the
     connection between the client and the OAuth 2.0 authorization
     server.

5.   The client will send a standard OAuth request to the token
     endpoint along with the Sec-Token-Binding HTTP header.

6.   The authorization server validates the value of Sec-Token-Binding
     header, including the signature, and records the token binding
     ID (which is also included in the token binding message) against
     the issued refresh token. To make the process stateless, the
     authorization server can include the hash of the token binding
     ID into the refresh token itself—so it does not need to remember/
     store it separately.

7.   Later, the OAuth 2.0 client tries to use the refresh token against the
     same token endpoint to refresh the access token. Now, the client
     has to use the same private key and public key pair used before
     to generate the token binding message and, once again, includes
     the base64url-encoded value of it to the Sec-Token-Binding HTTP
     header. The token binding message has to carry the same token
     binding ID as in the case where the refresh token was originally
     issued.

8.   The OAuth 2.0 authorization server now must validate the Sec-
     Token-Binding HTTP header and then needs to make sure that
     the token binding ID in the binding message is the same as the
     original token binding ID attached to the refresh token in the
     same request. This check will make sure that the refresh token
     cannot be used outside the original token binding. In case the
     authorization server decides to embed the hashed value of the

token binding ID to the refresh token itself, now it has to calculate the hash of the token binding ID in the Sec-Token-Binding HTTP header and compare it with what is embedded into the refresh token.

9. If someone steals the refresh token and is desperate to use it outside the original token binding, then he/she also has to steal the private/public key pair corresponding to the connection between the client and the server.

There are two types of token bindings—and what we discussed with respect to the refresh token is known as provided token binding. This is used when the token exchange happens directly between the client and the server. The other type is known as referred token binding, which is used when requesting tokens, which are intended to present to a different server—for example, the access token. The access token is issued in a connection between the client and the authorization server—but used in a connection between the client and the resource server.

Token Binding for OAuth 2.0 Authorization Code/Access Token

Let's see how the token binding works for access tokens, under the authorization code grant type. Under the OAuth 2.0 authorization code grant type, the client first gets the authorization code via the browser (user agent) and then exchanges it to an access token and a refresh token by talking to the token endpoint of the OAuth 2.0 authorization server (see Figure 11-5).

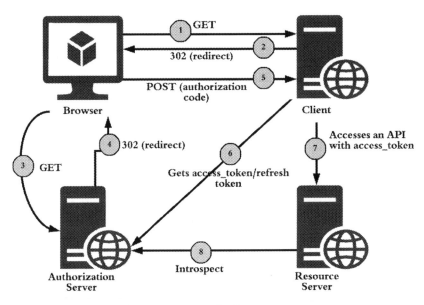

Figure 11-5. *OAuth 2.0 authorization code flow*

1.   When the end user clicks the login link on the OAuth 2.0 client
     application on the browser, the browser has to do an HTTP GET
     to the client application (which is running on a web server), and
     the browser has to establish a TLS connection with the OAuth
     2.0 client first. The browser, which supports OAuth 2.0 token
     binding, during the TLS handshake itself, negotiates the required
     parameters with the client application, which too supports OAuth
     2.0 token binding. Once the TLS handshake is completed, the
     browser will generate a private key and public key (for the client
     domain) and will sign the exported keying material (EKM) from
     the underlying TLS connection with the private key—and builds
     the token binding message. The base64url-encoded token binding
     message will be added as the value to the *Sec-Token-Binding* HTTP
     header to the connection between the browser and the OAuth 2.0
     client—which is the HTTP GET.

2.   In response to step 1 (assuming all the token binding validations
     are done), the client will send a 302 response to the browser, asking
     to redirect the user to the OAuth 2.0 authorization server. Also in
     the response, the client will include the HTTP header **Include-
     Referred-Token-Binding-ID**, which is set to *true*. This instructs the

browser to include the token binding ID established between the browser and the client in the request to the authorization server. Also, the client application will include two additional parameters in the request: **code_challenge** and **code_challenge_method**. These parameters are defined in the Proof Key for Code Exchange (PKCE) or RFC 7636 for OAuth 2.0. Under token binding, these two parameters will carry static values, **code_challenge=referred_tb** and **code_challenge_method=referred_tb**.

3. The browser, during the TLS handshake itself, negotiates the required parameters with the authorization server. Once the TLS handshake is completed, the browser will generate a private key and public key (for the authorization server domain) and will sign the exported keying material (EKM) from the underlying TLS connection with the private key—and builds the token binding message. The client will send the standard OAuth request to the authorization endpoint along with the *Sec-Token-Binding* HTTP header. This *Sec-Token-Binding* HTTP header now includes two token bindings (in one token binding message—see Figure 11-3), one for the connection between the browser and the authorization server, and the other one is for the browser and the client application (referred binding).

4. The authorization server redirects the user back to the OAuth client application via browser—along with the authorization code. The authorization code is issued against the token binding ID in the referred token binding.

5. The browser will do a POST to the client application, which also includes the authorization code from the authorization server. The browser will use the same token binding ID established between itself and the client application—and adds the *Sec-Token-Binding* HTTP header.

6. Once the client application gets the authorization code (and given that the *Sec-Token-Binding* validation is successful), it will now talk to the authorization server's token endpoint.

Prior to that, the client has to establish a token binding with the authorization server. The token request will also include the code_verifier parameter (defined in the PKCE RFC), which will carry the provided token binding ID between the client and the browser—which is also the token binding ID attached to the authorization code. Since the access token, which will be issued by the authorization server, is going to be used against a protected resource, the client has to include the token binding between itself and the resource server into this token binding message as a referred binding. Upon receiving the token request, the OAuth 2.0 authorization server now must validate the *Sec-Token-Binding* HTTP header and then needs to make sure that the token binding ID in the **code_verifier** parameter is the same as the original token binding ID attached to the authorization code at the point of issuing it. This check will make sure that the code cannot be used outside the original token binding. Then the authorization server will issue an access token, which is bound to the referred token binding, and a refresh token, which is bound to the connection between the client and the authorization server.

7. The client application now invokes an API in the resource server passing the access token. This will carry the token binding between the client and the resource server.

8. The resource server will now talk to the introspection endpoint of the authorization server—and it will return back the binding ID attached to the access token, so the resource server can check whether it's the same binding ID used between itself and the client application.

TLS Termination

Many production deployments do include a reverse proxy—which terminates the TLS connection. This can be at an Apache or Nginx server sitting between the client and the server. Once the connection is terminated at the reverse proxy, the server has no clue what happened at the TLS layer. To make sure the security tokens are bound to the incoming TLS connection, the server has to know the token binding ID. The *HTTPS Token Binding with TLS Terminating Reverse Proxies,* the draft specification (https:// tools.ietf.org/html/draft-ietf-tokbind-ttrp-09), standardizes how the binding IDs are passed from the reverse proxy to the back-end server, as HTTP headers. The **Provided-Token-Binding-ID** and **Referred-Token-Binding-ID** HTTP headers are introduced by this specification (see Figure 11-6).

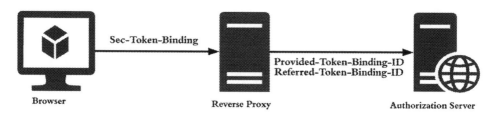

Figure 11-6.   The reverse proxy passes the Provided-Token-Binding-ID and Referred-Token-Binding-ID HTTP headers to the backend server

Summary

- OAuth 2.0 token binding proposal cryptographically binds security tokens to the TLS layer, preventing token export and replay attacks.

- Token binding relies on TLS—and since it binds the tokens to the TLS connection itself, anyone who steals a token cannot use it over a different channel.

- We can break down the token binding protocol into three main phases: negotiation phase, key generation phase, and proof of possession phase.

- During the negotiation phase, the client and the server negotiate a set of parameters to use for token binding between them.

- During the key generation phase, the client generates a key pair according to the parameters negotiated in the negotiation phase.

- During the proof of possession phase, the client uses the keys generated in the key generation phase to prove the possession.

CHAPTER 12

Federating Access to APIs

One of the research performed by Quocirca (analyst and research company) confirms that many businesses now have more external users who interact with enterprise applications than internal ones. In Europe, 58% of businesses transact directly with users from other firms and/or consumers. In the United Kingdom alone, the figure is 65%.

If you look at recent history, most enterprises today grow via acquisitions, mergers, and partnerships. In the United States alone, the volume of mergers and acquisitions totaled $865.1 billion in the first nine months of 2013, according to Dealogic. That's a 39% increase over the same period of the previous year and the highest nine-month total since 2008. What does this mean for securing APIs? You need to have the ability to deal with multiple heterogeneous security systems across borders.

Enabling Federation

Federation, in the context of API security, is about propagating user identities across distinct identity management systems or distinct enterprises. Let's start with a simple use case where you have an API exposed to your partners. How would you authenticate users for this API from different partners? These users belong to the external partners and are managed by them. HTTP Basic authentication won't work. You don't have access to the external users' credentials, and, at the same time, your partners won't expose an LDAP or a database connection outside their firewall to external parties. Asking for usernames and passwords simply doesn't work in a federation scenario. Would OAuth 2.0 work? To access an API secured with OAuth, the client must present an access token issued by the owner of the API or issued by an entity that your API trusts. Users from external parties have to authenticate first with the OAuth authorization server that the API trusts and then obtain an access token. Ideally, the authorization server the API trusts is from the same domain as the API.

Neither the authorization code grant type nor the implicit grant type mandates how to authenticate users at the authorization server. It's up to the authorization server to

257

© Prabath Siriwardena 2020
P. Siriwardena, *Advanced API Security*, https://doi.org/10.1007/978-1-4842-2050-4_12

decide. If the user is local to the authorization server, then it can use a username and password or any other direct authentication protocol. If the user is from an external entity, then you have to use some kind of brokered authentication.

Brokered Authentication

With brokered authentication, at the time of authentication, the local authorization server (running in the same domain as the API) does not need to trust each and every individual user from external parties. Instead, it can trust a broker from a given partner domain (see Figure 12-1). Each partner should have a trust broker whose responsibility is to authenticate its own users (possibly through direct authentication) and then pass the authentication decision back to the local OAuth authorization server in a reliable and trusted manner. In practice, an identity provider running in the user's (in our case, the partner employees') home domain plays the role of a trust broker.

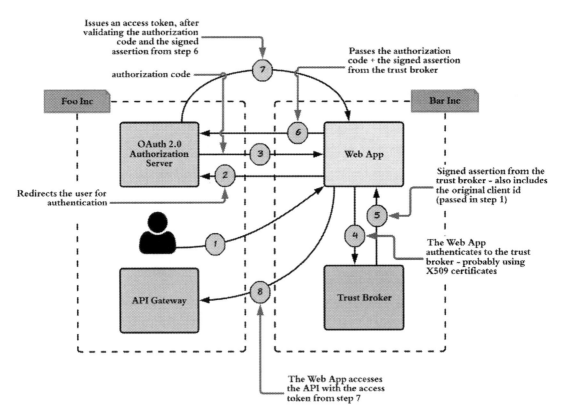

Figure 12-1. *Brokered authentication for OAuth client applications*

The trust relationship between the brokers from partners and the local OAuth authorization server (or between two federation domains) must be established out of band. In other words, it has to be established with a prior agreement between two parties. In most scenarios, trust between different entities is established through X.509 certificates. Let's walk through a sample brokered authentication use case.

Going back to OAuth principles, you need to deal with four entities in a federation scenario: the resource owner, the resource server, the authorization server, and the client application. All these entities can reside in the same domain or in different ones.

Let's start with the simplest scenario first. The resource owner (user), resource server (API gateway), and authorization server are in a single domain, and the client application (web app) is in a different domain. For example, you're an employee of Foo Inc. and want to access a web application hosted by Bar Inc. (see Figure 12-1). Once you log in to a web application at Bar Inc., it needs to access an API hosted in Foo Inc. on your behalf. Using OAuth terminology, you're the resource owner, and the API is hosted in the resource server. Both you and API are from the Foo domain. The web application hosted by Bar Inc. is the OAuth client application.

Figure 12-1 illustrates how brokered authentication works for an OAuth client application.

- The resource owner (user) from Foo Inc. visits the web application at Bar Inc. (step 1).

- To authenticate the user, the web application redirects the user to the OAuth authorization server at Foo Inc., which is also the home domain of the resource owner (step 2). To use the OAuth authorization code grant type, the web application also needs to pass its client ID along with the authorization code grant request during the redirection. At this time, the authorization server won't authenticate the client application but only validates its existence. In a federation scenario, the authorization server does not need to trust each and every individual application (or OAuth client); rather, it trusts the corresponding domain. The authorization server accepts authorization grant requests from any client that belongs to a trusted domain. This also avoids the cost of client registration. You don't need to register each client application from Bar Inc.—instead, you can build a trust relationship between the authorization server from

Foo Inc. and the trust broker from Bar Inc. During the authorization code grant phase, the authorization server only needs to record the client ID. It doesn't need to validate the client's existence.

Note   The OAuth client identifier (ID) isn't treated as a secret. It's publicly visible to anyone.

- Once the client application gets the authorization code from the authorization server (step 3), the next step is to exchange it for a valid access token. This step requires client authentication.

- Because the authorization server doesn't trust each individual application, the web application must first authenticate to its own trust broker in its own domain (step 4) and get a signed assertion (step 5). This signed assertion can be used as a token of proof against the authorization server in Foo Inc.

- The authorization server validates the signature of the assertion and, if it's signed by an entity it trusts, returns the corresponding access token to the client application (steps 6 and 7).

- The client application can use the access token to access the APIs in Foo Inc. on behalf of the resource owner (step 8), or it can talk to a user endpoint at Foo Inc. to get more information about the user.

Note   The definition of *assertion*, according to the Oxford English Dictionary, is "a confident and forceful statement of fact or belief." The fact or belief here is that the entity that brings this assertion is an authenticated entity at the trust broker. If the assertion isn't signed, anyone in the middle can alter it. Once the trust broker (or the asserting party) signs the assertion with its private key, no one in the middle can alter it. If it's altered, any alterations can be detected at the authorization server during signature validation. The signature is validated using the corresponding public key of the trust broker.

Security Assertion Markup Language (SAML)

Security Assertion Markup Language (SAML) is an OASIS standard for exchanging authentication, authorization, and identity-related data between interested parties in an XML-based data format. SAML 1.0 was adopted as an OASIS standard in 2002, and in 2003 SAML 1.1 was ratified as an OASIS standard. At the same time, the Liberty Alliance donated its Identity Federation Framework to OASIS. SAML 2.0 became an OASIS standard in 2005 by converging SAML 1.1, Liberty Alliance's Identity Federation Framework, and Shibboleth 1.3. SAML 2.0 has four basic elements:

- *Assertions*: `Authentication`, `Authorization`, and `Attribute` assertions.

- *Protocol*: `Request` and `Response` elements to package SAML assertions.

- *Bindings*: How to transfer SAML messages between interested parties. HTTP binding and SOAP binding are two examples. If the trust broker uses a SOAP message to transfer a SAML assertion, then it has to use the SOAP binding for SAML.

- *Profiles*: How to aggregate the assertions, protocol, and bindings to address a specific use case. A SAML 2.0 Web Single Sign-On (SSO) profile defines a standard way to establish SSO between different service providers via SAML.

Note   The blog post at `http://blog.facilelogin.com/2011/11/depth-of-saml-saml-summary.html` provides a high-level overview of SAML.

SAML 2.0 Client Authentication

To achieve client authentication with the SAML 2.0 profile for OAuth 2.0, you can use the parameter `client_assertion_type` with the value `urn:ietf:params:oauth:client-assertion-type:saml2-bearer` in the access token request (see step 6 in Figure 12-1). The OAuth flow starts from step 2.

Now let's dig into each step. The following shows a sample authorization code grant request initiated by the web application at Bar Inc.:

```
GET /authorize?response_type=code
                &client_id=wiuo879hkjhkjhk3232
                &state=xyz
                &redirect_uri=https://bar.com/cb
HTTP/1.1
Host: auth.foo.com
```

This results in the following response, which includes the requested authorization code:

```
HTTP/1.1 302 Found
Location: https://bar.com/cb?code=SplwqeZQwqwKJjklje&state=xyz
```

So far it's the normal OAuth authorization code flow. Now the web application has to talk to the trust broker in its own domain to obtain a SAML assertion. This step is outside the scope of OAuth. Because this is machine-to-machine authentication (from the web application to the trust broker), you can use a SOAP-based WS-Trust protocol to obtain the SAML assertion or any other protocol like OAuth 2.0 Token Delegation profile, which we discussed in Chapter 9. The web application does not need to do this each time a user logs in; it can be one-time operation that is governed by the lifetime of the SAML assertion. The following is a sample SAML assertion obtained from the trust broker:

```
<saml:Assertion >
      <saml:Issuer>bar.com</saml:Issuer>
      <ds:Signature>
        <ds:SignedInfo></ds:SignedInfo>
        <ds:SignatureValue></ds:SignatureValue>
        <ds:KeyInfo></ds:KeyInfo>
      </ds:Signature>
      <saml:Subject>
            <saml:NameID>18982198kjk2121</saml:NameID>
            <saml:SubjectConfirmation>
            <saml:SubjectConfirmationData
                    NotOnOrAfter="2019-10-05T19:30:14.654Z"
                    Recipient="https://foo.com/oauth2/token"/>
```

```
            </saml:SubjectConfirmation>
        </saml:Subject>
        <saml:Conditions
                NotBefore="2019-10-05T19:25:14.654Z"
                NotOnOrAfter="2019-10-05T19:30:14.654Z">
                <saml:AudienceRestriction>
                    <saml:Audience>
                        https://foo.com/oauth2/token
                    </saml:Audience>
                </saml:AudienceRestriction>
        </saml:Conditions>
        <saml:AuthnStatement AuthnInstant="2019-10-05T19:25:14.655Z">
                <saml:AuthnContext>
                    <saml:AuthnContextClassRef>
                        urn:oasis:names:tc:SAML:2.0:ac:classes:unspecified
                    </saml:AuthnContextClassRef>
                </saml:AuthnContext>
        </saml:AuthnStatement>
    </saml:Assertion>
</saml:Assertion>
```

To use this SAML assertion in an OAuth flow to authenticate the client, it must adhere to the following rules:

- The assertion must have a unique identifier for the `Issuer` element, which identifies the token-issuing entity. In this case, the broker of the Bar Inc.

- The assertion must have a `NameID` element inside the `Subject` element that uniquely identifies the client application (web app). This is treated as the client ID of the client application at the authorization server.

- The `SubjectConfirmation` method must be set to `urn:oasis:names:tc:SAML:2.0:cm:bearer`.

- If the assertion issuer authenticates the client, then the assertion must have a single `AuthnStatement`.

Note   WS-Trust is an OASIS standard for SOAP message security. WS-Trust, which is built on top of the WS-Security standard, defines a protocol to exchange identity information that is wrapped in a token (SAML), between two trust domains. The blog post at `http://blog.facilelogin.com/2010/05/ws-trust-with-fresh-banana-service.html` explains WS-Trust at a high level. The latest WS-Trust specification is available at `http://docs.oasis-open.org/ws-sx/ws-trust/v1.4/errata01/ws-trust-1.4-errata01-complete.html`.

Once the client web application gets the SAML assertion from the trust broker, it has to base64url-encode the assertion and send it to the authorization server along with the access token request. In the following sample HTTP POST message, `client_assertion_type` is set to `urn:ietf:params:oauth:client-assertion-type:saml2-bearer`, and the base64url-encoded (see Appendix E) SAML assertion is set to the `client_assertion` parameter:

```
POST /token HTTP/1.1
Host: auth.foo.com
Content-Type: application/x-www-form-urlencoded
grant_type=authorization_code&code=SplwqeZQwqwKJjklje
&client_assertion_type=urn:ietf:params:oauth:client-assertion-type:saml2-
bearer
&client_assertion=HdsjkkbKLew...[omitted for brevity]...OT
```

Once the authorization server receives the access token request, it validates the SAML assertion. If it's valid (signed by a trusted party), an access token is issued, along with a refresh token.

SAML Grant Type for OAuth 2.0

The previous section explained how to use a SAML assertion to authenticate a client application. That is one federation use case that falls under the context of OAuth. There the trust broker was running inside Bar Inc., where the client application was running. Let's consider a use case where the resource server (API), the authorization server, and the client application run in the same domain (Bar Inc.), while the user is from an outside domain (Foo Inc.). Here the end user authenticates to the web application with a SAML assertion (see Figure 12-2). A trust broker (a SAML identity provider) in the user's domain issues this assertion. The client application uses this assertion to talk to the local authorization server to obtain an access token to access an API on behalf of the logged-in user.

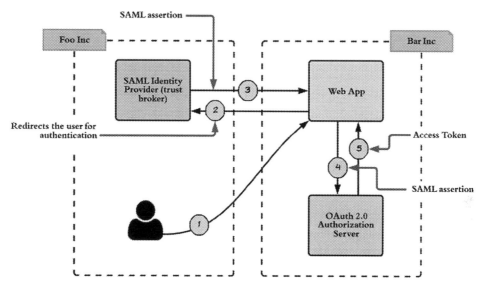

Figure 12-2. *Brokered authentication with the SAML grant type for OAuth 2.0*

Figure 12-2 illustrates how brokered authentication with a SAML grant type for OAuth 2.0 works.

- The first three steps are outside the scope of OAuth. The resource owner first logs in to the web application owned by Bar Inc. via SAML 2.0 Web SSO.

- The SAML 2.0 Web SSO flow is initiated by the web application by redirecting the user to the SAML identity provider at Foo Inc. (step 2).

- Once the user authenticates to the SAML identity provider, the SAML identity provider creates a SAML response (which wraps the assertion) and sends it back to the web application (step 3). The web application validates the signature in the SAML assertion and, if a trusted identity provider signs it, allows the user to log in to the web application.

- Once the user logs in to the web application, the web application has to exchange the SAML assertion for an access token by talking to its own internal authorization server (steps 4 and 5). The way to do this is defined in the SAML 2.0 Profile for OAuth 2.0 Client Authentication and Authorization Grants specification (RFC 7522).

The following is a sample POST message from the web application to the authorization server. There the value of `grant_type` must be `urn:ietf:params:oauth:grant-type:saml2-bearer`, and the base64url-encoded SAML assertion is set as the value of the `assertion` parameter:

Note   No refresh tokens are issued under the SAML Bearer grant type. The lifetime of the access token should not exceed the lifetime of the SAML bearer assertion by a significant amount.

```
POST /token HTTP/1.1
Host: auth.bar.com
Content-Type: application/x-www-form-urlencoded
grant_type=urn:ietf:params:oauth:grant-type:saml2-bearer
&assertion=QBNhbWxwOl...[omitted for brevity]...OT4
```

This request is validated at the authorization server. The SAML assertion is once again validated via its signature; and, if a trusted identity provider signs it, the authorization server issues a valid access token.

The scope of the access token issued under the SAML Bearer grant type should be set out of band by the resource owner. *Out of band* here indicates that the resource owner makes a pre-agreement with the resource server/authorization server with respect to the scope associated with a given resource when the SAML grant type is being used. The client application can include a scope parameter in the authorization grant request, but the value of the scope parameter must be a subset of the scope defined out of band by the resource owner. If no scope parameter is included in the authorization grant request, then the access token inherits the scope set out of band.

Both federation use cases discussed assume that the resource server and the authorization server are running in the same domain. If that isn't the case, the resource server must invoke an API exposed by the authorization server to validate the access token at the time the client tries to access a resource. If the authorization server supports the OAuth Introspection specification (discussed in Chapter 9), the resource server can talk to the introspection endpoint and find out whether the token is active or not and also what scopes are associated with the token. The resource server can then check whether the token has the required set of scopes to access the resource.

JWT Grant Type for OAuth 2.0

The JSON Web Token (JWT) profile for OAuth 2.0, which is defined in the RFC 7523, extends the OAuth 2.0 core specification by defining its own authorization grant type and a client authentication mechanism. An authorization grant in OAuth 2.0 is an abstract representation of the temporary credentials granted to the OAuth 2.0 client by the resource owner to access a resource. The OAuth 2.0 core specification defines four grant types: authorization code, implicit, resource owner password, and client credentials. Each of these grant types defines in a unique way how the resource owner can grant delegated access to a resource he/she owns to an OAuth 2.0 client. The JWT grant type, which we discuss in this chapter, defines how to exchange a JWT for an OAuth 2.0 access token. In addition to the JWT grant type, the RFC 7523 also defines a way to authenticate an OAuth 2.0 client in its interactions with an OAuth 2.0 authorization server. OAuth 2.0 does not define a concrete way for client authentication, even though in most of the cases it's the HTTP Basic authentication with client id and the client secret. The RFC 7523 defines a way to authenticate an OAuth 2.0 client using a JWT.

The JWT authorization grant type assumes that the client is in possession with a JWT. This JWT can be a self-issued JWT or a JWT obtained from an identity provider. Based on who signs the JWT, one can differentiate a self-issued JWT from an identity provider–issued JWT. The client itself signs a self-issued JWT, while an identity provider signs the identity provider–issued JWT. In either case, the OAuth authorization server must trust the issuer of the JWT. The following shows a sample JWT authorization grant request, where the value of the grant_type parameter is set to urn:ietf:params:oauth:grant-type:jwt-bearer.

```
POST /token HTTP/1.1
Host: auth.bar.com
Content-Type: application/x-www-form-urlencoded
```

```
grant_type=urn%3Aietf%3Aparams%3Aoauth%3Agrant-type%3Ajwt-bearer&assertion=
eyJhbGciOiJFUzI1NiIsImtpZCI6IjE2InO.
eyJpc3Mi[...omitted for brevity...].
J9l-ZhwP[...omitted for brevity...]
```

The Assertion Framework for OAuth 2.0 Client Authentication and Authorization Grants specification, which is the RFC 7521, defines the parameters in the JWT authorization grant request, as listed out in the following:

- grant_type: This is a required parameter, which defines the format of the assertion, as understood by the authorization server. The value of grant_type is an absolute URI, and it must be urn:ietf:params:oauth:grant-type:jwt-bearer.

- assertion: This is a required parameter, which carries the token. For example, in the case of JWT authorization grant type, the assertion parameter will carry the base64url-encoded JWT, and it must only contain a single JWT. If there are multiple JWTs in the assertion, then the authorization server will reject the grant request.

- scope: This is an optional parameter. Unlike in authorization code and implicit grant types, the JWT grant type does not have a way to get the resource owner's consent for a requested scope. In such case, the authorization server will establish the resource owner's consent via an out-of-band mechanism. If the authorization grant request carries a value for the scope parameter, then either it should exactly match the out-of-band established scope or less than that.

Note   The OAuth authorization server will not issue a refresh_token under the JWT grant type. If the access_token expires, then the OAuth client has to get a new JWT (if the JWT has expired) or use the same valid JWT to get a new access_token. The lifetime of the access_token should match the lifetime of the corresponding JWT.

Applications of JWT Grant Type

There are multiple applications of the JWT authorization grant type. Let's have a look at one common use case, where the end user or the resource owner logs in to a web application via OpenID Connect (Chapter 6), then the web application needs to access an API on behalf of the logged-in user, which is secured with OAuth 2.0. Figure 12-3 shows the key interactions related to this use case.

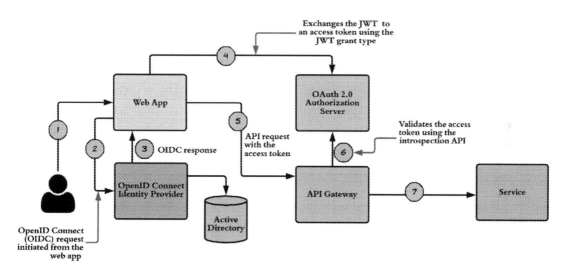

Figure 12-3. *JWT grant type, a real-world example*

The following lists out all the interactions as illustrated in Figure 12-3 by the number:

- The end user visits the web application (step 1).

- In step 2, the user gets redirected to the OpenID Connect server and authenticates against the Active Directory connected to it. After the authentication, the user gets redirected back to the web application, with an authorization code (assuming that we are using OAuth 2.0 authorization code grant type).

- The web application talks directly to the OpenID Connect server and exchanges the authorization code from the previous step to an ID token and an access token. The ID token itself is a JWT, which is signed by the OpenID Connect server (step 3).

- Now the web application needs to invoke an *API* on behalf of the logged-in user. It talks to the OAuth authorization server, trusted by the API, and using the JWT grant type, exchanges the JWT from step 3 to an OAuth access token. The OAuth authorization server validates the JWT and makes sure that it's being signed by a trusted identity provider. In this case, the OAuth authorization server trusts the OpenID Connect identity provider (step 4).

- In step 5, the web application invokes the API with the access token from step 4.

- The application server, which hosts the API, validates the access token by talking to the OAuth authorization server, which issued the access token (step 6).

JWT Client Authentication

The OAuth 2.0 core specification does not define a concrete way to authenticate OAuth clients to the OAuth authorization server. Mostly it's the HTTP Basic authentication with client_id and the client_secret. The RFC 7523 defines a way to authenticate OAuth clients with a JWT. The JWT client authentication is not just limited to a particular grant type; it can be used with any OAuth grant types. That's another beauty in OAuth 2.0—the OAuth grant types are decoupled from the client authentication. The following shows a sample request to the OAuth authorization server under the authorization code grant type, which uses JWT client authentication.

```
POST /token HTTP/1.1
Host: auth.bar.com
Content-Type: application/x-www-form-urlencoded

grant_type=authorization_code&
code=nOesc3NRze7LTCu7iYzS6a5acc3fOogp4&
client_assertion_type=urn%3Aietf%3Aparams%3Aoauth%3Aclient-assertion-
type%3Ajwt-bearer&
client_assertion=eyJhbGciOiJSUzI1NiIsImtpZCI6IjIyIn0.
eyJpc3Mi[...omitted for brevity...].
cC4hiUPo[...omitted for brevity...]
```

The RFC 7523 uses three additional parameters in the OAuth request to the token endpoint to do the client authentication: `client_assertion_type`, `client_assertion`, and `client_id` (optional). The Assertion Framework for OAuth 2.0 Client Authentication and Authorization Grants specification, which is the RFC 7521, defines these parameters. The following lists them out along with their definitions:

- `client_assertion_type`: This is a required parameter, which defines the format of the assertion, as understood by the OAuth authorization server. The value of `client_assertion_type` is an absolute URI. For JWT client authentication, this parameter must carry the value `urn:ietf:params:oauth:client-assertion-type:jwt-bearer`.

- `client_assertion`: This is a required parameter, which carries the token. For example, in the case of JWT client authentication, the `client_assertion` parameter will carry the base64url-encoded JWT, and it must only contain a single JWT. If there are multiple JWTs in the assertion, then the authorization server will reject the grant request.

- `client_id`: This is an optional parameter. Ideally, the `client_id` must be present inside the `client_assertion` itself. If this parameter carries a value, it must match the value of the `client_id` inside the `client_assertion`. Having the `client_id` parameter in the request itself could be useful, as the authorization server does not need to parse the assertion first to identify the client.

Applications of JWT Client Authentication

The JWT client authentication is used to authenticate a client to an OAuth authorization server with a JWT, instead of using HTTP Basic authentication with `client_id` and `client_secret`. Why would someone select JWT client authentication over HTTP Basic authentication?

Let's take an example. Say we have two companies called foo and bar. The foo company hosts a set of APIs, and the bar company has a set of developers who are developing applications against those APIs. Like in most of the OAuth examples we discussed in this book, the bar company has to register with the foo company to obtain a `client_id` and `client_secret`, in order to access its APIs. Since the bar company develops multiple applications (a web app, a mobile app, a rich client app), the same `client_id` and `client_secret` obtained from the foo company need to be shared between multiple developers. This is a bit risky as any one of those developers can pass over the secret keys to anyone else—or even misuse them. To fix this, we can use JWT client authentication. Instead of sharing the `client_id` and the `client_secret` with its developers, the bar company can create a key pair (a public key and a private key), sign the public key by the key of the company's certificate authority (CA), and hand them over to its developers. Now, instead of the shared `client_id` and `client_secret`, each developer will have its own public key and private key, signed by the company CA. When talking to the foo company's OAuth authorization server, the applications will use the JWT client authentication, where its own private key signs the JWT—and the token will carry the corresponding public key. The following code snippet shows a sample decoded JWS header and the payload, which matches the preceding criteria. Chapter 7 explains JWS in detail and how it relates to JWT.

```
{
  "alg": "RS256"
  "x5c": [
          "MIIE3jCCA8agAwIBAgICAwEwDQYJKoZIhvcNAQEFBQ......",
          "MIIE3jewlJJMddds9AgICAwEwDQYJKoZIhvUjEcNAQ......",
          ]
}
{
  "sub": "3MVG9uudbyLbNPZN8rZTCj6IwpJpGBv49",
  "aud": "https://login.foo.com",
  "nbf": 1457330111,
  "iss": "bar.com",
  "exp": 1457330711,
  "iat": 1457330111,
  "jti": "44688e78-2d30-4e88-8b86-a6e25cd411fd"
}
```

The authorization server at the foo company first needs to verify the JWT with the attached public key (which is the value of the x5c parameter in the preceding code snippet) and then needs to check whether the corresponding public key is signed by the bar company's certificate authority. If that is the case, then it's a valid JWT and would successfully complete the client authentication. Also note that the value of the original client_id created for the bar company is set as the subject of the JWT.

Still we have a challenge. How do we revoke a certificate that belongs to a given developer, in case he/she resigns or it is found that the certificate is misused? To facilitate this, the authorization server has to maintain a certificate revocation list (CRL) by the client_id. In other words, each client_id can maintain its own certificate revocation list. To revoke a certificate, the client (in this case, the bar company) has to talk to the CRL API hosted in the authorization server. The CRL API is a custom API that must be hosted at the OAuth authorization server to support this model. This API must be secured with OAuth 2.0 client credentials grant type. Once it receives a request to update the CRL, it will update the CRL corresponding to the client who invokes the API, and each time the client authentication happens, the authorization server must check the public certificate in the JWT against the CRL. If it finds a match, then the request should be turned down immediately. Also, at the time the CRL of a particular client is updated, all the access tokens and refresh tokens issued against a revoked public certificate must be revoked too. In case you worry about the overhead it takes to support a CRL, you probably can use short-lived certificates and forget about revocation. Figure 12-4 shows the interactions between the foo and the bar companies.

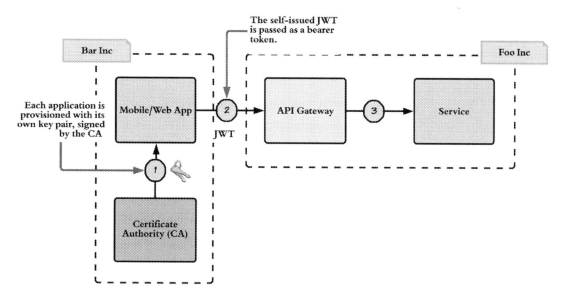

Figure 12-4. *JWT client authentication, a real-world example*

Parsing and Validating JWT

The OAuth authorization server must parse and validate the JWT, both in the JWT grant type and in the client authentication. The following lists out the criteria for token validation:

- The JWT must have the `iss` parameter in it. The `iss` parameter represents the issuer of the JWT. This is treated as a case-sensitive string value. Ideally, this represents the asserting party of the claims set. If Google issues the JWT, then the value of `iss` would be `accounts.google.com`. This is an indication to the receiving party who the issuer of the JWT is.

- The JWT must have the `sub` parameter in it. The token issuer or the asserting party issues the JWT for a particular entity, and the claims set embedded into the JWT normally represents this entity, which is identified by the `sub` parameter. The value of the `sub` parameter is a case-sensitive string value. For the JWT client authentication, the value of the sub parameter must carry the corresponding `client_id`, while for the authorization grant, it will be the authorized accessor or the resource server for which the access token is being requested.

- The JWT must have the `aud` parameter. The token issuer issues the JWT to an intended recipient or a list of recipients, which is represented by the `aud` parameter. The recipient or the recipient list should know how to parse the JWT and validate it. Prior to any validation check, the recipient of the token must first see whether the particular JWT is issued for its use and if not should reject immediately. The value of the `aud` parameter can be a case-sensitive string value or an array of strings. The token issuer should know, prior to issuing the token, who the intended recipient (or the recipients) of the token is, and the value of the `aud` parameter must be a pre-agreed value between the token issuer and the recipient. In practice, one can also use a regular expression to validate the audience of the token. For example, the value of the `aud` in the token can be `*.apress.com`, while each recipient under the `apress.com` domain can have its own aud values: `foo.apress.com`, `bar.apress.com` likewise.

Instead of finding an exact match for the aud value, each recipient can just check whether the aud value in the token matches a regular expression: (?:[a-zA-Z0-9]*|*).apress.com. This will make sure that any recipient can use a JWT, which is having any subdomain of apress.com.

- The JWT must have the exp parameter. Each JWT will carry an expiration time. The recipient of the JWT token must reject it, if that token has expired. The issuer can decide the value of the expiration time. The JWT specification does not recommend or provide any guidelines on how to decide the best token expiration time. It's a responsibility of the other specifications, which use JWT internally, to provide such recommendations. The value of the exp parameter is calculated by adding the expiration time (from the token issued time) in seconds to the time elapsed from 1970-01-01T00:00:00Z UTC to the current time. If the token issuer's clock is out of sync with the recipient's clock (irrespective of their time zone), then the expiration time validation could fail. To fix that, each recipient can add a couple of minutes as the clock skew.

- The JWT may have the nbf parameter. In other words, this is not a must. The recipient of the token should reject it, if the value of the nbf parameter is greater than the current time. The JWT is not good enough to use prior to the value indicated in the nbf parameter. The value of the nbf parameter is calculated by adding the not before time (from the token issued time) in seconds to the time elapsed from 1970-01-01T00:00:00Z UTC to the current time.

- The JWT may have the iat parameter. The iat parameter in the JWT indicates the issued time of the JWT as calculated by the token issuer. The value of the iat parameter is the number of seconds elapsed from 1970-01-01T00:00:00Z UTC to the current time, when the token is issued.

- The JWT must be digitally signed or carry a Message Authentication Code (MAC) defined by its issuer.

Summary

- Identity federation is about propagating user identities across boundaries. These boundaries can be between distinct enterprises or even distinct identity management systems within the same enterprise.

- Two OAuth 2.0 profiles—SAML 2.0 grant type and JWT grant type—focus on building federation scenarios for API security.

- The SAML profile for OAuth 2.0, which is defined in the RFC 7522, extends the capabilities of the OAuth 2.0 core specification. It introduces a new authorization grant type as well as a way of authenticating OAuth 2.0 clients, based on a SAML assertion.

- The JSON Web Token (JWT) profile for OAuth 2.0, which is defined in the RFC 7523, extends the capabilities of the OAuth 2.0 core specification. It introduces a new authorization grant type as well as a way of authenticating OAuth 2.0 clients, based on a JWT.

CHAPTER 13

User-Managed Access

OAuth 2.0 introduced an authorization framework for access delegation. It lets Bob delegate read access to his Facebook wall to a third-party application, without sharing Facebook credentials. User-Managed Access (UMA, pronounced "OOH-mah") extends this model to another level, where Bob can not only delegate access to a third-party application but also to Peter who uses the same third-party application.

UMA is an OAuth 2.0 profile. OAuth 2.0 decouples the resource server from the authorization server. UMA takes one step further: it lets you control a distributed set of resource servers from a centralized authorization server. Also the resource owner can define a set of policies at the authorization server, which can be evaluated at the time a client is granted access to a protected resource. This eliminates the need of having the presence of the resource owner to approve access requests from arbitrary clients or requesting parties. The authorization server can make the decision based on the policies defined by the resource owner.

The latest version of UMA, which we discuss in this chapter, is UMA 2.0. If you are interested in learning more about UMA evolution, please check Appendix D: UMA Evolution.

Use Cases

Let's say you have multiple bank accounts with Chase Bank, Bank of America, and Wells Fargo. You have hired a financial manager called Peter, who manages all your bank accounts through a personal financial management (PFM) application, which helps to budget better and understand the overall financial position, by often pulling information from multiple bank accounts. Here, you need to give limited access to Peter, to use the PFM to access your bank accounts. We assume all the banks expose their functionality over APIs and PFM uses banking APIs to retrieve data.

© Prabath Siriwardena 2020
P. Siriwardena, *Advanced API Security*, https://doi.org/10.1007/978-1-4842-2050-4_13

At a very high level, let's see how UMA solves this problem (see Figure 13-1). First you need to define an access control policy at the authorization server, which all your banks trust. This authorization policy would say Peter should be given read access via the PFM app to Wells Fargo, Chase, and Bank of America bank accounts. Then you also need to introduce each bank to the authorization server, so whenever Peter tries to access your bank accounts, each bank talks to the authorization server and asks whether Peter is allowed to do that. For Peter to access a bank account via PFM app, the PFM app first needs to talk to the authorization server and gets a token on behalf of Peter. During this process, before issuing the token, the authorization server evaluates the access control policy you defined.

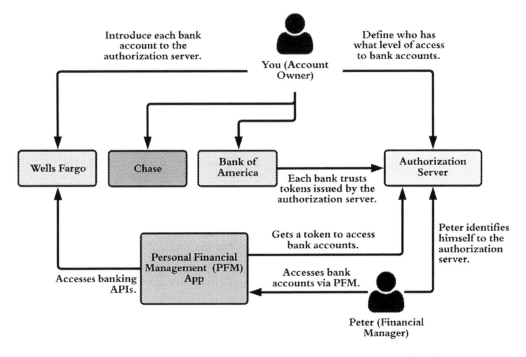

Figure 13-1. *An account owner delegates the administration of his/her accounts to a Financial Manager via a Personal Financial Management App*

Let's take another example. Say you have a Google Doc. You do not want to share this with everyone, but with anyone from the management team of foo and bar companies (see Figure 13-2). Let's see how this works with UMA.

First you have an authorization server, which Google trusts, so whenever someone wants to access your Google Doc, Google talks to the authorization server to see whether that person has the rights to do so. You also define a policy at the authorization server, which says only the managers from foo and bar companies can access your Google Doc.

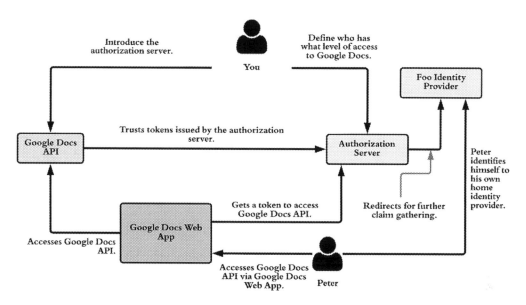

Figure 13-2. *A Google Doc owner delegates access to a Google Doc to a third party from a different company with specific roles*

When a person (say Peter) tries to access your Google Doc, Google will redirect you to the authorization server. Then the authorization server will redirect Peter to Foo identity provider (or the home identity provider of Peter). Foo identity provider will authenticate Peter and send back Peter's role as a claim to the authorization server. Now, since authorization server knows Peter's role, and also the company Peter belongs to, if Peter belongs to a manager role, it will issue a token to Google Docs app, which it can use to retrieve the corresponding Google Doc via the Google Docs API.

UMA 2.0 Roles

UMA introduces one more role in addition to the four roles (resource owner, resource server, client, and authorization server) we discussed under OAuth 2.0, in Chapter 4. The following lists out all five roles involved in UMA:

1. *Resource owner*: In the preceding two use cases, you are the resource owner. In the first case, you owned the bank account, and in the second use case, you owned the Google Doc.

2. *Resource server*: This is the place which hosts protected resources. In the preceding first use case, each bank is a resource server— and in the second use case, the server, which hosts Google Docs API, is the resource server.

3. *Client*: This is the application, which wants to access a resource on behalf of the resource owner. In the preceding first use case, the personal financial management (PFM) application is the client, and in the second use case, it is the Google Docs web application.

4. *Authorization server*: This is the entity, which acts as the security token service (STS) to issue OAuth 2.0 access tokens to client applications.

5. *Requesting party*: This is something new in UMA. In the preceding first use case, Peter, the financial manager, is the requesting party, and in the second use case, Peter who is a manager at Foo company is the requesting party. The requesting party accesses a resource via a client application, on behalf of the resource owner.

UMA Protocol

There are two specifications developed under Kantara Initiative, which define UMA protocol. The core specification is called UMA 2.0 Grant for OAuth 2.0 Authorization. The other one is the Federated Authorization for UMA 2.0, which is optional.

A grant type is an extension point in OAuth 2.0 architecture. UMA 2.0 grant type extends the OAuth 2.0 to support the requesting party role and defines the flow the client application should follow to obtain an access token on behalf of the requesting party from the authorization server.

Let's see in step by step how UMA 2.0 works, with the first use case we discussed earlier:

1. First, the account owner has to introduce each of his banks to the UMA authorization server. Here we possibly follow OAuth 2.0 authorization code grant type and provision an access token to the Chase Bank. UMA gives a special name to this token: Protection API Access Token (PAT).

2. The Chase Bank uses the provisioned access token or the PAT to register its resources with the authorization server. Following is a sample cURL command for resource registration. $PAT in the following command is a placeholder for the Protection API Access

Token. Here we register the account of the account owner as a resource.

```
\> curl -v -X POST -H "Authorization:Bearer $PAT"
-H "Content-Type: application/json" -d '{"resource_
scopes":["view"], "description":"bank account details",
"name":"accounts/1112019209", "type":"/accounts"}'
https://as.uma.example.com/uma/resourceregistration
```

3. Peter via the personal financial management (PFM) application tries to access the Chase Bank account with no token.

```
\> curl -X GET https://chase.com/apis/accounts/1112019209
```

4. Since there is no token in the request from PFM, the bank API responds back with a 401 HTTP error code, along with the endpoint of the authorization server and a permission ticket. This permission ticket represents the level of permissions PFM needs to do a GET to /accounts API of the Chase Bank. In other words, PFM should get an access token from the provided authorization server, with the provided permissions in the given permission ticket.

5. To generate the permission ticket, the Chase Bank has to talk to the authorization server. As per the following cURL command, Chase Bank also passes resource_id and the resource_scope. The permission API is protected via OAuth 2.0, so the Chase Bank has to pass a valid access token to access it. UMA gives a special name to this token: Protection API Access Token (PAT), which we provisioned to Chase Bank in step 1.

```
\> curl -v -X POST -H "Authorization:Bearer $PAT" -H
"Content-Type: application/json" -d '[{"resource_id":"
accounts/1112019209","resource_scopes":["view"]}]'
https://as.uma.example.com/uma/permission
{"ticket":"1qw32s-2q1e2s-1rt32g-r4wf2e"}
```

6. Now the Chase Bank will send the following 401 response to the PFM application.

```
HTTP/1.1 401 Unauthorized
WWW-Authenticate: UMA realm="chase" as_uri="https://as.uma.
example.com" ticket="1qw32s-2q1e2s-1rt32g-r4wf2e "
```

7. The client application or the PFM now has to talk to the authorization server. By this time, we can assume that Peter, or the requesting party, has already logged in to the client app. If that login happens over OpenID Connect, then PFM has an ID token, which represents Peter. PFM passes both the ID token (as `claim_token`) and the permission ticket (as `ticket`) it got from Chase Bank to the authorization server, in the following cURL command. The `claim_token` is an optional parameter in the request, and if it is present, then there must be `claim_token_format` parameter as well, which defines the format of the `claim_token`. In the following cURL command, use a `claim_token` of the ID token format, and it can be even a SAML token. Here the `$APP_CLIENTID` and `$APP_CLIENTSECRET` are the OAuth 2.0 client id and client secret, respectively, you get at the time you register your application (PFM) with the OAuth 2.0 authorization server. The `$IDTOKEN` is a placeholder for the OpenID Connect ID token, while `$TICKET` is a placeholder for the permission ticket. The value of the grant_type parameter must be set to `urn:ietf:params:oauth:grant-type:uma-ticket`. The following cURL command is only an example, and it does not carry all the optional parameters.

```
\> curl -v -X POST --basic -u $APP_CLIENTID:$APP_
CLIENTSECRET
    -H "Content-Type: application/x-www-form-urlencoded;
    charset=UTF-8" -k -d
    "grant_type=urn:ietf:params:oauth:grant-type:uma-ticket&
     claim_token=$IDTOKEN&
```

```
claim_token_format=http://openid.net/specs/openid-
connect-core-1_0.html#IDToken&
ticket=$TICKET"
https://as.uma.example.com/uma/token
```

8. As the response to the preceding request, the client application gets an access token, which UMA calls a requesting party token (RPT), and before authorization server returns back the access token, it internally evaluates any authorization policies defined by the account owner (or the resource owner) to see whether Peter has access to the corresponding bank account.

```
{
  "token_type":"bearer",
  "expires_in":3600,
  "refresh_token":"22b157546b26c2d6c0165c4ef6b3f736",
  "access_token":"cac93e1d29e45bf6d84073dbfb460"
}
```

9. Now the application (PFM) tries to access the Chase Bank account with the RPT from the preceding step.

```
\> curl -X GET -H "Authorization: Bearer
cac93e1d29e45bf6d84073dbfb460" https://chase.com/apis/
accounts/1112019209
```

10. The Chase Bank API will now talk to the introspection (see Chapter 9) endpoint to validate the provided RPT and, if the token is valid, will respond back with the corresponding data. If the introspection endpoint is secured, then the Chase Bank API has to pass the PAT in the HTTP authorization header to authenticate.

```
\> curl -H "Authorization:Bearer $PAT" -H 'Content-Type:
application/x-www-form-urlencoded' -X POST --data "token=
cac93e1d29e45bf6d84073dbfb460" https://as.uma.example.com/
uma/introspection

HTTP/1.1 200 OK
Content-Type: application/json
Cache-Control: no-store
```

```
{
  "active": true,
  "client_id":"s6BhdRkqt3",
  "scope": "view",
  "sub": "peter",
  "aud": "accounts/1112019209"
}
```

11. Once the Chase Bank finds the token is valid and carries all
    required scopes, it will respond back to the client application
    (PFM) with the requested data.

Note   A recording of a UMA 2.0 demo done by the author of the book to the
UMA working group with the open source WSO2 Identity Server is available here:
`www.youtube.com/watch?v=66aGc5AV7P4`.

Interactive Claims Gathering

In the previous section, in step 7, we assumed that the requesting party is already
logged in to the client application and the client application knows about the requesting
party's claims, say, for example, in the format of an ID token or a SAML token. The client
application passes these claims in the `claim_token` parameter along with the permission
ticket to the token endpoint of the authorization server. This request from the client
application to the authorization server is a direct request. In case the client application
finds that it does not have enough claims that are required by the authorization server
to make an authorization decision based on its policies, the client application can
decide to use interactive claim gathering. During the interactive claim gathering, the
client application redirects the requesting party to the UMA authorization server. This
is what we discussed under the second use case at the very beginning of the chapter,
with respect to sharing Google Docs with external companies. The following is a
sample request the client application generates to redirect the requesting party to the
authorization server.

```
Host: as.uma.example.com
GET /uma/rqp_claims?client_id=$APP_CLIENTID
&ticket=$TICKET
&claims_redirect_uri=https://client.example.com/redirect_claims
&state=abc
```

The preceding sample request is an HTTP redirect, which flows through the browser. Here the $APP_CLIENTID is the OAuth 2.0 client id you get at the time you register your application with the UMA authorization server, and $TICKET is a placeholder for the permission ticket the client application gets from the resource server (see step 6 in the previous section). The value of claim_redirect_uri indicates the authorization server, where to send the response back, which points to an endpoint hosted in the client application.

How the authorization server does claim gathering is out of the scope of the UMA specification. Ideally, it can be by redirecting the requesting party again to his/her own home identity provider and getting back the requested claims (see Figure 13-2). Once the claim gathering is completed, the authorization server redirects the user back to the claim_redirect_uri endpoint with a permission ticket, as shown in the following. The authorization server tracks all the claims it gathered against this permission ticket.

```
HTTP/1.1 302 Found
Location: https://client.example.com/redirect_claims?
ticket=cHJpdmFjeSBpcyBjb25zZXh0LCBjb25zcm9s&state=abc
```

The client application will now talk to the token endpoint of the authorization server with the preceding permission ticket to get a requesting party token (RPT). This is similar to what we discussed under step 7 in the previous section, but here we do not send a claim_token.

```
\> curl -v -X POST --basic -u $APP_CLIENTID:$APP_CLIENTSECRET
   -H "Content-Type: application/x-www-form-urlencoded;
   charset=UTF-8" -k -d
   "grant_type=urn:ietf:params:oauth:grant-type:uma-ticket&
   ticket=$TICKET"
   https://as.uma.example.com/uma/token
```

As the response to the preceding request, the client application gets an access token, which UMA calls a requesting party token (RPT), and before authorization server returns back the access token, it internally evaluates any authorization policies defined by the account owner (or the resource owner) to see whether Peter has access to the corresponding bank account.

```
{
  "token_type":"bearer",
  "expires_in":3600,
  "refresh_token":"22b157546b26c2d6c0165c4ef6b3f736",
  "access_token":"cac93e1d29e45bf6d84073dbfb460"
}
```

Summary

- User-Managed Access (UMA) is an emerging standard built on top of the OAuth 2.0 core specification as a profile.

- UMA still has very few vendor implementations, but it promises to be a highly recognized standard in the near future.

- There are two specifications developed under Kantara Initiative, which define the UMA protocol. The core specification is called the UMA 2.0 Grant for OAuth 2.0 Authorization. The other one is the Federated Authorization for UMA 2.0, which is optional.

- UMA introduces a new role called, requesting party, in addition to the four roles used in OAuth 2.0: the authorization server, the resource server, the resource owner and the client application.

CHAPTER 14

OAuth 2.0 Security

OAuth 2.0 is an authorization framework, as you know already. Being a framework, it gives multiple options for application developers. It is up to the application developers to pick the right options based on their use cases and how they want to use OAuth 2.0. There are few guideline documents to help you use OAuth 2.0 in a secure way. OAuth 2.0 Threat Model and Security Considerations (RFC 6819) produced by OAuth IETF working group defines additional security considerations for OAuth 2.0, beyond those in the OAuth 2.0 specification, based on a comprehensive threat model. The OAuth 2.0 Security Best Current Practice document, which is a draft proposal at the time of writing, talks about new threats related to OAuth 2.0, since the RFC 6819 was published. Also, the Financial-grade API (FAPI) working group under the OpenID foundation has published a set of guidelines on how to use OAuth 2.0 in a secure way to build financial grade applications. In this chapter, we go through a set of possible attacks against OAuth 2.0 and discuss how to mitigate those.

Identity Provider Mix-Up

Even though OAuth 2.0 is about access delegation, still people work around it to make it work for login. That's how login with Facebook works. Then again, the OpenID Connect (see Chapter 6), which is built on top of OAuth 2.0, is the right way of using OAuth 2.0 for authentication. A recent research done by one of the leading vendors in the Identity and Access Management domain confirmed that most of the new development happened over the past few years at the enterprise level picked OAuth 2.0/OpenID Connect over SAML 2.0. All in all, OAuth 2.0 security is a hot topic. In 2016, Daniel Fett, Ralf Küsters, and Guido Schmitz did a research on OAuth 2.0 security and published a paper.[1] Identity provider mix-up is one of the attacks highlighted in their paper. Identity provider is in

---

[1]A Comprehensive Formal Security Analysis of OAuth 2.0, `https://arxiv.org/pdf/1601.01229.pdf`

© Prabath Siriwardena 2020

P. Siriwardena, *Advanced API Security*, https://doi.org/10.1007/978-1-4842-2050-4_14

fact the entity that issues OAuth 2.0 tokens or the OAuth 2.0 authorization server, which we discussed in Chapter 4.

Let's try to understand how identity provider mix-up works (see Figure 14-1):

1. This attack happens with an OAuth 2.0 client application, which provides multiple identity provider (IdP) options for login. Let's say foo.idp and evil.idp. We assume that the client application does not know that evil.idp is evil. Also it can be a case where evil.idp is a genuine identity provider, which could possibly be under an attack itself.

2. The victim picks foo.idp from the browser and the attacker intercepts the request and changes the selection to evil.idp. Here we assume the communication between the browser and the client application is not protected with Transport Layer Security (TLS). The OAuth 2.0 specification does not talk about it, and it's purely up to the web application developers. Since there is no confidential data passed in this flow, most of the time the web application developers may not worry about using TLS. At the same time, there were few vulnerabilities discovered over the past on TLS implementations (mostly openssl). So, the attacker could possibly use such vulnerabilities to intercept the communication between the browser and the client application (web server), even if TLS is used.

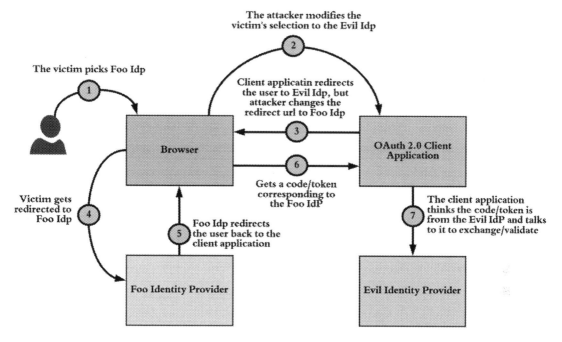

Figure 14-1. *Identity provider mix-up attack*

3. Since the attacker changed the identity provider selection of the user, the client application thinks it's evil.idp (even though the user picked foo.idp) and redirects the user to evil.idp. The client application only gets the modified request from the attacker, who intercepted the communication.

4. The attacker intercepts the redirection and modifies the redirection to go to the foo.idp. The way redirection works is the web server (in this case, the client application) sends back a response to the browser with a 302 status code—and with an HTTP Location header. If the communication between the browser and the client application is not on TLS, then this response is not protected, even if the HTTP Location header contains an HTTPS URL. Since we assumed already, the communication between the browser and the client application can be intercepted by the attacker, then the attacker can modify the Location header in the response to go to the foo.idp—which is the original selection—and no surprise to the user.

5. The client application gets either the code or the token (based on the grant type) and now will talk to the evil.idp to validate it. The authorization server (or the identity provider) will send back the authorization code (if the code grant type is used) to the callback URL, which is under the client application. Just looking at the authorization code, the client application cannot decide to which identity provider the code belongs to. So we assume it tracks the identity provider by some session variable—so as per step 3, the client application thinks it's the evil.idp and talks to the evil.idp to validate the token.

6. The evil.idp gets hold of the user's access token or the authorization code from the foo.idp. If it's the implicit grant type, then it would be the access token, otherwise the authorization code. In mobile apps, most of the time, people used to embed the same client id and the client secret into all the instances—so an attacker having root access to his own phone can figure it out what the keys are and then, with the authorization code, can get the access token.

There is no record that the preceding attack is being carried out in practice—but at the same time, we cannot totally rule it out. There are a couple of options to prevent such attacks, and our recommendation is to use the option 1 as it is quite straightforward and solves the problem without much hassle.

1. Have separate callback URLs by each identity provider. With this the client application knows to which identity provider the response belongs to. The legitimate identity provider will always respect the callback URL associated with the client application and will use that. The client application will also attach the value of the callback URL to the browser session and, once the user got redirected back, will see whether it's on the right place (or the right callback URL) by matching with the value of the callback URL from the browser session.

2. Follow the mitigation steps defined in the IETF draft specification: OAuth 2.0 IdP Mix-Up Mitigation (`https://tools.ietf.org/html/draft-ietf-oauth-mix-up-mitigation-01`). This specification proposes to send a set of mitigation data from

the authorization server back to the client, along with the authorization response. The mitigation data provided by the authorization server to the client includes an **issuer identifier**, which is used to identify the authorization server, and a **client id**, which is used to verify that the response is from the correct authorization server and is intended for the given client. This way the OAuth 2.0 client can verify from which authorization server it got the response back and based on that identify the token endpoint or the endpoint to validate the token.

Cross-Site Request Forgery (CSRF)

In general, Cross-Site Request Forgery (CSRF) attack forces a logged-in victim's browser to send a forged HTTP request, including the victim's session cookie and any other automatically included authentication information to a vulnerable web application. Such an attack allows the attacker to force a victim's browser to generate requests, where the vulnerable application thinks are legitimate requests from the victim. OWASP (Open Web Application Security Project) identifies this as one of the key security risks in web applications in its 2017 report.[2]

Let's see how CSRF can be used with OAuth 2.0 to exploit a vulnerable web application (see Figure 14-2):

1. The **attacker** tries to log in to the target web site (OAuth 2.0 client) with his account at the corresponding identity provider. Here we assume the attacker has a valid account at the identity provider, trusted by the corresponding OAuth 2.0 client application.

2. The **attacker** blocks the redirection to the target web site and captures the authorization code. The target web site never sees the code. In OAuth 2.0, the authorization code is only good enough for one-time use. In case the OAuth 2.0 client application sees it and then exchanges it to an access token, then it's no more valid—so the attacker has to make sure that the authorization code never reaches the client application. Since the authorization code flows through the attacker's browser to the client, it can be easily blocked.

---

[2]OWASP Top 10 2017, `www.owasp.org/images/7/72/OWASP_Top_10-2017_%28en%29.pdf`.pdf

3. The **attacker** constructs the callback URL for the target site—and makes the victim clicks on it. In fact, it would be the same callback URL the attacker can copy from step 2. Here the attacker can send the link to the victim's email or somehow fool him to click on the link.

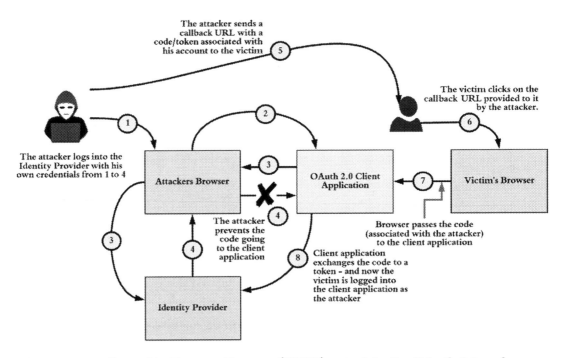

Figure 14-2. *Cross-Site Request Forgery (CSRF) attack in the OAuth 2.0 code flow*

4. The **victim** clicks on the link and logs in to the target web site, with the account attached to the attacker—and adds his/her credit card information. Since the authorization code belongs to the attacker, the victim logs in to the target web site with the attacker's account. This is a pattern many web sites follow to authenticate users with OAuth 2.0. Login with Facebook works in the same way. Once the web site gets the authorization code, it will talk to the authorization server and exchanges it to an access token. Then using that access token, the web site talks to another endpoint in the authorization server to find user information. In this case, since the code belongs to the attacker, the user information returned back from the authorization server will be related to

him—so the victim now logs in to the target web site with the attacker's account.

5. The **attacker** too logs in to the target web site with his/her valid credentials and uses victim's credit card to purchase goods.

The preceding attack can be mitigated by following these best practices:

- Use a short-lived authorization code. Making the authorization code expires soon gives very little time for the attacker to plant an attack. For example, the authorization code issued by LinkedIn expires in 30 seconds. Ideally, the lifetime of the authorization code should be in seconds.

- Use the **state** parameter as defined in the OAuth 2.0 specification. This is one of the key parameters to use to mitigate CSRF attacks in general. The client application has to generate a random number (or a string) and passes it to the authorization server along with the grant request. Further, the client application has to add the generated value of the **state** to the current user session (browser session) before redirecting the user to the authorization server. According to the OAuth 2.0 specification, the authorization server has to return back the same state value with the authorization code to the redirect_uri (to the client application). The client must validate the state value returned from the authorization server with the value stored in the user's current session—if it mismatches, it rejects moving forward. Going back to the attack, when the user clicks the crafted link sent to the victim by the attacker, it won't carry the same state value generated before and attached to the victim's session (or most probably victim's session has no state value), or the attacker does not know how to generate the exact same state value. So, the attack won't be successful, and the client application will reject the request.

- Use PKCE (Proof Key for Code Exchange). PKCE (RFC 7636) was introduced to protect OAuth 2.0 client applications from the authorization code interception attack, mostly targeting native mobile apps. The use of PKCE will also protect users from CSRF attacks, once the code_verifier is attached to the user's browser session. We talked about PKCE in detail in Chapter 10.

Token Reuse

OAuth 2.0 tokens are issued by the authorization server to a client application to access a resource on behalf of the resource owner. This token is to be used by the client—and the resource server will make sure it's a valid one. What if the resource server is under the control of an attacker and wants to reuse the token sent to it to access another resource, impersonating the original client? Here the basic assumption is there are multiple resource servers, which trust the same authorization server. For example, in a microservices deployment, there can be multiple microservices protected with OAuth 2.0, which trust the same authorization server.

How do we make sure at the resource server side that the provided token is only good enough to access it? One approach is to have properly scoped access tokens. The scopes are defined by the resource server—and update the authorization server. If we qualify each scope with a Uniform Resource Name (URN) specific to the corresponding resource server, then there cannot be any overlapping scopes across all the resource servers—and each resource server knows how to uniquely identify a scope corresponding to it. Before accepting a token, it should check whether the token is issued with a scope known to it.

This does not completely solve the problem. If the client decides to get a single access token (with all the scopes) to access all the resources, then still a malicious client can use that access token to access another resource by impersonating the original client. To overcome this, the client can first get an access token with all the scopes, then it can exchange the access token to get multiple access tokens with different scopes, following the OAuth 2.0 Token Exchange specification (which we discussed in Chapter 9). A given resource server will only see an access token having scopes only related to that particular resource server.

Let's see another example of token reuse. Here assume that you log in to an OAuth 2.0 client application with Facebook. Now the client has an access token, which is good enough to access the user info endpoint (`https://graph.facebook.com/me`) of Facebook and find who the user is. This client application is under an attacker, and now the attacker tries to access another client application, which uses the implicit grant type, with the same access token, as shown in the following.

```
https://target-app/callback?access_token=<access_token>
```

The preceding URL will let the attacker log in to the client application as the original user unless the target client application has proper security checks in place. How do we overcome this?

There are multiple options:

- Avoid using OAuth 2.0 for authentication—instead use OpenID Connect. The ID token issued by the authorization server (via OpenID Connect) has an element called **aud** (audience)—and its value is the client id corresponding to the client application. Each application should make sure that the value of the **aud** is known to it before accepting the user. If the attacker tries to replay the ID token, it will not work since the audience validation will fail at the second client application (as the second application expects a different **aud** value).

- Facebook login is not using OpenID Connect—and the preceding attack can be carried out against a Facebook application which does not have the proper implementation. There are few options introduced by Facebook to overcome the preceding threat. One way is to use the undocumented API, `https://graph.facebook.com/app?access_token=<access_token>`, to get access token metadata. This will return back in a JSON message the details of the application which the corresponding access token is issued to. If it's not yours, reject the request.

- Use the standard token introspection endpoint of the authorization server to find the token metadata. The response will have the client_id corresponding to the OAuth 2.0 application—and if it does not belong to you, reject the login request.

There is another flavor of token reuse—rather we call it token misuse. When implicit grant type is used with a single-page application (SPA), the access token is visible to the end user—as it's on the browser. It's the legitimate user—so the user seeing the access token is no big deal. But the issue is the user would probably take the access token out of the browser (or the app) and automate or script some API calls, which would generate more load on the server that would not expect in a normal scenario. Also, there is a cost of making API calls. Most of the client applications are given a throttle limit—meaning a given application can only do *n* number of calls during a minute or some fixed time period. If one user tries to invoke APIs with a script, that could possibly eat out the complete throttle limit of the application—making an undesirable impact on the other users of the same application. To overcome such scenarios, the recommended approach is to introduce throttle limits by user by application—not just by the application. In that way, if a user wants to eat out his own throttle limit, go out and do it! The other solution is to use Token Binding, which we discussed in Chapter 11. With token binding, the access token is bound to the underlying Transport Layer Security (TLS) connection, and the user won't be able to export it and use it from somewhere else.

Token Leakage/Export

More than 90% of the OAuth 2.0 deployments are based on bearer tokens—not just the public/Internet scale ones but also at the enterprise level. The use of a bearer token is just like using cash. When you buy a cup of coffee from Starbucks, paying by cash, no one will bother how you got that ten-dollar note—or if you're the real owner of it. OAuth 2.0 bearer tokens are similar to that. If someone takes the token out of the wire (just like stealing a ten-dollar note from your pocket), he/she can use it just as the original owner of it—no questions asked!

Whenever you use OAuth 2.0, it's not just recommended but a must to use TLS. Even though TLS is used, still a man-in-the-middle attack can be carried out with various techniques. Most of the time, the vulnerabilities in TLS implementations are used to intercept the TLS-protected communication channels. The Logjam attack discovered in May 2015 allowed a man-in-the-middle attacker to downgrade vulnerable TLS connections to 512-bit export-grade cryptography. This allowed the attacker to read and modify any data passed over the connection.

There are few things we need to worry about as precautions to keep the attacker away from having access to the tokens:

- Always be on TLS (use TLS 1.2 or later).

- Address all the TLS-level vulnerabilities at the client, authorization server, and the resource server.

- The token value should be >=128 bits long and constructed from a cryptographically strong random or pseudorandom number sequence.

- Never store tokens in cleartext—but the salted hash.

- Never write access/refresh tokens into logs.

- Use TLS tunneling over TLS bridging.

- Decide the lifetime of each token based on the risk associated with token leakage, duration of the underlying access grant (SAML grant (RFC 7522) or JWT grant (RFC 7523)), and the time required for an attacker to guess or produce a valid token.

- Prevent reuse of the authorization code—just once.

- Use one-time access tokens. Under the OAuth 2.0 implicit grant type, access token comes as a URI fragment—which will be in the browser history. In such cases, it can be immediately invalidated by exchanging it to a new access token from the client application (which is an SPA).

- Use strong client credentials. Most of the applications just use client id and client secret to authenticate the client application to the authorization server. Rather than passing credentials over the wire, client can use either the SAML or JWT assertion to authenticate.

In addition to the preceding measures, we can also cryptographically bind the OAuth 2.0 access/refresh tokens and authorization codes to a given TLS channel—so those cannot be exported and used elsewhere. There are few specifications developed under the IETF Token Binding working group to address this aspect.

The Token Binding Protocol, which we discussed in Chapter 11, allows client/server applications to create long-lived, uniquely identifiable TLS bindings spanning multiple TLS sessions and connections. Applications are then enabled to cryptographically bind security tokens to the TLS layer, preventing token export and replay attacks. To protect privacy, the Token Binding identifiers are only conveyed over TLS and can be reset by the user at any time.

The OAuth 2.0 Token Binding specification (which we discussed in Chapter 11) defines how to apply Token Binding to access tokens, authorization codes, and refresh tokens. This cryptographically binds OAuth tokens to a client's Token Binding key pair, the possession of which is proven on the TLS connections over which the tokens are intended to be used. The use of Token Binding protects OAuth tokens from man-in-the-middle, token export, and replay attacks.

Open Redirector

An open redirector is an endpoint hosted on the resource server (or the OAuth 2.0 client application) end, which accepts a URL as a query parameter in a request—and then redirects the user to that URL. An attacker can modify the redirect_uri in the authorization grant request from the resource server to the authorization server to include an open redirector URL pointing to an endpoint owned by him. To do this, the attacker has to intercept the communication channel between the victim's browser and the authorization server—or the victim's browser and the resource server (see Figure 14-3).

Once the request hits the authorization server and after the authentication, the user will be redirected to the provided redirect_uri, which also carries the open redirector query parameter pointing to the attacker's endpoint. To detect any modifications to the redirect_uri, the authorization server can carry out a check against a preregistered URL. But then again, some authorization server implementations will only worry about the domain part of the URL and will ignore doing an exact one-to-one match. So, any changes to the query parameters will be unnoticed.

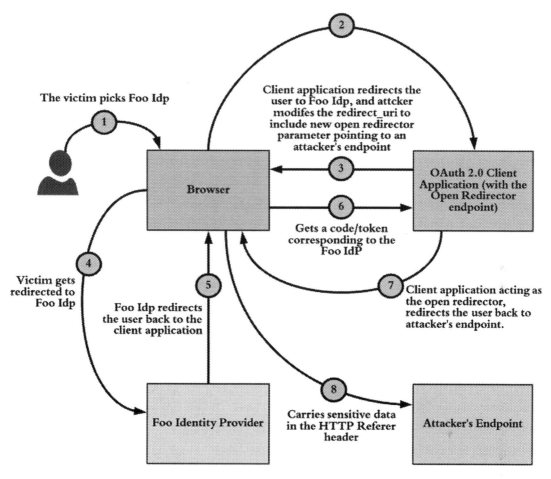

Figure 14-3. *Open Redirector attack*

Once the user got redirected to the open redirector endpoint, it will again redirect the user to the value (URL) defined in the open redirector query parameter—which will take him/her to the attacker's endpoint. In this request to the attacker's endpoint, the HTTP Referer header could carry some confidential data, including the authorization code (which is sent to the client application by the authorization server as a query parameter).

How to prevent an open redirector attack:

- Enforce strict validations at the authorization server against the redirect_uri. It can be an exact one-to-one match or regex match.

- Validate the redirecting URL at open redirector and make sure you only redirect to the domains you own.

- Use JWT Secured Authorization Request (JAR) or Pushed Authorization Requests (PAR) as discussed in Chapter 4 to protect the integrity of the authorization request, so the attacker won't be able to modify the request to include the open redirector query parameter to the redirect_uri.

Code Interception Attack

Code interception attack could possibly happen in a native mobile app. OAuth 2.0 authorization requests from native apps should only be made through external user agents, primarily the user's browser. The OAuth 2.0 for Native Apps specification (which we discussed in Chapter 10) explains in detail the security and usability reasons why this is the case and how native apps and authorization servers can implement this best practice.

The way you do single sign-on in a mobile environment is by spinning up the system browser from your app and then initiate OAuth 2.0 flow from there. Once the authorization code is returned back to the redirect_uri (from the authorization server) on the browser, there should be a way to pass it over to the native app. This is taken care by the mobile OS—and each app has to register for a URL scheme with the mobile OS. When the request comes to that particular URL, the mobile OS will pass its control to the corresponding native app. But, the danger here is, there can be multiple apps that get registered for the same URL scheme, and there is a chance a malicious app could get hold of the authorization code. Since many mobile apps embed the same client id and client secret for all the instances of that particular app, the attacker can also find out what they are. By knowing the client id and client secret, and then having access to the authorization code, the malicious app can now get an access token on behalf of the end user.

PKCE (Proof Key for Code Exchange), which we discussed in detail in Chapter 10, was introduced to mitigate such attacks. Let's see how it works:

1. The OAuth 2.0 client app generates a random number (code_verifier) and finds the SHA256 hash of it—which is called the code_challenge.

2. The OAuth 2.0 client app sends the code_challenge along with the hashing method in the authorization grant request to the authorization server.

3. Authorization server records the code_challenge (against the issued authorization code) and replies back with the code.

4. The client sends the code_verifier along with the authorization code to the token endpoint.

5. The authorization server finds the hash of the provided code_verifier and matches it against the stored code_challenge. If it does not match, rejects the request.

With this approach, a malicious app just having access to the authorization code cannot exchange it to an access token without knowing the value of the code_verifier.

Security Flaws in Implicit Grant Type

The OAuth 2.0 implicit grant type (see Figure 14-4) is now obsolete. This was mostly used by single-page applications and native mobile apps—but no more. In both the cases, the recommendation is to use the authorization code grant type. There are few security flaws, as listed in the following, identified in the implicit grant type, and the IETF OAuth working group officially announced that the applications should not use implicit grant type any more:

- With implicit grant type, the access token comes as a URI fragment and remains in the web browser location bar (step 5 in Figure 14-4). Since anything the web browser has in the location bar persevered as browser history, anyone having access to the browser history can steal the tokens.

- Since the access token remains in the web browser location bar, the API calls initiated from the corresponding web page will carry the entire URL in the location bar, along with the access token, in the HTTP Referer header. This will let external API endpoints to figure out (looking at the HTTP Referer header) what the access token is and possibly misuse it.

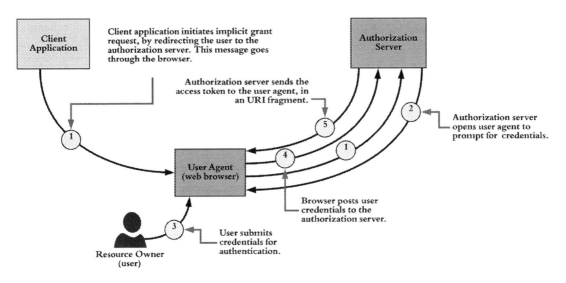

Figure 14-4. *OAuth 2.0 implicit grant flow.*

Google Docs Phishing Attack

An attacker used a fake OAuth 2.0 app called Google Docs as a medium to launch a massive phishing attack targeting Google users in May 2017. The first target was the media companies and public relations (PR) agencies. They do have a large amount of contacts—and the attacker used the email addresses from their contact lists to spread the attack. It went viral for an hour—before the app was removed by Google.

Is this a flaw in the OAuth 2.0 protocol exploited by the attacker or a flaw in how Google implemented it? Is there something we could have done better to prevent such attacks?

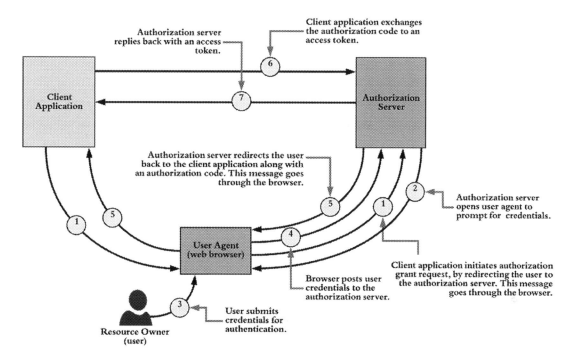

Figure 14-5. *OAuth 2.0 authorization grant flow.*

Almost all the applications you see on the Web today use the authorization code grant flow in OAuth 2.0. The attacker exploited step 3 in Figure 14-5 by tricking the user with an application name (Google Docs) known to them. Also, the attacker used an email template which is close to what Google uses in sharing docs, to make the user click on the link. Anyone who carefully looked at the email or even the consent screen could have caught up something fishy happening—but unfortunately, very few do care.

It's neither a flaw of OAuth 2.0 nor how Google implemented it. Phishing is a prominent threat in cybersecurity. Does that mean there is no way to prevent such attacks other than proper user education? There are basic things Google could do to prevent such attacks in the future. Looking at the consent screen, "Google Docs" is the key phrase used there to win user's trust. When creating an OAuth 2.0 app in Google, you can pick any name you want. This helps an attacker to misguide users. Google could easily filter out the known names and prevent app developers from picking names to trick the users.

Another key issue is Google does not show the domain name of the application (but just the application name) on the consent page. Having domain name prominently displayed on the consent page will provide some hint to the user where he is heading to. Also the image of the application on the consent page misleads the user. The attacker has intentionally picked the Google Drive image there. If all these OAuth applications can go through an approval process, before launching into public, such mishaps can be prevented. Facebook already follows such a process. When you create a Facebook app, first, only the owner of the application can log in—to launch it to the public, it has to go through an approval process.

G Suite is widely used in the enterprise. Google can give the domain admins more control to whitelist, which applications the domain users can access from corporate credentials. This prevents users under phishing attacks, unknowingly sharing access to important company docs with third-party apps.

The phishing attack on Google is a good wake-up call to evaluate and think about how phishing resistance techniques can be occupied in different OAuth flows. For example, Google Chrome security team has put so much effort when they designed the Chrome warning page for invalid certificates. They did tons of research even to pick the color, the alignment of text, and what images to be displayed. Surely, Google will bring up more bright ideas to the table to fight against phishing.

Summary

- OAuth 2.0 is the de facto standard for access delegation to cater real production use cases. There is a huge ecosystem building around it—with a massive adoption rate.

- Whenever you use OAuth, you should make sure that you follow and adhere to security best practices—and always use proven libraries and products, which already take care of enforcing the best practices.

- OAuth 2.0 Threat Model and Security Considerations (RFC 6819) produced by OAuth IETF working group defines additional security considerations for OAuth 2.0, beyond those in the OAuth 2.0 specification, based on a comprehensive threat model.

- The OAuth 2.0 Security Best Current Practice document, which is a draft proposal at the time of writing, talks about new threats related to OAuth 2.0, since the RFC 6819 was published.

- The Financial-grade API (FAPI) working group under OpenID Foundation has published a set of guidelines on how to use OAuth 2.0 in a secure way to build financial-grade applications.

CHAPTER 15

Patterns and Practices

Throughout the book so far over 14 chapters and 7 appendices, we discussed different ways of securing APIs and the theoretical background behind those. In this chapter, we present a set of API security patterns to address some of the most common enterprise security problems.

Direct Authentication with the Trusted Subsystem

Suppose a medium-scale enterprise has a number of APIs. Company employees are allowed to access these APIs via a web application while they're behind the company firewall. All user data are stored in Microsoft Active Directory (AD), and the web application is connected directly to the Active Directory to authenticate users. The web application passes the logged-in user's identifier to the back-end APIs to retrieve data related to the user.

The problem is straightforward, and Figure 15-1 illustrates the solution. You need to use some kind of direct authentication pattern. User authentication happens at the front-end web application, and once the user is authenticated, the web application needs to access the back-end APIs. The catch here is that the web application passes the logged-in user's identifier to the APIs. That implies the web application needs to invoke APIs in a user-aware manner.

Since both the web application and the APIs are in the same trust domain, we only authenticate the end user at the web application, and the back-end APIs trust whatever data passed on to those from the web application. This is called the *trusted subsystem* pattern. The web application acts as a trusted subsystem. In such case, the best way to secure APIs is through mutual Transport Layer Security (mTLS). All the requests generated from the web application are secured with mTLS, and no one but the web application can access the APIs (see Chapter 3).

© Prabath Siriwardena 2020
P. Siriwardena, *Advanced API Security*, https://doi.org/10.1007/978-1-4842-2050-4_15

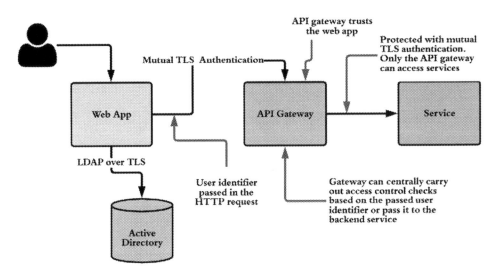

Figure 15-1. *Direct authentication with the trusted subsystem pattern*

Some do resist using TLS due to the overhead it adds and rely on building a controlled environment, where security between the web application and the container that hosts APIs is governed at the network level. Network-level security must provide the assurance that no component other than the web application server can talk to the container that hosts the APIs. This is called the trust-the-network pattern, and over the time, this has become an antipattern. The opposite of the ***trust-the-network*** pattern is zero-trust network. With the ***zero-trust network*** pattern, we do not trust the network. When we do not trust the network, we need to make sure we have enforced security checks as much as closer to the resource (or in our case, the APIs). The use of mTLS to secure the APIs is the most ideal solution here.

Single Sign-On with the Delegated Access Control

Suppose a medium-scale enterprise has a number of APIs. Company employees are allowed to access these APIs via web applications while they're behind the company firewall. All user data are stored in Microsoft Active Directory, and all the web applications are connected to an identity provider, which supports Security Assertion Markup Language (SAML) 2.0 to authenticate users. The web applications need to access back-end APIs on behalf of the logged-in user.

The catch here is the last statement: "The web applications need to access back-end APIs on behalf of the logged-in user." This suggests the need for an access delegation protocol: OAuth 2.0. However, users don't present their credentials directly to the web application—they authenticate through a SAML 2.0 identity provider.

In this case, you need to find a way to exchange the SAML token a web application receives via the SAML 2.0 Web SSO protocol for an OAuth access token, which is defined in the SAML grant type for the OAuth 2.0 specification (see Chapter 12). Once the web application receives the SAML token, as shown in step 3 of Figure 15-2, it has to exchange the SAML token to an access token by talking to the OAuth 2.0 authorization server.

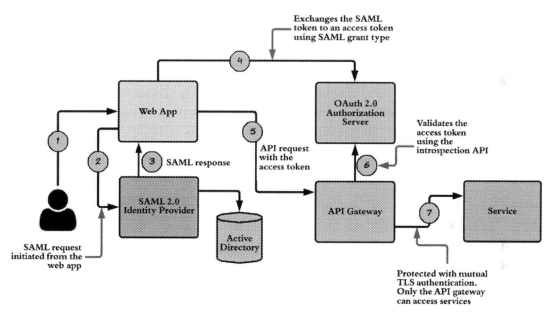

Figure 15-2. *Single sign-on with the Delegated Access Control pattern*

The authorization server must trust the SAML 2.0 identity provider. Once the web application gets the access token, it can use it to access back-end APIs. The SAML grant type for OAuth 2.0 doesn't provide a refresh token. The lifetime of the access token issued by the OAuth 2.0 authorization server must match the lifetime of the SAML token used in the authorization grant.

After the user logs in to the web application with a valid SAML token, the web application creates a session for the user from then onward, and it doesn't worry about the lifetime of the SAML token. This can lead to some issues. Say, for example, the SAML token expires, but the user still has a valid browser session in the web application. Because the SAML token has expired, you can expect that the corresponding OAuth

2.0 access token obtained at the time of user login has expired as well. Now, if the web application tries to access a back-end API, the request will be rejected because the access token is expired. In such a scenario, the web application has to redirect the user back to the SAML 2.0 identity provider, get a new SAML token, and exchange that token for a new access token. If the session at the SAML 2.0 identity provider is still live, then this redirection can be made transparent to the end user.

Single Sign-On with the Integrated Windows Authentication

Suppose a medium-scale enterprise that has a number of APIs. Company employees are allowed to access these APIs via multiple web applications while they're behind the company firewall. All user data are stored in Microsoft Active Directory, and all the web applications are connected to a SAML 2.0 identity provider to authenticate users. The web applications need to access back-end APIs on behalf of the logged-in user. All the users are in a Windows domain, and once they're logged in to their workstations, they shouldn't be asked to provide credentials at any point for any other application.

The catch here is the statement, "All the users are in a Windows domain, and once they're logged in to their workstations, they shouldn't be asked to provide credentials at any point for any other application."

You need to extend the solution we provided using single sign-on (SSO) with the Delegated Access Control pattern (the second pattern). In that case, the user logs in to the SAML 2.0 identity provider with their Active Directory username and password. Here, this isn't acceptable. Instead, you can use Integrated Windows Authentication (IWA) to secure the SAML 2.0 identity provider. When you configure the SAML 2.0 identity provider to use IWA, then once the user is redirected to the identity provider for authentication, the user is automatically authenticated; as in the case of SSO with the Delegated Access Control pattern, a SAML response is passed to the web application. The rest of the flow remains unchanged.

Identity Proxy with the Delegated Access Control

Suppose a medium-scale enterprise has a number of APIs. Company employees, as well as employees from trusted partners, are allowed to access these APIs via web applications. All the internal user data are stored in Microsoft Active Directory, and all the web applications are connected to a SAML 2.0 identity provider to authenticate users. The web applications need to access back-end APIs on behalf of logged-in users.

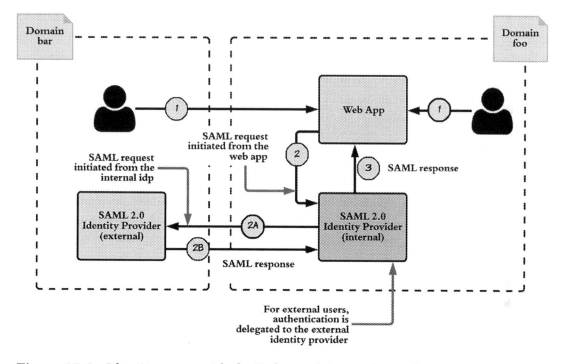

Figure 15-3. *Identity proxy with the Delegated Access Control pattern*

This use case is an extension of using SSO with the Delegated Access Control pattern. The catch here is the statement, "company employees, as well as employees from trusted partners, are allowed to access these APIs via web applications." You now have to go beyond the company domain. Everything in Figure 15-2 remains unchanged. The only thing you need to do is to change the authentication mechanism at the SAML 2.0 identity provider (see Figure 15-3).

Regardless of the end user's domain, the client web application only trusts the identity provider in its own domain. Internal as well as external users are first redirected to the internal (or local) SAML identity provider. The local identity provider should offer the user the option to pick whether to authenticate with their username and password (for internal users) or to pick their corresponding domain. Then the identity provider can redirect the user to the corresponding identity provider running in the external user's home domain. Now the external identity provider returns a SAML response to the internal identity provider.

The external identity provider signs this SAML token. If the signature is valid, and if it's from a trusted external identity provider, the internal identity provider issues a new SAML token signed by itself to the calling application. The flow then continues as shown in Figure 15-2.

Note   One benefit of this approach is that the internal applications only need to trust their own identity provider. The identity provider handles the brokering of trust between other identity providers outside its domain. In this scenario, the external identity provider also talks SAML, but that can't be expected all the time. There are also identity providers that support other protocols. In such scenarios, the internal identity provider must be able to transform identity assertions between different protocols.

Delegated Access Control with the JSON Web Token

Suppose a medium-scale enterprise that has a number of APIs. Company employees are allowed to access these APIs via web applications while they're behind the company firewall. All user data are stored in Microsoft Active Directory, and all the web applications are connected to an OpenID Connect identity provider to authenticate users. The web applications need to access back-end APIs on behalf of the logged-in user.

This use case is also an extension of the SSO with the Delegated Access Control pattern. The catch here is the statement, "all the web applications are connected to an OpenID Connect identity provider to authenticate users." You need to replace the SAML identity provider shown in Figure 15-2 with an OpenID Connect identity provider, as illustrated in Figure 15-4. This also suggests the need for an access delegation protocol (OAuth).

In this case, however, users don't present their credentials directly to the web application; rather, they authenticate through an OpenID Connect identity provider. Thus, you need to find a way to exchange the ID token received in OpenID Connect authentication for an OAuth access token, which is defined in the JWT grant type for

OAuth 2.0 specification (Chapter 12). Once the web application receives the ID token in step 3, which is also a JWT, it has to exchange it for an access token by talking to the OAuth 2.0 authorization server. The authorization server must trust the OpenID Connect identity provider. When the web application gets the access token, it can use it to access back-end APIs.

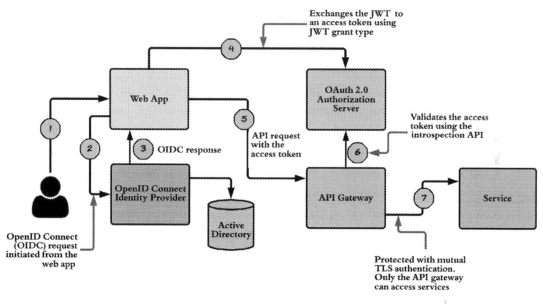

Figure 15-4. *Delegated Access Control with the JWT pattern*

Note Why would someone exchange the ID token obtained in OpenID Connect for an access token when it directly gets an access token along with the ID token? This is not required when both the OpenID Connect server and the OAuth authorization server are the same. If they aren't, you have to use the JWT Bearer grant type for OAuth 2.0 and exchange the ID token for an access token. The access token issuer must trust the OpenID Connect identity provider.

Nonrepudiation with the JSON Web Signature

Suppose a medium-scale enterprise in the finance industry needs to expose an API to its customers through a mobile application, as illustrated in Figure 15-5. One major requirement is that all the API calls should support nonrepudiation.

The catch here is the statement, "all the API calls should support nonrepudiation." When you do a business transaction via an API by proving your identity, you shouldn't be able to reject it later or repudiate it. The property that ensures the inability to repudiate is known as *nonrepudiation*. Basically, you do it once, and you own it forever (see Chapter 2 for details).

Nonrepudiation should provide proof of the origin and the integrity of data in an unforgeable manner, which a third party can verify at any time. Once a transaction is initiated, none of its content, including the user identity, date, time, and transaction details, should be altered while in transit, in order to maintain transaction integrity and to allow for future verifications. Nonrepudiation has to ensure that the transaction is unaltered and logged after it's committed and confirmed.

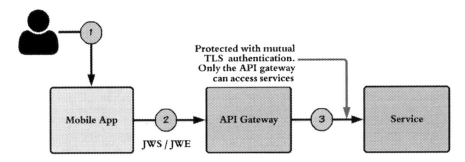

Figure 15-5. *Nonrepudiation with the JSON Web Signature pattern*

Logs must be archived and properly secured to prevent unauthorized modifications. Whenever there is a repudiation dispute, transaction logs, along with other logs or data, can be retrieved to verify the initiator, date, time, transaction history, and so on. The way to achieve nonrepudiation is via signature. A key known only to the end user should sign each message.

In this case, the financial institution must issue a key pair to each of its customers, signed by a certificate authority under its control. It should only store the corresponding public certificate, not the private key. The customer can install the private key in his or her mobile device and make it available to the mobile application. All API calls generated from the mobile application must be signed by the private key of the user and encrypted by the public key of the financial institution.

To sign the message, the mobile application can use JSON Web Signature (see Chapter 7); and for encryption, it can use JSON Web Encryption (see Chapter 8). When using both the signature and encryption on the same payload, the message must be signed first, and then the signed payload must be encrypted for legal acceptance.

Chained Access Delegation

Suppose a medium-scale enterprise that sells bottled water has an API (Water API) that can be used to update the amount of water consumed by a registered user. Any registered user can access the API via any client application. It could be an Android app, an iOS app, or even a web application.

The company only provides the API—anyone can develop client applications to consume it. All the user data of the Water API are stored in Microsoft Active Directory. The client applications shouldn't be able to access the API directly to find out information about users. Only the registered users of the Water API can access it. These users should only be able to see their own information. At the same time, for each update made by a user, the Water API must update the user's healthcare record maintained at MyHealth.org. The user also has a personal record at MyHealth.org, and it too exposes an API (MyHealth API). The Water API has to invoke the MyHealth API to update the user record on the user's behalf.

In summary, a mobile application accesses the Water API on behalf of the end user, and then the Water API has to access the MyHealth API on behalf of the end user. The Water API and the MyHealth API are in two independent domains. This suggests the need for an access delegation protocol.

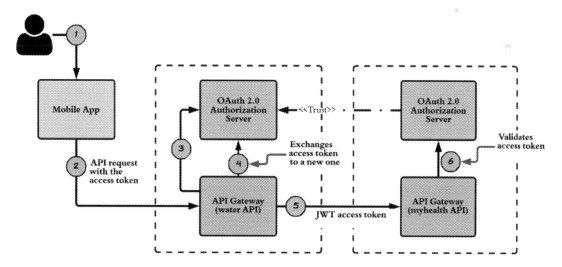

Figure 15-6. *Chained Access Delegation pattern*

Again, the catch here is the statement, "the Water API must also update the user's healthcare record maintained at MyHealth.org." This has two solutions. In the first solution, the end user must get an access token from MyHealth.org for the Water API (the Water API acts as the OAuth client), and then the Water API must store the token internally against the user's name. Whenever the user sends an update through a mobile application to the Water API, the Water API first updates its own record and then finds the MyHealth access token corresponding to the end user and uses it to access the MyHealth API. With this approach, the Water API has the overhead of storing the MyHealth API access token, and it should refresh the access token whenever needed.

The second solution is explained in Figure 15-6. It's built around the OAuth 2.0 Token Delegation profile (see Chapter 9). The mobile application must carry a valid access token to access the Water API on behalf of the end user. In step 3, the Water API talks to its own authorization server to validate the access token. Then, in step 4, the Water API exchanges the access token it got from the mobile application for a JWT access token. The JWT access token is a special access token that carries some meaningful data, and the authorization server in the Water API's domain signs it. The JWT includes the end user's local identifier (corresponding to the Water API) as well as its mapped identifier in the MyHealth domain. The end user must permit this action at the Water API domain.

In step 6, the Water API accesses the MyHealth API using the JWT access token. The MyHealth API validates the JWT access token by talking to its own authorization server. It verifies the signature; and, if it's signed by a trusted entity, the access token is treated as valid.

Because the JWT includes the mapped username from the MyHealth domain, it can identify the corresponding local user record. However, this raises a security concern. If you let users update their profiles in the Water API domain with the mapped MyHealth identifier, they can map it to any user identifier, and this leads to a security hole. To avoid this, the account mapping step must be secured with OpenID Connect authentication. When the user wants to add his or her MyHealth account identifier, the Water API domain initiates the OpenID Connect authentication flow and receives the corresponding ID token. Then the account mapping is done with the user identifier in the ID token.

Trusted Master Access Delegation

Suppose a large-scale enterprise that has a number of APIs. The APIs are hosted in different departments, and each department runs its own OAuth 2.0 authorization server due to vendor incompatibilities in different deployments. Company employees are allowed to access these APIs via web applications while they're behind the company firewall, regardless of the department which they belong to.

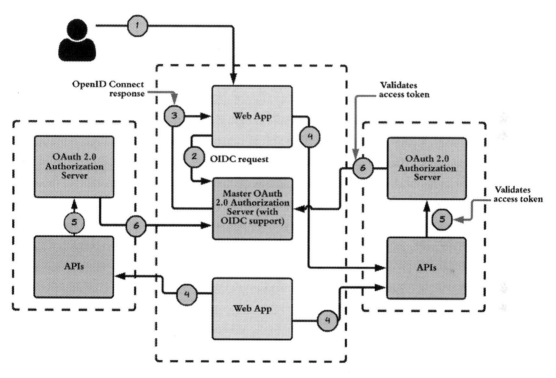

Figure 15-7. *Trusted Master Access Delegation pattern*

All user data are stored in a centralized Active Directory, and all the web applications are connected to a centralized OAuth 2.0 authorization server (which also supports OpenID Connect) to authenticate users. The web applications need to access back-end APIs on behalf of the logged-in user. These APIs may come from different departments, each of which has its own authorization server. The company also has a centralized OAuth 2.0 authorization server, and an employee having an access token from the centralized authorization server must be able to access any API hosted in any department.

Once again, this is an extended version of using SSO with the Delegated Access Control pattern. You have a master OAuth 2.0 authorization server and a set of secondary authorization servers. An access token issued from the master authorization server should be good enough to access any of the APIs under the control of the secondary authorization servers. In other words, the access token returned to the web application, as shown in step 3 of Figure 15-7, should be good enough to access any of the APIs.

To make this possible, you need to make the access token self-contained. Ideally, you should make the access token a JWT with the iss (issuer) field. In step 4, the web application accesses the API using the access token; and in step 5, the API talks to its own authorization server to validate the token. The authorization server can look at the JWT header and find out whether it issued this token or if a different server issued it. If the master authorization server issued it, then the secondary authorization server can talk to the master authorization server's OAuth introspection endpoint to find out more about the token. The introspection response specifies whether the token is active and identifies the scopes associated with the access token. Using the introspection response, the secondary authorization server can build an eXtensible Access Control Markup Language (XACML) request and call a XACML policy decision point (PDP). If the XACML response is evaluated to permit, then the web application can access the API. Then again XACML is a little too complex in defining access control policies, irrespective of how powerful it is. You can also check the Open Policy Agent (OPA) project, which has become quite popular recently in building fine-grained access control policies.

Resource Security Token Service (STS) with the Delegated Access Control

Suppose a global organization has APIs and API clients are distributed across different regions. Each region operates independently from the others. Currently, both clients and APIs are nonsecured. You need to secure the APIs without making any changes either at the API or the client end.

The solution is based on a simple theory in software engineering: introducing a layer of indirection can solve any problem. You need to introduce two interceptors. One sits in the client region, and all the nonsecured messages generated from the client are intercepted. The other interceptor sits in the API region, and all the API requests are intercepted. No other component except this interceptor can access the APIs in a nonsecured manner.

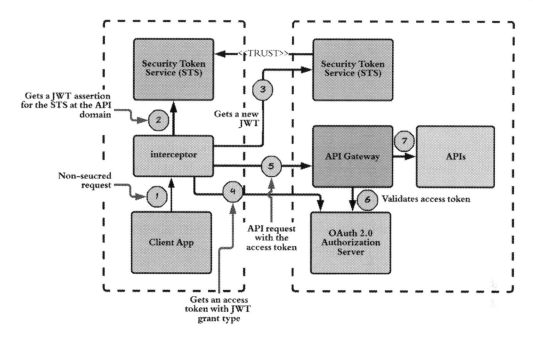

Figure 15-8. *Resource STS with the Delegated Access Control pattern*

This restriction can be enforced at the network level. Any request generated from outside has no path to the API other than through the API interceptor. Probably you deploy both API interceptor and the API in the same physical machine. You can also call this component a policy enforcement point (PEP) or API gateway. The PEP validates the security of all incoming API requests. The interceptor's responsibility, sitting in the client region, is to add the necessary security parameters to the nonsecured messages generated from the client and to send it to the API. In this way, you can secure the API without making changes at either the client or the API end.

Still, you have a challenge. How do you secure the API at the API gateway? This is a cross-domain scenario, and the obvious choice is to use JWT grant type for OAuth 2.0. Figure 15-8 explains how the solution is implemented. Nonsecured requests from the client application are captured by the interceptor component in step 1. Then it has to talk to its own security token service (STS). In step 2, the interceptor uses a default user account to access the STS using OAuth 2.0 client credentials grant type. The STS authenticates the request and issues a self-contained access token (a JWT), having the STS in the API region as the audience of the token.

In step 3, the client-side interceptor authenticates to the STS at the API region with the JWT token and gets a new JWT token, following OAuth 2.0 Token Delegation profile, which we discussed in Chapter 9. The audience of the new JWT is the OAuth 2.0

317

authorization server running in the API region. Before issuing the new JWT, the STS at the API region must validate its signature and check whether a trusted entity has signed it.

To make this scenario happen, the STS in the API region must trust the STS on the client side. The OAuth 2.0 authorization server only trusts its own STS. That is why step 4 is required. Step 4 initiates the JWT grant type for OAuth 2.0, and the client interceptor exchanges the JWT issued by the STS of the API region for an access token. Then it uses that access token to access the API in step 5.

The PEP in the API region intercepts the request and calls the authorization server to validate the access token. If the token is valid, the PEP lets the request hit the API (step 7).

Delegated Access Control with No Credentials over the Wire

Suppose a company wants to expose an API to its employees. However, user credentials must never go over the wire. This is a straightforward problem with an equally straightforward solution. Both OAuth 2.0 bearer tokens and HTTP Basic authentication take user credentials over the wire. Even though both these approaches use TLS for protection, still some companies worry about passing user credentials over communication channels—or in other words passing bearer tokens over the wire.

You have few options: use either HTTP Digest authentication or OAuth 2.0 MAC tokens (Appendix G). Using OAuth 2.0 MAC tokens is the better approach because the access token is generated for each API, and the user can also revoke the token if needed without changing the password. However, the OAuth 2.0 MAC token profile is not matured yet. The other approach is to use OAuth 2.0 with Token Binding, which we discussed in Chapter 11. Even though we use bearer tokens there, with Token Binding, we bind the token to the underneath TLS channel—so no one can export the token and use it somewhere else.

There are few more draft proposals discussed under the IETF OAuth working group to address this concern. The OAuth 2.0 Mutual-TLS Client Authentication and Certificate-Bound Access Tokens is one of them, available at `https://tools.ietf.org/html/draft-ietf-oauth-mtls-17`.

Summary

- API security is an ever-evolving subject.

- More and more standards and specifications are popping up, and most of them are built around the core OAuth 2.0 specification.

- Security around JSON is another evolving area, and the IETF JOSE working group is currently working on it.

- It's highly recommended that if you wish to continue beyond this book, you should keep an eye on the IETF OAuth working group, the IETF JOSE working group, the OpenID Foundation, and the Kantara Initiative.

APPENDIX A

The Evolution of Identity Delegation

Identity delegation plays a key role in securing APIs. Most of the resources on the Web today are exposed over APIs. The Facebook API exposes your Facebook wall, the Twitter API exposes your Twitter feed, Flickr API exposes your Flickr photos, Google Calendar API exposes your Google Calendar, and so on. You could be the owner of a certain resource (Facebook wall, Twitter feed, etc.) but not the direct consumer of an API. There may be a third party who wants to access an API on your behalf. For example, a Facebook app may want to import your Flickr photos on behalf of you. Sharing credentials with a third party who wants to access a resource you own on your behalf is an antipattern. Most web-based applications and APIs developed prior to 2006 utilized credential sharing to facilitate identity delegation. Post 2006, many vendors started developing their own proprietary ways to address this concern without credential sharing. Yahoo! BBAuth, Google AuthSub, and Flickr Authentication are some of the implementations that became popular.

A typical identity delegation model has three main roles: *delegator*, *delegate*, and *service provider*. The delegator owns the resource and is also known as the *resource owner*. The delegate wants to access a service on behalf of the delegator. The delegator delegates a limited set of privileges to the delegate to access the service. The service provider hosts the protected service and validates the legitimacy of the delegate. The service provider is also known as the *resource server*.

© Prabath Siriwardena 2020
P. Siriwardena, *Advanced API Security*, https://doi.org/10.1007/978-1-4842-2050-4_16

Direct Delegation vs. Brokered Delegation

Let's take a step back and look at a real-world example (see Figure A-1). Flickr is a popular cloud-based service for storing and sharing photos. Photos stored in Flickr are the resources, and Flickr is the resource server or the service provider. Say you have a Flickr account: you're the resource owner (or the delegator) of the photos under your account. You also have a Snapfish account. Snapfish is a web-based photo-sharing and photo-printing service that is owned by Hewlett-Packard. How can you print your Flickr photos from Snapfish? To do so, Snapfish has to first import those photos from Flickr and should have the privilege to do so, which should be delegated to Snapfish by you. You're the delegator, and Snapfish is the delegate. Other than the privilege to import photos, Snapfish won't be able to do any of the following with your Flickr photos:

- Access your Flickr account (including private content)

- Upload, edit, and replace photos and videos in the account

- Interact with other members' photos and videos (comment, add notes, favorite)

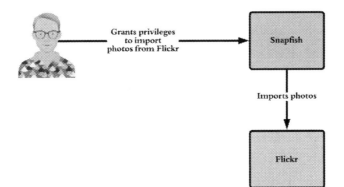

Figure A-1. *Direct delegation. The resource owner delegates privileges to the client application*

Snapfish can now access your Flickr account on your behalf with the delegated privileges. This model is called *direct delegation*: the delegator directly delegates a subset of his or her privileges to a delegate. The other model is called *indirect delegation*: the delegator first delegates to an intermediate delegate, and that delegate delegates to another delegate. This is also known as *brokered delegation* (see Figure A-2).

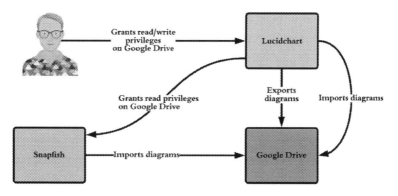

Figure A-2. *Brokered delegation. The resource owner delegates privileges to an intermediate application and that application delegates privileges to another application*

Let's say you have a Lucidchart account. Lucidchart is a cloud-based design tool that you can use to draw a wide variety of diagrams. It also integrates with Google Drive. From your Lucidchart account, you have the option to publish completed diagrams to your Google Drive. To do that, Lucidchart needs privileges to access the Google Drive API on your behalf, and you need to delegate the relevant permissions to Lucidchart. If you want to print something from Lucidchart, it invokes the Snapfish printing API. Snapfish needs to access the diagrams stored in your Google Drive. Lucidchart has to delegate a subset of the permissions you delegated to it to Snapfish. Even though you granted read/write permissions to Lucidchart, it only has to delegate read permission to Snapfish to access your Google Drive and print the selected drawings.

The Evolution

The modern history of identity delegation can be divided into two eras: pre-2006 and post-2006. Credential sharing mostly drove identity delegation prior to 2006. Twitter, SlideShare, and almost all the web applications used credential sharing to access third-party APIs. As shown in Figure A-3, when you created a Twitter account prior to 2006, Twitter asked for your email account credentials so it could access your email address book and invite your friends to join Twitter. Interestingly, it displayed the message "We don't store your login, your password is submitted securely, and we don't email without your permission" to win user confidence. But who knows—if Twitter wanted to read all your emails or do whatever it wanted to your email account, it could have done so quite easily.

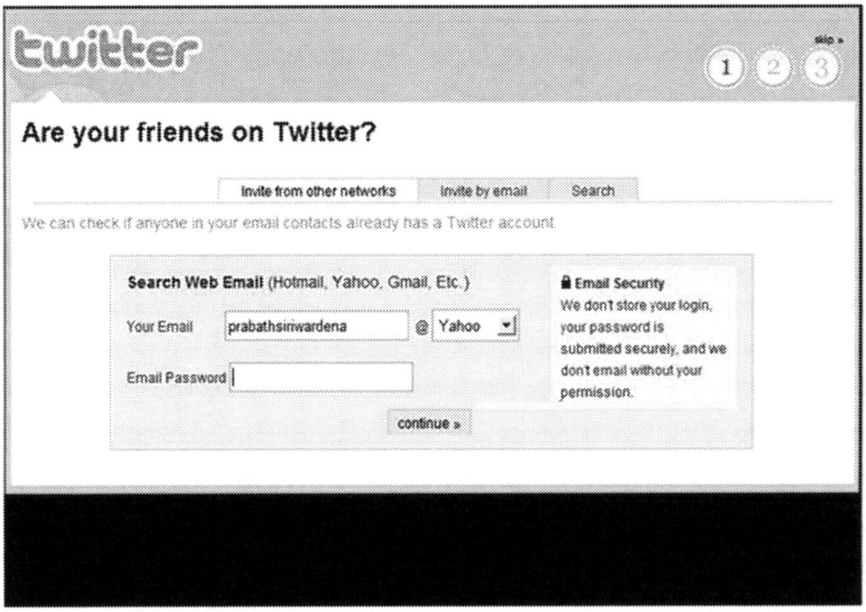

Figure A-3. *Twitter, pre-2006*

SlideShare did the same thing. SlideShare is a cloud-based service for hosting and sharing slides. Prior to 2006, if you wanted to publish a slide deck from SlideShare to a Blogger blog, you had to give your Blogger username and password to SlideShare, as shown in Figure A-4. SlideShare used Blogger credentials to access its API to post the selected slide deck to your blog. If SlideShare had wanted to, it could have modified published blog posts, removed them, and so on.

Figure A-4. *SlideShare, pre-2006*

These are just two examples. The pre-2006 era was full of such applications. Google Calendar, introduced in April 2006, followed a similar approach. Any third-party application that wanted to create an event in your Google Calendar first had to request your Google credentials and use them to access the Google Calendar API. This wasn't tolerable in the Internet community, and Google was pushed to invent a new and, of course, better way of securing its APIs. Google AuthSub was introduced toward the end of 2006 as a result. This was the start of the post-2006 era of identity delegation.

Google ClientLogin

In the very early stages of its deployment, the Google Data API was secured with two nonstandard security protocols: ClientLogin and AuthSub. ClientLogin was intended to be used by *installed applications*. An installed application can vary from a simple desktop application to a mobile application—but it can't be a web application. For web applications, the recommended way was to use AuthSub.

Note   The complete Google ClientLogin documentation is available at `https://developers.google.com/accounts/docs/AuthForInstalledApps`. The ClientLogin API was deprecated as of April 20, 2012. According to the Google deprecation policy, it operated the same until April 20, 2015.

As shown in Figure A-5, Google ClientLogin uses identity delegation with password sharing. The user has to share his Google credentials with the installed application in the first step. Then the installed application creates a request token out of the credentials, and it calls the Google Accounts Authorization service. After the validation, a CAPTCHA challenge is sent back as the response. The user must respond to the CAPTCHA and is validated again against the Google Accounts Authorization service. Once the user is validated successfully, a token is issued to the application. Then the application can use the token to access Google services.

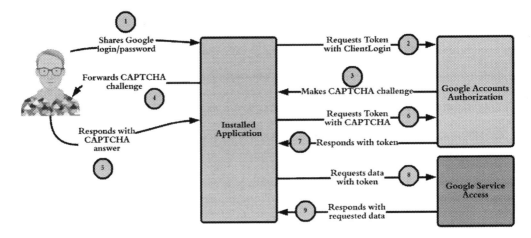

Figure A-5. *Google ClientLogin*

Google AuthSub

Google AuthSub was the recommended authentication protocol to access Google APIs via web applications in the post-2006 era. Unlike ClientLogin, AuthSub doesn't require credential sharing. Users don't need to provide credentials for a third-party web application—instead, they provide credentials directly to Google, and Google shares a temporary token with a limited set of privileges with the third-party web application. The third-party application uses the temporary token to access Google APIs. Figure A-6 explains the protocol flow in detail.

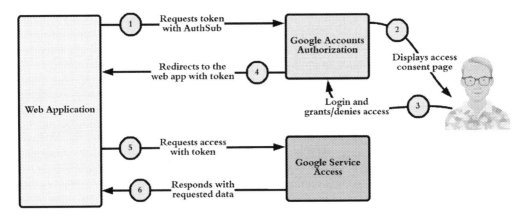

Figure A-6. *Google AuthSub*

The end user initiates the protocol flow by visiting the web application. The web application redirects the user to the Google Accounts Authorization service with an AuthSub request. Google notifies the user of the access rights (or the privileges) requested by the application, and the user can approve the request by login. Once approved by the user, Google Accounts Authorization service provides a temporary token to the web application. Now the web application can use that temporary token to access Google APIs.

Note   The complete Google AuthSub documentation is available at `https://developers.google.com/accounts/docs/AuthSub`. How to use AuthSub with the Google Data API is explained at `https://developers.google.com/gdata/docs/auth/authsub`. The AuthSub API was deprecated as of April 20, 2012. According to the Google deprecation policy, it operated the same until April 20, 2015.

Flickr Authentication API

Flickr is a popular image/video hosting service owned by Yahoo!. Flickr was launched in 2004 (before the acquisition by Yahoo! in 2005), and toward 2005 it exposed its services via a public API. It was one of the very few companies at that time that had a public API; this was even before the Google Calendar API. Flickr was one of the very few applications that followed an identity delegation model without credential sharing prior to 2006. Most of the implementations that came after that were highly influenced by the Flickr Authentication API. Unlike in Google AuthSub or ClientLogin, the Flickr model was signature based. Each request should be signed by the application from its application secret.

Yahoo! Browser–Based Authentication (BBAuth)

Yahoo! BBAuth was launched in September 2006 as a generic way of granting third-party applications access to Yahoo! data with a limited set of privileges. Yahoo! Photos and Yahoo! Mail were the first two services to support BBAuth. BBAuth, like Google AuthSub, borrowed the same concept used in Flickr (see Figure A-7).

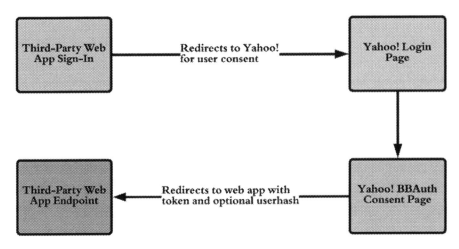

Figure A-7. *Yahoo! BBAuth*

The user first initiates the flow by visiting the third-party web application. The web application redirects the user to Yahoo!, where the user has to log in and approve the access request from the third-party application. Once approved by the user, Yahoo! redirects the user to the web application with a temporary token. Now the third-party web application can use the temporary token to access user's data in Yahoo! with limited privileges.

Note   The complete guide to Yahoo! BBAuth is available at `http://developer.yahoo.com/bbauth/`.

OAuth

Google AuthSub, Yahoo! BBAuth, and Flickr Authentication all made considerable contributions to initiate a dialog to build a common standardized delegation model. OAuth 1.0 was the first step toward identity delegation standardization. The roots of OAuth go back to November 2006, when Blaine Cook started developing an OpenID implementation for Twitter. In parallel, Larry Halff of Magnolia (a social bookmarking site) was thinking about integrating an authorization model with OpenID (around this time, OpenID began gaining more traction in the Web 2.0 community). Larry started discussing the use of OpenID for Magnolia with Twitter and found out there is no way to delegate access to Twitter APIs through OpenID. Blaine and Larry, together with Chris Messina, DeWitt Clinton, and Eran Hammer, started a discussion group in April 2007 to build a standardized access delegation protocol—which later became OAuth. The access delegation model proposed in OAuth 1.0 wasn't drastically different from what Google, Yahoo!, and Flickr already had.

Note   OpenID is a standard developed by the OpenID Foundation for decentralized single sign-on. The OpenID 2.0 final specification is available at `http://openid.net/specs/openid-authentication-2_0.html`.

The OAuth 1.0 core specification was released in December 2007. Later, in 2008, during the 73rd Internet Engineering Task Force (IETF) meeting, a decision was made to develop OAuth under the IETF. It took some time to be established in the IETF, and OAuth 1.0a was released as a community specification in June 2009 to fix a security issue related to a session fixation attack.[1] In April 2010, OAuth 1.0 was released as RFC 5849 under the IETF.

Note   The OAuth 1.0 community specification is available at `http://oauth.net/core/1.0/`, and OAuth 1.0a is at `http://oauth.net/core/1.0a/`. Appendix B explains OAuth 1.0 in detail.

In November 2009, during the Internet Identity Workshop (IIW), Dick Hardt of Microsoft, Brian Eaton of Google, and Allen Tom of Yahoo! presented a new draft specification for access delegation. It was called Web Resource Authorization Profiles (WRAP), and it was built on top of the OAuth 1.0 model to address some of its limitations. In December 2009, WRAP was deprecated in favor of OAuth 2.0.

Note   The WRAP specification contributed to the IETF OAuth working group is available at `http://tools.ietf.org/html/draft-hardt-oauth-01`.

While OAuth was being developed under the OAuth community and the IETF working group, the OpenID community also began to discuss a model to integrate OAuth with OpenID. This effort, initiated in 2009, was called OpenID/OAuth hybrid extension

---

[1]Session fixation, `www.owasp.org/index.php/Session_fixation`

(see Figure A-8). This extension describes how to embed an OAuth approval request into an OpenID authentication request to allow combined user approval. For security reasons, the OAuth access token isn't returned in the OpenID authentication response. Instead, a mechanism to obtain the access token is provided.

Note   The finalized specification for OpenID/OAuth extension is available at `http://step2.googlecode.com/svn/spec/openid_oauth_extension/latest/openid_oauth_extension.html`.

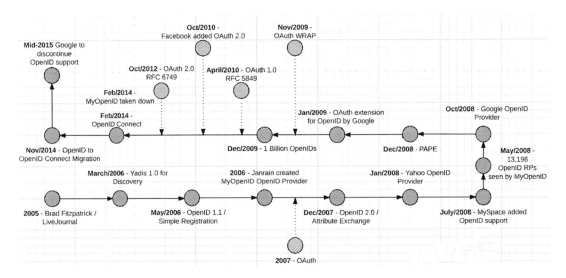

Figure A-8. *The evolution of identity protocols from OpenID to OpenID Connect*

OAuth 1.0 provided a good foundation for access delegation. However, criticism arose against OAuth 1.0, mainly targeting its usability and extensibility. As a result, OAuth 2.0 was developed as an authorization framework, rather than a standard protocol. OAuth 2.0 became the RFC 6749 in October 2012 under the IETF.

OAuth 1.0

OAuth 1.0 was the first step toward the standardization of identity delegation. OAuth involves three parties in an identity delegation transaction. The delegator, also known as the user, assigns access to his or her resources to a third party. The delegate, also known as the consumer, accesses a resource on behalf of its user. The application that hosts the actual resource is known as the service provider. This terminology was introduced in the first release of the OAuth 1.0 specification under `oauth.net`. It changed a bit when the OAuth specification was brought into the IETF working group. In OAuth 1.0, RFC 5849, the user (delegator) is known as the *resource owner*, the consumer (delegate) is known as the *client*, and the service provider is known as the *server*.

Note   The OAuth 1.0 community specification is available at `http://oauth.net/core/1.0/`, and OAuth 1.0a is at `http://oauth.net/core/1.0a/`. OAuth 1.0, RFC 5849, made OAuth 1.0 (community version) and 1.0a obsolete. RFC 5849 is available at `http://tools.ietf.org/html/rfc5849`.

The Token Dance

Token-based authentication goes back to 1994, when the Mosaic Netscape 0.9 beta version added support for cookies. For the first time, cookies were used to identify whether the same user was revisiting a given web site. Even though it's not a strong form of authentication, this was the first time in history that a cookie was used for identification. Later, most browsers added support for cookies and started using them as a form of authentication. To log in to a web site, the user gives his or her username and password. Once the user is successfully authenticated, the web server creates a session for that user, and the session identifier is written into a cookie. To reuse the already

© Prabath Siriwardena 2020
P. Siriwardena, *Advanced API Security*, https://doi.org/10.1007/978-1-4842-2050-4_17

authenticated session for each request from then onward, the user must attach the cookie. This is the most widely used form of token-based authentication.

Note   RFC 6265 defines the cookie specification in the context of HTTP: see `http://tools.ietf.org/html/rfc6265`.

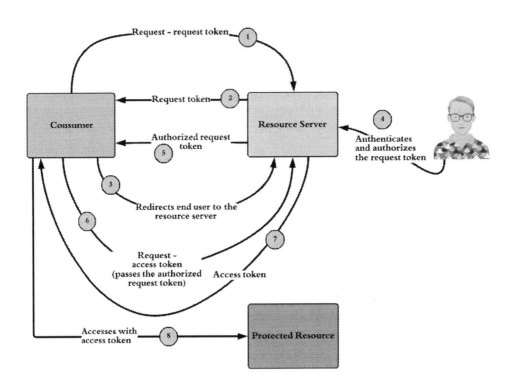

Figure B-1. *OAuth 1.0 token dance*

> ***Token***: *A unique identifier issued by the server and used by the client to associate authenticated requests with the resource owner whose authorization is requested or has been obtained by the client. Tokens have a matching shared-secret that is used by the client to establish its ownership of the token, and its authority to represent the resource owner.*
>
> —OAuth 1.0 RFC 5849

This appendix helps you digest the formal definition given for *token* by RFC 5849. OAuth uses tokens at different phases in its protocol flow (see Figure B-1). Three main phases are defined in the OAuth 1.0 handshake: the temporary-credential request phase, the resource-owner authorization phase, and the token-credential request phase.

Note   All three phases in the OAuth 1.0 token dance *must* happen over Transport Layer Security (TLS). These are bearer tokens, so anyone who steals them can use them. A bearer token is like cash. If you steal 10 bucks from someone, you can still use it at a Starbucks to buy a coffee, and the cashier will not question whether you own or how you earned that 10 bucks.

Temporary-Credential Request Phase

During the temporary-credential request phase, the OAuth client sends an HTTP POST to the temporary-credential request endpoint hosted in the resource server:

```
POST /oauth/request-token HTTP/1.1
Host: server.com
Authorization: OAuth realm="simple",
oauth_consumer_key="dsdsddDdsdsds",
oauth_signature_method="HMAC-SHA1",
oauth_callback="http://client.net/client_cb",
oauth_signature="dsDSdsdsdsdddsdsdsd"
```

The authorization header in the request is constructed with the following parameters:

- OAuth: The keyword used to identify the type of the authorization header. It must have the value OAuth.

- realm: An identifier known to the resource server. Looking at the realm value, the resource server can find out how to authenticate the OAuth client. The value of realm here serves the same purpose as in HTTP Basic authentication, which we discuss in Appendix F.

- oauth_consumer_key: A unique identifier issued to the OAuth client by the resource server. This key is associated with a secret key that is known both to the client and to the resource server.

- oauth_signature_method: The method used to generate the oauth_signature. This can be PLAINTEXT, HMAC-SHA1, or RSA-SHA1. PLAINTEXT means no signature, HMAC-SHA1 means a shared key has been used for the signature, and RSA-SHA1 means an RSA private key has been used for the signature. The OAuth specification doesn't mandate any signature method. The resource server can enforce any signature method, based on its requirements.

- oauth_signature: The signature, which is calculated according to the method defined in oauth_signature_method.

Note   With PLAINTEXT as the oauth_signature_method, the oauth_signature is the consumer secret followed by &. For example, if the consumer secret associated with the corresponding consumer_key is Ddedkljlj878dskjds, then the value of oauth_signature is Ddedkljlj878dskjds&.

- oauth_callback: An absolute URI that is under the control of the client. In the next phase, once the resource owner has authorized the access request, the resource server has to redirect the resource owner back to the oauth_callback URI. If this is preestablished between the client and the resource server, the value of oauth_callback should be set to oob to indicate that it is out of band.

The temporary-credential request authenticates the client. The client must be a registered entity at the resource server. The client registration process is outside the scope of the OAuth specification. The temporary-credential request is a direct HTTP POST from the client to the resource server, and the user isn't aware of this phase. The client gets the following in response to the temporary-credential request. Both the temporary-credential request and the response must be over TLS:

```
HTTP/1.1 200 OK
Content-Type: application/x-www-form-urlencoded
oauth_token=bhgdjgdds&
oauth_token_secret=dsdasdasdse&
oauth_callback_confirmed=true
```

Let's examine the definition of each parameter:

- oauth_token: An identifier generated by the resource server. This is used to identify the value of the oauth_token_secret in future requests made by the client to the resource server. This identifier links the oauth_token_secret to the oauth_consumer_key.

- oauth_token_secret: A shared secret generated by the resource server. The client will use this in the future requests to generate the oauth_signature.

- oauth_callback_confirmed: This must be present and set to true. It helps the client to confirm that the resource server received the oauth_callback sent in the request.

To initiate the temporary-credential request phase, the client must first be registered with the resource server and have a consumer key/consumer secret pair. At the end of this phase, the client will have an oauth_token and an oauth_token_secret.

Resource-Owner Authorization Phase

During the resource-owner authorization phase, the client must get the oauth_token received in the previous phase authorized by the user or the resource owner. The client redirects the user to the resource server with the following HTTP GET request. The oauth_token received in the previous phase is added as a query parameter. Once the request hits the resource server, the resource server knows the client corresponding to the provided token and displays the name of the client to the user on its login page. The user must authenticate first and then authorize the token:

```
GET /authorize_token?oauth_token= bhgdjgdds HTTP/1.1
Host: server.com
```

After the resource owner's approval, the resource server redirects the user to the oauth_callback URL corresponding to the client:

```
GET /client_cb?x=1&oauth_token=dsdsdsdd&oauth_verifier=dsdsdsds HTTP/1.1
Host: client.net
```

Let's examine the definition of each parameter:

- oauth_token: An identifier generated by the resource server. It's used to identify the value of the oauth_verifier in future requests made by the client to the resource server. This identifier links the oauth_verifier to the oauth_consumer_key.

- oauth_verifier: A shared verification code generated by the resource server. The client will use this in the future requests to generate the oauth_signature.

Note   If no oauth_callback URL is registered by the client, the resource server displays a verification code to the resource owner. The resource owner must take it and provide it to the client manually. The process by which the resource owner provides the verification code to the client is outside the scope of the OAuth specification.

To initiate the resource-owner authorization phase, the client must have access to the oauth_token and the oauth_token_secret. At the end of this phase, the client has a new oauth_token and an oauth_verifier.

Token-Credential Request Phase

During the token-credential request phase, the client makes a direct HTTP POST or a GET request to the access token endpoint hosted at the resource server:

```
POST /access_token HTTP/1.1
Host: server.com
Authorization: OAuth realm="simple",
oauth_consumer_key="dsdsddDdsdsds",
oauth_token="bhgdjgdds",
```

```
oauth_signature_method="PLAINTEXT",
oauth_verifier="dsdsdsds",
oauth_signature="fdfsdfdfdfdfsfffdf"
```

The authorization header in the request is constructed with the following parameters:

- OAuth: The keyword used to identify the type of the authorization header. It must have the value OAuth.

- realm: An identifier known to the resource server. Looking at the realm value, the resource server can decide how to authenticate the OAuth client. The value of realm here serves the same purpose as in HTTP Basic authentication.

- oauth_consumer_key: A unique identifier issued to the OAuth client by the resource server. This key is associated with a secret key that is known to both the client and the resource server.

- oauth_signature_method: The method used to generate the oauth_signature. This can be PLAINTEXT, HMAC-SHA1, or RSA-SHA1. PLAINTEXT means no signature, HMAC-SHA1 means a shared key has been used for the signature, and RSA-SHA1 means an RSA private key has been used for the signature. The OAuth specification doesn't mandate any signature method. The resource server can enforce any signature method, based on its requirements.

- oauth_signature: The signature, which is calculated according to the method defined in oauth_signature_method.

- oauth_token: The temporary-credential identifier returned in the temporary-credential request phase.

- oauth_verifier: The verification code returned in the resource-owner authorization phase.

After the resource server validates the access token request, it sends back the following response to the client:

```
HTTP/1.1 200 OK
Content-Type: application/x-www-form-urlencoded
oauth_token=dsdsdsdsdweoio998s&oauth_token_secret=ioui789kjhk
```

Let's examine the definition of each parameter:

- oauth_token: An identifier generated by the resource server. In future requests made by the client, this will be used to identify the value of oauth_token_secret to the resource server. This identifier links oauth_token_secret to the oauth_consumer_key.

- oauth_token_secret: A shared secret generated by the resource server. The client will use this in future requests to generate the oauth_signature.

To initiate the token-credential request phase, the client must have access to the oauth_token from the first phase and the oauth_verifier from the second phase. At the end of this phase, the client will have a new oauth_token and a new oauth_token_secret.

Invoking a Secured Business API with OAuth 1.0

At the end of the OAuth token dance, the following tokens should be retained at the OAuth client end:

- oauth_consumer_key: An identifier generated by the resource server to uniquely identify the client. The client gets the oauth_consumer_key at the time of registration with the resource server. The registration process is outside the scope of the OAuth specification.

- oauth_consumer_secret: A shared secret generated by the resource server. The client will get the oauth_consumer_secret at the time of registration, with the resource server. The registration process is outside the scope of the OAuth specification. The oauth_consumer_secret is never sent over the wire.

- oauth_token: An identifier generated by the resource server at the end of the token-credential request phase.

- oauth_token_secret: A shared secret generated by the resource server at the end of the token-credential request phase.

Following is a sample HTTP request to access a secured API with OAuth 1.0. Here we send an HTTP POST to the student API with one argument called name. In addition to the previously described parameters, it also has oauth_timestamp and oauth_nonce. An API gateway (or any kind of an interceptor) intercepts the request and talks to the token issuer to validate the authorization header. If all looks good, the API gateway routes the request to the business service (behind the API) and then sends back the corresponding response:

```
POST /student?name=pavithra HTTP/1.1
Host: server.com
Content-Type: application/x-www-form-urlencoded
Authorization: OAuth realm="simple",
oauth_consumer_key="dsdsddDdsdsds ",
oauth_token="dsdsdsdsdweoio998s",
oauth_signature_method="HMAC-SHA1",
oauth_timestamp="1474343201",
oauth_nonce="rerwerweJHKjhkdsjhkhj",
oauth_signature="bYT5CMsGcbgUdFHObYMEfcx6bsw%3D"
```

Let's examine the definition of the oauth_timestamp and oauth_nonce parameters:

- oauth_timestamp: A positive integer that is the number of seconds counted since January 1, 1970, 00:00:00 GMT.

- oauth_nonce: A randomly generated unique value added to the request by the client. It's used to avoid replay attacks. The resource server must reject any request with a nonce that it has seen before.

Demystifying oauth_signature

Out of the three phases we discussed in the section "The Token Dance," oauth_signature is required in two: the temporary-credential request phase and the token-credential request phase. In addition, oauth_signature is required in all client requests to the protected resource or to the secured API. The OAuth specification defines three kinds of signature methods: PLAINTEXT, HMAC-SHA1, and RSA-SHA1. As explained earlier, PLAINTEXT means no signature, HMAC-SHA1 means a shared key has been used for the signature, and RSA-SHA1 means an RSA private key has been used for the signature.

The OAuth specification doesn't mandate any signature method. The resource server can enforce a signature method, based on its requirements. The challenge in each signature method is how to generate the base string to sign. Let's start with the simplest case, PLAINTEXT (see Table B-1).

Table B-1. *Signature Calculation with the PLAINTEXT Signature Method*

Phase	oauth_signature
Temporary-credential request phase	consumer_secret&
Token-credential request phase	consumer_secret&oauth_token_secret

With the PLAINTEXT oauth_signature_method, the oauth_signature is the encoded consumer secret followed by &. For example, if the consumer secret associated with the corresponding consumer_key is Ddedkljlj878dskjds, the value of oauth_signature is Ddedkljlj878dskjds&. In this case, TLS must be used to protect the secret key going over the wire. This calculation of oauth_signature with PLAINTEXT is valid only for the temporary-credential request phase. For the token-credential request phase, oauth_signature also includes the shared token secret after the encoded consumer secret. For example, if the consumer secret associated with the corresponding consumer_key is Ddedkljlj878dskjds and the value of the shared token secret is ekhjkhkhrure, then the value of oauth_signature is Ddedkljlj878dskjds&ekhjkhkhrure. The shared token secret in this case is the oauth_token_secret returned in the temporary-credential request phase.

For both HMAC-SHA1 and RSA-SHA1 signature methods, first you need to generate a base string for signing, which we discuss in the next section.

Generating the Base String in Temporary-Credential Request Phase

Let's start with the temporary-credential request phase. The following is a sample OAuth request generated in this phase:

```
POST /oauth/request-token HTTP/1.1
Host: server.com
Authorization: OAuth realm="simple",
oauth_consumer_key="dsdsddDdsdsds",
oauth_signature_method="HMAC-SHA1",
```

```
oauth_callback="http://client.net/client_cb",
oauth_signature="dsDSdsdsdsdddsdsdsd"
```

Step 1: Get the uppercase value of the HTTP request header (GET or POST):

```
POST
```

Step 2: Get the value of the scheme and the HTTP host header in lowercase. If the port has a nondefault value, it needs to be included as well:

```
http://server.com
```

Step 3: Get the path and the query components in the request resource URI:

```
/oauth/request-token
```

Step 4: Get all the OAuth protocol parameters, excluding oauth_signature, concatenated by & (no line breaks):

```
oauth_consumer_key="dsdsddDdsdsds"&
oauth_signature_method="HMAC-SHA1"&
oauth_callback="http://client.net/client_cb"
```

Step 5: Concatenate the outputs from steps 2 and 3:

```
http://server.com/oauth/request-token
```

Step 6: Concatenate the output from steps 5 and 4 with & (no line breaks):

```
http://server.com/oauth/access-token&
oauth_consumer_key="dsdsddDdsdsds"&
oauth_signature_method="HMAC-SHA1"&
oauth_callback="http://client.net/client_cb"
```

Step 7: URL-encode the output from step 6 (no line breaks):

```
http%3A%2F%2Fserver.com%2Foauth%2F
access-token&%26%20oauth_consumer_key%3D%22dsdsddDdsdsds%22%26
oauth_signature_method%3D%22HMAC-SHA1%22%26
oauth_callback%3D%22http%3A%2F%2Fclient.net%2Fclient_cb%22
```

Step 8: Concatenate the output from steps 1 and 7 with &. This produces the final base string to calculate the oauth_signature (no line breaks):

```
POST&http%3A%2F%2Fserver.com%2Foauth%2F
access-token&%26%20oauth_consumer_key%3D%22dsdsddDdsdsds%22%26
oauth_signature_method%3D%22HMAC-SHA1%22%26
oauth_callback%3D%22http%3A%2F%2Fclient.net%2Fclient_cb%22
```

Generating the Base String in Token Credential Request Phase

Now, let's see how to calculate the base string in the token-credential request phase. The following is a sample OAuth request generated in this phase:

```
POST /access_token HTTP/1.1
Host: server.com
Authorization: OAuth realm="simple",
oauth_consumer_key="dsdsddDdsdsds",
oauth_token="bhgdjgdds",
oauth_signature_method="HMAC-SHA1",
oauth_verifier="dsdsdsds",
oauth_signature="fdfsdfdfdfdfsfffdf"
```

Step 1: Get the uppercase value of the HTTP request header (GET or POST):

```
POST
```

Step 2: Get the value of the scheme and the HTTP host header in lowercase. If the port has a nondefault value, it needs to be included as well:

```
http://server.com
```

Step 3: Get the path and the query components in the request resource URI:

```
/oauth/access-token
```

Step 4: Get all the OAuth protocol parameters, excluding oauth_signature, concatenated by & (no line breaks):

```
oauth_consumer_key="dsdsddDdsdsds"&
oauth_token="bhgdjgdds"&
```

```
oauth_signature_method="HMAC-SHA1"&
oauth_verifier="dsdsdsds"
```

Step 5: Concatenate the output from steps 2 and 3:

```
http://server.com/oauth/access-token
```

Step 6: Concatenate the output from steps 5 and 4 with & (no line breaks):

```
http://server.com/oauth/request-token&
oauth_consumer_key="dsdsddDdsdsds"&
oauth_token="bhgdjgdds"&
oauth_signature_method="HMAC-SHA1"&
oauth_verifier="dsdsdsds"
```

Step 7: URL-encode the output from step 6 (no line breaks):

```
http%3A%2F%2Fserver.com%2Foauth%2F
request-token%26oauth_consumer_key%3D%22dsdsddDdsdsds%22%26
oauth_token%3D%22%20bhgdjgdds%22%26
oauth_signature_method%3D%22HMAC-SHA1%22%26
oauth_verifier%3D%22%20dsdsdsds%22%20
```

Step 8: Concatenate the output from steps 1 and 7 with &. This produces the final base string to calculate the oauth_signature (no line breaks):

```
POST&http%3A%2F%2Fserver.com%2Foauth%2F
request-token%26oauth_consumer_key%3D%22dsdsddDdsdsds%22%26
oauth_token%3D%22%20bhgdjgdds%22%26
oauth_signature_method%3D%22HMAC-SHA1%22%26
oauth_verifier%3D%22%20dsdsdsds%22%20
```

Building the Signature

Once you've calculated the base string for each phase, the next step is to build the signature based on the signature method. For the temporary-credential request phase, if you use HMAC-SHA1 as the signature method, the signature is derived in the following manner:

```
oauth_signature= HMAC-SHA1(key, text)
oauth_signature= HMAC-SHA1(consumer_secret&, base-string)
```

For the token-credential request phase, the key also includes the shared token secret after the consumer secret. For example, if the consumer secret associated with the corresponding consumer_key is Ddedkljlj878dskjds and the value of the shared token secret is ekhjkhkhrure, then the value of the key is Ddedkljlj878dskjds&ekhjkh khrure. The shared token secret in this case is the oauth_token_secret returned in the temporary-credential request phase:

```
oauth_signature= HMAC-SHA1(consumer_secret&oauth_token_secret, base-string)
```

In either phase, if you want to use RSA-SHA1 as the oauth_signature_method, the OAuth client must register an RSA public key corresponding to its consumer key, at the resource server. For RSA-SHA1, you calculate the signature in the following manner, regardless of the phase:

```
oauth_signature= RSA-SHA1(RSA private key, base-string)
```

Generating the Base String in an API Call

In addition to the token dance, you also need to build the oauth_signature in each business API invocation. In the following sample request, the OAuth client invokes the student API with a query parameter. Let's see how to calculate the base string in this case:

```
POST /student?name=pavithra HTTP/1.1
Host: server.com
Content-Type: application/x-www-form-urlencoded
Authorization: OAuth realm="simple",
oauth_consumer_key="dsdsddDdsdsds ",
oauth_token="dsdsdsdsdweoio998s",
oauth_signature_method="HMAC-SHA1",
oauth_timestamp="1474343201",
oauth_nonce="rerwerweJHKjhkdsjhkhj",
oauth_signature="bYT5CMsGcbgUdFHObYMEfcx6bsw%3D"
```

Step 1: Get the uppercase value of the HTTP request header (GET or POST):

```
POST
```

Step 2: Get the value of the scheme and the HTTP host header in lowercase. If the port has a nondefault value, it needs to be included as well:

```
http://server.com
```

Step 3: Get the path and the query components in the request resource URI:

```
/student?name=pavithra
```

Step 4: Get all the OAuth protocol parameters, excluding oauth_signature, concatenated by & (no line breaks):

```
oauth_consumer_key="dsdsddDdsdsds"&
oauth_token="dsdsdsdsdweoio998s"&
oauth_signature_method="HMAC-SHA1"&
oauth_timestamp="1474343201"&
oauth_nonce="rerwerweJHKjhkdsjhkhj"
```

Step 5: Concatenate the output from steps 2 and 3 (no line breaks):

```
http://server.com/student?name=pavithra
```

Step 6: Concatenate the output from steps 5 and 4 with & (no line breaks):

```
http://server.com/student?name=pavithra&
oauth_consumer_key="dsdsddDdsdsds"&
oauth_token="dsdsdsdsdweoio998s"&
oauth_signature_method="HMAC-SHA1"&
oauth_timestamp="1474343201"&
oauth_nonce="rerwerweJHKjhkdsjhkhj"
```

Step 7: URL-encode the output from step 6 (no line breaks):

```
http%3A%2F%2Fserver.com%2Fstudent%3Fname%3Dpavithra%26
oauth_consumer_key%3D%22dsdsddDdsdsds%20%22%26
oauth_token%3D%22dsdsdsdsdweoio998s%22%26
oauth_signature_method%3D%22HMAC-SHA1%22%26
oauth_timestamp%3D%221474343201%22%26
oauth_nonce%3D%22rerwerweJHKjhkdsjhkhj%22
```

Step 8: Concatenate the output from steps 1 and 7 with &. This produces the final base string to calculate the oauth_signature (no line breaks):

```
POST& http%3A%2F%2Fserver.com%2Fstudent%3Fname%3Dpavithra%26
oauth_consumer_key%3D%22dsdsddDdsdsds%20%22%26
oauth_token%3D%22dsdsdsdsdweoio998s%22%26
oauth_signature_method%3D%22HMAC-SHA1%22%26
oauth_timestamp%3D%221474343201%22%26
oauth_nonce%3D%22rerwerweJHKjhkdsjhkhj%22
```

Once you have the base string, the OAuth signature is calculated in the following manner with the HMAC-SHA1 and RSA-SHA1 signature methods. The value of oauth_token_secret is from the token-credential request phase:

```
oauth_signature= HMAC-SHA1(consumer_secret&oauth_token_secret,
base-string)
oauth_signature= RSA-SHA1(RSA private key, base-string)
```

Three-Legged OAuth vs. Two-Legged OAuth

The OAuth flow discussed so far involves three parties: the resource owner, the client, and the resource server. The client accesses a resource hosted in the resource server on behalf of the resource owner. This is the most common pattern in OAuth, and it's also known as *three-legged OAuth* (three parties involved). In two-legged OAuth, you have only two parties: the client becomes the resource owner. There is no access delegation in two-legged OAuth.

Note   Two-legged OAuth never made it to the IETF. The initial draft specification is available at `http://oauth.googlecode.com/svn/spec/ext/consumer_request/1.0/drafts/2/spec.html`.

If the same student API discussed earlier is secured with two-legged OAuth, the request from the client looks like the following. The value of oauth_token is an empty string. There is no token dance in two-legged OAuth. You only need oauth_consumer_key and consumer_secret. The HMAC-SHA1 signature is generated using consumer_secret as the key:

```
POST /student?name=pavithra HTTP/1.1
Host: server.com
Content-Type: application/x-www-form-urlencoded
Authorization: OAuth realm="simple",
oauth_consumer_key="dsdsddDdsdsds ",
oauth_token="",
oauth_signature_method="HMAC-SHA1",
oauth_timestamp="1474343201",
oauth_nonce="rerwerweJHKjhkdsjhkhj",
oauth_signature="bYT5CMsGcbgUdFHObYMEfcx6bsw%3D"
```

> **Note**   In both HTTP Basic authentication and two-legged OAuth, the resource owner acts as the client and directly invokes the API. With HTTP Basic authentication, you pass the credentials over the wire; this must be over TLS. With two-legged OAuth, you never pass the `consumer_secret` over the wire, so it need not be on TLS.

HTTP Digest authentication looks very similar to two-legged OAuth. In both cases, you never pass credentials over the wire. The difference is that HTTP Digest authentication authenticates the user, whereas two-legged OAuth authenticates the application on behalf of the resource owner. A given resource owner can own multiple applications, and each application can have its own consumer key and consumer secret.

OAuth WRAP

In November 2009, a new draft specification for access delegation called Web Resource Authorization Profiles (WRAP) was proposed, built on top of the OAuth 1.0 model. WRAP was later deprecated in favor of OAuth 2.0.

> **Note**   The initial draft of the WRAP profile submitted to the IETF is available at `http://tools.ietf.org/html/draft-hardt-oauth-01`.

Unlike OAuth 1.0, WRAP didn't depend on a signature scheme. At a high level, the user experience was the same as in OAuth 1.0, but WRAP introduced a new component into the access delegation flow: the authorization server. Unlike in OAuth 1.0, all the communications with respect to obtaining a token now happens between the client and the authorization server (not with the resource server). The client first redirects the user to the authorization server with its consumer key and the callback URL. Once the user authorized the access rights to the client, the user is redirected back to the callback URL with a verification code. Then the client has to do a direct call to the access token endpoint of the authorization server with the verification code to get the access token. Thereafter, the client only needs to include the access token in all API calls (all API calls must be on TLS):

```
https://friendfeed-api.com/v2/feed/home?wrap_access_token=dsdsdrwerwr
```

> **Note**   In November 2009, Facebook joined the Open Web Foundation, together with Microsoft, Google, Yahoo!, and many others, with a commitment to support open standards for web authentication. Keeping that promise, in December 2009, Facebook added OAuth WRAP support to FriendFeed, which it had acquired a few months earlier.

OAuth WRAP was one of the initial steps toward OAuth 2.0. WRAP introduced two types of profiles for acquiring an access token: autonomous client profiles and user delegation profiles. In autonomous client profiles, the client becomes the resource owner, or the client is acting on behalf of itself. In other words, the resource owner is the one who accesses the resource. This is equivalent to the two-legged OAuth model in OAuth 1.0. In user delegation profiles, the client acts on behalf of the resource owner. OAuth 1.0 didn't have this profile concept, and was limited to a single flow. This extensibility introduced by OAuth WRAP later became a key part of OAuth 2.0.

Client Account and Password Profile

The OAuth WRAP specification introduced two autonomous client profiles: the Client Account and Password Profile and the Assertion Profile. The Client Account and Password Profile uses the client's or the resource owner's credentials at the authorization server to obtain an access token. This pattern is mostly used for server-to-server authentication where no end user is involved. The following cURL command does an HTTP POST to the WRAP token endpoint of the authorization server, with three attributes: wrap_name is the username, wrap_password is the password corresponding to the username, and wrap_scope is the expected level of access required by the client. wrap_scope is an optional parameter:

```
\> curl -v -k -X POST
    -H "Content-Type: application/x-www-form-urlencoded;charset=UTF-8"
    -d "wrap_name=admin&
       wrap_password=admin&
       wrap_scope=read_profile"
       https://authorization-server/wrap/token
```

This returns wrap_access_token, wrap_refresh_token, and wrap_access_token_expires_in parameters. wrap_access_token_expires_in is an optional parameter that indicates the lifetime of wrap_access_token in seconds. When wrap_access_token expires, wrap_refresh_token can be used to get a new access token. OAuth WRAP introduced for the first time this token-refreshing functionality. The access token refresh request only needs wrap_refresh_token as a parameter, as shown next, and it returns a new wrap_access_token. It doesn't return a new wrap_refresh_token. The same wrap_refresh_token obtained in the first access token request can be used to refresh subsequent access tokens:

```
\> curl -v -k -X POST
    -H "Content-Type: application/x-www-form-urlencoded;charset=UTF-8"
    -d "wrap_refresh_token=Xkjk78iuiuh876jhhkwkjhewew"
       https://authorization-server/wrap/token
```

Assertion Profile

The Assertion Profile is another profile introduced by OAuth WRAP that falls under the autonomous client profiles. This assumes that the client somehow obtains an assertion—say, for example, a SAML token—and uses it to acquire a wrap_access_token. The following example cURL command does an HTTP POST to the WRAP token endpoint of the authorization server, with three attributes: wrap_assertion_format is the type of the assertion included in the request in a way known to the authorization server, wrap_assertion is the encoded assertion, and wrap_scope is the expected level of access required by the client. wrap_scope is an optional parameter:

```
\> curl -v -k -X POST
    -H "Content-Type: application/x-www-form-urlencoded;charset=UTF-8"
    -d "wrap_assertion_format=saml20&
        wrap_assertion=encoded-assertion&
        wrap_scope=read_profile"
        https://authorization-server/wrap/token
```

The response is the same as in the Client Account and Password Profile, except that in the Assertion Profile, there is no wrap_refresh_token.

Username and Password Profile

The WRAP user delegation profiles introduced three profiles: the Username and Password Profile, the Web App Profile, and the Rich App Profile. The Username and Password Profile is mostly recommended for installed trusted applications. The application is the client, and the end user or the resource owner must provide their username and password to the application. Then the application exchanges the username and password for an access token and stores the access token in the application.

The following cURL command does an HTTP POST to the WRAP token endpoint of the authorization server, with four attributes: wrap_client_id is an identifier for the application, wrap_username is the username of the end user, wrap_password is the password corresponding to the username, and wrap_scope is the expected level of access required by the client (wrap_scope is an optional parameter):

```
\> curl -v -k -X POST
    -H "Content-Type: application/x-www-form-urlencoded;charset=UTF-8"
    -d "wrap_client_id=app1&
        wrap_username=admin&
        wrap_password=admin&
        wrap_scope=read_profile"
        https://authorization-server/wrap/token
```

This returns wrap_access_token and wrap_access_token_expires_in parameters. wrap_access_token_expires_in is an optional parameter that indicates the lifetime of wrap_access_token in seconds. If the authorization server detects any malicious access patterns, then instead of sending wrap_access_token to the client application, it returns a wrap_verification_url. It's the responsibility of the client application to load this URL into the user's browser or advise them to visit that URL. Once the user has completed that step, the user must indicate to the client application that verification is complete. Then the client application can initiate the token request once again. Instead of sending a verification URL, the authorization server can also enforce a CAPTCHA verification through the client application. There the authorization server sends back a wrap_captcha_url, which points to the location where the client application can load the CAPTCHA. Once it's loaded and has the response from the end user, the client application must POST it back to the authorization server along with the token request:

```
\> curl -v -k -X POST
    -H "Content-Type: application/x-www-form-urlencoded;charset=UTF-8"
    -d "wrap_captcha_url=url-encoded-captcha-url&
        wrap_captch_solution-solution&
        wrap_client_id=app1&
        wrap_username=admin&
        wrap_password=admin&
        wrap_scope=read_profile"
        https://authorization-server/wrap/token
```

Web App Profile

The Web App Profile defined under the WRAP user delegation profiles is mostly recommended for web applications, where the web application must access a resource belonging to an end user on his or her behalf. The web application follows a two-step process to acquire an access token: it gets a verification code from the authorization server and then exchanges that for an access token. The end user must initiate the first step by visiting the client web application. Then the user is redirected to the authorization server. The following example shows how the user is redirected to the authorization server with appropriate WRAP parameters:

```
https://authorization-server/wrap/authorize?
        wrap_client_id=OrhQErXIX49svVYoXJGtoDWBuFca&
        wrap_callback=https%3A%2F%2Fmycallback&
        wrap_client_state=client-state&
        wrap_scope=read_profile
```

wrap_client_id is an identifier for the client web application. wrap_callback is the URL where the user is redirected after a successful authentication at the authorization server. Both wrap_client_state and wrap_scope are optional parameters. Any value in wrap_client_state must be returned back to the client web application. After the end user's approval, a wrap_verification_code and other related parameters are returned to the callback URL associated with the client web application as query parameters.

The next step is to exchange this verification code to an access token:

```
\> curl -v -k -X POST
    -H "Content-Type: application/x-www-form-urlencoded;charset=UTF-8"
    -d "wrap_client_id=OrhQErXIX49svVYoXJGtoDWBuFca &
        wrap_client_secret=weqeKJHjhkhkihjk&
        wrap_verification_code=dsadkjljljrrer&
        wrap_callback=https://mycallback"
        https://authorization-server/wrap/token
```

This cURL command does an HTTP POST to the WRAP token endpoint of the authorization server, with four attributes: wrap_client_id is an identifier for the application, wrap_client_secret is the password corresponding to wrap_client_id, wrap_verification_code is the verification code returned in the previous step, and wrap_callback is the callback URL where the verification code was sent. This returns wrap_access_token, wrap_refresh_token, and wrap_access_token_expires_in parameters. wrap_access_token_expires_in is an optional parameter that indicates the lifetime of wrap_access_token in seconds. When wrap_access_token expires, wrap_refresh_token can be used to get a new access token.

Rich App Profile

The Rich App Profile defined under the WRAP user delegation profiles is most commonly used in scenarios where the OAuth client application is an installed application that can also work with a browser. Hybrid mobile apps are the best example. The protocol flow is very similar to that of the Web App Profile. The rich client application follows a two-step process to acquire an access token: it gets a verification code from the authorization server and then exchanges that for an access token. The end user must initiate the first step by visiting the rich client application. Then the application spawns a browser and redirects the user to the authorization server:

```
https://authorization-server/wrap/authorize?
        wrap_client_id=OrhQErXIX49svVYoXJGtODWBuFca&
        wrap_callback=https%3A%2F%2Fmycallback&
        wrap_client_state=client-state&
        wrap_scope=read_profile
```

wrap_client_id is an identifier for the rich client application. wrap_callback is the URL where the user is redirected after a successful authentication at the authorization server. Both wrap_client_state and wrap_scope are optional parameters. Any value in wrap_client_state is returned back to the callback URL. After the end user's approval, a wrap_verification_code is returned to the rich client application.

The next step is to exchange this verification code for an access token:

```
\> curl -v -k -X POST
    -H "Content-Type: application/x-www-form-urlencoded;charset=UTF-8"
    -d "wrap_client_id=OrhQErXIX49svVYoXJGtODWBuFca&
        wrap_verification_code=dsadkjljljrrer&
        wrap_callback=https://mycallback"
        https://authorization-server/wrap/token
```

This cURL command does an HTTP POST to the WRAP token endpoint of the authorization server, with three attributes: wrap_client_id is an identifier for the application, wrap_verification_code is the verification code returned in the previous step, and wrap_callback is the callback URL where the verification code was sent. This returns wrap_access_token, wrap_refresh_token, and wrap_access_token_expires_in parameters. wrap_access_token_expires_in is an optional parameter that indicates the lifetime of wrap_access_token in seconds. When wrap_access_token expires, wrap_refresh_token can be used to get a new access token. Unlike in the Web App Profile, the Rich App Profile doesn't need to send wrap_client_secret in the access token request.

Accessing a WRAP-Protected API

All the previous profiles talk about how to get an access token. Once you have the access token, the rest of the flow is independent of the WRAP profile. The following cURL command shows how to access a WRAP-protected resource or an API, and it must happen over TLS:

```
\> curl -H "Authorization: WRAP
        access_token=cac93e1d29e45bf6d84073dbfb460"
        https://localhost:8080/recipe
```

WRAP to OAuth 2.0

OAuth WRAP was able to sort out many of the limitations and drawbacks found in OAuth 1.0: primarily, extensibility. OAuth 1.0 is a concrete protocol for identity delegation that has its roots in Flickr Authentication, Google AuthSub, and Yahoo! BBAuth. Another key difference between OAuth 1.0 and WRAP is the dependency on signatures: OAuth WRAP eliminated the need for signatures and mandated using TLS for all types of communications.

OAuth 2.0 is a big step forward from OAuth WRAP. It further improved the extensibility features introduced in OAuth WRAP and introduced two major extension points: grant types and token types.

How Transport Layer Security Works?

After the exposure of certain secret operations carried out by the National Security Agency (NSA) of the United States, by its former contractor, Edward Snowden, most of the governments, corporations, and even individuals started to think more about security. Edward Snowden is a traitor for some while a whistle-blower for others. *The Washington Post* newspaper published details from a document revealed by Edward Snowden on October 30, 2013. This was a disturbing news for two Silicon Valley tech giants, Google and Yahoo!. This highly confidential document revealed how NSA intercepted communication links between data centers of Google and Yahoo! to carry out a massive surveillance on its hundreds of millions of users. Further, according to the document, NSA sends millions of records every day from the Yahoo! and Google internal networks to data warehouses at the agency's headquarters in Fort Meade, Md. After that, field collectors process these data records to extract out metadata, which indicate who sent or received emails and when, as well as the content such as text, audio, and video.[1]

How is this possible? How come an intruder (in this case, it's the government) intercepts the communication channels between two data centers and gets access to the data? Even though Google used a secured communication channel from the user's browser to the Google front-end servers, from there onward, and between the data centers, the communication was in cleartext. As a response to this incident, Google started securing all its communication links between data centers with encryption. Transport Layer Security (TLS) plays a major role in securing data transferred over

---

[1]NSA infiltrates links to Yahoo, Google data centers worldwide, Snowden documents say, `www.washingtonpost.com/world/national-security/nsa-infiltrates-links-to-yahoo-google-data-centers-worldwide-snowden-documents-say/2013/10/30/e51d661e-4166-11e3-8b74-d89d714ca4dd_story.html`

© Prabath Siriwardena 2020
P. Siriwardena, *Advanced API Security*, https://doi.org/10.1007/978-1-4842-2050-4_18

communication links. In fact, Google is one of the first out of all tech giants to realize the value of TLS. Google made TLS the default setting in Gmail in January 2010 to secure all Gmail communications and four months later introduced an encrypted search service located at `https://encrypted.google.com`. In October 2011, Google further enhanced its encrypted search and made google.com available on HTTPS, and all Google search queries and the result pages were delivered over HTTPS. HTTPS is in fact the HTTP over TLS.

In addition to establishing a protected communication channel between the client and the server, TLS also allows both the parties to identify each other. In the most popular form of TLS, which everyone knows and uses in day-to-day life on the Internet, only the server authenticates to the client—this is also known as *one-way TLS*. In other words, the client can identify exactly the server it communicates with. This is done by observing and matching the server's certificate with the server URL, which the user hits on the browser. As we proceed in this appendix, we will further discuss how exactly this is done in detail. In contrast to one-way TLS, mutual authentication identifies both the parties—the client and the server. The client knows exactly the server it communicates with, and the server knows who the client is.

The Evolution of Transport Layer Security (TLS)

TLS has its roots in SSL (Secure Sockets Layer). Netscape Communications (then Mosaic Communications) introduced SSL in 1994 to build a secured channel between the Netscape browser and the web server it connects to. This was an important need at that time, just prior to the dot-com bubble.[2] The SSL 1.0 specification was never released to the public, because it was heavily criticized for the weak cryptographic algorithms that were used. In February 1995, Netscape released the SSL 2.0 specification with many improvements.[3] Most of its design was done by Kipp Hickman, with much less participation from the public community. Even though it had its own vulnerabilities, it

---

[2]Dot-com bubble refers to the rapid rise in equity markets fueled by investments in Internet-based companies. During the dot-com bubble of the late 1990s, the value of equity markets grew exponentially, with the technology-dominated Nasdaq index rising from under 1,000 to 5,000 between 1995 and 2000.

[3]Adam Shostack, the well-known author of *The New School of Information Security,* provides an overview of SSL 2.0 at `www.homeport.org/~adam/ssl.html`

earned the trust and respect of the public as a strong protocol. The very first deployment of SSL 2.0 was in Netscape Navigator 1.1. In late 1995, Ian Goldberg and David Wagner discovered a vulnerability in the random number generation logic in SSL 2.0.[4] Mostly due to US export regulations, Netscape had to weaken its encryption scheme to use 40-bit long keys. This limited all possible key combinations to a million million, which were tried by a set of researchers in 30 hours with many spare CPU cycles; they were able to recover the encrypted data.

SSL 2.0 was completely under the control of Netscape and was developed with no or minimal inputs from others. This encouraged many other vendors including Microsoft to come up with their own security implementations. As a result, Microsoft developed its own variant of SSL in 1995, called Private Communication Technology (PCT).[5] PCT fixed many security vulnerabilities uncovered in SSL 2.0 and simplified the SSL handshake with fewer round trips required in establishing a connection. Among the differences between SSL 2.0 and PCT, the non-encrypted operational mode introduced in PCT was quite prominent. With non-encrypted operational mode, PCT only provides authentication—no data encryption. As discussed before, due to the US export regulation laws, SSL 2.0 had to use weak cryptographic keys for encryption. Even though the regulations did not mandate to use weak cryptographic keys for authentication, SSL 2.0 used the same weak cryptographic keys used for encryption, also for authentication. PCT fixed this limitation in SSL 2.0 by introducing a separate strong key for authentication.

Netscape released SSL 3.0 in 1996 having Paul Kocher as the key architect. This was after an attempt to introduce SSL 2.1 as a fix for the SSL 2.0. But it never went pass the draft stage, and Netscape decided it was the time to design everything from ground up. In fact, Netscape hired Paul Kocher to work with its own Phil Karlton and Allan Freier to build SSL 3.0 from scratch. SSL 3.0 introduced a new specification language as well as a new record type and a new data encoding technique, which made it incompatible with the SSL 2.0. It fixed issues in its predecessor, introduced due to MD5 hashing. The new version used a combination of the MD5 and SHA-1 algorithms to build a hybrid hash. SSL 3.0 was the most stable of all. Even some of the issues found in Microsoft PCT were fixed in SSL 3.0, and it further added a set of new features that were not in PCT. In 1996,

---

[4]Ian Goldberg and David Wagner, "Randomness and the Netscape Browser: How Secure Is the World Wide Web?" `www.cs.berkeley.edu/~daw/papers/ddj-netscape.html`, January 1996.

[5]Microsoft proposed PCT to the IETF in October 1995: `http://tools.ietf.org/html/draft-benaloh-pct-00`. This was later superseded by SSL 3.0 and TLS.

Microsoft came up with a new proposal to merge SSL 3.0 and its own SSL variant PCT 2.0 to build a new standard called Secure Transport Layer Protocol (STLP).[6]

Due to the interest shown by many vendors in solving the same problem in different ways, in 1996 the IETF initiated the *Transport Layer Security* working group to standardize all vendor-specific implementations. All the major vendors, including Netscape and Microsoft, met under the chairmanship of Bruce Schneier in a series of IETF meetings to decide the future of TLS. TLS 1.0 (RFC 2246) was the result; it was released by the IETF in January 1999. The differences between TLS 1.0 and SSL 3.0 aren't dramatic, but they're significant enough that TLS 1.0 and SSL 3.0 don't interoperate. TLS 1.0 was quite stable and stayed unchanged for seven years, until 2006. In April 2006, RFC 4346 introduced TLS 1.1, which made few major changes to TLS 1.0. Two years later, RFC 5246 introduced TLS 1.2, and in August 2018, almost 10 years after TLS 1.2, RFC 8446 introduced TLS 1.3.

Transmission Control Protocol (TCP)

Understanding how Transmission Control Protocol (TCP) works provides a good background to understand how TLS works. TCP is a layer of abstraction of a reliable network running over an unreliable channel. IP (Internet Protocol) provides host-to-host routing and addressing. TCP/IP is collectively known as the *Internet Protocol Suite*, which was initially proposed by Vint Cerf and Bob Kahn.[7] The original proposal became the RFC 675 under the network working group of IETF in December 1974. After a series of refinements, the version 4 of this specification was published as two RFCs: RFC 791 and RFC 793. The former talks about the Internet Protocol (IP), while the latter is about the Transmission Control Protocol (TCP).

The TCP/IP protocol suite presents a four-layered model for network communication as shown in Figure C-1. Each layer has its own responsibilities and communicates with each other using a well-defined interface. For example, the Hypertext Transfer Protocol (HTTP) is an *application layer* protocol, which is *transport layer* protocol agnostic. HTTP does not care how the packets are transported from one host to another. It can be over TCP or UDP (User Datagram Protocol), which are defined at the *transport layer*. But

---

[6]Microsoft Strawman Proposal for a Secure Transport Layer Protocol ("STLP"), http://cseweb.ucsd.edu/~bsy/stlp.ps

[7]A Protocol for Packet Network Intercommunication, www.cs.princeton.edu/courses/archive/fall06/cos561/papers/cerf74.pdf

in practice, most of the HTTP traffic goes over TCP. This is mostly due to the inherent characteristics of TCP. During the data transmission, TCP takes care of retransmission of lost data, ordered delivery of packets, congestion control and avoidance, data integrity, and many more. Almost all the HTTP traffic is benefitted from these characteristics of TCP. Neither the TCP nor the UDP takes care of how the *Internet layer* operates. The Internet Protocol (IP) functions at the *Internet layer*. Its responsibility is to provide a hardware-independent addressing scheme to the messages pass-through. Finally, it becomes the responsibility of the network access layer to transport the messages via the physical network. The network access layer interacts directly with the physical network and provides an addressing scheme to identify each device the messages pass through. The Ethernet protocol operates at the network access layer.

Our discussion from here onward focuses only on TCP, which operates at the transport layer. Any TCP connection bootstraps with a three-way handshake. In other words, TCP is a connection-oriented protocol, and the client has to establish a connection with the server prior to the data transmission. Before the data transmission begins between the client and the server, each party has to exchange with each other a set of parameters. These parameters include the starting packet sequence numbers and many other connection-specific parameters. The client initiates the TCP three-way handshake by sending a TCP packet to the server. This packet is known as the SYN packet. SYN is a flag set in the TCP packet. The SYN packet includes a randomly picked sequence number by the client, the source (client) port number, destination (server) port number, and many other fields as shown in Figure C-2. If you look closely at Figure C-2, you will notice that the source (client) IP address and the destination (server) IP address are outside the TCP packet and are included as part of the IP packet. As discussed before, IP operates at the network layer, and the IP addresses are defined to be hardware independent. Another important field here that requires our attention is the TCP Segment Len field. This field indicates the length of the application data this packet carries. For all the messages sent during the TCP three-way handshake, the value of the TCP Segment Len field will be zero, as no exchange has started yet.

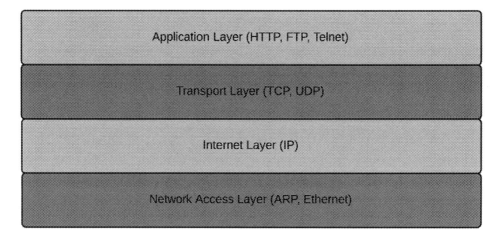

Figure C-1. *TCP/IP stack: protocol layer*

```
▶ Frame 1: 74 bytes on wire (592 bits), 74 bytes captured (592 bits)
▶ Ethernet II, Src: AsustekC_b3:01:84 (00:1d:60:b3:01:84), Dst: Actionte_2f:47:87 (00:26:62:2f:47:87)
▶ Internet Protocol Version 4, Src: 192.168.1.2, Dst: 174.143.213.184
▼ Transmission Control Protocol, Src Port: 54841 (54841), Dst Port: 80 (80), Seq: 0, Len: 0
      Source Port: 54841
      Destination Port: 80
      [Stream index: 0]
      [TCP Segment Len: 0]
      Sequence number: 0     (relative sequence number)
      Acknowledgment number: 0
      Header Length: 40 bytes
    ▶ Flags: 0x002 (SYN)
      Window size value: 5840
      [Calculated window size: 5840]
    ▶ Checksum: 0x85f0 [validation disabled]
      Urgent pointer: 0
    ▶ Options: (20 bytes), Maximum segment size, SACK permitted, Timestamps, No-Operation (NOP), Window scale
```

Figure C-2. *TCP SYN packet captured by Wireshark, which is an open source packet analyzer*

Once the server receives the initial message from the client, it too picks its own random sequence number and passes it back in the response to the client. This packet is known as the SYN ACK packet. The two main characteristics of TCP, error control (recover from lost packets) and ordered delivery, require each TCP packet to be identified uniquely. The exchange of sequence numbers between the client and the server helps to keep that promise. Once the packets are numbered, both sides of the communication channel know which packets get lost during the transmission and duplicate packets and how to order a set of packets, which are delivered in a random order. Figure C-3 shows a sample TCP SYN ACK packet captured by Wireshark. This includes the source (server) port, destination (client) port, server sequence number, and the acknowledgement number. Adding one to the client sequence number found in the SYN packet derives the acknowledgement number. Since we are still in the three-way handshake, the value of the *TCP Segment Len field is zero*.

```
▶ Frame 2: 74 bytes on wire (592 bits), 74 bytes captured (592 bits)
▶ Ethernet II, Src: Actionte_2f:47:87 (00:26:62:2f:47:87), Dst: AsustekC_b3:01:84 (00:1d:60:b3:01:84)
▶ Internet Protocol Version 4, Src: 174.143.213.184, Dst: 192.168.1.2
▼ Transmission Control Protocol, Src Port: 80 (80), Dst Port: 54841 (54841), Seq: 0, Ack: 1, Len: 0
    Source Port: 80
    Destination Port: 54841
    [Stream index: 0]
    [TCP Segment Len: 0]
    Sequence number: 0     (relative sequence number)
    Acknowledgment number: 1      (relative ack number)
    Header Length: 40 bytes
  ▶ Flags: 0x012 (SYN, ACK)
    Window size value: 5792
    [Calculated window size: 5792]
  ▶ Checksum: 0x4ff1 [validation disabled]
    Urgent pointer: 0
  ▶ Options: (20 bytes), Maximum segment size, SACK permitted, Timestamps, No-Operation (NOP), Window scale
  ▶ [SEQ/ACK analysis]
```

Figure C-3. *TCP SYN ACK packet captured by Wireshark*

```
▶ Frame 3: 66 bytes on wire (528 bits), 66 bytes captured (528 bits)
▶ Ethernet II, Src: AsustekC_b3:01:84 (00:1d:60:b3:01:84), Dst: Actionte_2f:47:87 (00:26:62:2f:47:87)
▶ Internet Protocol Version 4, Src: 192.168.1.2, Dst: 174.143.213.184
▼ Transmission Control Protocol, Src Port: 54841 (54841), Dst Port: 80 (80), Seq: 1, Ack: 1, Len: 0
    Source Port: 54841
    Destination Port: 80
    [Stream index: 0]
    [TCP Segment Len: 0]
    Sequence number: 1     (relative sequence number)
    Acknowledgment number: 1      (relative ack number)
    Header Length: 32 bytes
  ▶ Flags: 0x010 (ACK)
    Window size value: 46
    [Calculated window size: 5888]
    [Window size scaling factor: 128]
  ▶ Checksum: 0x9529 [validation disabled]
    Urgent pointer: 0
  ▶ Options: (12 bytes), No-Operation (NOP), No-Operation (NOP), Timestamps
  ▶ [SEQ/ACK analysis]
```

Figure C-4. *TCP ACK packet captured by Wireshark*

To complete the handshake, the client will once again send a TCP packet to the server to acknowledge the SYN ACK packet it received from the server. This is known as the ACK packet. Figure C-4 shows a sample TCP ACK packet captured by Wireshark. This includes the source (client) port, destination (server) port, initial client sequence number + 1 as the new sequence number, and the acknowledgement number. Adding one to the server sequence number found in the SYN ACK packet derives the acknowledgement number. Since we are still in the three-way handshake, the value of the TCP Segment Len field is zero.

Once the handshake is complete, the application data transmission between the client and the server can begin. The client sends the application data packets to the server immediately after it sends the ACK packet. The transport layer gets the application data from the application layer. Figure C-5 is a captured message from Wireshark, which shows the TCP packet corresponding to an HTTP GET request to download an image. The HTTP, which operates at the application layer, takes care of building the HTTP message with all relevant headers and passes it to the TCP at the transport layer. Whatever the data it receives from the application layer, the TCP encapsulates with its own headers and passes it through the rest of the layers in the TCP/IP stack. How TCP derives the sequence number for the first TCP packet, which carries the application data, is explained under the side bar "How does TCP sequence numbering work?" If you look closely at the value of the TCP Segment Len field in Figure C-5, you will notice that it is now set to a nonzero value.

```
▸ Frame 4: 791 bytes on wire (6328 bits), 791 bytes captured (6328 bits)
▸ Ethernet II, Src: AsustekC_b3:01:84 (00:1d:60:b3:01:84), Dst: Actionte_2f:47:87 (00:26:62:2f:47:87)
▸ Internet Protocol Version 4, Src: 192.168.1.2, Dst: 174.143.213.184
▾ Transmission Control Protocol, Src Port: 54841 (54841), Dst Port: 80 (80), Seq: 1, Ack: 1, Len: 725
      Source Port: 54841
      Destination Port: 80
      [Stream index: 0]
      [TCP Segment Len: 725]
      Sequence number: 1      (relative sequence number)
      [Next sequence number: 726      (relative sequence number)]
      Acknowledgment number: 1      (relative ack number)
      Header Length: 32 bytes
   ▸ Flags: 0x018 (PSH, ACK)
      Window size value: 46
      [Calculated window size: 5888]
      [Window size scaling factor: 128]
   ▸ Checksum: 0x48ee [validation disabled]
      Urgent pointer: 0
   ▸ Options: (12 bytes), No-Operation (NOP), No-Operation (NOP), Timestamps
   ▸ [SEQ/ACK analysis]
▾ Hypertext Transfer Protocol
   ▸ GET /images/layout/logo.png HTTP/1.1\r\n
      Host: packetlife.net\r\n
      User-Agent: Mozilla/5.0 (X11; U; Linux x86_64; en-US; rv:1.9.2.3) Gecko/20100423 Ubuntu/10.04 (lucid) Firefox/3.6.3\r\n
      Accept: text/html,application/xhtml+xml,application/xml;q=0.9,*/*;q=0.8\r\n
      Accept-Language: en-us,en;q=0.5\r\n
      Accept-Encoding: gzip,deflate\r\n
      Accept-Charset: ISO-8859-1,utf-8;q=0.7,*;q=0.7\r\n
      Keep-Alive: 115\r\n
      Connection: keep-alive\r\n
```

Figure C-5. *TCP packet corresponding to an HTTP GET request to download an image captured by Wireshark*

Once the application data transmission between the client and the server begins, the other should acknowledge each data packet sent by either party. As a response to the first TCP packet sent by the client, which carries application data, the server will respond with a TCP ACK packet, as shown in Figure C-6. How TCP derives the sequence number and the acknowledgement number for this TCP ACK packet is explained under the side bar "How does TCP sequence numbering work?"

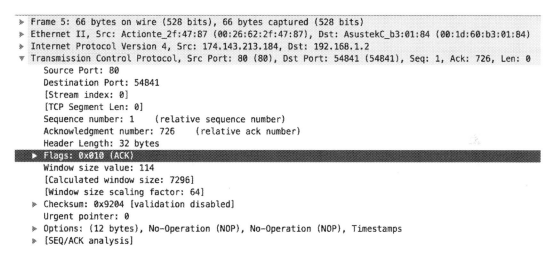

```
▶ Frame 5: 66 bytes on wire (528 bits), 66 bytes captured (528 bits)
▶ Ethernet II, Src: Actionte_2f:47:87 (00:26:62:2f:47:87), Dst: AsustekC_b3:01:84 (00:1d:60:b3:01:84)
▶ Internet Protocol Version 4, Src: 174.143.213.184, Dst: 192.168.1.2
▼ Transmission Control Protocol, Src Port: 80 (80), Dst Port: 54841 (54841), Seq: 1, Ack: 726, Len: 0
      Source Port: 80
      Destination Port: 54841
      [Stream index: 0]
      [TCP Segment Len: 0]
      Sequence number: 1      (relative sequence number)
      Acknowledgment number: 726     (relative ack number)
      Header Length: 32 bytes
   ▶ Flags: 0x010 (ACK)
      Window size value: 114
      [Calculated window size: 7296]
      [Window size scaling factor: 64]
   ▶ Checksum: 0x9204 [validation disabled]
      Urgent pointer: 0
   ▶ Options: (12 bytes), No-Operation (NOP), No-Operation (NOP), Timestamps
   ▶ [SEQ/ACK analysis]
```

Figure C-6. *TCP ACK from the server to the client captured by Wireshark*

HOW DOES TCP SEQUENCE NUMBERING WORK?

Whenever either of the two parties at either end of the communication channel wants to send a message to the other, it sends a packet with the ACK flag as an acknowledgement to the last received sequence number from that party. If you look at the very first SYN packet (Figure C-2) sent from the client to the server, it does not have an ACK flag, because prior to the SYN packet, the client didn't receive anything from the server. From there onward, every packet sent either by the server or the client has the ACK flag and the *Acknowledgement Number* field in the TCP packet.

In the SYN ACK packet (Figure C-3) from the server to the client, the value of the *Acknowledgement Number* is derived by adding one to the sequence number of the last packet received by the server (from the client). In other words, the *Acknowledgement Number* field here, from the server to the client, represents the sequence number of the next expected packet. Also if you closely look at the TCP Segment Len field in each TCP packet of the three-way handshake, the value of it is set to zero. Even though we mentioned before that the

Acknowledgement Number field in SYN ACK is derived by adding one to the sequence number found in the SYN packet from the client, precisely what happens is the server adds 1 + the value of the TCP Segment Len field from the client to the current sequence number to derive the value of the *Acknowledgement Number* field. The same applies to the ACK packet (Figure C-4) sent from the client to the server. Adding 1 + the value of the TCP Segment Len field from the server to the sequence number of the last packet received by the client (from the server) derives the *Acknowledgement Number* field there. The value of the sequence number in the ACK packet is the same as the value of the *Acknowledgement Number* in the SYN ACK packet from the server.

The client starts sending real application data only after the three-way handshake is completed. Figure C-5 shows the first TCP packet, which carries application data from the client to the server. If you look at the sequence number in that TCP packet, it's the same from the previous packet (ACK packet as shown in Figure C-4) sent from the client to the server. After client sends the ACK packet to the server, it receives nothing from the server. That implies the server still expects a packet with a sequence number, which matches the value of the *Acknowledgement Number* in the last packet it sent to the client. If you look at Figure C-5, which is the first TCP packet with application data, the value of the TCP Segment Len field is set to a nonzero value, and as per Figure C-6, which is the ACK to the first packet with the application data sent by the client, the value of *Acknowledgement Number* is set correctly to the value of the TCP Segment Len field + 1 + the current sequence number from the client.

How Transport Layer Security (TLS) Works

Transport Layer Security (TLS) protocol can be divided into two phases: the handshake and the data transfer. During the handshake phase, both the client and the server get to know about each other's cryptographic capabilities and establish cryptographic keys to protect the data transfer. The data transfer happens at the end of the handshake. The data is broken down into a set of records, protected with the cryptographic keys established in the first phase, and transferred between the client and the server. Figure C-7 shows how TLS fits in between other transport and application layer protocols. TLS was initially designed to work on top of a reliable transport protocol like TCP (Transmission Control Protocol). However, TLS is also being used with unreliable transport layer protocols like UDP (User Datagram Protocol). The RFC 6347 defines the

Datagram Transport Layer Security (DTLS) 1.2, which is the TLS equivalent in the UDP world. The DTLS protocol is based on the TLS protocol and provides equivalent security guarantees. This chapter only focuses on TLS.

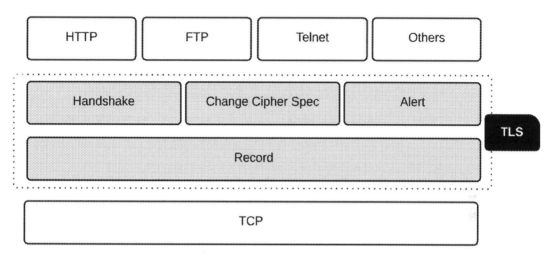

Figure C-7. *TLS protocol layers*

Transport Layer Security (TLS) Handshake

Similar to the three-way TCP handshake (see Figure C-8), TLS too introduces its own handshake. The TLS handshake includes three subprotocols: the *Handshake* protocol, the *Change Cipher Spec* protocol, and the *Alert* protocol (see Figure C-7). The *Handshake* protocol is responsible for building an agreement between the client and the server on cryptographic keys to be used to protect the application data. Both the client and the server use the *Change Cipher Spec* protocol to indicate to each other that it's going to switch to a cryptographically secured channel for further communication. The *Alert* protocol is responsible for generating alerts and communicating them to the parties involved in the TLS connection. For example, if the server certificate the client receives during the TLS handshake is a revoked one, the client generates the *certificate_revoked* alert.

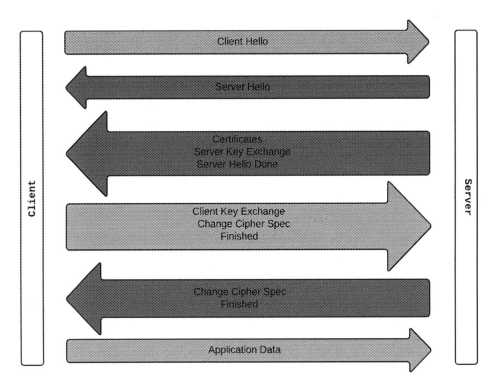

Figure C-8. *TLS handshake*

The TLS handshake happens after the TCP handshake. For the TCP or for the transport layer, everything in the TLS handshake is just application data. Once the TCP handshake is completed, the TLS layer will initiate the TLS handshake. The *Client Hello* is the first message in the TLS handshake from the client to the server. As you can see in Figure C-9, the sequence number of the TCP packet is 1, as expected, since this is the very first TCP packet, which carries application data. The *Client Hello* message includes the highest version of the TLS protocol the client supports, a random number generated by the client, cipher suites and the compression algorithm supported by the client, and an optional session identifier (see Figure C-9). The session identifier is used to resume an existing session rather than doing the handshake again from scratch. The TLS handshake is very CPU intensive, but with the support for session resumption, this overhead can be minimized.

```
▶ Frame 1517: 264 bytes on wire (2112 bits), 264 bytes captured (2112 bits) on interface 0
▶ Ethernet II, Src: Apple_1f:5b:bd (28:cf:e9:1f:5b:bd), Dst: 2wireInc_bf:de:ed (f8:18:97:bf:de:ed)
▶ Internet Protocol Version 4, Src: 192.168.1.65, Dst: 216.58.192.34
▼ Transmission Control Protocol, Src Port: 51669 (51669), Dst Port: 443 (443), Seq: 1, Ack: 1, Len: 198
      Source Port: 51669
      Destination Port: 443
      [Stream index: 29]
      [TCP Segment Len: 198]
      Sequence number: 1     (relative sequence number)
      [Next sequence number: 199     (relative sequence number)]
      Acknowledgment number: 1     (relative ack number)
      Header Length: 32 bytes
   ▶ Flags: 0x018 (PSH, ACK)
      Window size value: 4121
      [Calculated window size: 131872]
      [Window size scaling factor: 32]
   ▶ Checksum: 0x9a87 [validation disabled]
      Urgent pointer: 0
   ▶ Options: (12 bytes), No-Operation (NOP), No-Operation (NOP), Timestamps
   ▶ [SEQ/ACK analysis]
▼ Secure Sockets Layer
   ▼ TLSv1.2 Record Layer: Handshake Protocol: Client Hello
         Content Type: Handshake (22)
         Version: TLS 1.0 (0x0301)
         Length: 193
      ▶ Handshake Protocol: Client Hello
```

Figure C-9. *TLS Client Hello captured by Wireshark*

Note   TLS session resumption has a direct impact on performance. The master key generation process in the TLS handshake is extremely costly. With session resumption, the same master secret from the previous session is reused. It has been proven through several academic studies that the performance enhancement resulting from TLS session resumption can be up to 20%. Session resumption also has a cost, which is mostly handled by servers. Each server has to maintain the TLS state of all its clients and also to address high-availability aspects; it needs to replicate this state across different nodes in the cluster.

```
▶ Frame 1517: 264 bytes on wire (2112 bits), 264 bytes captured (2112 bits) on interface 0
▶ Ethernet II, Src: Apple_1f:5b:bd (28:cf:e9:1f:5b:bd), Dst: 2wireInc_bf:de:ed (f8:18:97:bf:de:ed)
▶ Internet Protocol Version 4, Src: 192.168.1.65, Dst: 216.58.192.34
▶ Transmission Control Protocol, Src Port: 51669 (51669), Dst Port: 443 (443), Seq: 1, Ack: 1, Len: 198
▼ Secure Sockets Layer
   ▼ TLSv1.2 Record Layer: Handshake Protocol: Client Hello
        Content Type: Handshake (22)
        Version: TLS 1.0 (0x0301)
        Length: 193
      ▼ Handshake Protocol: Client Hello
           Handshake Type: Client Hello (1)
           Length: 189
           Version: TLS 1.2 (0x0303)
         ▶ Random
           Session ID Length: 0
           Cipher Suites Length: 22
         ▶ Cipher Suites (11 suites)
           Compression Methods Length: 1
         ▶ Compression Methods (1 method)
           Extensions Length: 126
         ▶ Extension: server_name
         ▶ Extension: renegotiation_info
         ▶ Extension: elliptic_curves
         ▶ Extension: ec_point_formats
         ▶ Extension: SessionTicket TLS
         ▶ Extension: next_protocol_negotiation
         ▶ Extension: Application Layer Protocol Negotiation
         ▶ Extension: status_request
         ▶ Extension: signature_algorithms
```

Figure C-10. *TLS Client Hello expanded version captured by Wireshark*

One key field in the *Client Hello* message is the *Cipher Suites*. Figure C-12 expands the *Cipher Suites* field of Figure C-10. The *Cipher Suites* field in the *Client Hello* message carries all the cryptographic algorithms supported by the client. The message captured in Figure C-12 shows the cryptographic capabilities of the Firefox browser version 43.0.2 (64-bit). A given cipher suite defines the server authentication algorithm, the key exchange algorithm, the bulk encryption algorithm, and the message integrity algorithm. For example, in TLS_ECDHE_RSA_WITH_AES_128_GCM_SHA256 cipher suite, RSA is the authentication algorithm, ECDHE is the key exchange algorithm, AES_128_GCM is the bulk encryption algorithm, and SHA256 is the message integrity algorithm. Any cipher suite that starts with TLS is only supported by the TLS protocols. As we proceed in this appendix, we will learn the purpose of each algorithm.

Once the server receives the *Client Hello* message from the client, it responds back with the *Server Hello* message. The *Server Hello* is the first message from the server to the client. To be precise, the *Server Hello* is the first message from the server to the client, which is generated at the TLS layer. Prior to that, the TCP layer of the server responds back to the client with a TCP ACK message (see Figure C-11). All TLS layer messages are treated as application data by the TCP layer, and each message will be acknowledged either by the client or the server. From here onward, we will not talk about TCP ACK messages.

```
▶ Frame 1521: 66 bytes on wire (528 bits), 66 bytes captured (528 bits) on interface 0
▶ Ethernet II, Src: 2wireInc_bf:de:ed (f8:18:97:bf:de:ed), Dst: Apple_1f:5b:bd (28:cf:e9:1f:5b:bd)
▶ Internet Protocol Version 4, Src: 216.58.192.34, Dst: 192.168.1.65
▼ Transmission Control Protocol, Src Port: 443 (443), Dst Port: 51669 (51669), Seq: 1, Ack: 199, Len: 0
      Source Port: 443
      Destination Port: 51669
      [Stream index: 29]
      [TCP Segment Len: 0]
      Sequence number: 1     (relative sequence number)
      Acknowledgment number: 199     (relative ack number)
      Header Length: 32 bytes
    ▶ Flags: 0x010 (ACK)
      Window size value: 341
      [Calculated window size: 43648]
      [Window size scaling factor: 128]
    ▶ Checksum: 0xde83 [validation disabled]
      Urgent pointer: 0
    ▶ Options: (12 bytes), No-Operation (NOP), No-Operation (NOP), Timestamps
    ▶ [SEQ/ACK analysis]
```

Figure C-11. *TCP ACK message from the server to the client*

The *Server Hello* message includes the highest version of TLS protocol that both the client and the server can support, a random number generated by the server, the strongest cipher suite, and the compression algorithm that both the client and the server can support (see Figure C-13). Both parties use the random numbers generated by each other (the client and the server) independently to generate the master secret. This master secret will be used later to derive encryption keys. To generate a session identifier, the server has several options. If no session identifier is included in the *Client Hello* message, the server generates a new one. Even the client includes one; but if the server can't resume that session, then once again a new identifier is generated. If the server is capable of resuming the TLS session corresponding to the session identifier specified in the *Client Hello* message, then the server includes it in the *Server Hello* message. The server may also decide not to include any session identifiers for any new sessions that it's not willing to resume in the future.

```
▶ Frame 1517: 264 bytes on wire (2112 bits), 264 bytes captured (2112 bits) on interface 0
▶ Ethernet II, Src: Apple_1f:5b:bd (28:cf:e9:1f:5b:bd), Dst: 2wireInc_bf:de:ed (f8:18:97:bf:de:ed)
▶ Internet Protocol Version 4, Src: 192.168.1.65, Dst: 216.58.192.34
▶ Transmission Control Protocol, Src Port: 51669 (51669), Dst Port: 443 (443), Seq: 1, Ack: 1, Len: 198
▼ Secure Sockets Layer
  ▼ TLSv1.2 Record Layer: Handshake Protocol: Client Hello
      Content Type: Handshake (22)
      Version: TLS 1.0 (0x0301)
      Length: 193
    ▼ Handshake Protocol: Client Hello
        Handshake Type: Client Hello (1)
        Length: 189
        Version: TLS 1.2 (0x0303)
      ▶ Random
        Session ID Length: 0
        Cipher Suites Length: 22
      ▼ Cipher Suites (11 suites)
          Cipher Suite: TLS_ECDHE_ECDSA_WITH_AES_128_GCM_SHA256 (0xc02b)
          Cipher Suite: TLS_ECDHE_RSA_WITH_AES_128_GCM_SHA256 (0xc02f)
          Cipher Suite: TLS_ECDHE_ECDSA_WITH_AES_256_CBC_SHA (0xc00a)
          Cipher Suite: TLS_ECDHE_ECDSA_WITH_AES_128_CBC_SHA (0xc009)
          Cipher Suite: TLS_ECDHE_RSA_WITH_AES_128_CBC_SHA (0xc013)
          Cipher Suite: TLS_ECDHE_RSA_WITH_AES_256_CBC_SHA (0xc014)
          Cipher Suite: TLS_DHE_RSA_WITH_AES_128_CBC_SHA (0x0033)
          Cipher Suite: TLS_DHE_RSA_WITH_AES_256_CBC_SHA (0x0039)
          Cipher Suite: TLS_RSA_WITH_AES_128_CBC_SHA (0x002f)
          Cipher Suite: TLS_RSA_WITH_AES_256_CBC_SHA (0x0035)
          Cipher Suite: TLS_RSA_WITH_3DES_EDE_CBC_SHA (0x000a)
```

Figure C-12. *Cipher suites supported by the TLS client captured by Wireshark*

Note In the history of TLS, several attacks have been reported against the TLS handshake. Cipher suite rollback and version rollback are a couple of them. This could be a result of a man-in-the-middle attack, where the attacker intercepts the TLS handshake and downgrades either the cipher suite or the TLS version, or both. The problem was fixed from SSL 3.0 onward with the introduction of the *Change Cipher Spec* message. This requires both parties to share the hash of all TLS handshake messages up to the *Change Cipher Spec* message exactly as each party read them. Each has to confirm that they read the messages from each other in the same way.

```
► Frame 1522: 1484 bytes on wire (11872 bits), 1484 bytes captured (11872 bits) on interface 0
► Ethernet II, Src: 2wireInc_bf:de:ed (f8:18:97:bf:de:ed), Dst: Apple_1f:5b:bd (28:cf:e9:1f:5b:bd)
► Internet Protocol Version 4, Src: 216.58.192.34, Dst: 192.168.1.65
► Transmission Control Protocol, Src Port: 443 (443), Dst Port: 51669 (51669), Seq: 1, Ack: 199, Len: 1418
▼ Secure Sockets Layer
   ▼ TLSv1.2 Record Layer: Handshake Protocol: Server Hello
        Content Type: Handshake (22)
        Version: TLS 1.2 (0x0303)
        Length: 72
     ▼ Handshake Protocol: Server Hello
          Handshake Type: Server Hello (2)
          Length: 68
          Version: TLS 1.2 (0x0303)
        ► Random
          Session ID Length: 0
          Cipher Suite: TLS_ECDHE_RSA_WITH_AES_128_GCM_SHA256 (0xc02f)
          Compression Method: null (0)
          Extensions Length: 28
        ► Extension: renegotiation_info
        ► Extension: server_name
        ► Extension: SessionTicket TLS
        ► Extension: Application Layer Protocol Negotiation
        ► Extension: ec_point_formats
```

Figure C-13. *TLS Server Hello captured by Wireshark*

After the *Server Hello* message is sent to the client, the server sends its public
certificate, along with other certificates, up to the root certificate authority (CA) in the
certificate chain (see Figure C-14). The client must validate these certificates to accept
the identity of the server. It uses the public key from the server certificate to encrypt
the premaster secret key later. The *premaster key* is a shared secret between the client
and the server to generate the master secret. If the public key in the server certificate
isn't capable of encrypting the premaster secret key, then the TLS protocol mandates
another extra step, known as the *Server Key Exchange* (see Figure C-14). During this step,
the server has to create a new key and send it to the client. Later the client will use it to
encrypt its premaster secret key.

If the server demands TLS mutual authentication, then the next step is for the
server to request the client certificate. The client certificate request message from the
server includes a list of certificate authorities trusted by the server and the type of the
certificate. After the last two optional steps, the server sends the *Server Hello Done*
message to the client (see Figure C-14). This is an empty message that only indicates to
the client that the server has completed its initial phase in the handshake.

If the server demands the client certificate, now the client sends its public certificate
along with all other certificates in the chain up to the root certificate authority (CA)
required to validate the client certificate. Next is the *Client Key Exchange* message,
which includes the TLS protocol version as well as the premaster secret key

(see Figure C-15). The TLS protocol version must be the same as specified in the initial *Client Hello* message. This is a guard *against* any rollback attacks to force the server to use an unsecured TLS/SSL version. The premaster secret key included in the message should be encrypted with the server's public key obtained from the server certificate or with the key passed in the *Server Key Exchange* message.

The *Certificate Verify* message is the next in line. This is optional and is needed only if the server demands client authentication. The client has to sign the entire set of TLS handshake messages that have taken place so far with its private key and send the signature to the server. The server validates the signature using the client's public key, which was shared in a previous step. The signature generation process varies depending on which signing algorithm picked during the handshake. If RSA is being used, then the hash of all the previous handshake messages is calculated with both MD5 and SHA-1. Then the concatenated hash is encrypted using the client's private key. If the signing algorithm picked during the handshake is DSS (Digital Signature Standard), only a SHA-1 hash is used, and it's encrypted using the client's private key.

```
▶ Frame 1524: 760 bytes on wire (6080 bits), 760 bytes captured (6080 bits) on interface 0
▶ Ethernet II, Src: 2wireInc_bf:de:ed (f8:18:97:bf:de:ed), Dst: Apple_1f:5b:bd (28:cf:e9:1f:5b:bd)
▶ Internet Protocol Version 4, Src: 216.58.192.34, Dst: 192.168.1.65
▶ Transmission Control Protocol, Src Port: 443 (443), Dst Port: 51669 (51669), Seq: 2837, Ack: 199, Len: 694
▶ [3 Reassembled TCP Segments (3106 bytes): #1522(1341), #1523(1418), #1524(347)]
▼ Secure Sockets Layer
   ▼ TLSv1.2 Record Layer: Handshake Protocol: Certificate
       Content Type: Handshake (22)
       Version: TLS 1.2 (0x0303)
       Length: 3101
     ▼ Handshake Protocol: Certificate
         Handshake Type: Certificate (11)
         Length: 3097
         Certificates Length: 3094
       ▶ Certificates (3094 bytes)
▼ Secure Sockets Layer
   ▼ TLSv1.2 Record Layer: Handshake Protocol: Server Key Exchange
       Content Type: Handshake (22)
       Version: TLS 1.2 (0x0303)
       Length: 333
     ▼ Handshake Protocol: Server Key Exchange
         Handshake Type: Server Key Exchange (12)
         Length: 329
       ▶ EC Diffie-Hellman Server Params
   ▼ TLSv1.2 Record Layer: Handshake Protocol: Server Hello Done
       Content Type: Handshake (22)
       Version: TLS 1.2 (0x0303)
       Length: 4
     ▼ Handshake Protocol: Server Hello Done
         Handshake Type: Server Hello Done (14)
         Length: 0
```

Figure C-14. *Certificate, Server Key Exchange, and Server Hello Done captured by Wireshark*

At this point, the client and the server have exchanged all the required materials to generate the master secret. The master secret is generated using the client random number, the server random number, and the premaster secret. The client now sends the *Change Cipher Spec* message to the server to indicate that all messages generated from here onward are protected with the keys already established (see Figure C-15).

The *Finished* message is the last one from the client to the server. It's the hash of the complete message flow in the TLS handshake encrypted by the already established keys. Once the server receives the *Finished* message from the client, it responds back with the *Change Cipher Spec* message (see Figure C-16). This indicates to the client that the server is ready to start communicating with the secret keys already established. Finally, the server will send the *Finished* message to the client. This is similar to the *Finished* message generated by the client and includes the hash of the complete message flow in the handshake encrypted by the generated cryptographic keys. This completes the TLS handshake, and here onward both the client and the server can send data over an encrypted channel.

```
▸ Frame 1527: 192 bytes on wire (1536 bits), 192 bytes captured (1536 bits) on interface 0
▸ Ethernet II, Src: Apple_1f:5b:bd (28:cf:e9:1f:5b:bd), Dst: 2wireInc_bf:de:ed (f8:18:97:bf:de:ed)
▸ Internet Protocol Version 4, Src: 192.168.1.65, Dst: 216.58.192.34
▸ Transmission Control Protocol, Src Port: 51669 (51669), Dst Port: 443 (443), Seq: 199, Ack: 3531, Len: 126
▾ Secure Sockets Layer
   ▾ TLSv1.2 Record Layer: Handshake Protocol: Client Key Exchange
        Content Type: Handshake (22)
        Version: TLS 1.2 (0x0303)
        Length: 70
      ▾ Handshake Protocol: Client Key Exchange
           Handshake Type: Client Key Exchange (16)
           Length: 66
         ▸ EC Diffie-Hellman Client Params
   ▾ TLSv1.2 Record Layer: Change Cipher Spec Protocol: Change Cipher Spec
        Content Type: Change Cipher Spec (20)
        Version: TLS 1.2 (0x0303)
        Length: 1
        Change Cipher Spec Message
   ▾ TLSv1.2 Record Layer: Handshake Protocol: Multiple Handshake Messages
        Content Type: Handshake (22)
        Version: TLS 1.2 (0x0303)
        Length: 40
      ▸ Handshake Protocol: Hello Request
      ▸ Handshake Protocol: Hello Request
```

Figure C-15. *Client Key Exchange and Change Cipher Spec captured by Wireshark*

```
▶ Frame 1529: 328 bytes on wire (2624 bits), 328 bytes captured (2624 bits) on interface 0
▶ Ethernet II, Src: 2wireInc_bf:de:ed (f8:18:97:bf:de:ed), Dst: Apple_1f:5b:bd (28:cf:e9:1f:5b:bd)
▶ Internet Protocol Version 4, Src: 216.58.192.34, Dst: 192.168.1.65
▶ Transmission Control Protocol, Src Port: 443 (443), Dst Port: 51669 (51669), Seq: 3531, Ack: 325, Len: 262
▼ Secure Sockets Layer
   ▼ TLSv1.2 Record Layer: Handshake Protocol: New Session Ticket
        Content Type: Handshake (22)
        Version: TLS 1.2 (0x0303)
        Length: 206
      ▶ Handshake Protocol: New Session Ticket
   ▼ TLSv1.2 Record Layer: Change Cipher Spec Protocol: Change Cipher Spec
        Content Type: Change Cipher Spec (20)
        Version: TLS 1.2 (0x0303)
        Length: 1
        Change Cipher Spec Message
   ▼ TLSv1.2 Record Layer: Handshake Protocol: Multiple Handshake Messages
        Content Type: Handshake (22)
        Version: TLS 1.2 (0x0303)
        Length: 40
      ▶ Handshake Protocol: Hello Request
      ▶ Handshake Protocol: Hello Request
```

Figure C-16. *Server Change Cipher Spec captured by Wireshark*

TLS VS. HTTPS

HTTP operates at the application layer of the TCP/IP stack, while the TLS operates between the application layer and the transport layer (see Figure C-1). The agent (e.g., the browser) acting as the HTTP client should also act as the TLS client to initiate the TLS handshake, by opening a connection to a specific port (default 443) at the server. Only after the TLS handshake is completed, the agent should initiate the application data exchange. All HTTP data are sent as TLS application data. HTTP over TLS was initially defined by the RFC 2818, under the IETF network working group. The RFC 2818 further defines a URI format for HTTP over TLS traffic, to differentiate it from plain HTTP traffic. HTTP over TLS is differentiated from HTTP URIs by using the *https* protocol identifier in place of the *http* protocol identifier. The RFC 2818 was later updated by two RFCs: RFC 5785 and RFC 7230.

Application Data Transfer

After the TLS handshake phase is complete, sensitive application data can be exchanged between the client and the server using the TLS Record protocol (Figure C-18). This protocol is responsible for breaking all outgoing messages into blocks and assembling all incoming messages. Each outgoing block is compressed; Message Authentication Code (MAC) is calculated and encrypted. Each incoming block is decrypted, decompressed, and MAC verified. Figure C-17 summarizes all the key messages exchanged in the TLS handshake.

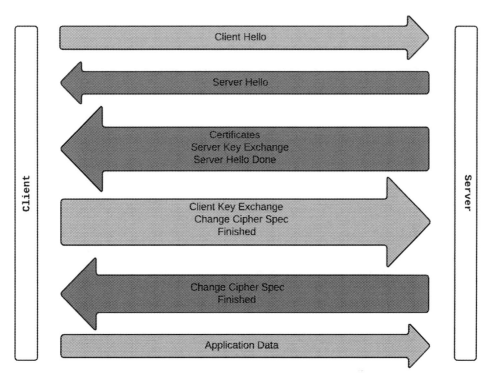

Figure C-17. *TLS handshake*

During the TLS handshake, each side derives a master secret using the client-generated random key, the server-generated random key, and the client-generated premaster secret. All these three keys are shared between each other during the TLS handshake. The master secret is never transferred over the wire. Using the master secret, each side generates four more keys. The client uses the first key to calculate the MAC for each outgoing message. The server uses the same key to validate the MAC of all incoming messages from the client. The server uses the second key to calculate the MAC for each outgoing message. The client uses the same key to validate the MAC of all incoming messages from the server. The client uses the third key to encrypt outgoing messages, and the server uses the same key to decrypt all incoming messages. The server uses the fourth key to encrypt outgoing messages, and the client uses the same key to decrypt all incoming messages.

```
▶ Frame 1531: 122 bytes on wire (976 bits), 122 bytes captured (976 bits) on interface 0
▶ Ethernet II, Src: 2wireInc_bf:de:ed (f8:18:97:bf:de:ed), Dst: Apple_1f:5b:bd (28:cf:e9:1f:5b:bd)
▶ Internet Protocol Version 4, Src: 216.58.192.34, Dst: 192.168.1.65
▶ Transmission Control Protocol, Src Port: 443 (443), Dst Port: 51669 (51669), Seq: 3793, Ack: 325, Len: 56
▼ Secure Sockets Layer
  ▼ TLSv1.2 Record Layer: Application Data Protocol: http
      Content Type: Application Data (23)
      Version: TLS 1.2 (0x0303)
      Length: 51
      Encrypted Application Data: 000000000000000014046831b4ff3a6075a5eb26feddc383a...
```

Figure C-18. *Server Change Cipher Spec captured by Wireshark*

REVERSE-ENGINEERING TLS

For each session, TLS creates a master secret and derives four keys from it for hashing and encryption. What if the private key of the server leaked out? If all the data transferred between clients and the server is being recorded, can it be decrypted? Yes, it can. If the TLS handshake is recorded, you can decrypt the premaster secret if you know the server's private key. Then, using the client-generated random number and the server-generated random number, you can derive the master secret—and then the other four keys. Using these keys, you can decrypt the entire set of recorded conversations.

Using perfect forward secrecy (PFS) can prevent this. With PFS, just as in TLS, a session key is generated, but the session key can't later be derived back from the server's master secret. This eliminates the risk of losing the confidentiality of the data if a private key leaks out. To add support for PFS, both the server and the client participating in the TLS handshake should support a cipher suite with Ephemeral Diffie-Hellman (DHE) or the elliptic-curve variant (ECDHE).

Note   Google enabled forward secrecy for Gmail, Google+, and Search in November 2011.

UMA Evolution

User-Managed Access (UMA, pronounced "OOH-mah") is an OAuth 2.0 profile. OAuth 2.0 decouples the resource server from the authorization server. UMA takes one step forward: it lets you control a distributed set of resource servers from a centralized authorization server. It also enables the resource owner to define a set of policies at the authorization server, which can be evaluated at the time a client is granted access to a protected resource. This eliminates the need for the resource owner's presence to approve access requests from arbitrary clients or requesting parties. The authorization server can make the decision based on the policies defined by the resource owner.

ProtectServe

UMA has its roots in the Kantara Initiative. The Kantara Initiative is a nonprofit professional association focused on building digital identity management standards. The first meeting of the UMA working group was held on August 6, 2009. There were two driving forces behind UMA: ProtectServe and vendor relationship management (VRM). ProtectServe is a standard that was heavily influenced by VRM. The goal of ProtectServe was to build a permission-based data-sharing model that was simple, secure, efficient, RESTful, powerful, OAuth-based, and system identity agnostic. ProtectServe defines four parties in its protocol flow: the user, the authorization manager, the service provider, and the consumer.

The *service provider* (SP) manages the user's resources and exposes them to the rest of the world. The *authorization manager* (AM) keeps track of all service providers associated with a given user. The *user* is the resource owner, who introduces all the service providers (or the applications he or she works with) to the authorization manager and builds access control policies that define the basis on which to share resources with others. The *consumer* consumes the user's resources via the SP. Before consuming any services or resources, the consumer must request an access grant from the AM.

© Prabath Siriwardena 2020
P. Siriwardena, *Advanced API Security*, https://doi.org/10.1007/978-1-4842-2050-4_19

The requested access grant is evaluated against the policies defined on the associated service by its owner, at the AM. ProtectServe uses OAuth 1.0 (see Appendix B) as the protocol for access delegation.

The steps in the ProtectServe protocol flow are as follows:

Step 1: The user or the resource owner introduces the SP to the AM (see Figure D-1).

1. The user provides the metadata URL of the AM to the SP.

2. The SP talks to the metadata endpoint of the AM and gets details related to the consumer key issuer, the request token issuer, the access token issuer, and the associated policies (OAuth 1.0 specification defines consumer key, request token, and access token).

3. The SP initiates an OAuth 1.0 flow by requesting an OAuth request token from the request token issuer (which could be the same AM).

4. The AM generates an authorization request token and sends it back to the SP along with other parameters defined under OAuth 1.0 specification.

5. The SP redirects the user to the AM with a token reference along with other parameters defined under OAuth 1.0 specification, to get it authorized.

6. Once authorized by the user, the authorization manager returns the authorized request token along with other parameters defined under OAuth 1.0 specification to the SP.

7. To complete the OAuth 1.0 flow, the SP exchanges the authorized request token for an access token, with the AM.

8. Once the OAuth flow is completed, the SP talks to the AM endpoint (which is secured with OAuth 1.0) to get an SP handle.

9. The AM validates the OAuth signature and, once verified, issues an SP handle to the SP. An SP handle is a unique identifier generated by the AM to identify the SP in future communications.

That completes the initial step in the ProtectServe protocol flow.

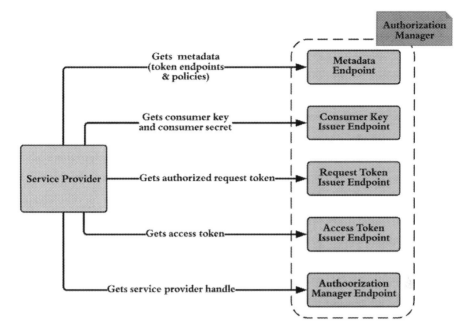

Figure D-1. *The service provider bootstraps trust with the authorization manager*

Note   The service provider handle is a key that uniquely identifies the service provider at the authorization manager. This information is publicly available. A given service provider can have multiple service provider handles—one for each associated authorization manager.

Step 2: Each consumer who wants to get access to protected resources must be provisioned with corresponding consumer keys:

1. The consumer tries to access a protected resource hosted in an SP.

2. The SP detects the unauthenticated access attempt and returns an HTTP 401 status code with required details to get the SP metadata (see Figure D-2).

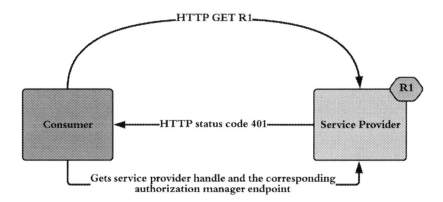

Figure D-2. *The consumer is rejected by the service provider with a 401 response. R1 represents a resource*

3. With the details in the 401 response, the consumer talks to the SP's metadata endpoint (see Figure D-2).

4. The SP metadata endpoint returns the SP handle (which is registered at the AM) and the corresponding AM endpoint.

5. The consumer talks to the AM endpoint to obtain a consumer key and a consumer secret (see Figure D-3).

6. The consumer requests an access token from the AM, with its consumer key and the SP handle. The request must be digitally signed by the corresponding consumer secret.

7. The AM validates the parameters in the access token request and issues an access token and a token secret to the consumer.

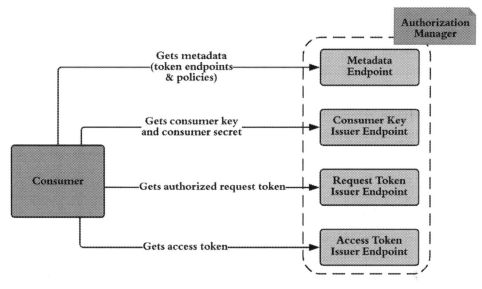

Figure D-3. *The consumer gets an access token from the authorization manager*

Step 3: A consumer with a valid access token can access the protected resource hosted in the SP (see Figure D-4):

1. The consumer tries to access the protected resource in the SP with its access token, signed with the access token secret.

2. The SP talks to the AM and gets the secret key corresponding to the consumer's access token. If required, the SP can store it locally.

3. The SP validates the signature of the request using the access token secret.

4. If the signature is valid, the SP talks to the policy decision endpoint of the AM, passing the access token and the SP handle. The request must be digitally signed by the corresponding access token secret.

5. The AM first validates the request, next evaluates the corresponding policies set by the user or the resource owner, and then sends the decision to the SP.

6. If the decision is a Deny, the location of the terms is returned to the SP, and the SP returns the location to the consumer with a 403 HTTP status code.

7. The consumer requests the terms by talking to the terms endpoint hosted in the AM. The request includes the consumer key, signed with the consumer secret.

8. When the consumer receives the terms, it evaluates them and talks to the AM with additional information to prove its legitimacy. This request includes the consumer key and is signed with the consumer secret.

9. The AM evaluates the additional information and claims provided by the consumer. If those meet the required criteria, the AM creates an agreement resource and sends the location of the agreement resource to the consumer.

10. If this requires the user's consent, the AM must send it for the user's approval before sending the location of the agreement resource.

11. Once the consumer receives the location of the agreement resource, it can talk to the corresponding endpoint hosted in the AM and get the agreement resource to see the status.

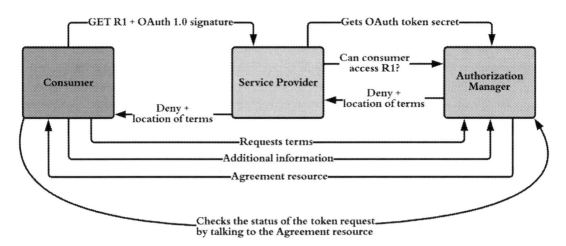

Figure D-4. *The consumer accesses a resource hosted at the service provider with valid OAuth credentials, but with limited privileges*

Step 4: Once approved by the authorization manager, the consumer can access the protected resource with its access token and the corresponding secret key (see Figure D-5):

1. The consumer tries to access the protected resource at the SP with its access token, signed with the access token secret.

2. The SP talks to the AM and gets the secret key corresponding to the consumer's access token. If required, the SP can store it locally.

3. The SP validates the signature of the request using the access token secret.

4. If the signature is valid, the SP talks to the policy decision endpoint of the AM, passing the access token and SP handle, signed with the corresponding access token secret.

5. The AM first validates the request, next evaluates the corresponding policies set by the user or the resource owner, and then sends the decision to the SP.

6. If the decision is an Allow from the AM, the SP returns the requested resource to the corresponding consumer.

7. The SP can cache the decision from the AM. Subsequent calls by the same consumer for the resource can utilize the cache instead of going to the AM.

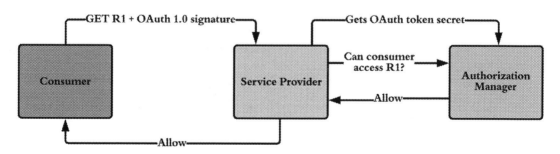

Figure D-5. *The consumer accesses a resource hosted at the SP with valid OAuth credentials and with required privileges*

UMA and OAuth

Over the years, ProtectServe evolved into UMA. ProtectServe used OAuth 1.0 to protect its APIs, and UMA moved from OAuth 1.0 to OAuth WRAP to OAuth 2.0. The UMA specification, which was developed under the Kantara Initiative for almost three years, was submitted to the IETF OAuth working group on July 9, 2011, as a draft recommendation for a user-managed data access protocol.

UMA 1.0 Architecture

The UMA architecture has five main components (see Figure D-6): the *resource owner* (analogous to the user in ProtectServe), the *resource server* (analogous to the service provider in ProtectServe), the *authorization server* (analogous to the authorization manager in ProtectServe), the *client* (analogous to the consumer in ProtectServe), and the *requesting party*. These five components interact with each other during the three phases as defined in the UMA core specification.

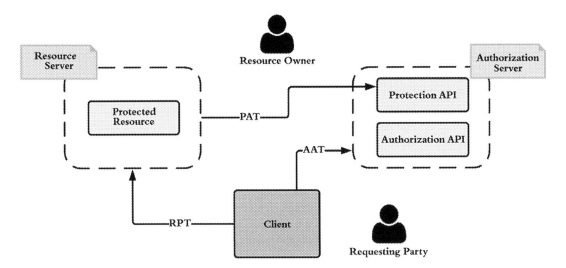

Figure D-6. *UMA high-level architecture*

UMA 1.0 Phases

The first phase of UMA[1] is to protect the resource. The resource owner initiates this phase by introducing the resource servers associated with him or her to a centralized authorization server.

The client initiates the second phase when it wants to access a protected resource. The client talks to the authorization server and obtains the required level of authorization to access the protected resource that's hosted in the resource server. Finally, in the third phase, the client directly accesses the protected resource.

UMA Phase 1: Protecting a Resource

Resources are owned by the resource owner and may be at different resource servers. Let's look at an example. Suppose my photos are with Flickr, my calendar is with Google, and my friend list is with Facebook. How can I protect all these resources, which are distributed across different resource servers, with a centralized authorization server? The first step is to introduce the centralized authorization server to Flickr, Google, and Facebook—to all the resource servers. The resource owner must do this. The resource owner can log in to each resource server and provide the authorization server configuration endpoint to each of them. The authorization server must provide its configuration data in JSON format.

The following is a set of sample configuration data related to the authorization server. The data in this JSON format should be understood by any of the resource servers that support UMA. This section digs into the details of each configuration element as you proceed:

```
{
    "version":"1.0",
    "issuer":"https://auth.server.com",
    "pat_profiles_supported":["bearer"],
    "aat_profiles_supported":["bearer"],
    "rpt_profiles_supported":["bearer"],
    "pat_grant_types_supported":["authorization_code"],
    "aat_grant_types_supported":["authorization_code"],
```

---

[1]https://docs.kantarainitiative.org/uma/rec-uma-core.html

```
  "claim_profiles_supported":["openid"],
  "dynamic_client_endpoint":"https://auth.server.com/dyn_client_reg_uri",
  "token_endpoint":"https://auth.server.com/token_uri",
  "user_endpoint":"https://auth.server.com/user_uri",
  "resource_set_registration_endpoint":"https://auth.server.com/rs/rsrc_uri",
  "introspection_endpoint":"https://auth.server.com/rs/status_uri",
  "permission_registration_endpoint":"https://auth.server.com/perm_uri",
  "rpt_endpoint":"https://auth.server.com/rpt",
  "authorization_request_endpoint":"https://auth.server.com/authorize"
}
```

Once the resource server is introduced to the authorization server via its configuration data endpoint, the resource server can talk to the dynamic client registration (RFC 7591) endpoint (dynamic_client_endpoint) to register it at the authorization server.

The client registration endpoint exposed by the authorization server can be secured or not. It can be secured with OAuth, HTTP Basic authentication, Mutual TLS, or any other security protocol as desired by the authorization server. Even if the Dynamic Client Registration profile (RFC 7591) doesn't enforce any authentication protocols over the registration endpoint, it must be secured with TLS. If the authorization server decides to allow the endpoint to be public and let anyone be registered, it can do so. To register a client, you have to pass all its metadata to the registration endpoint. Here's a sample JSON message for client registration:

```
POST /register HTTP/1.1
Content-Type: application/json
Accept: application/json
Host: authz.server.com
{
    "redirect_uris":["https://client.org/callback","https://client.org/
    callback2"],
    "token_endpoint_auth_method":"client_secret_basic",
    "grant_types": ["authorization_code" , "implicit"],
    "response_types": ["code" , "token"],
}
```

A successful client registration results in the following JSON response, which includes the client identifier and the client secret to be used by the resource server:

```
HTTP/1.1 200 OK
Content-Type: application/json
Cache-Control: no-store
Pragma: no-cache
{
    "client_id":"iuyiSgfgfhffgfh",
    "client_secret": "hkjhkiiu89hknhkjhuyjhk",
    "client_id_issued_at":2343276600,
    "client_secret_expires_at":2503286900,
    "redirect_uris":["https://client.org/callback","https://client.org/
    callback2"],
    "grant_types": "authorization_code",
    "token_endpoint_auth_method": "client_secret_basic",
}
```

Note   You aren't required to use the Dynamic Client Registration API. Resource servers can use any method they prefer to register at the authorization server. The registration at the authorization server is one-time operation, not per resource owner. If a given resource server has already been registered with a given authorization server, then it doesn't need to register again at the authorization server when the same authorization server is introduced by a different resource owner.

Once the initial resource server registration process is complete, the next step in the first phase is for the resource server to obtain a Protection API token (PAT) to access the Protection API exposed by the authorization server. (You learn more on PAT in the section "Protection API," later in the appendix.) PAT is issued per resource server, per resource owner. In other words, each resource owner must authorize a PAT so the resource server can use it to protect resources with the centralized authorization server. The authorization server configuration file declares the types of PATs it supports. In the previous example, the authorization server supports OAuth 2.0 bearer tokens:

```
pat_profiles_supported":["bearer"]
```

In addition to the PAT token type, the authorization server configuration file also declares the way to obtain the PAT. In this case, it should be via the OAuth 2.0 authorization code grant type. The resource server must initiate an OAuth flow with the authorization code grant type to obtain the PAT in bearer format:

```
"pat_grant_types_supported":["authorization_code"]
```

Note   The scope of the PAT token must be `http://docs.kantarainitiative.org/uma/scopes/prot.json`. This must be included in the scope value of the authorization code grant request.

The following is a sample authorization code grant request to obtain a PAT:

```
GET /authorize?response_type=code
    &client_id=dsdasDdsdsdsdsdas
    &state=xyz
    &redirect_uri=https://flickr.com/callback
    &scope=http://docs.kantarainitiative.org/uma/scopes/prot.json
HTTP/1.1 Host: auth.server.com
```

Once the resource server gets the PAT, it can be used to access the Resource Set Registration API exposed by the authorization server, to register a set of resources that needs to be protected by the given authorization server. The endpoint of the Resource Set Registration API is defined under the authorization server configuration file (you learn more about the Resource Set Registration API in the section "Protection API"):

```
"resource_set_registration_endpoint":"https://auth.server.com/rs/rsrc_uri",
```

UMA Phase 2: Getting Authorization

According to the UMA specification, phase 2 begins after a failed access attempt by the client. The client tries to access a resource hosted in the resource server and gets an HTTP 403 status code (see Figure D-7). In addition to the 403 response, the resource server includes the endpoint (as_uri) of the corresponding authorization server where the client can obtain a requesting party token (RPT):

```
HTTP/1.1 403 Forbidden
WWW-Authenticate: UMA realm="my-realm",
                      host_id="photos.flickr.com",
                      as_uri=https://auth.server.com
```

According to UMA, to access a protected resource, the client must present a valid RPT. (You learn more about RPT in the section "Authorization API.") The RPT endpoint that must be included in the 403 response is declared in the authorization server configuration file:

```
"rpt_endpoint":"https://auth.server.com/rpt"
```

Once rejected by the resource server with a 403, the client has to talk to the RPT endpoint of the authorization server. To do so, the client must have an Authorization API token (AAT). To get an AAT, the client must be registered at the corresponding authorization server. The client can use the OAuth Dynamic Client Registration API or any other way it prefers to register. After it's registered with the authorization server, the client gets a client key and a client secret. The requesting party can be a different entity from the client. For example, the client can be a mobile application or a web application, whereas the requesting party could be a human user who uses either the mobile application or the web application. The ultimate goal is for the requesting party to access an API owned by a resource owner, hosted in a resource server, via a client application. To achieve this, the requesting party should get an RPT from an authorization server trusted by the resource server. To get an RPT, the requesting party should first get an AAT via the client application. To get an AAT, the client must follow an OAuth grant type supported by the authorization server to issue AATs. That is declared in the authorization server's configuration file. In this case, the authorization server supports the authorization code grant type to issue AATs:

```
"aat_grant_types_supported":["authorization_code"]
```

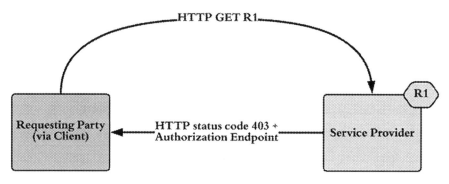

Figure D-7. *The resource server rejects any request without an RPT*

Once the client is registered at the authorization server, to get an AAT on behalf of the requesting party, it must initiate the OAuth authorization code grant type flow, with the scope: `http://docs.kantarainitiative.org/uma/scopes/authz.json`. The following is a sample authorization code grant request to obtain an AAT:

```
GET /authorize?response_type=code
    &client_id=dsdasDdsdsdsdsdas
    &state=xyz
    &redirect_uri=https://flickr.com/callback
    &scope=http://docs.kantarainitiative.org/uma/scopes/authz.json
HTTP/1.1 Host: auth.server.com
```

Note   You aren't required to use the Dynamic Client Registration API. The client can use any method it prefers to register at the authorization server. The registration at the authorization server is one-time operation and not per resource server or per requesting party. If a given client has already been registered with a given authorization server, then it doesn't need to register again when a different requesting party uses the same authorization server. The AAT is per client per requesting party per authorization server and is independent from the resource server.

Once you have the AAT, upon the 403 response from the resource server, the client can talk to the authorization server's RPT endpoint and get the corresponding RPT (see Figure D-8). To get an RPT, the client must authenticate with the AAT. In the following example, the AAT is used in the HTTP Authorization header as an OAuth 2.0 bearer token:

```
POST /rpt HTTP/1.1
Host: as.example.com
Authorization: Bearer GghgjhsuyuE8heweds
```

Note   The RPT endpoint is defined under the `rpt_endpoint` attribute of the authorization server's configuration.

The following shows a sample response from the RPT endpoint of the authorization server. If this is the first issuance of the RPT, it doesn't have any authorization rights attached. It can only be used as a temporary token to get the "real" RPT:

```
HTTP/1.1 201 Created
Content-Type: application/json
{
    "rpt": "dsdsJKhkiuiuoiwewjewkej"
}
```

When the client is in possession of the initial RPT, it can once again try to access the resource. In this case, the RPT goes as an OAuth 2.0 bearer token in the HTTP Authorization header. Now the resource server extracts the RPT from the resource request and talks to the Introspection API exposed by the authorization server. The Introspection API can tell whether the RPT is valid and, if it is, the permissions associated with it. In this case, because you're still using the initial RPT, there are no permissions associated with it, even though it's a valid token.

Note   The Introspection API exposed by the authorization server is OAuth 2.0 protected. The resource server must present a valid PAT to access it. The PAT is another bearer token that goes in the HTTP `Authorization` header.

If the RPT doesn't have enough permission to access the resource, the resource server talks to the Client Requested Permission Registration API exposed by the authorization server and registers the required set of permissions to access the desired resource. When permission registration is successfully completed, the authorization server returns a permission ticket identifier.

Note   The Client Requested Permission Registration endpoint is defined under the `permission_registration_endpoint` attribute in the authorization server's configuration. This endpoint, which is part of the UMA Protection API, is secured with OAuth 2.0. The resource server must present a valid PAT to access the API.

The following is a sample request to the permission registration endpoint of the authorization server. It must include a unique resource_set_id corresponding to the requested resource and the required set of scopes associated with it:

```
POST /perm_uri HTTP/1.1
Content-Type: application/json
Host: auth.server.com
{
    "resource_set_id": "1122wqwq23398100",
    "scopes": [
        "http://photoz.flickr.com/dev/actions/view",
        "http://photoz.flickr.com/dev/actions/all"
          ]
}
```

In response to this request, the authorization server generates a permission ticket:

```
HTTP/1.1 201 Created
Content-Type: application/json
{"ticket": "016f88989-f9b9-11e0-bd6f-0cc66c6004de"}
```

When the permission ticket is created at the authorization server, the resource server sends the following response to the client:

```
HTTP/1.1 403 Forbidden
WWW-Authenticate: UMA realm="my-realm",
                  host_id=" photos.flickr.com ",
                  as_uri="https://auth.server.com"
                  error="insufficient_scope"
```

```
{"ticket": "016f88989-f9b9-11e0-bd6f-0cc66c6004de"}
```

Now the client has to get a new RPT with the required set of permissions. Unlike in the previous case, this time the RPT request also includes the ticket attribute from the previous 403 response:

```
POST /rpt HTTP/1.1
Host: as.example.com
Authorization: Bearer GghgjhsuyuE8heweds
{
    "rpt": "dsdsJKhkiuiuoiwewjewkej",
    "ticket": "016f88989-f9b9-11e0-bd6f-0cc66c6004de"
}
```

Note   The RPT endpoint of the authorization server is secured with OAuth 2.0. To access the RPT endpoint, the client must use an AAT in the HTTP `Authorization` header as the OAuth bearer token.

At this point, prior to issuing the new RPT to satisfy the requested set of permissions, the authorization server evaluates the authorization policies set by the resource owner against the client and the requesting party. If the authorization server needs more information regarding the requesting party while evaluating the policies, it can interact directly with the requesting party to gather the required details. Also, if it needs further approval by the resource owner, the authorization server must notify the resource owner and wait for a response. In any of these cases, once the authorization server decides to associate permissions with the RPT, it creates a new RPT and sends it to the client:

```
HTTP/1.1 201 Created
Content-Type: application/json
{"rpt": "dsdJhkjhkhk879dshkjhkj877979"}
```

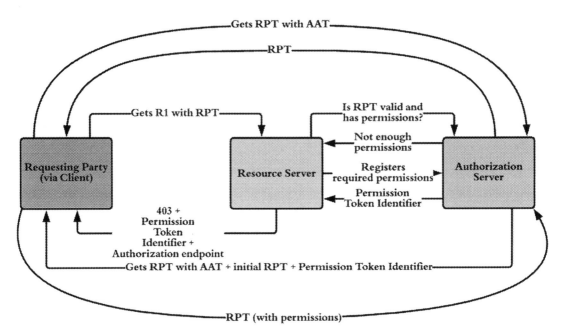

Figure D-8. *The client gets an authorized RPT from the authorization server*

UMA Phase 3: Accessing the Protected Resource

At the end of phase 2, the client got access to a valid RPT with the required set of permissions. Now the client can use it to access the protected resource. The resource server again uses the Introspection API exposed by the authorization server to check the validity of the RPT. If the token is valid and has the required set of permissions, the corresponding resource is returned to the client.

UMA APIs

UMA defines two main APIs: the Protection API and the Authorization API (see Figure D-9). The Protection API sits between the resource server and the authorization server, and the Authorization API sits between the client and the authorization server. Both APIs are secured with OAuth 2.0. To access the Protection API, the resource server must present a PAT as the bearer token; and to access the Authorization API, the client must present an AAT as the bearer token.

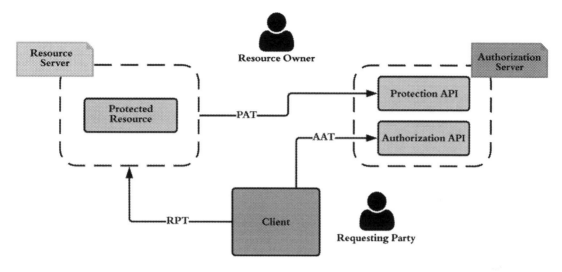

Figure D-9. *UMA APIs*

Protection API

The Protection API is the interface exposed to the resource server by the authorization server. It consists of three subelements: the OAuth Resource Set Registration endpoint,[2] the Client Requested Permission Registration endpoint, and the OAuth Token Introspection (RFC 7662) endpoint.

These three APIs that fall under the Protection API address different concerns. The resource server uses the Resource Set Registration API to publish semantics and discovery properties of its resources to the authorization server. The resource server does this in an ongoing manner. Whenever it finds a resource set that needs to be protected by an external authorization server, it talks to the corresponding Resource Set Registration endpoint to register new resources. This action can be initiated by the resource server itself or by the resource owner. The following example shows a JSON request to the Resource Set Registration API of the authorization server. The value of the name attribute should be human-readable text, and the optional icon_uri can point to any image that represents this resource set. The scope array should list all the scope values required to

---

[2]The latest draft of the OAuth Resource Set Registration specification is available at
https://tools.ietf.org/html/draft-hardjono-oauth-resource-reg-07

access the resource set. The type attribute describes the semantics associated with the resource set; the value of this attribute is meaningful only to the resource server and can be used to process the associated resources:

```
{
  "name": "John's Family Photos",
  "icon_uri": "http://www.flickr.com/icons/flower.png",
  "scopes": [
        "http://photoz. flickr.com/dev/scopes/view",
        "http://photoz. flickr.com/dev/scopes/all"
  ],
  "type": "http://www. flickr.com/rsets/photoalbum"
}
```

This JSON message is also known as the *resource description*. Each UMA authorization server must present a REST API to create (POST), update (PUT), list (GET), and delete (DELETE) resource set descriptions. The resource server can utilize this endpoint either during phase 1 or in an ongoing manner.

The resource server accesses the Client Requested Permission Registration endpoint during phase 2 of UMA flow. The resource server uses this API to inform the authorization server about the level of permissions required for the client to access the desired resource. The resource server uses the Introspection API to check the validity of the RPT.

Authorization API

The Authorization API is the interface between the client and the authorization server. The main responsibility of this API is to issue RPTs.

APPENDIX E

Base64 URL Encoding

Base64 encoding defines how to represent binary data in an ASCII string format. The objective of base64 encoding is to transmit binary data such as keys or digital certificates in a printable format. This type of encoding is needed if these objects are transported as part of an email body, a web page, an XML document, or a JSON document.

To do base64 encoding, first the binary data are grouped into 24-bit groups. Then each 24-bit group is divided into four 6-bit groups. Now, a printable character can represent each 6-bit group based on its bit value in decimal (see Figure E-1). For example, the decimal value of the 6-bit group 000111 is 7. As per Figure E-1, the character H represents this 6-bit group. Apart from the characters shown in Figure E-1, the character = is used to specify a special processing function, which is to pad. If the length of the original binary data is not an exact multiple of 24, then we need padding. Let's say the length is 232, which is not a multiple of 24. Now we need to pad this binary data to make its length equal to the very next multiple of the 24, which is 240. In other words, we need to pad this binary data by 8 to make its length 240. In this case, padding is done by adding eight 0s to the end of the binary data. Now, when we divide this 240 bits by 6 to build 6-bit groups, the last 6-bit group will be of all zeros—and this complete group will be represented by the padding character =.

© Prabath Siriwardena 2020
P. Siriwardena, *Advanced API Security*, https://doi.org/10.1007/978-1-4842-2050-4_20

0	A	16	Q	32	g	48	w
1	B	17	R	33	h	49	x
2	C	18	S	34	I	50	y
3	D	19	T	35	j	51	z
4	E	20	U	36	k	52	0
5	F	21	V	37	l	53	1
6	G	22	W	38	m	54	2
7	H	23	X	39	n	55	3
8	I	24	Y	40	o	56	4
9	J	25	Z	41	p	57	5
10	K	26	a	42	q	58	6
11	L	27	b	43	r	59	7
12	M	28	c	44	s	60	8
13	N	29	d	45	t	61	9
14	O	30	e	46	u	62	+
15	P	31	f	47	v	63	/

Figure E-1. *Base64 encoding*

The following example shows how to base64-encode/decode binary data with Java 8. The `java.util.Base64` class was introduced from Java 8.

```
byte[] binaryData = // load binary data to this variable
// encode
String encodedString = Base64.getEncoder().encodeToString(binaryData);
// decode
binary[] decodedBinary = Base64.getDecoder().decode(encodedString);
```

One issue with base64 encoding is that it does not work quite well with URLs. The + and / characters in base64 encoding (see Figure E-1) have a special meaning when used within a URL. If we try to send a base64-encoded image as a URL query parameter and if the base64-encoded string carries any of the preceding two characters, then the browser will interpret the URL in a wrong way. The base64url encoding was introduced to address this problem. The way base64url encoding works is exactly the same as base64 encoding other than two exceptions: the character - is used in base64url encoding instead of the character + in base64 encoding, and the character _ is used in base64url encoding instead of the character / in base64 encoding.

The following example shows how to base64url-encode/decode binary data with Java 8. The java.util.Base64 class was introduced from Java 8.

```
byte[] binaryData = // load binary data to this variable
// encode
String encodedString = Base64.getUrlEncoder().encodeToString(binaryData);
// decode
binary[] decodedBinary = Base64.getUrlEncoder().decode(encodedString);
```

APPENDIX F

Basic/Digest Authentication

HTTP Basic authentication and Digest authentication are two authentication schemes, used for protecting resources on the Web. Both are based on username- and password-based credentials. When trying to log in to a web site, if the browser presents you a dialog box asking your username and password, then most probably this web site is protected with HTTP Basic or Digest authentication. Asking the browser to challenge the user to authenticate is one of the quick and dirty ways of protecting a web site. None or at least very few web sites on the Internet today use HTTP Basic or Digest authentication. Instead, they use a nice form-based authentication or their own custom authentication schemes. But still some use HTTP Basic/Digest authentication to secure direct API-level access to resources on the Web.

HTTP Basic authentication is first standardized through the HTTP/1.0 RFC (Request For Comments)[1] by IETF (Internet Engineering Task Force). It takes the username and password over the network as an HTTP header in cleartext. Passing user credentials over the wire in cleartext is not secure, unless it's used over a secured transport channel, like HTTP over TLS (Transport Layer Security). This limitation was addressed in the RFC 2617, which defined two authentication schemes for HTTP: *Basic Access Authentication* and *Digest Access Authentication*. Unlike Basic authentication, the Digest authentication is based on cryptographic hashes and never sends user credentials over the wire in cleartext.

---

[1]Hypertext Transfer Protocol—HTTP/1.0, `www.rfc-base.org/txt/rfc-1945.txt`

401

© Prabath Siriwardena 2020
P. Siriwardena, *Advanced API Security*, https://doi.org/10.1007/978-1-4842-2050-4_21

HTTP Basic Authentication

The HTTP/1.0 specification first defined the scheme for HTTP Basic authentication and got further refined by RFC 2617. The RFC 2617 was proposed as a companion to the HTTP 1.1 specification or the RFC 2616.[2] Then again in 2015, the RFC 2617 was obsoleted by the new RFC 7617. It's a challenge-response-based authentication scheme, where the server challenges the user to provide valid credentials to access a protected resource. With this model, the user has to authenticate him for each realm. The realm can be considered as a protection domain. A realm allows the protected resources on a server to be partitioned into a set of protection spaces, each with its own authentication scheme and/or authorization database.[3] A given user can belong to multiple realms simultaneously. The value of the realm is shown to the user at the time of authentication—it's part of the authentication challenge sent by the server. The realm value is a string, which is assigned by the authentication server. Once the request hits the server with Basic authentication credentials, the server will authenticate the request only if it can validate the username and the password, for the protected resource, against the corresponding realm.

```
┌──────────────────────────────────────────────────────────────────────────┐
│         ACCESSING THE GITHUB API WITH HTTP BASIC AUTHENTICATION            │
└──────────────────────────────────────────────────────────────────────────┘
```

GitHub is a web-based git repository hosting service. Its REST API[4] is protected with HTTP Basic authentication. This exercise shows you how to access the secured GitHub API to create a git repository. You need to have a GitHub account to try out the following, and in case you do not have one, you can create an account from `https://github.com`.

Let's try to invoke the following GitHub API with cURL. It's an open API that doesn't require any authentication and returns pointers to all available resources, corresponding to the provided GitHub username.

```
\> curl  -v  https://api.github.com/users/{github-user}
```

For example:

```
\> curl  -v  https://api.github.com/users/prabath
```

---

[2]Hypertext Transfer Protocol—HTTP/1.1, `www.ietf.org/rfc/rfc2616.txt`
[3]HTTP Authentication: Basic and Digest Access Authentication, `www.ietf.org/rfc/rfc2617.txt`
[4]GitHub REST API, `http://developer.github.com/v3/`

The preceding command returns back the following JSON response.

```json
{
    "login":"prabath",
    "id":1422563,
    "avatar_url":"https://avatars.githubusercontent.com/u/1422563?v=3",
    "gravatar_id":"",
    "url":"https://api.github.com/users/prabath",
    "html_url":"https://github.com/prabath",
    "followers_url":"https://api.github.com/users/prabath/followers",
    "following_url":"https://api.github.com/users/prabath/following
    {/other_user}",
    "gists_url":"https://api.github.com/users/prabath/gists{/gist_id}",
    "starred_url":"https://api.github.com/users/prabath/starred{/owner}
    {/repo}",
    "subscriptions_url":"https://api.github.com/users/prabath/subscriptions",
    "organizations_url":"https://api.github.com/users/prabath/orgs",
    "repos_url":"https://api.github.com/users/prabath/repos",
    "events_url":"https://api.github.com/users/prabath/events{/privacy}",
    "received_events_url":"https://api.github.com/users/prabath/received_
    events",
    "type":"User",
    "site_admin":false,
    "name":"Prabath Siriwardena",
    "company":"WSO2",
    "blog":"http://blog.faciellogin.com",
    "location":"San Jose, CA, USA",
    "email":"prabath@apache.org",
    "hireable":null,
    "bio":null,
    "public_repos":3,
    "public_gists":1,
    "followers":0,
    "following":0,
    "created_at":"2012-02-09T10:18:26Z",
    "updated_at":"2015-11-23T12:57:36Z"
}
```

Note   All the cURL commands used in this book are broken into multiple lines just for clarity. When you execute them, make sure to have it as a single line, with no line breaks.

Now let's try out another API. Here you create a GitHub repository with the following API call. This returns a negative response with the HTTP status code *401 Unauthorized*. The API is secured with HTTP Basic authentication, and you need to provide credentials to access it:

```
\> curl -i  -X POST -H 'Content-Type: application/x-www-form-urlencoded'
       -d '{"name": "my_github_repo"}'  https://api.github.com/user/repos
```

The preceding command returns back the following HTTP response, indicating that the request is not authenticated. Observing the response from GitHub for the unauthenticated API call to create a repository, it looks as though the GitHub API isn't fully compliant with the HTTP 1.1 specification. According to the HTTP 1.1 specification, whenever the server returns a 401 status code, it also must return the HTTP header *WWW-Authenticate*.

```
HTTP/1.1 401 Unauthorized
Content-Type: application/json; charset=utf-8
Content-Length: 115
Server: GitHub.com
Status: 401 Unauthorized
{
  "message": "Requires authentication",
  "documentation_url": "https://developer.github.com/v3/repos/#create"
}
```

Let's invoke the same API with proper GitHub credentials. Replace $GitHubUserName and $GitHubPassword with your credentials:

```
curl  -i -v -u $GitHubUserName:$GitHubPassword
       -X POST -H 'Content-Type: application/x-www-form-urlencoded'
       -d '{"name": "my_github_repo"}'  https://api.github.com/user/repos
```

Next, let's look at the HTTP request generated from the cURL client:

```
POST /user/repos HTTP/1.1
Authorization: Basic cHJhYmF0OaDpwcmFiYXRoMTIz
```

The HTTP Authorization header in the request is generated from the username and password you provided. The formula is simple: `Basic Base64Encode(username:password)`. Any base64-encoded text is no better than cleartext—it can be decoded quite easily back to the cleartext. That is why Basic authentication on plain HTTP isn't secured. It must be used in conjunction with a secured transport channel, like HTTPS.

The preceding command returns back the following HTTP response (truncated for clarity), indicating that the git repository was created successfully.

```
HTTP/1.1 201 Created
Server: GitHub.com
Content-Type: application/json; charset=utf-8
Content-Length: 5261
Status: 201 Created
{
  "id": 47273092,
  "name": "my_github_repo",
  "full_name": "prabath/my_github_repo"
}
```

Note   To add HTTP Basic authentication credentials to a request generated from a cURL client, you can use the option **–u username:password**. This creates the base64-encoded HTTP basic authorization header. **–i** is used to include HTTP headers in the output, and **–v** is used to run cURL in verbose mode. **–H** is used to set HTTP headers in the outgoing request, and **–d** is used to post data to the endpoint.

HTTP Digest Authentication

HTTP Digest authentication was initially proposed by the RFC 2069[5] as an extension to the HTTP/1.0 specification to overcome certain limitations in HTTP Basic authentication. Later this specification was made obsolete by the RFC 2617. The RFC 2617 removed some optional elements specified by the RFC 2069 due to problems found since its publication and introduced a set of new elements for compatibility, and those new elements have been made optional. Digest authentication is an authentication scheme based on a challenge-response model, which never sends the user credentials over the wire. Because the credentials are never sent over the wire with the request, Transport Layer Security (TLS) isn't a must. Anyone intercepting the traffic won't be able to discover the password in cleartext.

To initiate Digest authentication, the client has to send a request to the protected resource with no authentication information, which results in a challenge (in the response). The following example shows how to initiate a Digest authentication handshake from cURL (this is just an example, don't try it till we set up the cute-cupcake sample later in this appendix):

```
\> curl -k --digest -u userName:password -v https://localhost:8443/recipe
```

Note   To add HTTP Digest authentication credentials to a request generated from a cURL client, use the option **--digest -u username: password**.

Let's look at the HTTP headers in the response. The first response is a 401[6] with the HTTP header WWW-Authenticate, which in fact is the challenge:

```
HTTP/1.1 401 Unauthorized
WWW-Authenticate: Digest realm="cute-cupcakes.com", qop="auth",
nonce="1390781967182:c2db4ebb26207f6ed38bb08eeffc7422",
opaque="F5288F4526B8EAFFC4AC79F04CA8A6ED"
```

---

[5]An Extension to HTTP: Digest Access Authentication, www.ietf.org/rfc/rfc2069.txt

[6]The 401 HTTP status code is returned back in the HTTP response when the request is not authenticated to access the corresponding resource. All HTTP/1.1 status codes are defined here: www.w3.org/Protocols/rfc2616/rfc2616-sec10.html

Note   You learn more about the Recipe API and how to deploy it locally as you proceed through this appendix. The "Securing the Recipe API with HTTP Digest Authentication" exercise at the end of the appendix explains how to secure an API with Digest authentication.

The challenge from the server consists of the following key elements. Each of these elements is defined in the RFC 2617:

- `realm`: A string to be displayed to users so they know which username and password to use. This string should contain at least the name of the host performing the authentication and may additionally indicate the collection of users who may have access.

- `domain`: This is an optional element, not present in the preceding response. It's a comma-separated list of URIs. The intent is that the client could use this information to know the set of URIs for which the same authentication information should be sent. The URIs in this list may exist on different servers. If this keyword is omitted or empty, the client should assume that the domain consists of all URIs on the responding server.

- `nonce`: A server-specified data string, which should be uniquely generated each time a 401 response is made. The value of the nonce is implementation dependent and is opaque to the client. The client should not try to interpret the value of nonce.

- `opaque`: A string of data, specified by the server, that should be returned by the client unchanged in the *Authorization* header of subsequent requests with URIs in the same protection space (which is the realm). Because the client is returning back the value of the *opaque* element given to it by the server for the duration of a session, the *opaque* data can be used to transport authentication session state information or can be used as a session identifier.

- `stale`: A flag, indicating that the previous request from the client was rejected because the nonce value was stale. If stale is TRUE (case insensitive), the client may wish to simply retry the request with a new nonce value, without reprompting the user for a new username and password. The server should only set stale to TRUE if it receives a request for which the nonce is invalid but with a valid digest for that nonce (indicating that the client knows the correct username/password). If stale is FALSE, or anything other than TRUE, or the stale directive is not present, the username and/or password are invalid, and new values must be obtained. This flag is not shown in the preceding response.

- algorithm: This is an optional element, not shown in the preceding response. The value of algorithm is a string indicating a pair of algorithms used to produce the digest and a checksum. If the client does not understand the algorithm, the challenge should be ignored, and if it is not present, it is assumed to be MD5.

- qop: The *quality of protection* options applied to the response by the server. The value *auth* indicates authentication; while the value *auth-int* indicates authentication with integrity protection. This is an optional element and introduced to be backward compatible with the RFC 2069.

Once the client gets the response from the server, it has to respond back. Here's the HTTP request with the response to the challenge:

```
Authorization: Digest username="prabath", realm="cute-cupcakes.com",
nonce="1390781967182:c2db4ebb26207f6ed38bb08eeffc7422", uri="/recipe",
cnonce="MTM5MDc4", nc=00000001, qop="auth",
response="f5bfb64ba8596d1b9ad1514702f5a062",
opaque="F5288F4526B8EAFFC4AC79F04CA8A6ED"
```

The following are the key elements in the response from the client:

- username: The unique identifier of the user who's going to invoke the API.

- realm/qop/nonce/opaque: The same as in the initial challenge from the server. The value of qop indicates what *quality of protection* the client has applied to the message. If present, its value MUST be one of the alternatives the server indicated it supports in the WWW-Authenticate header.

- cnonce: This MUST be specified if a qop directive is sent and MUST NOT be specified if the server did not send a qop directive in the WWW-Authenticate header field. The value of cnonce is an opaque quoted string value provided by the client and used by both the client and the server to avoid chosen plaintext attacks,[7] to provide mutual authentication, and to provide some message integrity protection. This is not shown in the preceding response.

- nc: This MUST be specified if a qop directive is sent and MUST NOT be specified if the server did not send a qop directive in the WWW-Authenticate header field. The value of nc is the hexadecimal count of the number of requests (including the current request) that the client has sent with the same nonce value. For example, in the first request sent in response to a given nonce value, the client sends "nc=00000001". The purpose of this directive is to allow the server to detect request replays by maintaining its own copy of this count—if the same nc value is seen twice for the same nonce value, then the request is a replay.

- digest-uri: The request URI from the request line. Duplicated here because proxies are allowed to change the Request-Line in transit. The value of the digest-uri is used to calculate the value of the response element, as explained later in the chapter.

- auth-param: This is an optional element not shown in the preceding response. It allows for future extensions. The server MUST ignore any unrecognized directive.

- response: The response to the challenge sent by the server, calculated by the client. The following section explains how the value of response is calculated.

---

[7]Chosen plaintext attack is an attack model where the attacker has access to both the encrypted text and the corresponding plaintext. The attacker can specify his own plaintext and get it encrypted or signed by the server. Further he can carefully craft the plaintext to learn characteristics about the encryption/signing algorithm. For example, he can start with an empty text, a text with one letter, with two letters likewise, and get corresponding encrypted/signed text. This kind of an analysis on encrypted/signed text is known as cryptanalysis.

The value of `response` is calculated in the following manner. Digest authentication supports multiple algorithms. RFC 2617 recommends using MD5 or MD5-sess (MD5-session). If no algorithm is specified in the server challenge, MD5 is used. Digest calculation is done with two types of data: security-related data (A1) and message-related data (A2). If you use MD5 as the hashing algorithm or if it is not specified, then you define security-related data (A1) in the following manner:

```
A1 = username:realm:password
```

If you use MD5-sess as the hashing algorithm, then you define security-related data (A1) in the following manner. cnonce is an opaque quoted string value provided by the client and used by both the client and the server to avoid chosen plaintext attacks. The value of nonce is the same as in the server challenge. If the MD5-sess is picked as the hashing algorithm, then A1 is calculated only once on the first request by the client following receipt of a WWW-Authenticate challenge from the server:

```
A1 = MD5 (username:realm:password):nonce:cnonce
```

RFC 2617 defines message-related data (A2) in two ways, based on the value of qop in the server challenge. If the value is auth or undefined, then the message-related data (A2) is defined in the following manner. The value of the request-method element can be GET, POST, PUT, DELETE, or any HTTP verb, and the value of the uri-directive-value element is the request URI from the request line:

```
A2 = request-method:uri-directive-value
```

If the value of qop is `auth-int`, then you need to protect the integrity of the message, in addition to authenticating. A2 is derived in the following manner. When you have MD5 or MD5-sess as the hashing algorithm, the value of H is MD5:

```
A2 = request-method:uri-directive-value:H(request-entity-body)
```

The final value of the digest is calculated in the following way, based on the value of qop. If qop is set to `auth` or `auth-int`, then the final digest value is as shown next. The nc value is the hexadecimal count of the number of requests (including the current request) that the client has sent with the nonce value in this request. This directive helps the server detect replay attacks. The server maintains its own copy of nonce and the nonce count (nc); if any are seen twice, that indicates a possible replay attack:

```
MD5(MD5(A1):nonce:nc:cnonce:qop:MD5(A2))
```

If qop is undefined, then the final digest value is

`MD5(MD5(A1):<nonce>:MD5(A2))`

This final digest value will be set as the value of the *response* element in the HTTP request from the client to the server. Once the client responds back to the server's initial challenge, the subsequent requests from there onward do not need all the preceding three message flows (the initial unauthenticated request from the client, the challenge from the server, and the response to the challenge from the client). The server will send a challenge to the client only if there is no valid authorization header in the request. Once the client gets the initial challenge, for the subsequent requests, the same parameters from the challenge will be used. In other words, the response by the client to a *WWW-Authenticate* challenge from the server for a protection space starts an authentication session with that protection space. The authentication session lasts until the client receives another *WWW-Authenticate* challenge from any server in the protection space. The client should remember the *username, password, nonce, nonce count*, and *opaque* values associated with the authentication session to use to construct the authorization header in the subsequent requests within that protection space. For example, the authorization header from the client should have the *nonce* value in each request. This *nonce* value is picked from the initial challenge from the server, but the value of the *nc* element will be increased by one, for each request. Table F-1 provides a comparison between HTTP Basic authentication and Digest authentication.

Table F-1. *HTTP Basic Authentication vs. HTTP Digest Authentication*

HTTP Basic Authentication	HTTP Digest Authentication
Sends credentials in cleartext over the wire.	Credentials are never sent in cleartext. A digest derived from the cleartext password is sent over the wire.
Should be used in conjunction with a secured transport channel, like HTTPS.	Doesn't depend on the security of the underneath transport channel.
Only performs authentication.	Can be used to protect the integrity of the message, in addition to authentication (with qop=auth-int).
User store can store passwords as a salted hash.	User store should store passwords in cleartext or should store the hash value of username:realm:password.

Note   With HTTP Digest authentication, a user store has to store passwords either in cleartext or as the hashed value of `username:password:realm`. This is required because the server has to validate the digest sent from the client, which is derived from the cleartext password (or the hash of `username:realm:password`).

CUTE-CUPCAKE FACTORY: DEPLOYING THE RECIPE API IN APACHE TOMCAT

In this example, you deploy a prebuilt web application with the Recipe API in Apache Tomcat. The Recipe API is hosted and maintained by the Cute-Cupcake factory. It's a public API with which the customers of Cute-Cupcake factory can interact. The Recipe API supports the following five operations:

- `GET /recipe`: Returns all the recipes in the system

- `GET /recipe/{$recipeNo}`: Returns the recipe with the given recipe number

- `POST /recipe`: Creates a new recipe in the system

- `PUT /recipe`: Updates the recipe in the system with the given details

- `DELETE /recipe/{$recipeNo}`: Deletes the recipe from the system with the provided recipe number

You can download the latest version of Apache Tomcat from `http://tomcat.apache.org`. All the examples discussed in this book use Tomcat 9.0.20.

To deploy the API, download the `recipe.war` file from `https://github.com/apisecurity/samples/blob/master/appendix-f/recipe.war` and copy it to `[TOMCAT_HOME]\webapps`. To start Tomcat, run the following from the `[TOMCAT_HOME]\bin` directory:

```
[Linux] sh catalina.sh run
[Windows] catalina.bat run
```

Once the server is started, use cURL to execute the following command. Here it's assumed that Tomcat is running on its default HTTP port 8080:

```
\> curl  http://localhost:8080/recipe
```

This returns all the recipes in the system as a JSON payload:

```
{
    "recipes":[
        {
            "recipeId":"10001",
            "name":"Lemon Cupcake",
            "ingredients":"lemon zest, white sugar,unsalted butter, flour,salt,
            milk",
            "directions":"Preheat oven to 375 degrees F (190 degrees C). Line 30
            cupcake pan cups with paper liners...."
        },
        {
            "recipeId":"10002",
            "name":"Red Velvet Cupcake",
            "ingredients":"cocoa powder, eggs, white sugar,unsalted butter,
            flour,salt, milk",
            "directions":" Preheat oven to 350 degrees F. Mix flour, cocoa
            powder,
                                baking soda and salt in medium bowl. Set
                                aside...."
        }
    ]
}
```

To get the recipe of any given cupcake, use the following cURL command, where 10001 is the ID of the cupcake you just created:

```
\> curl  http://localhost:8080/recipe/10001
```

This returns the following JSON response:

```
{
        "recipeId":"10001",
        "name":"Lemon Cupcake",
        "ingredients":"lemon zest, white sugar,unsalted butter, flour,salt,
        milk",
        "directions":"Preheat oven to 375 degrees F (190 degrees C). Line 30
        cupcake pan cups with paper liners...."
}
```

To create a new recipe, use the following cURL command:

```
curl  -X POST -H 'Content-Type: application/json'
      -d '{"name":"Peanut Butter Cupcake",
          "ingredients":"peanut butter, eggs, sugar,unsalted butter,
          flour,salt, milk",
          "directions":"Preheat the oven to 350 degrees F (175 degrees C).
          Line a cupcake pan with paper liners, or grease and flour
          cups..."
          }' http://localhost:8080/recipe
```

This returns the following JSON response:

```
{
        "recipeId":"10003",
        "location":"http://localhost:8080/recipe/10003",
}
```

To update an existing recipe, use the following cURL command:

```
curl  -X PUT -H 'Content-Type: application/json'
      -d '{"name":"Peanut Butter Cupcake",
          "ingredients":"peanut butter, eggs, sugar,unsalted butter,
          flour,salt, milk",
          "directions":"Preheat the oven to 350 degrees F (175 degrees C).
          Line a cupcake pan with
           paper liners, or grease and flour cups..."
          }' http://localhost:8080/recipe/10003
```

This returns the following JSON response:

```
{
        "recipeId":"10003",
        "location":"http://localhost:8080/recipe/10003",
}
```

To delete an existing recipe, use the following cURL command:

```
\> curl  -X DELETE http://localhost:8080/recipe/10001
```

Note   To do remote debugging with Apache Tomcat, start the server under Linux operating system as *sh catalina.sh jpda run* or under Windows operating system as *catalina.bat jpda run.* This opens port 8000 for remote debugging connections.

CONFIGURING APACHE DIRECTORY SERVER (LDAP)

Apache Directory Server is an open source LDAP server distributed under Apache 2.0 license. You can download the latest version from `http://directory.apache.org/studio/`. It's recommended that you download the Apache Directory Studio[8] itself, as it comes with a set of very useful tools to configure LDAP. We use Apache Directory Studio 2.0.0 in the following example.

The following steps are needed only if you don't have an LDAP server set up to run. First you need to start Apache Directory Studio. This provides a management console to create and manage LDAP servers and connections. Then proceed with the following steps:

1. From Apache Directory Studio, go to the LDAP Servers view. If it's not there already, go to Window ➤ Show View ➤ LDAP Servers.

2. Right-click LDAP Servers View, choose New ➤ New Server, and select ApacheDS 2.0.0. Give any name to the server in the Server Name text box, and click Finish.

3. The server you created appears in the LDAP Servers view. Right-click the server, and select Run. If it's started properly, State is updated to Started.

4. To view or edit the configuration of the server, right-click it and select Open Configuration. By default, the server starts on LDAP port 10389 and LDAPS port 10696.

---

[8]Apache Directory Studio user guide for setting up and getting started is available at `http://directory.apache.org/studio/users-guide/apache_directory_studio/`

Now you have an LDAP server up and running. Before you proceed any further, let's create a test connection to it from the Apache Directory Studio:

1. From Apache Directory Studio, get to the Connections view. If it's not there already, go to Window ➤ Show View ➤ Connections.

2. Right-click Connections View, and select New Connection.

3. In the Connection Name text box, give a name to the connection.

4. The Host Name field should point to the server where you started the LDAP server. In this case, it's `localhost`.

5. The Port field should point to the port of your LDAP server, which is 10389 in this case.

6. Keep Encryption Method set to No Encryption for the time being. Click Next.

7. Type `uid=admin,ou=system` as the Bind DN and `secret` as the Bind Password, and click Finish. These are the default Bind DN and password values for Apache Directory Server.

8. The connection you just created appears in the Connections view. Double-click it, and the data retrieved from the underlying LDAP server appears in the LDAP Browser view.

In the sections that follow, you need some users and groups in the LDAP server. Let's create a user and a group. First you need to create an organizational unit (OU) structure under the `dc=example,dc=com` domain in Apache Directory Server:

1. In Apache Directory Studio, get to the LDAP browser by clicking the appropriate LDAP connection in the Connections view.

2. Right-click `dc=example,dc=com`, and choose New ➤ New Entry ➤ Create Entry From Scratch. Pick organizationalUnit from Available Object Classes, click Add, and then click Next. Select ou for the RDN, and give it the value `groups`. Click Next and then Finish.

3. Right-click `dc=example,dc=com`, and choose New ➤ New Entry ➤ Create Entry From Scratch. Pick organizationalUnit from Available Object Class, click Add, and then click Next. Select ou for the RDN, and give it the value `users`. Click Next and then Finish.

4.   Right-click dc=example,dc=com/ou=users, and choose New ➤ New Entry
     ➤ Create Entry From Scratch. Pick inetOrgPerson from Available Object Class,
     click Add, and then click Next. Select uid for the RDN, give it a value, and click
     Next. Complete the empty fields with appropriate values. Right-click the same
     pane, and choose New Attribute. Select userPassword as the Attribute Type, and
     click Finish. Enter a password, select SSHA-256 as the hashing method, and
     click OK.

5.   The user you created appears under dc=example,dc=com/ou=users in the
     LDAP browser.

6.   To create a group, right-click dc=example,dc=com/ou=groups ➤ New
     ➤ New Entry ➤ Create Entry From Scratch. Pick groupOfUniqueNames from
     Available Object Class, click Add, and click Next. Select cn for the RDN, give it
     a value, and click Next. Give the DN of the user created in the previous step as
     the uniqueMember (e.g., uid=prabath,ou=users,ou=system), and click
     Finish.

7.   The group you created appears under dc=example,dc=com/ou=groups in
     the LDAP browser.

CONNECTING APACHE TOMCAT TO APACHE DIRECTORY SERVER (LDAP)

You've already deployed the Recipe API in Apache Tomcat. Let's see how you can configure
Apache Tomcat to talk to the LDAP server you configured, following these steps:

1.   Shut down the Tomcat server if it's running.

2.   By default, Tomcat finds users from the conf/tomcat-users.xml file via
     org.apache.catalina.realm.UserDatabaseRealm.

3.   Open [TOMCAT_HOME]\conf\server.xml, and comment out the following
     line in it:

```
<Resource
        name="UserDatabase" auth="Container"
        type="org.apache.catalina.UserDatabase"
        description="User database that can be updated and saved"
```

```
            factory="org.apache.catalina.users.MemoryUserDatabaseFactory"
            pathname="conf/tomcat-users.xml" />
```

4. In [TOMCAT_HOME]\conf\server.xml, comment out the following line,
    which points to the UserDatabaseRealm:

```
<Realm  className="org.apache.catalina.realm.UserDatabaseRealm"
        resourceName="UserDatabase"/>
```

5. To connect to the LDAP server, you should use the JNDIRealm. Copy and paste
    the following configuration into [TOMCAT_HOME]\conf\server.xml just after
    <Realm className="org.apache.catalina.realm.LockOutRealm">:

```
<Realm  className="org.apache.catalina.realm.JNDIRealm"
        debug="99"
        connectionURL="ldap://localhost:10389"
        roleBase="ou=groups , dc=example, dc=com"
        roleSearch="(uniqueMember={0})"
        roleName="cn"
        userBase="ou=users, dc=example, dc=com"
        userSearch="(uid={0})"/>
```

SECURING AN API WITH HTTP BASIC AUTHENTICATION

The Recipe API that you deployed in Apache Tomcat is still an open API. Let's see how to
secure it with HTTP Basic authentication. You want to authenticate users against the corporate
LDAP server and also use access control based on HTTP operations (GET, POST, DELETE,
PUT). The following steps guide you on how to secure the Recipe API with HTTP Basic
authentication:

1. Shut down the Tomcat server if it's running, and make sure connectivity to the
    LDAP server works correctly.

2. Open [TOMCAT_HOME]\webapps\recipe\WEB-INF\web.xml and add the
    following under the root element <web-app>. The security-role element
    at the bottom of the following configuration lists all the roles allowed to use this
    web application:

```
<security-constraint>
 <web-resource-collection>
        <web-resource-name>Secured Recipe API</web-resource-name>
        <url-pattern>/*</url-pattern>
 </web-resource-collection>
 <auth-constraint>
        <role-name>admin</role-name>
 </auth-constraint>
</security-constraint>
<login-config>
        <auth-method>BASIC</auth-method>
        <realm-name>cute-cupcakes.com</realm-name>
</login-config>
<security-role>
        <role-name>admin</role-name>
</security-role>
```

This configuration will protect the complete Recipe API from unauthenticated access attempts. A legitimate user should have an account in the corporate LDAP server and also should be in the *admin* group. If you don't have a group called *admin*, change the preceding configuration appropriately.

3. You can further enable fine-grained access control to the Recipe API by HTTP operation. You need to have a `<security-constraint>` element defined for each scenario. The following two configuration blocks will let any user that belongs to the *admin* group perform GET/POST/PUT/DELETE on the Recipe API, whereas a user that belongs to the *user* group can only do a GET. When you define an `http-method` inside a `web-resource-collection` element, only those methods are protected. The rest can be invoked by anyone if no other security constraint has any restrictions on those methods. For example, if you only had the second block, then any user would be able to do a POST. Having the first block that controls POST will allow only the legitimate user to do a POST to the Recipe API. The `security-role` element at the bottom of the following configuration lists all the roles allowed to use this web application:

```
<security-constraint>
    <web-resource-collection>
        <web-resource-name>Secured Recipe API</web-resource-name>
```

```
                    <url-pattern>/*</url-pattern>
                    <http-method>GET</http-method>
                    <http-method>PUT</http-method>
                    <http-method>POST</http-method>
                    <http-method>DELETE</http-method>
            </web-resource-collection>
            <auth-constraint>
                    <role-name>admin</role-name>
            </auth-constraint>
    </security-constraint>
    <security-constraint>
        <web-resource-collection>
                    <web-resource-name>Secured Recipe API</web-resource-name>
                    <url-pattern>/*</url-pattern>
                    <http-method>GET</http-method>
            </web-resource-collection>
        <auth-constraint>
                    <role-name>user</role-name>
        </auth-constraint>
    </security-constraint>
    <login-config>
                    <auth-method>BASIC</auth-method>
                    <realm-name>cute-cupcakes.com</realm-name>
    </login-config>
    <security-role>
                    <role-name>admin</role-name>
                    <role-name>user</role-name>
    </security-role>
```

ENABLING TLS IN APACHE TOMCAT

The way you configured HTTP Basic authentication in the previous exercise isn't secure enough. It uses HTTP to transfer credentials. Anyone who can intercept the channel can see the credentials in cleartext. Let's see how to enable Transport Layer Security (TLS) in Apache Tomcat and restrict access to the Recipe API only via TLS:

1. To enable TLS, first you need to have a keystore with a public/private key pair. You can create a keystore using Java keytool. It comes with the JDK distribution, and you can find it in [JAVA_HOME]\bin. The following command creates a Java keystore with the name catalina-keystore.jks. This command uses catalina123 as the keystore password as well as the private key password.

Note   JAVA_HOME refers to the directory where you've installed the JDK. To run the keytool, you need to have Java installed in your system.

```
\> keytool    -genkey -alias localhost -keyalg RSA -keysize 1024
              -dname "CN=localhost"
              -keypass catalina123
              -keystore catalina-keystore.jks
              -storepass catalina123
```

2. Copy catalina-keystore.jks to [TOMCAT_HOME]\conf, and add the following element to [TOMCAT_HOME]\conf\server.xml under the <Service> parent element. Replace the values of keyStoreFile and keystorePass elements appropriately:

```
<Connector
        port="8443"
        maxThreads="200"
        scheme="https"
        secure="true"
        SSLEnabled="true"
        keystoreFile="absolute/path/to/catalina-keystore.jks"
        keystorePass="catalina123"
        clientAuth="false"
        sslProtocol="TLS"/>
```

3. Start the Tomcat server, and execute the following cURL command to validate the TLS connectivity. Make sure you replace the values of username and password appropriately. They must come from the underlying user store:

```
\> curl -k  -u username:password  https://localhost:8443/recipe
```

You've configured Apache Tomcat to work with TLS. Next you need to make sure that the Recipe API only accepts connections over TLS.

Open `[TOMCAT_HOME]\webapps\recipe\WEB-INF\web.xml`, and add the following under each `<security-constraint>` element. This makes sure only TLS connections are accepted:

```
<user-data-constraint>
    <transport-guarantee>CONFIDENTIAL</transport-guarantee>
</user-data-constraint>
```

SECURING THE RECIPE API WITH HTTP DIGEST AUTHENTICATION

The Tomcat `JNDIRealm` that you used previously to connect to the LDAP server doesn't support HTTP Digest authentication. If you need HTTP Digest authentication support, you have to write your own `Realm`, extending Tomcat `JNDIRealm`, and override the `getPassword()` method. To see how to secure an API with Digest authentication, we need to switch back to the Tomcat `UserDatabaseRealm`:

1. Open `[TOMCAT_HOME]\conf\server.xml`, and make sure that the following line is there. If you commented this out during a previous exercise, revert it back:

    ```
    <Resource
            name="UserDatabase"
            auth="Container"
            type="org.apache.catalina.UserDatabase"
            description="User database that can be updated and saved"
            factory="org.apache.catalina.users.MemoryUserDatabaseFactory"
            pathname="conf/tomcat-users.xml" />
    ```

2. In `[TOMCAT_HOME]\conf\server.xml`, make sure that the following line, which points to `UserDatabaseRealm`, is there. If you commented it out during a previous exercise, revert it back:

    ```
    <Realm  className="org.apache.catalina.realm.UserDatabaseRealm"
            resourceName="UserDatabase"/>
    ```

3. Open [TOMCAT_HOME]\webapps\recipe\WEB-INF\web.xml, and add the following under the root element <web-app>:

```
<security-constraint>
  <web-resource-collection>
            <web-resource-name>Secured Recipe API</web-resource-
            name>
            <url-pattern>/* </url-pattern>
  </web-resource-collection>
  <auth-constraint>
            <role-name>admin</role-name>
  </auth-constraint>
</security-constraint>
<login-config>
            <auth-method>DIGEST</auth-method>
            <realm-name>cute-cupcakes.com</realm-name>
</login-config>
<security-role>
            <role-name>admin</role-name>
</security-role>
```

4. Open [TOMCAT_HOME]\conf\tomcat-users.xml, and add the following under the root element. This adds a role and a user to Tomcat's default file system–based user store:

```
<role rolename="admin"/>
<user username="prabath" password="prabath123" roles="admin"/>
```

5. Invoke the API with the cURL command shown next. The --digest -u username:password option used here generates the password in digest mode and adds it to the HTTP request. Replace username:password with appropriate values:

```
\> curl -k -v --digest -u username:password https://localhost:8443/
recipe
```

OAuth 2.0 MAC Token Profile

The OAuth 2.0 core specification doesn't mandate any specific token type. It's one of the extension points introduced in OAuth 2.0. Almost all public implementations use the OAuth 2.0 Bearer Token Profile. This came up with the OAuth 2.0 core specification, but as an independent profile, documented under RFC 6750. Eran Hammer, who was the lead editor of the OAuth 2.0 specification by that time, introduced the Message Authentication Code (MAC) Token Profile for OAuth 2.0. (Hammer also led the OAuth 1.0 specification.) Since its introduction to the OAuth 2.0 IETF working group in November 2011, the MAC Token Profile has made a slow progress. The slow progress was mostly due to the fact that the working group was interested in building a complete stack around bearer tokens before moving into another token type. In this chapter, we will take a deeper look into the OAuth 2.0 MAC Token Profile and its applications.

OAUTH 2.0 AND THE ROAD TO HELL

One of the defining moments of OAuth 2.0 history was the resignation of OAuth 2.0 specification lead editor Eran Hammer. On July 26, 2012, he wrote a famous blog post titled "OAuth 2.0 and the Road to Hell"[1] after announcing his resignation from the OAuth 2.0 IETF working group. As highlighted in the blog post, Hammer thinks OAuth 2.0 is a bad protocol, just like any WS-* (web services) standard. In his comparison, OAuth 1.0 is much better than OAuth 2.0 in terms of complexity, interoperability, usefulness, completeness, and security. Hammer was worried about the direction in which OAuth 2.0 was heading, because it was not what was intended by the web community that initially formed the OAuth 2.0 working group.

---

[1]Available at `http://hueniverse.com/2012/07/oauth-2-0-and-the-road-to-hell/`

© Prabath Siriwardena 2020

P. Siriwardena, *Advanced API Security*, https://doi.org/10.1007/978-1-4842-2050-4_22

According to Hammer, the following were the initial objectives of the OAuth 2.0 working group:

- Build a protocol very similar to OAuth 1.0.

- Simplify the signing process.

- Add a light identity layer.

- Address native applications.

- Add more flows to accommodate more client types.

- Improve security.

In his blog post, Hammer highlighted the following architectural changes from OAuth 1.0 to 2.0 (extracted from `http://hueniverse.com/2012/07/oauth-2-0-and-the-road-to-hell/`):

- *Unbounded tokens*: In 1.0, the client has to present two sets of credentials on each protected resource request, the token credentials and the client credentials. In 2.0, the client credentials are no longer used. This means that tokens are no longer bound to any particular client type or instance. This has introduced limits on the usefulness of access tokens as a form of authentication and increased the likelihood of security issues.

- *Bearer tokens*: 2.0 got rid of all signatures and cryptography at the protocol level. Instead, it relies solely on TLS. This means that 2.0 tokens are inherently less secure as specified. Any improvement in token security requires additional specifications, and as the current proposals demonstrate, the group is solely focused on enterprise use cases.

- *Expiring tokens*: 2.0 tokens can expire and must be refreshed. This is the most significant change for client developers from 1.0, as they now need to implement token state management. The reason for token expiration is to accommodate self-encoded tokens—encrypted tokens, which can be authenticated by the server without a database look-up. Because such tokens are self-encoded, they cannot be revoked and therefore must be short-lived to reduce their exposure. Whatever is gained from the removal of the signature is lost twice in the introduction of the token state management requirement.

- *Grant types*: In 2.0, authorization grants are exchanged for access tokens. Grant is an abstract concept representing the end user approval. It can be a code received after the user clicks "Approve" on an access request, or the user's actual username and password. The original idea behind grants was to enable multiple flows. 1.0 provides a single flow, which aims to accommodate multiple client types. 2.0 adds significant amount of specialization for different client types.

Most of all, Hammer wasn't in favor of the authorization framework built by OAuth 2.0 and the extensibility introduced. His argument was that the Web doesn't need another security framework: what it needs is a simple, well-defined security protocol. Regardless of these arguments, over the years OAuth 2.0 has become the de facto standard for API security—and the extensibility introduced by OAuth 2.0 is paying off.

Bearer Token vs. MAC Token

Bearer tokens are just like cash. Whoever owns one can use it. At the time you use it, you don't need to prove you're the legitimate owner. It's similar to the way you could use stolen cash with no problem; what matters is the validity of the cash, not the owner.

MAC tokens, on the other hand, are like credit cards. Whenever you use a credit card, you have to authorize the payment with your signature. If someone steals your card, the thief can't use it unless they know how to sign exactly like you. That's the main advantage of MAC tokens.

With bearer tokens, you always have to pass the token secret over the wire. But with MAC tokens, you never pass the token secret over the wire. The key difference between bearer tokens and MAC tokens is very similar to the difference between HTTP Basic authentication and HTTP Digest authentication, which we discussed in Appendix F.

Note   Draft 5 of the OAuth 2.0 MAC Token Profile is available at `http://tools.ietf.org/html/draft-ietf-oauth-v2-http-mac-05`. This chapter is based on draft 5, but this is an evolving specification. The objective of this chapter is to introduce the MAC Token Profile as an extension of OAuth token types. The request/response parameters discussed in this chapter may change as the specification evolves, but the basic concepts will remain the same. It's recommended that you keep an eye on `https://datatracker.ietf.org/doc/draft-ietf-oauth-v2-http-mac/` to find out the latest changes taking place.

Obtaining a MAC Token

The OAuth 2.0 core specification isn't coupled with any of the token profiles. The OAuth flows discussed in Chapter 4 applies in the same way for MAC tokens. OAuth grant types don't have any dependency on the token type. A client can obtain a MAC token by using any grant type. Under the authorization code grant type, the resource owner that visits the application initiates the flow. The client, which must be a registered application at the authorization server, redirects the resource owner to the authorization server to get the approval. The following is a sample HTTP redirect, which takes the resource owner to the OAuth authorization server:

```
https://authz.server.com/oauth2/authorize?response_type=code&
```

```
client_id=OrhQErXIX49svVYoXJGtODWBuFca&
```

```
redirect_uri=https%3A%2F%2Fmycallback
```

The value of response_type must be code. This indicates to the authorization server that the request is for an authorization code. client_id is an identifier for the client application. Once the client application is registered with the authorization server, the client gets a client_id and a client_secret. The value of redirect_uri should be same as the value registered with the authorization server. During the client registration phase, the client application must provide a URL under its control as the redirect_uri. The URL-encoded value of the callback URL is added to the request as the redirect_uri parameter. In addition to these parameters, a client application can also include a scope parameter. The value of the scope parameter is shown to the resource owner on the approval screen. It indicates to the authorization server the level of access the client needs on the target resource/API. The previous HTTP redirect returns the requested code to the registered callback URL:

```
https://mycallback/?code=9142d4cad58c66d0a5edfad8952192
```

The value of the authorization code is delivered to the client application via an HTTP redirect and is visible to the resource owner. In the next step, the client must exchange the authorization code for an OAuth access token by talking to the OAuth token endpoint exposed by the authorization server. This can be an authenticated request with the client_id and the client_secret of the client application in the HTTP authorization header, if the token endpoint is secured with HTTP Basic authentication. The value of the grant_type parameter must be the authorization_code, and the value of the code should be the one returned from the previous step. If the client application set a value for the redirect_uri parameter in the previous request, then it must include the same value in the token request. The client can't suggest to the authorization server the type of token it expects: it's entirely up to the authorization server to decide, or it can be based on a pre-agreement between the client and the authorization server at the time of client registration, which is outside the scope of OAuth.

The following cURL command to exchange the authorization code for a MAC token is very similar to what you saw for the Bearer Token Profile (in Chapter 4). The only difference is that this introduces a new parameter called audience, which is a *must* for a MAC token request:

```
\> curl -v -X POST --basic
    -u OrhQErXIX49svVYoXJGtODWBuFca:eYOFkL756W8usQaVNgCNkz9C2D0a
    -H "Content-Type: application/x-www-form-urlencoded;charset=UTF-8"
    -k -d "grant_type=authorization_code&
    code=9142d4cad58c66d0a5edfad8952192&
    redirect_uri=https://mycallback&
    audience=https://resource-server-URI"
    https://authz.server.com/oauth2/token
```

The previous cURL command returns the following response:

```
HTTP/1.1 200 OK
Content-Type: application/json
Cache-Control: no-store
 {
        "access_token": "eyJhbGciOiJSUOExXzUiLCJlbmMiOiJBM",
        "token_type":"mac",
        "expires_in":3600,
        "refresh_token":"8xLOxBtZp8",
        "kid":"22BIjxU93h/IgwEb4zCRu5WF37s=",
        "mac_key":"adijq39jdlaska9asud",
        "mac_algorithm":"hmac-sha-256"
}
```

Let's examine the definition of each parameter:

access_token: The OAuth 2.0 access token, which binds the client, the resource owner, and the authorization server together. With the introduction of the audience parameter, this now binds all of those with the resource server as well. Under the MAC Token Profile, by decoding the access token, you should be able to find the audience of the access token. If someone tampers with the access token to change the audience, that will make the token validation fail automatically at the authorization server.

token_type: Type of the token returned from the authorization server. The client should first try to understand the value of this parameter and begin processing accordingly. The processing rules differ from one token type to another. Under the MAC Token Profile, the value of the token type must be mac.

expires_in: The lifetime of the access token in seconds.

refresh_token: The refresh token associated with the access token. The refresh token can be used to acquire a new access token.

kid: Stands for *key identifier*. This is an identifier generated by the authorization server. It's recommended that you generate the key identifier by base64 encoding the hashed access token: kid = base64encode (sha-1 (access_token)). This identifier uniquely identifies the mac_key used later to generate the MAC while invoking the resource APIs.

mac_key: A session key generated by the authorization server, having the same lifetime as the access token. The mac_key is a shared secret used later to generate the MAC while invoking the resource APIs. The authorization server should never reissue the same mac_key or the same kid.

mac_algorithm: The algorithm to generate the MAC during API invocation. The value of the mac_algorithm should be well understood by the client, authorization server, and resource server.

The OAuth 2.0 access token is opaque to anyone outside the authorization server. It may or may not carry meaningful data, but no one outside the authorization server should try to interpret it. The OAuth 2.0 MAC Token Profile defines a more meaningful structure for the access token; it's no longer an arbitrary string. The resource server should understand the structure of the access token generated by the authorization server. Still, the client should not try to interpret it.

The access token returned from the authorization server to the client is encoded with the audience, key identifier, and encrypted value of the mac_key. The mac_key must be encrypted with the public key of the resource server or with a shared key established between the resource server and the authorization server via a prior agreement outside the scope of OAuth. When accessing a protected API, the client must send the access token along with the request. The resource server can decode the access token and get the encrypted mac_key, which it can later decrypt from its own private key or the shared key.

OAUTH 2.0 AUDIENCE INFORMATION

The audience parameter is defined in the OAuth 2.0: Audience Information Internet draft available at `http://tools.ietf.org/html/draft-tschofenig-oauth-audience-00`. This is a new parameter introduced into the OAuth token request flow and is independent of the token type. Once it's approved as an IETF proposed standard, the Bearer Token Profile also will be updated to include this in the access token request.

The objective of the audience parameter introduced by the OAuth 2.0: Audience Information Internet draft is to identify the audience of an issued access token. With this, the access token issued by the authorization server is for a specific client, to be used against a specific resource server or a specific set of resource servers. All resource servers should validate the audience of the access token before considering it valid.

After completing the authorization-granting phase, the client must decide which resource server to access and should find the corresponding audience URI. That must be included in the access token request to the token endpoint. Then the authorization server must check whether it has any associated resource servers that can be identified by the provided audience URI. If not, it must send back the error code invalid_request. If all validations pass at the authorization server, the new Internet draft suggests including the allowed audience in the access token. While invoking an API hosted in the resource server, it can decode the access token and find out whether the allowed audience matches its own.

Invoking an API Protected with the OAuth 2.0 MAC Token Profile

Following any of the grant types, you can obtain a MAC token from the authorization server. Unlike with the Bearer Token Profile, this needs more processing at the client end before you invoke an API protected with the MAC Token Profile. Prior to invoking the protected API, the client must construct an authenticator. The value of the authenticator is then added to the HTTP authorization header of the outgoing request. The authenticator is constructed from the following parameters:

kid: The key identifier from the authorization grant response.

ts: Timestamp, in milliseconds, since January 1, 1970.

seq-nr: Indicates the initial sequence number to be used during the message exchange between the client and the resource server, from client to server.

access_token: The value of the access token from the authorization grant response.

mac: The value of the MAC for the request message. Later, this appendix discusses how to calculate the MAC.

h: Colon-separated header fields, used to calculate the MAC.

cb: Specifies the channel binding. Channel bindings are defined in "Channel Bindings for TLS," RFC 5929, available at http://tools.ietf.org/html/rfc5929. The Channel Bindings for TLS RFC defines three bindings: tls-unique, tls-server-endpoint, and tls-unique-for-telnet.

The following is a sample request to access an API secured with an OAuth 2.0 MAC Token Profile.

```
GET /patient?name=peter&id=10909HTTP/1.1
Host: medicare.com
Authorization: MAC  kid="22BIjxU93h/IgwEb4zCRu5WF37s=",
                    ts="1336363200",
                    seq-nr="12323",
                    access_token="eyJhbGciOiJSUOExXzUiLCJlbmMiOiJBM",
                    mac="bhCQXTVyfj5cmA9uKkPFx1zeOXM=",
                    h="host",
                    cb="tls-unique:9382c93673d814579ed1610d3"
```

Calculating the MAC

The OAuth 2.0 MAC Token Profile defines two algorithms to calculate the MAC: HMAC-SHA1 and HMAC-SHA256. It also provides an extension for additional algorithms.

The Message Authentication Code (MAC) provides integrity and authenticity assurance for the associated message. The MAC algorithm accepts a message and a secret key to produce the associated MAC. To verify the MAC, the receiving party should have the same key and calculate the MAC of the received message. If the calculated MAC is equal to the MAC in the message, that guarantees integrity and authenticity.

A Hash-based Message Authentication Code (HMAC) is a specific way of calculating the MAC using a hashing algorithm. If the hashing algorithm is SHA-1, it's called HMAC-SHA1. If the hashing algorithm is SHA256, then it's called HMAC-SHA256. More information about HMAC is available at `http://tools.ietf.org/html/rfc2104`. The HMAC-SHA1 and HMAC-SHA256 functions need to be implemented in the corresponding programming language.

Here's the calculation with `HMAC-SHA1`:

```
mac = HMAC-SHA1(mac_key, input-string)
```

And here it is with `HMAC-SHA256`:

```
mac = HMAC-SHA256(mac_key, input-string)
```

For an API invocation request, the value of `input-string` is the `Request-Line` from the HTTP request, the timestamp, the value of `seq-nr`, and the concatenated values of the headers specified under the parameter h.

HTTP REQUEST-LINE

The HTTP `Request-Line` is defined in Section 5 of the HTTP RFC, available at `www.w3.org/Protocols/rfc2616/rfc2616-sec5.html`. The request line is defined as follows:

```
Request-Line = Method SP Request-URI SP HTTP-Version CRLF
```

The value of `Method` can be `OPTIONS`, `GET`, `HEAD`, `POST`, `PUT`, `DELETE`, `TRACE`, `CONNECT`, or any extension method. SP stands for space—to be technically accurate, it's ASCII code 32. `Request-URI` identifies the representation of the resource where the request is sent. According to the HTTP specification, there are four ways to construct a `Request-URI`:

```
Request-URI = "*" | absoluteURI | abs_path | authority
```

The asterisk (*) means the request targets not a specific resource but the server itself, for example, OPTIONS * HTTP/1.1.

The `absoluteURI` must be used when the request is made through a proxy, for example, GET `https://resource-server/myresource HTTP/1.1`.

`abs_path` is the most common form of a `Request-URI`. In this case, the absolute path with respect to the host server is used. The URI or the network location of the server is transmitted in the HTTP `Host` header. For example:

```
GET /myresource HTTP/1.1
Host: resource-server
```

The `authority` form of the `Request-URI` is only used with HTTP CONNECT method. This method is used to make a connection through a proxy with tunneling, as in the case of TLS tunneling.

After the `Request-URI` must be a space and then the HTTP version, followed by a carriage return and a line feed.

Let's take the following example:

```
POST /patient?name=peter&id=10909&blodgroup=bpositive HTTP/1.1
Host: medicare.com
```

The value of the `input-string` is

```
POST /patient?name=peter&id=10909&blodgroup=bpositive HTTP/1.1 \n
1336363200 \n
12323 \n
medicare.com \n
```

1336363200 is the timestamp, 12323 is the sequence number, and `medicare.com` is the value of the `Host` header. The value of the Host header is included here because it is set in the h parameter of the API request under the HTTP Authorization header. All of these entries should be separated by a newline separator character, denoted by \n in the example. Once the input string is derived, the MAC is calculated on it using the `mac_key` and the MAC algorithm specified under `mac_algorithm`.

MAC Validation by the Resource Server

To access any API secured with the OAuth 2.0 MAC Token Profile, the client should send the relevant parameters with the API invocation request. If any of the parameters are lacking in the request or the provided values are invalid, the resource server will respond with an HTTP 401 status code. The value of the WWW-Authenticate header should be set to MAC, and the value of the error parameter should explain the nature of the error:

```
HTTP/1.1 401 Unauthorized
WWW-Authenticate: MAC error="Invalid credentials"
```

Let's consider the following valid API request, which comes with a MAC header:

```
GET /patient?name=peter&id=10909HTTP/1.1
Host: medicare.com
Authorization: MAC  kid="22BIjxU93h/IgwEb4zCRu5WF37s=",
                    ts="1336363200",
                    seq-nr="12323",
                    access_token="eyJhbGciOiJSU0ExXzUiLCJlbmMiOiJBM",
                    mac="bhCQXTVyfj5cmA9uKkPFx1zeOXM=",
                    h="host",
                    cb="tls-unique:9382c93673d814579ed1610d3"
```

To validate the MAC of the request, the resource server has to know the mac_key. The client must pass the mac_key to the resource server, encoded in the access_token. The first step in validation is to extract the mac_key from the access_token in the request. Once the access_token is decoded, the resource server has to verify its audience. The authorization server encodes the audience of the access_token into the access_token.

Once the access_token is verified and the scopes associated with it are validated, the resource server can cache the mac_key by the kid. The cached mac_key can be used in future message exchanges.

According to the MAC Token Profile, the access_token needs to be included only in the first request from the client to the resource server. The resource server must use the cached mac_key (against the kid) to validate subsequent messages in the message exchange. If the initial access_token doesn't have enough privileges to invoke a later

API, the resource server can request a new access_token or a complete authenticator by responding with an HTTP WWW-Authenticate header.

The resource server must calculate the MAC of the message the same way the client did before and compare the calculated MAC with the value included in the request. If the two match, the request can be considered a valid, legitimate one. But you still need to make sure there are no replay attacks. To do that, the resource server must verify the timestamp in the message by comparing it with its local timestamp.

An attacker that can eavesdrop on the communication channel between the client and the resource server can record messages and replay them at a different time to gain access to the protected resource. The OAuth 2.0 MAC Token Profile uses timestamps as a way of detecting and mitigating replay attacks.

OAuth Grant Types and the MAC Token Profile

OAuth grant types and token types are two independent extension points introduced in the OAuth 2.0 core specification. They don't have any direct dependency between each other. This chapter only talks about the authorization code grant type, but all the other grant types work in the same manner: the structure of the access token returning from the implicit grant type, the resource owner password credentials grant type, and the client credentials grant type is the same.

OAuth 1.0 vs. OAuth 2.0 MAC Token Profile

Eran Hammer (who was initially the lead editor of the OAuth 2.0 specification) submitted the initial OAuth 2.0 MAC Token Profile draft to the OAuth working group in May 2011, and the first draft (also submitted by Hammer) followed with some improvements in February 2012. Both drafts were mostly influenced by the OAuth 1.0 architecture. After a long break, and after Hammer's resignation from the OAuth working group, the Internet draft 4 of the MAC Token Profile introduced a revamped architecture. This architecture, which was discussed in this chapter, has many architectural differences from OAuth 1.0 (see Table G-1).

Table G-1. *OAuth 1.0 vs. OAuth 2.0 MAC Token Profile*

OAuth 1.0	OAuth 2.0 MAC Token Profile
Requires a signature both during the initial handshake and during the business API invocation.	Requires a signature only for the business API invocation.
The resource server must know the secret key used to sign the message beforehand. The shared secret doesn't have an associated lifetime. Doesn't have any audience restrictions. Tokens can be used against any resource server.	The encrypted shared secret used to sign the message is passed to the resource server, embedded in the `access_token`. A lifetime is associated with the `mac_key`, which is used as the key to sign. The authorization server enforces an audience restriction on the issued `access_tokens`, so that those access tokens can't be used against any resource server.

Index

A

Access delegation problem, 81

Access token, 86, 93, 251

access_token parameter, 220

Additional authentication data (AAD), 185, 192, 194, 200

Advanced encryption standard (AES), 49, 192

Alert protocol, 365

alias argument, 74

Amazon Web Services (AWS), 3, 51, 52, 103

Apache Directory Server (LDAP)

    connections, 415

    connecting Apache Tomcat, 417

    organizational unit structure, creation, 416

    test connection, 416

Application programming interface (API)

    Amazon, 3, 4

    Big Data, 2

    Business models, 12

    database implementations, 15

    definition, 13

    Facebook, 6, 7

    governments, 9

    healthcare industry, 10

    IBM Watson technology, 9

    IoT, 2

    Java RMI, 16

    JDBC, 14

    kernel, 13, 14

    lifecycle, 22

    management platform, 23

    marshalling/unmarshalling technique, 16

    Netflix, 7

    Open Bank, 10

    ProgrammableWeb, 19

    reasons, 3

    Salesforce, 5

    SOAP, 17

    swagger, 24

    Uber, 5, 6

    UDDI, 23

    Walgreens, 8

    wearable industry, 11

Auditing, 65, 89

Authenticated Encryption with Associated Data (AEAD), 191, 192, 194

Authentication, 59

    biometric-based, 62

    brute-force attack, 60

    certificates and smart card–based, 61

    identity provider, 59

Authorization, 62

    access control list, 63

    DAC, 62

    MAC, 63

Authorization API, 389, 394, 396

Authorization API token (AAT), 389–391

© Prabath Siriwardena 2020
P. Siriwardena, *Advanced API Security*, https://doi.org/10.1007/978-1-4842-2050-4

I

J